FIG. 21·2

NEW GUINEA

Gulf of Carpentaria

HERN

TORY

Cooktown

Cairns

FIG. 24·2

Townsville

Repulse Bay

QUEENSLAND

Rockhampton

Curtis I

Fraser I.

Brisbane

Stradbroke I.

SOUTH

USTRALIA

NEW

SOUTH

WALES

Sydney

Botany Bay

Eyre
Pen.

Adelaide

angaroo I.

VICTORIA

FIG.
19·1

Melbourne

FIG. 18·1

BIGHT

TASMANIA

Launceston

Hobart

Pedra Branca

THE SECRET DISCOVERY OF AUSTRALIA

THE SECRET DISCOVERY OF AUSTRALIA

Portuguese Ventures 200 Years Before Captain Cook

KENNETH GORDON McINTYRE
O.B.E.,M.A.,LL.B.(Melb.)

SOUVENIR PRESS

Printed in Great Britain by
J. W. Arrowsmith Ltd., Bristol, England

TO MY WIFE
BETTY CONSTANCE McINTYRE

'It is *Justice* that leads me to lay this most *Wondrous Historie*
at Your Feet'

CONTENTS

What knew the Portuguese of this great country?
Something, for sure: which in their rivalry
With Spain they kept a secret. Old-time charts
Bespeak some knowledge . . .

LIST OF ILLUSTRATIONS

PLATES

LINE-DRAWINGS

A Map of Australia, showing the main places mentioned in the text, will be found in the end-papers of this book.

ACKNOWLEDGEMENTS

The author does not have a long list of acknowledgements, for in this unexplored field little assistance was available. He wishes to thank Mr Graham McCallum of Box Hill and Mr Evan Richard of Brisbane, mathematicians, for their help with the mathematical chapters of this book, and Dr F. E. M. Lilley of Canberra for help with Magnetic Deviation; Mr J. Ware, Registrar, Department of the Australian Navy, for valuable information concerning the finding of the Portuguese cannon at Carronade Island; and Mr S. R. Brookes of Camberwell for drawing attention to the ruins at Bittangabee Bay. Thanks are due to Mr L. J. Blake, formerly State Historian, for the research into La Trobe's papers, which served as the basis for the chapter on the Geelong Keys. Praise is due to the Geelong Historial Society for its continued interest in these keys; to the Warrnambool (Flagstaff Hill) Maritime Museum for continually keeping the story of the Mahogany Ship before the public, and to Mr Ian McKiggan, whose scientific probes for the Mahogany Ship generate such high hopes that it will be located and uncovered.

The following persons and firms are thanked for their kind permission to include in the text quotations from the works mentioned against their names, namely: Mrs E. E. Ingamells (Rex Ingamells, *The Great South Land*), Dr Howard Fry (*Alexander Dalrymple*), The Royal Society of Canada (W. F. Ganong, *Crucial Maps in the Early Cartography of Canada*), Oxford University Press (S. E. Morison, *The European Discovery of America*), Cambridge University Press (J. A. Williamson, article in *Cambridge History of the British Empire*), Macmillan Administration (Basingstoke) Limited (J. A. Williamson, *Short History of British Expansion*), Chas. J. Sawyer, Grafton Street, London (J. A. Williamson, *The Observations of Sir Richard Hawkins*), G. Bell & Sons Ltd, London (Raymond Lister, *Antique Maps and their Cartographers*), Livros Horizonte Limitada, Lisboa (Jaime Cortesão, *Os descobrimentos portugueses*), and University of Coimbra Press (Armando Cortesão, *The Nautical Chart of 1424*); and especial thanks are due to The Bodley Head of

London, the holders of the rights to that indispensable study in the history of early navigation, *The Haven-Finding Art,* by the late Professor Eva Taylor, and to Professor Armando Cortesão and Commander Avelino Teixeira da Mota, not only for their permission to quote from their works, but for the inspiration that their scholarship has been over many years of study.

On the New Zealand side, Miss Robyn Jenkin's interesting book *New Zealand Mysteries* first drew the author's attention to these fascinating clues, and her collection of references greatly facilitated the author's research. Gratitude is expressed to the Honourable Kevin Kelly, then Australian Ambassador to Portugal, for smoothing the author's path to research in that country, and to the library and archives staffs both in Portugal and Australia for their expert assistance.

For permission to reproduce illustrations, the author and publisher wish to thank: the late Frank Bamford (Plate I), the British Library (Plates IV, VI and VIII), Mr B. Egan, of Eden, N.S.W. (Plate II), the Mansell Collection, London (Plate III), the Rijksmuseum, Nederlands Scheepvaart Museum, Amsterdam (Plate VII), the John Rylands Collection, University of Manchester Library (Plate V), and the State Library of South Australia (Fig. 6.2).

Since the author first began lecturing on this subject, he has been heartened by the interest shown by the Australian news media, the Universities and the various historical societies. It encourages the hope that the publication of this book will lead to widespread interest in this forgotten chapter in early Australian history.

Box Hill, Australia, August 1977

A Historia não é apenas o relato de factos per-
feitamente averiguados, ma a reposta sempre
renovada a problemas muitas vezes sem solucão
evidente, e que nos deixam, como neste caso, à beira
de certeza.

JAIME CORTESÃO

(History is not only the relation of facts which have
been fully authenticated. Rather it is the probing,
revised and again revised, at problems which most
of the time appear to be without obvious solution,
by which we are led – as in this case – to the very
threshold of conviction.)

Introduction

THE QUESTION

What knew the Portuguese of this great country?
Something, for sure: which in their rivalry
With Spain they kept a secret. Old-time charts
Bespeak some knowledge ...

Rex Ingamells,
from *The Great South Land*

ALEXANDER von Humboldt said that there are three
stages in the popular attitude towards a great discovery:
first men doubt its existence, next they deny its importance,
and finally they give the credit to someone else. This, no
doubt, is intended to be a humorous exaggeration, but it
contains an element of truth. Its validity can be seen by
considering the analogy of the discovery of a lode of gold in
some gold-bearing frontier land where the King's Writ, as yet,
does not strongly run.

Suppose that some lone, unsupported fossicker, in the
uproarious gold-rush days of Victoria or California in the
1850s, came upon a rich find of gold. Fearful of his stronger
neighbours, his first instinct would be to keep his find secret,
to work it for himself, and to deny that any find had been
made. Then, when his neighbours grew suspicious, he would
say Yes, he had found some traces, but barely worth the
trouble of digging it. Finally, when the truth became known
and the gunmen of the strong-arm syndicates moved in, the
original discoverer would be edged out and forgotten, and the
new syndicate would take all the gold from the ground, and
gain all the plaudits of posterity.

This applied to the discovery of islands, lands and even
continents in the sixteenth century. Today International Law
is imperfect; in those days it was almost nonexistent. Even
today it is difficult for a militarily weak country to establish
any claim to a discovered island which is coveted by a stronger
power, even a friendly stronger power. If today Iceland
discovered an entirely new island, rich in fish or other wealth,
off the North Russian coast (or, for that matter, off the North

British coast), its best plan would be to work the find in secret and make no announcement of the discovery. But when the discovery is made by a Great Power then everything is different: the Great Power, sure of its military might, hastens to announce its new dominion to the world, and dins in the fact that it, the Great Power, was the discoverer. The mighty publicity given to Columbus's discoveries in America and to Cook's discoveries in Australia might have been muted and silenced if Spain and England had not, at the respective times, been super-powers of incontestable strength.

This consideration alone leads to the conjecture that there might have been pre-Columbian (and pre-Cook) discoveries of the respective continents by lesser powers which, under the Humboldt doctrine, would be denied, minimised, and finally forgotten; and it has been the task of scholars of this century, especially on the American side, to ferret out the clues and to piece together the evidence of these earlier voyages which achieved and discovered, but which were not broadcast to the world. This has led to the immense modern literature of 'Pre-Columbian Discoveries', a literature still growing and not yet exhausted.

It is not the purpose of this book to canvass the history of pre-Columbian discoveries in America, except in so far as they throw light, by analogy or otherwise, on the pre-Cook discoveries in Australia. But it can be mentioned here that they are many, and they stretch back many centuries. The Scandinavian discoveries and settlements in Greenland, Baffin Island and (more controversially) Vinland have very solid historical foundations. In the centuries that followed, there have been voyages to the west, documented but never fully documented, of Irishmen under St Brendan, Welshmen under Madoc, Danes under Pining and Pothurst, Portuguese under de Tieve and Cortereal, Englishmen from Bristol, and many others. On the continent of America there have been found relics and ruins, ranging from the undoubted relics at L'Anse-aux-meadows to hotly-debated curiosities like the Kensington Stone and the Dighton Rock. It is an intriguing, tantalising and sometimes exasperating branch of history – intriguing because circumstantial evidence builds up so strongly, exasperating because the most vital clues are always so hard to find.

And Australia, too, has the counterpart of these 'pre-orthodox' discoveries. Unfortunately, there is no Australian phrase which conveniently corresponds with the American phrase 'pre-Columbian'. The present official view is that the continent of Australia was first sighted by the Dutchman Willem Jantzoon in 1606; and that the fertile and important east coast was discovered by the Englishman James Cook in 1770. This duality causes this book to use two expressions, 'pre-Dutch' and 'pre-Cook', alternating as the context requires.

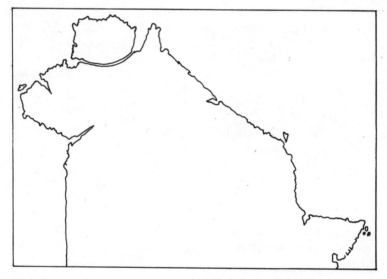

Fig. 0.1   THE DAUPHIN MAP on its original projection. (A more detailed copy of the same map is given in Fig. 8.1.)

The evidence of pre-Cook, pre-Dutch visits by other Europeans points only in one direction – to the proposition that, in the ninety years before the first Dutch sighting, the Portuguese sighted and visited and charted the Australian coasts. The historical detective story which follows will do its best to lay all of this evidence, all of the clues, all of the deductions, before the reader; the minor pieces of evidence will be met with as the story unfolds. The major piece of evidence is a set of Portuguese (or Franco-Portuguese) maps known as the

Fig. 0.2 THE DAUPHIN ON MERCATOR'S PROJECTION, with correction of the distortions caused by Magnetic Deviation and Erration.

Dieppe Maps, and much of this book will be taken up with their presentation and interpretation. It seems wise that the reader should be introduced to them at this stage.

In Fig. 0.1 is shown the outline of one of these maps – the so-called 'Dauphin' Map – and it must be evident at first sight that this 1536 Map does significantly resemble the real shape of Australia. Actually, the representation is an even closer likeness than superficially appears. After studying the projection upon which this Map was constructed, and after allowing for such things as the Magnetic Variation of the day and the

Erration error which was inherent in the Portuguese system of navigation then in use, it becomes possible to redraw the Dauphin Map on some projection with which the reader is more familiar, making due compensation for these calculable distortions. In Fig. 0.2 the Dauphin Map is redrawn on the familiar Mercator Projection: it can now be seen how unmistakably this Portuguese map of the sixteenth century portrays the real shape of Australia. So the Portuguese did know 'something, for sure'.

During the first half of the nineteenth century – say from 1786 to 1850 – these Dieppe Maps were known in England and France; and in those countries, in those years, they were openly accepted by the greatest geographers of the day as undoubted evidence of Portuguese discovery of Australia. The list of those who have left on record their acceptance is itself a rollcall of the geographical greats of the day: in England, Alexander Dalrymple, Matthew Flinders, Sir Joseph Banks, Major Rennell, John Pinkerton, James Burney; in France, Charles de Brosses, Barbie du Bocage, de la Rochette, Buache, Malte-Brun, Frederic Metz, Coquebert Montbret. It is hard to think of one leading English or French geographer of the time whose name does not appear on this list.

But from 1850 onwards acceptance of this Portuguese priority began to wane in England; and despite the advocacy of George Collingridge and a few other individuals it was never really accepted in Australia. There are underlying reasons for this – national prejudices, personal jealousies, official ignorance. But these prejudices reached their climax early this century, when the leading Australian professors of history, Professor G. Arnold Wood[1] and Professor Sir Ernest Scott,[2] came out in bitter denunciation of Collingridge and his theories. The present book, in its turn, has some harsh things to say about the Wood–Scott case.

In spite of the obvious interest that this subject must hold for Australia and for the world, little has been done to put the facts before those who wish to consider them. There has been only one full-length study, and three of essay length. The full-length study was George Collingridge's *The Discovery of Australia* (Sydney 1895), but this was so mauled by the critics, so stifled by the Establishment, so suppressed by the authorities, that it had little impact on contemporary or subsequent Australian thought: even the prestigious La Trobe Library, the repository of Australian historical books and materials, does not possess one single copy of this rare work. R. H. Major's[3] chapter in *Early Voyages to Terra Australis* (pro, twenty pages) and Professor G. A. Wood's chapter in his *The Discovery of Australia* (contra, eight pages) barely scratch the surface of the subject. The only modern work of substance – and it is a work of great value – is Professor O. H. K. Spate's[4] essay 'Terra Australia Cognita', in his book of essays, *Let Me Enjoy.* It is an oasis in a desert, but it is still only of essay length – twenty-eight valuable pages, but still only twenty-eight pages. So this present in-depth study is, at least, long overdue.

Perhaps one reason for the paucity of works on this subject is the deficiency of Portuguese scholarship in Australia. Professors Wood and Scott presumed to hand down their thundering (and adverse) rulings on this branch of Portuguese history without either the inclination or the ability to read one word in the Portuguese language. Only the Portuguese linguists, John Stevens and R. H. Major in Britain, George Collingridge and O. H. K. Spate in Australia, have captured the vision which gleams in the Portuguese chronicles of the Golden Age, and in the continuing Portuguese literature of their own day.

When John Stevens,[5] in 1694, published his translation of Faria y Sousa's *Asia Portuguesa,* introducing the British people, perhaps for the first time, to the enthralling story of how the Portuguese discovered the world, he dedicated his book to Catherine of Bragança, the Portuguese princess who had become Queen of England, with the words: 'It is *Justice* that leads me to lay this most *Wondrous Historie* at Your Majesty's Feet.' It is *Justice* that impels the present author to lay before his readers the equally *Wondrous Historie* of the Portuguese discoverers on the Australian coasts. It is only belated Justice that their exploits be now made known, that their part in unveiling the continent be now recognised, that the denigrated George Collingridge be now vindicated, and his detractors be now condemned.

J. R. McClymont[6] likened early Australian history to the junctioning of three streams:

> The [early Australian history] may be compared to the history of three streams which have their source in an unknown and half-mystical country. There is the stream of Portuguese ascendancy in the East. That stream undergoes changes, beginning in the end of the sixteenth century, and from being Portuguese became first Spanish and then Dutch . . . . To trace the course of these parent streams, and to discriminate them from their tributary waters, is the task of the man who would map out the various origins of the history of Australia.

It is the tracing of the first of these streams, the Portuguese, that is the task of this book. To trace it, we must roam far in the rich and romantic terrain of Portuguese history. We must meet the great navigators of Portugal's Golden Age of Discoveries, and sail with Gil Eannes and Diogo Cão, with Bartolomeu Dias and Vasco de Gama, and all the other *barões sinalados* of whom Luis Camões sang so eloquently. We must seek out the discoverers who reached the shores of Australia, and who brought home the charts on which the Dauphin Map is based. And first we must meet, and our story must start with, the greatest of them all, the man who began it all and who inspired them all – O Infante Dom Henrique, Prince Henry the Navigator.

PART ONE

'What knew the Portuguese of this great country?'

Chapter 1

PRINCE HENRY THE NAVIGATOR

THE national heroes of the Portuguese are the Great Discoverers of their Golden Age. Other countries may glorify their painters or their musicians, their statesmen or their warriors. The Portuguese glorify their mariners. Their national shrines are the tomb of Prince Henry at Batalha and the ruins of his College at Sagres. Vasco da Gama lies in state in the Jeronimos at Belém. Their greatest modern tribute is the Discoverers' Monument at the mouth of the Tagus. *The Lusiads* of Luis Camões are a paean of praise honouring da Gama and his peers.

One common tribute to the Discoverers is the wall map – a monument consisting of a mosaic map of the world on a stone wall, with proud ribbons radiating from Lisbon along the tracks of their heroes. One ribbon traces Gil Eannes past Cape Bojador; another traces Bartolomeu Dias to the Cape of Good Hope; others trace Vasco de Gama to India, Abreu and Serrão to the Islands of Spice, Cabral to Brazil. These, and many others, are well-known, well-documented voyages of discovery, of which the whole world is aware.

But there are other ribbons too, tracing tracks not so well known outside of Portugal, and sometimes with their roots more in tradition and legend than in documentation. One of these less authenticated ribbons traces João Vaz Cortereal to America, twenty years before Columbus.[1] Another, more doubtfully, traces David Melgueiro through the Bering Straits to the Siberian Arctic. Another traces a voyage to the sub-Antarctic South.

But, to Australians, the most interesting and the most intriguing is the ribbon which runs to Australia. It is clearly a Portuguese claim that their mariners discovered Australia too; and the more one delves into old maps and chronicles, the more this claim becomes substantiated. The chief barrier to its acceptance is the inability of the English mind, the Australian mind, to approach this thesis with any initial feeling other than shocked disbelief. Have we not been taught

from our schooldays that Captain Cook discovered
Australia – after some unimportant and impertinent intru-
sions by the Dutch in the preceding century? Do we not
consider Portugal weak, small and poor, a most unlikely
competitor in events of this kind? Do we not, in our secret
minds, share the sentiment expressed by Professor G. Arnold
Wood, when he concluded that the fact that Captain Cook
had had difficulties on the Great Barrier Reef coast, was a
sure indication that the Portuguese would not have been able
to navigate it at all?[2]

To dispel these prejudices from our minds, we must therefore be reminded of the great and glorious record of the
Portuguese in the fifteenth and sixteenth centuries – the age
in which this small country sprang to pre-eminence among the
nations of Europe, discovered the whole world, became
mistress of half of the world, established an Empire that was
larger than the Roman Empire and lasted longer than the
British Empire, climbed to the dazzling wealth of her Man-
oeline period, and opened the eyes of men to the new way of
life, ushering in the modern age.

What actuated this small and unlikely country in this way
has been the subject of unending conjecture and debate.
Scholars have found religious, political, commercial and mystical motives, all present and so entwined that no one can
satisfactorily disentangle them. These deeper motives are
probably more cogent than the one that will be expressed
here. But the half-truth of a good metaphor often illuminates
where pedestrian exposition of the whole truth only obscures.
So the symbol of the Golden Age, rich in legend and folklore,
ensainted by five centuries of a nation's adoration, mystically
alive today in the hearts of the Portuguese people, demands
our inquiry and contemplation, if we wish to understand the
question here posed. And that symbol is Prince Henry the
Navigator.

Prince Henry was born in 1394, the fourth son of a Portuguese prince (later King João I) and an English princess –
Philippa of Lancaster, daughter of John of Gaunt. It should
be a matter of pride to all people of English stock that this
great man whose vision and determination launched Portugal
on two centuries of voyaging, discovery and conquest was, on
his mother's side, of English descent. His earlier life, though

important, does not concern us here. The legend of Prince Henry starts in 1419, when he removed to Sagres and set up his establishment there.

Sagres is one of the twin headlands of Cape St Vincent, that long and desolate peninsula which is the Land's End of south-western Europe. The long Atlantic rollers break on the cliffs, their thunder only accentuating the silence, their rhythmic surge underlining the stillness. On one headland stands the St Vincent lighthouse, itself a symbol of the end of the land; and on the other headland – the sacred headland, as the name Sagres implies – stands the cluster of buildings which marks the spot to which Henry came to meditate.

The waves roll in from the horizon, and their question is always the same – from whence do they come? What is beyond? We today know that America is beyond to the west. But the men of Henry's era did not know that. They did not know if there was land there at all. They did not even know if there was ocean all the way. Perhaps somewhere out there – at Cape Bojador, the wise men said – the world came to an end, and the ocean went over the nameless precipice. Abyssus Abyssum.

This Cape Bojador has its important place in history. It is understandable that the Atlantic presented a water barrier to the west. But, in theory, there should have been no barrier to the south. The Portuguese and other Europeans knew the north-west coast of Africa – Morocco and its vicinity. We know today that the coast of Africa extends continuously, even monotonously, south from Morocco to the Cape of Good Hope. What stopped them from gradual mile-by-mile extension of travel down the coast until the Cape of Good Hope was reached?

The answer was Cape Bojador. The Cape can be found in any Atlas, in the colony of Spanish Sahara or Rio d'oro (or whatever its present name may be in this fast-changing world) almost at the nearest mainland point to the off-shore Canary Islands. To the scientific men of the day it was, geographically, the end of the *habitable* world, for the lands grow more and more arid as Cape Bojador is approached from the north, and at the Cape itself the poor lands give way to the uninhabited and trackless wastes of the Sahara. To the faithful of the day, it was God's boundary – 'a quae Deos deu por termo da

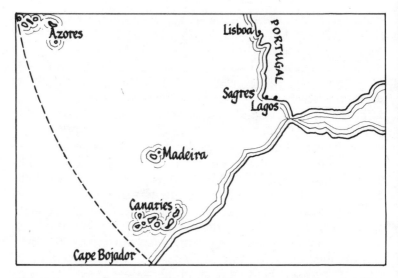

Fig. 1.1 CAPE BOJADOR (The supposed edge of the world is shown by dotted line).

habitação dos homens'.[3] To the mariners of the day, it was something incomparably worse.

Looked at from the sea today, Cape Bojador is not very significant and certainly not very terrifying. But in the days of sail a combination of circumstances – broken water, change of direction of the current, wind problems, reefs, fogs, storms – made it a difficult point to pass, a natural barrier at which to turn back. And because for a thousand years no one had passed that point, legend grew that the powers of darkness had made it impassable. The superstitious sailors of the day believed that its water was infested with sea-serpents and evil spirits. The end of the world was there, where the waters of the deep went over the edge like a waterfall. The waters boiled,[4] the ships disintegrated – even more darkly, the gates of Hell opened on the other side of the point. One hundred years earlier some Venetians, greatly daring, took their ship right to the point of the cape, so that they could see around the corner. There they glimpsed the black hand and fore-arm of Satan sticking out of the sea. The Venetians discontinued their investigations and returned to Venice. It is said that they clocked up such incredible time on the return passage that it stood as the record until the days of steam.

Most of this was medieval nonsense, as Henry himself was quick to point out. 'I wonder much at the notion you have all taken on so uncertain a matter,' he said, 'for even if these things that are reported had any authority, however small, I would not blame you: but you tell me only the opinions of four mariners who came but from the Flanders Trade, or from some other ports that are very commonly sailed to, and who know nothing of the needle or sailing-chart.' And the last part of this quotation from Azurara[5] shows that Henry was already on the way to the solution of the problem.

The difficulty, Henry could see, was one of technique, which could be overcome by research and education. Up to this date navigation had been developed in the Mediterranean, based on short-distance sailing in landlocked waters. For preference, the seamen kept close to the sight of land, sailing from landmark to landmark. It was obvious to Henry that Cape Bojador was nothing more than a local hazard, impassible for inshore sailing, but quite passable further out to sea. Therefore what was needed was a complete change-over from inshore sailing to blue-water sailing. The design of the ships, the principles of the rigging, the methods of navigation, the training of the crews – every facet of maritime science, indeed – would have to be changed to enable the ships to sail the empty ocean, far out of sight of land. There would no longer be use for the sailors who 'knew only the Flanders Trade', who could only find and enter 'ports that are commonly sailed to', who were too ignorant to navigate 'by [compass] needle and sailing-chart'.

The great ambition of Henry, and of the Portuguese, was to find a sea passage to Asia, especially to India and the Islands of Spice. They were not looking for empty lands to colonise (although when they discovered the empty Madeira and Azores Islands they did set up colonies there), for they were a small nation with no emigrants to spare. Consequently, the American lands to the west, even if they knew of them, were no attraction, although the first European settlement on the North American mainland was set up by the Portuguese at Ingonish[6] (Nova Scotia) in 1550. The American continent, when found, was to the Portuguese only a nuisance, a barrier stopping their passage to China. And as the Portuguese, far better than the Spaniards, had a realistic conception of the size of the earth, they discounted completely all tales of short passages to India across the Western Ocean. To Henry and the Portuguese, the way to India must be around the bottom of Africa, so first Cape Bojador had to be passed.

But as Henry puzzled and brooded at his cliff-top eyrie at Sagres, looking out over the empty Atlantic, suddenly the solution came to him. To pass to the tip of Africa, no less than to cross the ocean to America, one must first *travel west*, away from land, out into the deep ocean. Then by a semicircular sweep the ship could be brought to make landfall beyond Cape Bojador. If land was still there, next time a deeper and wider circle must be described, and this process repeated until at last one sweep would take the ship beyond the point of Africa into the Indian Ocean, and on its way to India. Vasco de Gama's sailing instructions swept him around the cape in this manner; Cabral swept out so wide that he discovered Brazil in the process.

This idea was revolutionary. It caused much the sensation that would have been created in the 1930s (though not in the 1970s) if some visionary had suggested that the quickest air route from London to Paris is not south-east but *straight up* – up into the stratosphere, then down to Paris by parachute. And in much the way that our men of the Space Age worked from a germ of an idea of this kind, collecting all available space knowledge from all the eminent physicists and mathematicians of the twentieth century, establishing a research station at Cape Kennedy, designing and perfecting the necessary spacecraft, recruiting and training the volunteer astronauts who were pledged to man them, and finally, to the world's wonder and amazement, setting a man on the moon – so Henry established his research station at Sagres for research, design, invention, training and all-over strategy, and there he succeeded in solving the secrets of the Ocean as our century has solved the secrets of Space.

For that is what Henry's 'College' at Sagres was. The word 'College' is used here, although it is a misnomer. It was · Henry's residence, his Fortaleza or Little Fort, to which were informally invited, for discussion and for the pooling of knowledge, all who could throw any light on the new knowledge that Henry required. He gathered there travellers, explorers, geographers, mapmakers, instrument makers, ship designers, astronomers, mathematicians, scientists, men of knowledge of all kinds. Each one contributed a little. And out of it all grew the new maritime knowledge which was soon to be put into practice.

The two great achievements of the Sagres 'think tank' were the new science of ocean navigation, and the Portuguese caravel. In the next chapter something will be said of the new navigation – the compass, the projections, the calculations and the rest. Very little was really new. But all available knowledge was there synthesised, rationalised, improved and made available, and the outcome was that indispensable knowledge which from Henry's day to our own enables the mariner to find his way across the trackless sea.

The other great achievement was in ship design: the evolution of the wonderful caravel. Here again no single feature was really new. The most revolutionary feature, the lateen sail, was clearly adapted from the Arab dhows. Most other features, the lines of the hull, the positioning of the masts etc, evolved from trial and error. But what was new was the deliberate scrapping of all of the old ideas applicable to coast-wise sailing, and the deliberate planning of the ship to meet the exigencies of ocean crossing. How well the designers succeeded is a matter of history. The miracle of the caravel (Plate III) was perhaps Portugal's greatest gift to the world.

When all was ready, Henry sent out his first ships in their great semicircular sweeps. The first results, as might be predicted, were the discoveries of the islands to the west and south-west, which (as previously mentioned) were immediately colonised. Then the Moment of Truth was at hand. Gil Eannes of Lagos was chosen to break the barrier at Cape Bojador.

The enlightened and rational Henry might scoff at the dark threat of Cape Bojador. To the less-educated Gil Eannes the in-built fears and superstitions of generations must have been paralysing. To his illiterate crew, the thought of braving Bojador was little removed from the thought of braving Hell itself. It took all of Henry's tact and patience to urge his captain on – even Gil Eannes turned back twice. How he kept control over his crew is beyond comprehension. The uncharitable say that the actual passage of Bojador was made in a fog, with the seamen unaware of their whereabouts. But the passage was made. In 1433 Gil Eannes passed Cape Bojador and made a landing on the Sahara coast, south of the dreaded cape. And to prove that he had really landed on land, and not on brimstone, he picked the only living things that he could find – some little wildflowers now known as St Mary's Roses, rosas da Santa Maria – and took them back to his prince. They were planted in the Algarve, where they flourished; and the Rosa da Santa Maria became the emblem and the trademark of the Portuguese discoverers in the century to come. The reader is requested to remember this little rose, for we shall next encounter it in Garden Island in Sydney.

On the sea front at Lagos stands the statue of Gil Eannes, diffidently holding his little bucket of wildflowers. Outside of Portugal his name is little known today. But if ever a man made 'one small step for a man, one leap forward for mankind' it was Gil Eannes in that memorable voyage.

The passage of Cape Bojador was one of the great turning-points in human history. It can only be likened to that day, in our own age, when the Space Barrier was broken for the first time. The breaking of the Space Barrier did not mean that distant stars could then be visited in the next ten minutes, but it made the world see that their eventual exploration is now possible and indeed inevitable. Likewise, distant lands and islands were not finally reached until decades, even centuries, after the Bojador Passage; but the world, and especially the Portuguese people, could at once see that they could be and would be so reached, given faith and enthusiasm, given time, men and money, given knowledge and technique. To Portugal, this was the unfolding of her Manifest Destiny. To Henry, it was the end of his period of dreaming, and the beginning of the hard, practical work that would translate his dreams into achievement.

Portugal was lucky that she had, at that moment of destiny, a leader so uniquely fitted to provide all that was required.

The world is fortunate that there was then, at Sagres, that man and that vision. 'If from the pinnacle of our present knowledge', wrote R. H. Major,[7] 'we mark on the world of waters those bright tracks which have led to the discovery of mighty continents, we shall find them all lead back to that same inhospitable point of Sagres, and to the motive which gave to it a Royal Inhabitant'.

Chapter 2

THE PORTOLANS

Iᴛ is easy to be dreamy-eyed with Henry, but it is necessary to be practical with him too. As Henry bent again over his maps, we need to bend over the same maps, to understand what they were and how they had developed, how they were made and how they are to be interpreted. Portolans were seamen's charts – charts of a special kind, no doubt, but essentially made for mariners to carry in their ships and to use at sea. The ornate, artistic Dauphin Map is a glorified portolan; its substance and form are taken from a portolan, representative of the Portuguese portolans of the 1520s, just prior to their radical overhaul by Pedro Nunes in 1537.[1] The portolans of Gil Eannes' day were even more simple, and had barely altered from the Mediterranean portolans of a century before.

The portolan was of Catalan origin, suited to the short distances and sheltered waters of the Mediterranean. The graticule of latitude and longitude had been invented by Ptolemy centuries before, but the portolans of the Mediterranean had no need of such sophistication. To the seaman sailing by portolan, to the navigator or cartographer constructing a portolan chart, only two ingredients were needed – direction and distance. Unknown to themselves, they were anticipating by two centuries the dictum of René Descartes that every point on a plane surface can be adequately represented, in relation to a point of origin, by these two ingredients only. And just as Descartes then proceeded to organise his 'direction and distance' points by articulating them on a grid of perpendicular and horizontal coordinates, so in due course the portolan mapmakers sought to articulate their points of reference on a grid of latitude and longitude coordinates.

But this was not yet. In its undeveloped stage in the early times, a portolan chart looked more like the 'direction-finder' which we find on a panoramic lookout at a tourist resort – a wind-rose of direction rays, each pointing (with distances

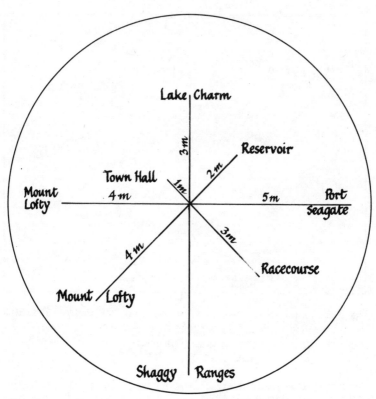

Fig. 2.1 DIRECTION FINDER. Locating features by distance and bearing, showing bearing (by rays) and distances (by figures).

shown in miles) to some point of interest (see Fig. 2.1). In Fig. 2.2 an imaginary Mediterranean direction-finder of this kind is shown, and from this the portolan grew.

The next step was to combine two or more 'direction-finders' into the one chart. Geometrically, this is not sound, as the curve of the earth introduces error; but for small areas, reasonably close to the Equator, this error was not significant, and it was convenient to have a chart which gave, or purported to give, direction and distance for more than one port. This proliferation of many wind-roses on the one chart gave birth to the special characteristic of the portolan – the beautiful intersecting rays of many wind-roses, with artistic embellishment at the centre of each. Where once the various

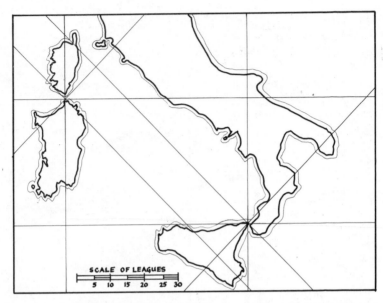

Fig. 2.2   EMBRYONIC PORTOLAN. Showing bearings (by rays) and distances (by scale). The centres of the wind-roses were later moved away from the coasts. (Diagram only.)

wind-roses were centred on their respective ports of origin, now the centres were shifted away from the ports to empty spaces on the chart, in the interest of legibility. The rays ceased to be direct radiating direction lines, and became instead a kind of in-built protractor, which could be read by means of a parallel straight-edge at any point on the chart. The mariners did not carry a protractor, but they were invited by the rays of the wind-roses to find their bearing or direction by comparison with the nearest parallel ray. The charts therefore purported to advise the true bearing or direction from any one point on the chart to any other point. The portolan is essentially a direction-finder or bearing chart: on the face of it, it purports to offer nothing else.

This assumes that the mariner, whether chart-maker or user, knew how to establish his bearing – that is, how to establish the direction of True North whether on land or on sea. This he was able to do. On land, where the ground is stable and time is unlimited, it was always known how to establish Local North by observation of the sun's shadow. First, a perpendicular pole (or gnomon) was erected. In mid-morning, its shadow was marked, and a circle of that radius was drawn around the gnomon. In mid-afternoon the lengthening shadow was watched, and its position marked again at the exact moment at which it again touched the circle. Bisecting the angle between the two marked positions of the shadow gave True North. Then, on the following day, the moment at which the shadow fell on the bisecting line was noon, thus giving true local time as well.

This performance was not possible on a moving and heaving ship. But in the northern hemisphere observation of the North Star (with necessary adjustments, which had been worked out by the astronomers) was an age-old and still practised method of finding direction. And, most important of all, since the thirteenth century the mariners of southern Europe had the instrumental aid of the lodestone, by the fifteenth century recognisably developed into the mariner's magnetic compass.

The early models, no doubt, were very crude, at first consisting of a needle inserted in a straw and floating in a basin of water. This crude device possibly read no finer than the four point of north, east, south and west. Gradually the instrument-makers improved on this, again with much of the impetus coming from Sagres. First the needle was boxed, then pivoted, then supplied with a compass-card, then the card itself was pivoted. All the time the instrument became more precise; and the card, which at first showed only eight points, blossomed to thirty-two. A compass with a 32-point card purported to be accurate to $11\frac{1}{4}°$, and no better; but at least it gave results as good as that, and in sailing ships no better was demanded. The wind-roses on the portolans are accordingly 32-ray roses, and the rays fan out at intervals of $11\frac{1}{4}°$. Where our trigonometrical and navigational tables read degree by degree from 1° to 90°, breaking down to minutes and where necessary to fractions of minutes, their tables covered only the eight 'winds' of each quadrant, and for all practical purposes these were the only bearings that mattered:

Portuguese wind	Modern bearing	Angle in degrees
0	E	0
1	E by S	$11\frac{1}{4}$
2	ESE	$22\frac{1}{2}$
3	SE by E	$33\frac{3}{4}$
4	SE	45
5	SE by S	$56\frac{1}{4}$
6	SSE	$67\frac{1}{2}$
7	S by E	$78\frac{3}{4}$
8	S	90

Within this rather broad limit of tolerance, the bearings shown on a fifteenth-century chart and the bearings followed by a fifteenth-century mariner were therefore scientifically sound; and so long as they did not journey too far away from home were quite accurate.

Magnetic deviation was not unknown to them, and at first did not cause much trouble. By comparing the compass with the local gnomon (on land), local deviation could be calculated and allowed for. In the next century Pedro Nunes invented the ingenious 'shadow-instrument', a compass-card with an inbuilt gnomon for self-correction. When Columbus and others began their trans-ocean crossings, magnetic deviation became of more importance, and its full impact will be considered in a later chapter.[2] The other magnetic variation, due to the proximity of iron in the ship, was not recognized as an error. In their small wooden ships it may not have caused much trouble. So, for better or for worse, the Portuguese of the fifteenth century had faith in their compass and their gnomon and their North Star. They believed implicitly in their ability to establish bearings, and all of their charts, tables and usages are based upon that faith.

The other ingredient in the early portolan chart was distance.[3] Here there was no instrumental help. The mariner had to guess the distance travelled by a form of dead-reakoning, palpably unscientific. Speed was judged by throwing a log overboard from the bow of the ship and timing the period that it took to clear the stern. Even this timing presented a problem, for they had no stopwatch, and it is amusing to note that the timing of the seconds as they slipped by could best be achieved by the sailors singing or chanting some doggerel shanty, and then counting the syllables chanted during the passage of the log. It was, clearly, very primitive. But even if it could be assumed that this log and time method gave good results – even assuming perfect results – it still only measured speed through the water as distinct from speed over the terrestial globe. Cook, with more sophisticated methods of gauging speed and distance, was very candid about their limitations. Off the Cape of Good Hope he was able to check his dead-reckoning by an astronomical fix, and admitted that 'if we had made no such [observation] we should have found an error of $10°$ $13'$ – such an effect the currents must have had upon the ship'.[4] And ten degrees is almost five hundred miles – a sizeable error in anyone's calculations.

An even better example is afforded by Abel Tasman (1642), who was wholly dependent upon dead-reckoning in estimating longitude, lacking the sophisticated astronomical fixes with which Cook and Green could cancel out their errors when opportunity offered. Tasman's methods of calculating were much the same, and quite as unreliable, as those of a century before. The first leg of his famous voyage to Tasmania and New Zealand was from Java to Mauritius, a traverse of about fifty degrees of longitude, and over that distance he was obliged to calculate his westing by the old methods. When he arrived at Mauritius he thought that he was in Long. $83°$ $48'$ (Tenerife) E, whereas that island is actually in Long. $74°$ (Tenerife) E. So Tasman made an error of nine degrees in a traverse of fifty degrees of sailing: in other words, his calculation of longitude was 18 percent in error.[5]

Yet the Portuguese navigator's ability to judge speed and distance was surprisingly good. From experience he knew his winds, he knew his currents, he knew what his ship could do. He knew that on a good day he normally travelled x miles, on a moderate day y miles, on a bad day z miles. If he had a reasonably straight and even run, the experienced navigator could judge his distance with an accuracy that is quite surprising.

And these distances, so calculated, were carried forward into the portolan charts. The figures, in miles or leagues, were not often inserted on the chart itself, but a scale of leagues was given, which could be pricked off with a pair of dividers. On setting out, the navigator noted the direction (by wind-rose) and the distance (by scale) of his next port of call. He endeavoured to sail that bearing by compass, and to calculate the distance sailed by his reckoning. The two together should bring him to port.

But a ship, particularly a sailing ship, is rarely allowed to sail on a line of constant bearing. Winds blow it off its course, it becomes necessary to veer and to tack, to zigzag from this side to that. The navigator had to have some means of reconciling the crooked course actually sailed with the constant bearing upon which he was attempting to sail. The first

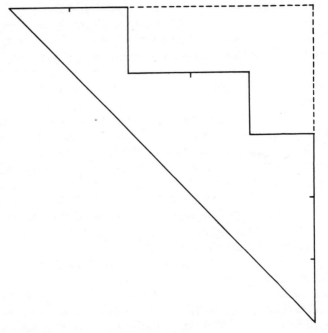

Fig. 2.3 COMPOUNDING BEARINGS. The position of the ship can be calculated on the simplified triangle, after the broken bearings have been compounded.

necessity was to count the legs of the tacks. If a ship, desiring to sail south-east, has to tack two miles east, then one mile south, then two miles east, then one south, then one east and then three south, it is back on its desired course (Fig. 2.3). To facilitate this counting, they invented the Traverse Board (Fig. 2.4). This was a wooden wind-rose, usually of 32 rays (although the illustration shows only eight), with holes bored along each ray and with wooden pegs to peg into the holes. The steersman recorded each half-hour's run by pegging the appropriate ray, and at the end of the day the navigating officer cleared the board and recorded the tally.

It was soon realised that these legs could be compounded. The complicated zigzag detailed above is the equivalent of a

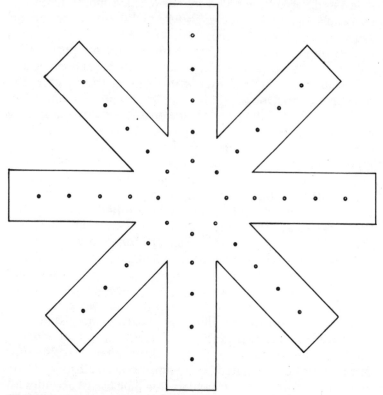

Fig. 2.4 THE TRAVERSE BOARD. The peg-holes enable the number of legs sailed on each bearing to be recorded.

total run of five miles east, then five miles south, as the dotted line shows in Fig. 2.3. So the pegging of the Traverse Board enabled the navigator to forget all the minor tacks, and to compound his day's run into (hopefully) one large and simple triangle. But whether he was working on one compounded triangle or on a multiplicity of small triangles, he still had to work out the position of the ship, the distance travelled, the distance made good, and the resultant angle of bearing; and for this he had to call in the aid of some trigonometry.

The reader should not be surprised to hear that they had trigonometry in those days. Invented by the Arabs and the Jews, it had passed into Portugal through her Moorish antecedents and her Jewish coteries, and was thoroughly understood and capably handled by her learned mathematicians, especially the astronomers. But few of these august beings sailed in ships, and they did not deign to give much direct help to the common mariner – though one of Henry's purposes at Sagres was to pick the brains of the mathematicians and astronomers in the interests of navigation. In any case, the uneducated mariners would not have had the ability to wrestle with complex trigonometrical problems. But they could add and subtract, multiply and divide, and find the answer to problems of proportion by the Rule of Three. And gradually some simplified trigonometrical tables seeped down from the astronomers, and the simple set of trigonometrical tables and trigonometrical rules needed for these problems of veering and tacking found their way into the books of sailing instructions. The best known of these was the handbook known as *The Rule of Marteloio*.[6]

If a ship is forced to veer or tack on an angle away from its true course, its distance from the true course at any moment can be calculated if the angle of divergence and the distance travelled are known. As said before, the two established ingredients of portolan sailing were bearing and distance; to these were now added a third ingredient, a trigonometrical table of proportions: and these three enabled off-course distance to be calculated. If a ship travels 100 miles at an angle of $22\frac{1}{2}°$ from its true course, it will be about 38 miles off course; if it travels 100 miles at an angle of 45°, it will be 71 miles off course, and so on. These proportions are the *sines* of the angle of bearing, and are given in the fourth column in Fig. 2.5.

The Portuguese did not know decimals, and all of their tables are expressed in awkward fractions. Similarly, their books of sailing instructions did not necessarily use modern terms such as sine and cosine. And again, their tables did not cover all angles, but only the eight sailing bearings. Fig. 2.5 is therefore not a facsimile of their material, but a modern equivalent. Nevertheless, it can be seen that these tables were versatile enough to solve all problems inherent in veering and tacking. The fifth column in Fig. 2.5 (giving the cosine of the angle) enabled the navigator to work out how many miles of his true course had been made good; and as he would already know the total distance from port to port, by subtraction he would then know the distance still to be sailed.

1	2	3	4	5	6
Portuguese wind	Illustrative bearing	Angle	Sine	Cosine	Tangent
0	S	0	.00	1.00	.00
1	S by E	$11\frac{1}{4}$	.20	.98	.20
2	SSE	$22\frac{1}{2}$	.38	.92	.41
3	SE by S	$33\frac{3}{4}$	.55	.83	.67
4	SE	45	.71	.71	1.00
5	SE by E	$56\frac{1}{4}$	.83	.55	1.50
6	ESE	$67\frac{1}{2}$	.92	.38	2.41
7	E by S	$78\frac{3}{4}$	.98	.20	5.03
8	E	90	1.00	.00	—

Fig. 2.5 MODERN EQUIVALENT OF MARTELOIO TABLES.

This can be seen in Fig. 2.6. The ship has to travel 150 miles from A to B. Having sailed 100 miles on an ENE ($22\frac{1}{2}°$) bearing, it is 38 miles off course (column 4), and has made good 92 miles of easting (column 5), so that 58 miles of easting remain to be sailed. The method with least mathematical subtlety would be to sail south the necessary 38 miles to rejoin the true course, then to turn at right-angles and sail east 58 miles to the port of destination. Incredible as it may seem, this clumsy

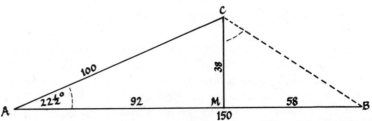

Fig. 2.6 MARINERS' TRIGONOMETRY. The Marteloio Tables enable the distance off course (CM) to be calculated. When this is known, the bearing required can be calculated and selected.

method was the one preferred and selected if winds and currents permitted those courses to be sailed. It is called 'right-angled sailing', and thereafter plays an important role in the development of Portuguese navigation. It was by this method that the successors of Gil Eannes proceeded down the African coast.

But before leaving the Marteloio Tables it is desirable to anticipate a little, to consider the sixth column in the figure. To travel from C to B by right-angled sailing, down the perpendicular and along the horizontal, was clearly not the shortest route from C to B, and was not always the most practicable. But if a mariner decided to cut the corner to sail direct from C to B, on what bearing should he sail? The tables had already provided sines and cosines, but this new problem entailed the third trigonometric ratio, the *tangent* of the angle, and the sixth column gives the set of tangents for the eight sailing bearings; but they had to be applied in a different way. The navigator would note that the ratio of his proposed easting (58 miles) to his proposed southing (38 miles) was approximately one and a half. Looking down the sixth column in the Tables, he would see that the ratio 1.5 is opposite angle $56\frac{1}{2}°$ (that is, the tangent of angle $56\frac{1}{4}°$ is 1.5), and he would therefore set his course south-east by east to sail from C to B. The invention of this method also had far-reaching results, as we shall see; and it was the prime cause of the phenomenon known as Erration.

The aids to navigation examined here were probably the limit of the navigational equipment carried by Gil Eannes, or any sailor before his time. He had his portolan, with a straight-edge to find the parallels to the rays of the wind-roses, and his dividers with which to measure off from the scale of leagues. He had his hourglass and his log of wood, for calculating speed and estimating distances. He had his traverse board for recording the legs of his tacks, and his Marteloio Tables for calculating his traverses. Above all, he had his magnetic compass, his faith in his Prince, and his faith in God. In 1433 no more was needed.

But the exploit of Gil Eannes at Cape Bojador produced not only a psychological revolution but a navigational one as well. Other mariners followed Eannes down the African coast. Nuno Tristão doubled Cabo Branco, and the first Portuguese fort was set up at Arguim. Dinis Dias passed Senegal and reached Cabo Verde. Alvaro Fernandes reached the Gambia, and Diogo Gomes added the Cape Verde Islands to the Portuguese Empire. The farthest point south in Henry's lifetime was reached by Pedro de Sintra, who reached and passed the Lion Mountains which are still today called Sierra Leone. From Cape Bojador to Sierra Leone was the incredible advance down unknown coasts, achieved by the will-power of one Prince, during that Prince's own lifetime.

To all of these successive mariners the instruction was the same: sail down the north-south meridian until you reach the latitude of your immediate predecessor's Furthest South; then turn east, and sail due east until you make landfall on the African coast; then battle down the coast as best you can, exploring and charting, until you can go no further; then return home. This was the old right-angled sailing, but right-angled sailing suddenly expanded to trans-oceanic proportions, raising enormous new navigational problems. How was the mariner to know when and where to make his turn to the east? Guesswork dead-reckoning may have been useful for one-day voyaging in the Mediterranean, but it could not cope with thousands of miles of open ocean travel in the Atlantic, out of sight of land. So some other means had to be found to tell the mariner where to make his turn.

The answer was found in Altura – not quite Latitude, but getting close to that conception. It was the recognition that the North Star (and, with modifications, other heavenly bodies, including the sun) sank in the heavens as the ship proceeded south, and that each place on the African coast, each port, cape or river-mouth, could be located by the angle which that heavenly body presented at each geographical point. By knowing the relevant angle (the Altura) and by having an instrument capable of measuring it, the mariner would know when he had reached a point opposite his required destination, and if he made his right-angled turn there he must coast in on his east-bound bearing. So all that he needed was an Altura Instrument, and a set of Altura tables.

This method was known by the Arabs before it was known to the Portuguese, and the Altura Instrument was an Arab invention. Once again it was Prince Henry's researches at Sagres that brought these benefits to the Western world. The instrument used by the Arab sailors was the Kamal – a cross-staff tethered to a knotted cord, which measured the decreasing distance between the North Star and the horizon, with the knots in the cord providing a rough scale of degrees. The European astronomers had a similar, but more complicated, instrument called the Astrolabe, which could similarly measure the Altura of the North Star, or of any other star, or of the sun. A simplified version of this called the Mariner's Astrolabe was soon invented, showing the angle of the sun by the bright spot which the sun cast through a pinhole in the perimeter of the cylinder. Better still was the cross-staff, which the Portuguese called the Balestilha, a firmer and more scientific version of the Kamal, but constructed on the same principle. Later the quadrant, with its plumb-line, was invented. There is no need to describe these instruments[7] further here, except to say that they all had the same purpose – to measure the angle of the heavenly body, and thus to ascertain terrestrial latitude. Probably all would be carried on the same ship: the cross-staff was best for sighting the North Star when a horizon was visible, the quadrant (using a plumb-line instead of a horizon) when it was not; the astrolabe was better for shooting the sun, for both quadrant and cross-staff entailed sighting the sun with the naked eye, often bringing blindness to the operator; the heavy metal ring of the astrolabe created less difficulty than the flimsy plumb-bob of the quadrant in rough seas or high winds. All had their uses, and when time allowed averages could be taken of the readings of all three instruments. To avoid having to differentiate between astrolabe, cross-staff and quadrant in later pages, the generic term Altura Instrument will be used.

At first these instruments did not display calibrations, graduated scales or numbered parallels of latitude. When the mariner found that he was level with (say) Cabo Branco, he wrote 'Cabo Branco' at the appropriate spot on his instrument. Similarly, he wrote in 'Arguim', 'Cabo Verde' and all other ports and points to which he needed reference. Then, as he sailed south, he waited until his instrument pointed to the name of his destination, and made his right-angled turn there.

Soon the clumsy method of writing in the names gave way to the more scientific system of a numbered calibration, and so the numbered parallels of latitude came into use. Following this, a latitudinal scale came to be printed on a suitable north-south line on the portolan charts – although ruled parallels (other than the Equator and the two Tropics) did not appear for another century. No longer were the portolans constituted by two ingredients, bearing and distance: now there were three – bearing, distance and latitude.

But the introduction of the latitude scale produced a new revolution in navigation. It took the guesswork out of the calculation of distance, and set up 'mile-posts in the sea'. The distance between any two parallels is uniform, 69.172 miles, or 60 sea-miles in English, $17\frac{1}{2}$ leagues in Portuguese; so a ship sailing down a meridian could clock up $17\frac{1}{2}$ leagues each time its Altura Instruments observed a change in latitude. On a north-south run, Latitude Observed was also Distance Observed.

It must be stressed that this new method did not abolish the need for dead-reckoning, but it superimposed a paramount check on the dead-reckoning; and where there was a discrepancy, the Altura calculation prevailed. All books[8] speak of 'checking' dead-reckoning by Altura, but this is a misnomer. 'Checking' in this case really means 'correcting' the dead-reckoning by the new calculation, and that is still the practice today. The navigator on a modern ship marks the hour-by-hour progress of his ship on his chart by reckoning from compass, engine speed, patent log etc. He pencils in his reckoned course on the chart. But when he makes his instrumental fix, he adopts the latter. If his reckoning does not agree with his instrumental fix, then his reckoning is wrong, probably due to ocean currents; and he sends his two readings – the correct instrumental position, the incorrect reckoned position – to Copenhagen, where the information helps the computers to work out the ocean currents in that part of the ocean where the ship is reported. The point is that 'checking' dead-reckoning means simply correcting it and superseding it.

Similarly, the system of southing and easting ('right-angled sailing') did not obviate the need for the Marteloio Tables. The ships were sailing ships, unable to sail due south on a constant bearing, without veering and tacking. Traverse boards and traverse tables were still needed to adjust the deviations from course that were bound to occur. And in the last column of the Marteloio Tables (the sixth column in Fig. 2.5) there lurked the germ of an idea which was to create still another step forward in navigation.

While the explorers were battling their way down the bulge of Africa, they were content to sail south down the meridian, turn at right-angles at the required latitude, and coast in on the easting (see Fig. 11.1). But once the coast turned inwards to the Gulf of Guinea, the general trend of their required courses became south-east rather than due south, and strict compliance with right-angled sailing became tedious. There was a temptation to cut the corner, to make diagonally for the mouth of the Congo or whatever other port was required. And the technique for setting the course for such oblique bearing was already established (see Fig. 2.5). By referring to that important last column in the Marteloio Tables (giving the tangents of the eight sailing bearings) the navigator could select the bearing which would run him directly in to port. And this was done.

But this new method, convenient though it appeared, had one disadvantage. It immediately destroyed the 'mile-posts in the sea' which were of such value to those mariners who adhered to the system of running down the meridian; and the navigator on the oblique course was driven back to the old guesswork of dead-reckoning. Yet by his Altura Instruments he could still fix each parallel of latitude as he crossed it. Could not the advantage be retained by some new method of calculation?

And this method was found, or was believed to have been found. It is of such importance in the story of the Portuguese Discovery of Australia which unfolds in this book that a full explanation is given here, and the reader is invited to study it carefully. In Fig. 2.7, a ship is at point A in Latitude 10°s, and requires to travel to B, 175 leagues south and 265 leagues east of the ship's position. Because it is 175 leagues south, B must be in Latitude 20°s, as shown on the diagram. The navigator could adopt the method of right-angled sailing, by sailing down the meridian to X (checking his position by Altura) then running east 265 leagues by dead-reckoning. But he elects to 'cut the corner'. He notes that his ratio of easting to southing, 265 to 175, is 1.506 (see Fig. 2.5, sixth column), which gives him a bearing of south-east by east, or $56\frac{1}{4}°$; and so he sails

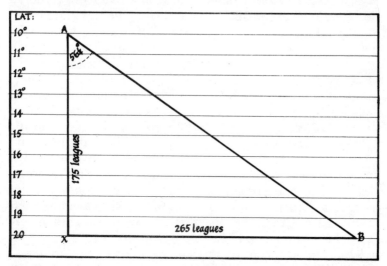

Fig. 2.7 THE INTERSECTION OF BEARING SAILED AND LATITUDE OBSERVED. Finding port by selecting the required bearing and sailing down that bearing until the required latitude is reached.[9]

along the line AB on that bearing. There is now, theoretically, no need for him to reckon by dead-reckoning at all. His Altura Instruments will tell him when he reaches Lat. 20°s; and as port B is at the intersection of lines AB and XB, that is, the intersection of the line of bearing sailed and the line of latitude observed, he should reach his port by trigonometry alone.

'*The intersection of Bearing Sailed and Latitude Observed*'. These were the new magical words of Portuguese navigation. Here for the first time is the breakthrough, the ability to ascertain latitude, giving the ability to ascertain distances at sea. It seemed at that time that they had solved all of their problems, for it promised that even longitude could now be calculated. Unfortunately these hopes were not completely justified, for later we shall find that one difficulty had been overlooked – they had failed to allow for Erration.

The switch to this new method of establishing distances – southing by direct Altura observation, easting by the tangent tables – is evidenced by the publication in Lisbon of a new set of tables, the *Regimento do Astrolábio e do Quadrante*,[10] which gave the table of tangents in an improved form, tailored for this new method of calculation. Here the ratios are based on the unit of $17\frac{1}{2}$ leagues (one degree of latitude), inviting the navigator to use the method here outlined. Pedro Nunes[11] gives illustrations of this method in use. He calculates the distance from Lisbon to Madeira by multiplying the difference in latitudes (eight degrees, or 140 leagues) by the trigonometrical ratio. He also demonstrates how the distance from Madeira to Terceira can be calculated, and then the distance from Lisbon to Terceira by combining the two. And then, a much more difficult problem, he calculates the distances of the remote South Atlantic island of Tristão da Cunha. But Nunes then went further, and the problems of longitude and Erration which he raised will have to be left until a later chapter. For the moment, we are concerned only with the new method of calculating distances.

Until the next century this system remained a Portuguese secret. No manuals or treatises were published, and no written exposition of the method survives in any Portuguese work until Pedro Nunes. But in 1520 Spain cracked the secret by enticing the expert hydrographer Ruy Faleiro to Spanish service; and Magellan, who went with him, was probably the most knowledgeable of Portuguese mariners – 'He was always busied with charts and questions of longitude,' as João de Barros said.[12] Martim Cortes, another Portuguese who went over to Spanish service, has left the best practical exposition of how the navigators applied this method in practice. Eva Taylor amusedly smiles at the unconscious humour of his long-winded explanation,[13] but as it is important to this discussion, it is explained here by Fig. 2.8. The ship

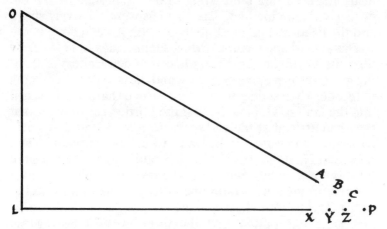

Fig. 2.8 THE METHOD OF MARTIM CORTES. Finding position at sea by the intersecting of bearing sailed and latitude observed. By opening the two pairs of dividers progressively, the position of the ship is eventually located at P.

left point O, sailing on bearing OP, and is now in latitude L. By dead-reckoning, the distance sailed is OA. If A is in fact in latitude L, then dead-reckoning and triangulation agree, and the position of the ship is confirmed. But if A is short of latitude L, or beyond latitude L, then the navigator takes two pairs of dividers: the dividers in the right hand prick the points O and A, the dividers in the left hand prick the points L and X. He then opens both a little to OB, LY – still not enough – then to OC, LZ, and finally to OP, LP where they join. That is where the ship is, at the intersection of Bearing Sailed and Latitude Observed.

Admiral S. E. Morison[14] warns us not to fall into the error of assuming that at the moment a new technique is invented it is immediately put into practice in all ships. It is not. The Portuguese mariners only slowly mastered this new method of navigating by triangulation, and it was not until after they had rounded the Cape of Good Hope that it became imperative for them to utilise it. Down the African coast the old methods still served, for the African coast trends mainly north-south, and it was sufficient to fix southing (latitude) by instrument, leaving the easting to be established by the old dead-reckoning method. The eastings were relatively short, and the dead-reckoning could cope with it well enough.

This at least applied until Prince Henry's death, or later. By then the Portuguese pioneers had rounded Cape Verde, at the most western bulge of Africa, and the coast was beginning to recede. Then suddenly the coast turned sharply to the east, into the Gulf of Guinea. At first the Portuguese thought that they had arrived at the end of African land, and that water passage all the way to India was now in front of them. When they found that this was not so, they built a fort at El Mina (in what is now Ghana), and most Atlantic navigators thereafter worked off the north-south line of Cape Three Points as the prime meridian for chart-making.

It is to this period that the three greatest Portuguese voyages belong – those of Diogo Cão, Bartolomeu Dias and Vasco da Gama. These three must be regarded as a team, each one passing on his knowledge to the next, even the crew of one sailing on the voyage of the next. It seems a pity that the fame of the first two has been so overshadowed by the glory of the third. Each left port in Portugal in the national atmosphere of emotion that betook of the quality of the launching of a Crusade – as indeed it was. Each carried a *padrão*, a commemorative stone cross to be set up at his furthest south; and these are today collector's pieces for which the world's historical museums vie in jealous competition.

Diogo Cão reached the Congo and beyond, and set up his *padrão* at Cape Cross in what is now Namibia (South-West

Africa). Bartolomeu Dias sailed from Lisbon in 1487, having on board the noted cartographer Alenquer (who later sailed with da Gama and to whom so much is owing in the development of Portuguese maps). Dias rounded the Cape, and set up his *padrão* at Kaarhoek, beyond the Great Fish River.

On 7 July 1497 Vasco da Gama, his officers and crew knelt in prayer in the little chapel at Belém. The next day all Lisbon was at the waterfront to see off the three ships whose voyage was felt to be epoch-making even before they had sailed. Prince Henry the Navigator slept more easily in his stone tomb at Batalha as the destiny which he had chosen for himself and his nation neared its great fulfilment. The next day the *São Rafael*, the *São Gabriel* and the *Berrio* passed across the bar of the Tejo into history.

The three ships rounded the Cape of Good Hope, and sailed on right across the Indian Ocean to make landfall in India. All that Henry had worked for and dreamed of was now crowned with success. The Indian Ocean became a Portuguese lake, with its capital and centre at Goa. And on the eastern boundary of that Portuguese lake was the land which the Portuguese were to discover and name 'India Meridional'; the land which later the Dutch were to sight and name 'New Holland'; the land which still later the British were to annex and name 'Western Australia'.

Chapter 3

THE TREATY OF TORDESILLAS

THIS book is the story of the Portuguese pre-Cook discovery of Australia. But the story has an elder sister – the story of the Portuguese pre-Columbian discovery of America – and the latter seems to jolt and surprise Americans as much as the former jolts and surprises the English and the Australians. Many a tourist has had the tranquility of his quiet stroll down the Avenida da Liberdade in Lisbon disturbed by viewing the mosaic memorial to 'The Discoverer of America' – commemorating not Columbus, but the voyage of João Vaz Cortereal, twenty years earlier. Many an American has been surprised to learn that the first European settlement in North America was not that of the English in North Carolina or Virginia, not even that of the Spanish in Florida, but that of the Portuguese at Ingonish in Nova Scotia.[1] Many a Canadian has been amazed to hear that the laconic and disappointed Portuguese expression *'ca nada'* ('there is nothing here') gave form to the name of his nation.

To delve fully into this American story would require another book as thick as this one; and attempting to unravel all the skeins of the Portuguese-American story would not be relevant to present purposes. Nevertheless, something must be said by way of background to the voyage of Columbus and its sequel; and those who are interested might be urged to study further, for the motives and policies and undercurrents latent in the American story have their parallels in and throw light upon the Australian story as well.

As told in Chapter 1, the Portuguese discovered and settled the Azores Islands in Prince Henry's time, and reached the outermost islands of Flores and Corvo by 1452. Now Corvo is only 1100 miles from Cape Race (Cabo Raso, itself a Portuguese name). To Australians accustomed to the vastness of the Pacific, it comes as a surprise to learn that only 1100 miles separates the last European outpost from the first American cape, that the longest ocean hop in the Atlantic is no more than the distance from Australia to New Zealand. And this proximity to Newfoundland gives Corvo much the role in the American story that Timor plays in the Australian story: it is such a natural jumping-off point that some contact with the continent beyond was almost inevitable.

The Azoreans then, as now, were fishermen. North-west of the Azores, between Corvo and Newfoundland (though favouring the Newfoundland side), are the great Fishing Banks, so important in subsequent Azorean and Portuguese history. The Azorean de Tieve discovered both Corvo and the Fishing Banks in 1452, though legends that he discovered the American coast in the process should be discounted; but whether he made his find a hundred or five hundred or a thousand miles from Corvo we do not know. It probably does not matter. Fishermen traditionally follow the fish; and if de Tieve's own first find was close to Corvo (of which island he was the discoverer[2]), his successors undoubtedly struck out further and further to the north-west, the fishing grounds getting richer and richer every mile, and it would be surprising if they did not eventually reach or at least sight the New-foundland coast. If they did so sight it, they were probably so busy hauling in fish that they took little notice.

And fishermen traditionally do not publicise their catches, or publish guides to assist their competitors. The fish garnered on the Great Banks was the cod, the famous Portuguese bacalhau. Immediately it made a most welcome addition to the Portuguese larder, and even today, in the twentieth century, the Portuguese would starve if they were deprived of it. It is therefore understandable that they did much exploring in the Fishing Banks area, and equally understandable that they did not tell the world much about it. Whether in the course of this activity they sighted the Iceland, Greenland, Labrador or Newfoundland coasts need not be debated here.[3]

Of course, the Greenland, Labrador and Newfoundland coasts were not unknown to Europeans. Since about AD 1000 the Scandinavians had set up colonies in Iceland, Greenland and Baffin Island, and had at least visited Newfoundland. The Greenland colonies subsisted until 1385, when contact was lost with the last of them. Now the year 1385 is only nine years before the birth of Prince Henry the Navigator. In Henry's own lifetime there were old men living in Denmark who had been in Greenland or Baffin Island. There were, in Denmark, maps and documents and oral traditions of the freshest kind.

The reader already knows that Prince Henry's 'College' at Sagres was set up as a clearing-house for all geographical information. Its primary purpose, no doubt, was to facilitate a sea route to India. But Henry and his colleagues at Sagres were actuated by a thirst for geographical knowledge of all sorts; and maps and travellers' tales concerning all parts of the world were eagerly collected. Henry's own brother, Prince Pedro the Traveller, made outstanding trips through central and eastern Europe, bringing back maps and information from those countries; and it is natural that Henry would seek information concerning these northern and western lands, which might throw light on oceanographic problems (the size of the earth, for example), even though they were not directly relevant to the Quest for the Indies.

And fortunately for Henry, the reigning king of Denmark, Eric II, was a kinsman of the Royal House of Portugal. From him, Henry obtained Clavus's map of Iceland and Greenland, and the Danish theory that there was a north-west passage beyond Baffin Island to China. All of this was at least filed in the geographical fact room at Sagres.

During the next two decades Portuguese familiarity with the north-west Atlantic grew, and Terra do Bacalhau became a familiar term. Codfish-*land* would seem to indicate coasts, though it may be only a mode of speech, as when we speak of fishing *grounds*. Columbus made his first voyage, as a deck-hand in a Portuguese ship, to these fishing grounds, 'a hundred leagues beyond Iceland'; and as Greenland is only a hundred leagues beyond Iceland, Columbus must have gone perilously near to sighting American soil on this voyage, fifteen years before his own more famous voyage of 1492.

But even earlier we have record of Portuguese interest in Greenland waters. In 1551 the burgomaster of Kiel wrote a letter to the then King of Denmark, speaking of Iceland and Greenland, and adding:

'Two skippers, Pining and Pothorst, were sent forth with several ships, at the request of the King of Portugal, to search for new islands and continents in the north. These were the skippers who set up the great beacon on the rock of Windzick off the coast of Greenland.'

This refers to the year 1472. And in Portuguese records[4] we learn that this expedition to 'Codfish-land', made at the request of the King of Portugal, was accompanied by the Portuguese navigator João Vaz Cortereal, who was made Governor of Terceira for his services. Subsequent maps show 'Terra do Bacalhau' or 'Stockfish-land' or even 'Terra Cortereal', where Newfoundland exists today. Again, it is not the purpose of this book to debate whether Cortereal discovered Greenland, Newfoundland or Nova Scotia. The point for our purposes is that as early as 1472 the Portuguese were on the Fishing Banks, and had more than a passing acquaintance with the waters around the coasts here mentioned.

The most important impact made by these north-west adventures was on the mind of a young man, then in Portuguese employ, named Christopher Columbus. He was Genoese by birth, but after being shipwrecked and washed up on the Portuguese coast he was befriended by the people of Lagos, and accepted Portugal as his adopted home. His brother, Bartolomeo, was already set up in Lisbon as a chart-maker, and Christopher went up to Lisbon to join him. But his interest was in the sea, and soon he was sailing in Portuguese ships. In 1477 he sailed to the northwest, beyond Iceland, where no doubt he heard talk of de Tieve and Cortereal, of the real or imagined coast of Stockfish-land, and of shadowy coasts still further west. Then he removed to Porto Santo, in the Madeira group, attracted by its reputation as a centre for exploration, as Professor Madariaga confirms.[5] He married a Portuguese girl, Felipa Perestrella, the daughter of the Captain of Porto Santo – thus joining a sea-faring family possessing traditional knowledge of Portuguese thrusts to the north-west. In every way he was well placed to imbibe Portuguese maritime lore. Everything was there to fire his interest in Lands to the West. He crossed over to the service of Spain, and made his great journey to the West Indies in 1492.

The details of this famous voyage are well known, and need not be repeated here. But two points are worth mentioning. First Columbus believed, and believed until his dying day, that he had in fact reached Asia: the term 'West Indies' on our modern maps reminds us of this.* Secondly, Columbus on his first voyage did not sight the mainland of America, but coasted along the islands of Cuba and Haiti. It would be splitting straws to say that he 'only' dscovered the islands: everyone accepts that his discovery of the islands two or three hundred miles off-shore is in fact the substantive discovery of the continent itself. And therefore, when twenty years (yes, only twenty years) later the Portuguese discoverer Abreu reached the Island of Timor, 285 miles off the Australian coast, an off-shore island of Australia in the same sense that Haiti is an off-shore island of America, the same line of reasoning must apply. More will be said of this in Chapter 5.

Portugal now had a competitor in her trans-oceanic explorations. Lacking Spain's military power, Portugal could not hope to throw the Spaniards out. At the same time, she could not brook competition down the African coast, or in her hoped-for monopoly of the Indian trade. Spain's excitement about the Columbian lands to the west might be irritating, but those lands could be written off by Portugal as not within the Portuguese grand design in any case. So Portugal sought compromise,[6] and the two countries laid their dispute before Pope Alexander VI for arbitration.

Earlier than this, in the 1450s, Portugal had sought a 'Charter of Imperialism' (as C. R. Boxer[7] calls it) from the Vatican, obtaining permission through three Papal Bulls (*Dum Diversis* 1452, *Romanus Pontifex* 1455 and the celebrated *Inter Caetera* 1456) to subjugate and convert non-Christian people from Cape Bojador to India. This, of course, has a religious purpose, clearly within the Pope's spiritual powers. But as the advance down the African coast progressed, the territorial acquisition of lands gained in importance over the earlier religious motive: and when King Manoel started checking through these old Bulls he found, especially in Inter Caetera, a very useful Papal foundation for Portuguese imperialism. So when Spain reached America and

* See dotted line on Fig. 10.1, p. 135, below.

began disputing with Portugal about the ownership of the new lands, the Portuguese King retorted that Spain was infringing *Inter Caetera*. Spain, in reply, argued that America does not lie between Cape Bojador and India, and claimed that therefore *Inter Caetera* did not apply.

This was the dispute that Pope Alexander VI was called upon to arbitrate. He was himself a Spaniard, a point which worried the Portuguese; but in his arbitration he seems to have shown tact, understanding and justice. He could see clearly that Portugal's great interest was in Africa and the East. He could also see that Portugal valued her Atlantic Islands – Madeira, the Azores and the Cape Verde Islands – and needed some territorial waters around them, say one hundred leagues of territorial waters. To the west of that, Spain's American New World began. Portugal had not yet discovered Brazil, or publicly had not admitted it; and similarly Portugal had not publicly admitted what, if anything, she had found in the north-west. So the Pope could not see how or why Portugal could be interested at all in lands to the west. Therefore he drew a line down the middle of the Atlantic, one hundred leagues west of the Azores or Cape Verde Islands, and adjudicated that all non-Christian lands to the east of that line were available for Portugal's exploitation, and all lands to the west for Spain's.

But King João II of Portugal was not satisfied with the line that the Pope had drawn. We have already seen that Portugal was vitally interested in much more than one hundred leagues of sea beyond the Azores, for the Fishing Banks extended three hundred leagues beyond those islands. João knew of Greenland and Newfoundland and Nova Scotia, probably believing them to be a little nearer than they actually are, and probably he was jockeying to obtain fishing ports on those coasts. Even more interesting is the suggestion that he already had secret reports of the discovery of Brazil. Dr Edgar Prestage[8] has found several manuscripts in the Lisbon archives which point strongly to that conclusion; and there is the extraordinarily interesting letter which Robert Thorne[9] wrote to Dr Ley in 1527, which asserts in clear words that 'when this foresaid consent of the division of the world was agreed of between them, the King of Portugal had already

discovered . . . certaine part of the maine land . . . and called it
the land of Brasil'. Brazil was not officially discovered until
the voyage of Pedro Alvares Cabral in 1500. But if Portugal
was negotiating a treaty, with secret knowledge of a new
continent held back as a hidden card, it serves as a precedent
for later negotiations at Saragossa, when the secret knowledge of the existence of the continent of Australia was
likewise held back by the Portuguese negotiators, and helps
to make more credible the theories put forward in Chapter
22.

So João fought hard to shift the Pope's Line further west,
and succeeded in having a new line fixed three hundred and
seventy leagues west of the Cape Verde Islands. As it was
then estimated that about 750 leagues lay between the Cape
Verde Islands and Columbus's discoveries in America, this
was probably arranged as a 'split-the-difference' compromise. The new line is often, even today, referred to loosely as
'the Pope's Line'; but as it is 270 leagues further west than the
Pope's Line, in this study it will be referred to as 'the Line of
Demarcation'. And this amended agreement was formally
written into the Treaty of Tordesillas in 1494.[10]

It should first be noted that this Treaty is a normal international treaty, made between Spain and Portugal, binding on
Spain and Portugal, and from its nature not intended to be
binding on anyone else. The fact that the Pope later ratified it
is a formality. It was not a papal handout to favoured nations,
to be derided and disrespected as the English and the Dutch
later claimed. It deserves the respect due to any other formal
international treaty, no more and no less. For a hundred years
and more it did keep the ring in the rivalry between the two
Iberian powers. It was substantially amended by the Treaty of
Saragossa in 1529. It was dishonourably breached by Spain,
when she seized the Philippines, in 1562. It was finally
abrogated and repealed by the Treaty of Madrid in 1750; but
even later, at times, its terms have had legal and international
significance. It became the matter of high legal argument in
the international litigation between Venezuela and Great
Britain over the British Guiana boundary in 1898.[11] And as
we shall see, it had bearing on the delimitation and annexation of the State of Western Australia.

It should be especially noted that the Treaty did not purport to vest the beneficiary nations with any lands other than non-Christian lands; and it only purported to cover those lands 'which up to the present and henceforth may be found and discovered'. Above all, it conferred no rights over the seas. But in later years both nations attempted to interpret the Treaty as meaning that the whole of the sea within the allotted hemispheres belonged to them, to the exclusion of all others, and therefore that no other nations could enter those seas to do any exploring. If this were true, all lands and islands, whether discovered or not, were theirs. This is the doctrine of the 'mare clausum', claimed by Portugal in respect of the Indian Ocean, claimed by Spain with respect to the whole of the Pacific.

Actually nothing was said, nor in a bilateral treaty could be said, about other nations having no rights to enter. But the Treaty did, in the strongest terms, forbid the Portuguese to cross the Line of Demarcation into the Spanish zone, and vice versa, with provisions jeopardising the whole treaty if this clause were disobeyed. As the weaker military power of the two, Portugal observed this provision with the utmost strictness (publicly, at least), for it was so much to her advantage to uphold the sanctity of the Treaty – to be able to appeal to the Pope, or to international conscience, whenever Spain breached it. It will be seen later with what nicety Portugal drew the Line of Demarcation on her charts.

But the most controversial clause in the Treaty was the most important clause: where is the Line of Demarcation actually located? This clause is worth quoting in full, to be compared with the similar clause which later appeared in the amendment of 1529. It reads:

'There shall be made and marked out on the said ocean a mark or line straight from Pole to Pole north to south, drawn straight at 370 leagues from the islands of Cape Verde to the west, by degrees or by any other manner.'

This says 'from the islands of Cape Verde', without specifying which island. The Arquipelago do Cabo Verde sprawls three degrees, about 180 miles, over the ocean. The Portuguese rather naturally measured from the most westerly of the islands, Santo Antão, while Spain ungenerously measured from the most easterly island, Boavista. Pope Alexander's arbitration probably intended and implied that the distance was to be measured in Italian leagues, while the Spanish–Portuguese treaty presumably used Iberian leagues – a matter of some moment, as these differed by almost one mile. Another ground for controversy appeared later, when longitude was understood better, for then it became necessary to know along which parallel the 370 leagues should be measured. And lastly, as the existence of a hemisphere on the other side of the world was then only dimly recognised, the Treaty did not properly contemplate – it certainly did not properly state – that the Atlantic Line of Demarcation was to be carried over the Poles to mark the corresponding boundary on the Asiatic side as well. This last difficulty seems of less importance, as later both nations seemed to accept the implication that the earth had been 'cut like an orange', that it had been intended that the Line was to run right around the earth in a Great Circle, providing a dividing boundary on the Asiatic side as well.

But even had they reached agreement on all of these disputed points – say, for example, that they had agreed to start at the island of Santo Antão and measure in Iberian leagues along the latitude in which that island is found – one insuperable practical difficulty remained. No one in 1494 had the instruments or the technique to locate the Line on the land or on the sea, or to define it beyond dispute on their charts, by longitude or other means. The best that anyone could suggest was to sail west from the selected starting island, calculating the 370 leagues by the crude dead-reckoning methods outlined in Chapter 2 – throwing logs over the side, and all the rest – and then turning at right-angles to run south down the meridian until the South American coast was reached. This method is actually prescribed in the text of the Treaty itself. Obviously the crudity of the method and the distances involved made the suggestion close to valueless.

Perhaps these practical navigational problems were not present to the minds of the plenipotentiaries who hammered out the Treaty in 1494. But a few years of confusion and controversy showed that the problems were real, and in 1524 the Kings of Spain and Portugal, flanked by experts of all kinds, navigators, mathematicians and lawyers, met in the frontier no-man's-land between Badajoz and Elvas (known as the Junta of Badajoz) to straighten out the difficulties. No practical solution was found. If the Portuguese knew a better method for fixing the Line (and by 1524 they believed that they did, based upon the tangent tables which were discussed in the last chapter), they were not talking. The meeting broke up on the understanding that each nation should fix its own Line of Demarcation, without prejudice to the right of the other nation to have it rectified if and when more accurate surveys were possible.

This was the Junta of Badajoz, 1524. And two years *before* the delegates assembled at Badajoz, a Portuguese expedition had already passed down the east coast of Australia. The track of those Portuguese discoverers is enshrined in the Dauphin Map.

Chapter 4

THE LINE OF
DEMARCATION

A GLANCE at a modern map of Brazil shows that the terminal point of the north coast, where it junctions with French Guiana, and the terminal point of the south coast, where it junctions with Uruguay, are almost exactly north and south of each other. The line joining these two points, running across Central Brazil, is, in the numbering of longitude which we use today, the 51st meridian west of Greenwich (Fig. 4.1); and following the Treaty of Tordesillas that was the then western boundary of the Brazilian territory claimed by the Portuguese. At that time, of course, not much of inland Brazil had been explored, and none of the interior was occupied; and therefore for many years the question of the inland boundary was not important – although in 1541–2, when Orellano's Spanish expedition came down the Amazon from its headwaters towards the sea, the Portuguese disputed their passage at this meridian.[1] But on the coast, it was early necessary to fix a boundary point, and the point fixed by the Portuguese on the north coast was the mouth of the Waipoco River, where the 51st meridian strikes the sea.

On the south coast, on the Uruguay boundary, there is no physical feature as distinctive as the Waipoco, and the actual boundary point wavered a few miles first this way and then that way; but substantially it has always been at or near the same meridian. The 51st crosses the Lagoa dos Patos, the swamps around it, and the spit of sand between it and the sea, so that the southern terminus was more a line on a map rather than a point on the ground. Lopo Homem's map of 1554 shows the Waipoco meridian clearly.[2] So do the maps of Jorge Reinel, the greatest of the early Lisbon map-makers – continuing to show this boundary even after he had gone over the service of Spain. On the other hand, there are many Spanish maps which attempt to push the conjectured boundary much further to the east, to Spain's advantage and Portugal's detriment.[3]

The treaty of Tordesillas implied, and the Junta of Badajoz confirmed, that each nation should unilaterally fix its own boundary, subject to later rectification. The Treaty itself provided further:

> 'And if it shall happen that the said line shall encounter any island or mainland, some signal or tower shall be made, and shall continue from that place onward by other signals through such island or land, and the subjects of the said parties shall not dare to cross the said signal and boundary.'

Acting on this invitation, Portugal did unilaterally mark its Brazilian frontier, not perhaps with a tower, but with an outpost settlement at Vila Velha ('the old settlement') just east of the Waipoco River. Predictably, however, Spain did not agree with the Portuguese line. Purporting to measure from Boavista, the most easterly of the Cape Verde Islands, and in other ways disagreeing with the Portuguese method of fixing the Line, Spain worked out that it should run just behind Rio de Janeiro, in what is today Long. 45° (Greenwich) w, which would have left Portugal with only a narrow coastal belt on the South American continent. This 'Spanish Claim' line[3] was used by Spain as a political talking-point, and was raised by Spain whenever the Line came up for discussion, at the Junta of Badajoz and at the Treaty of Saragossa. But in practical politics, on the actual ground in South America, Spain never seriously questioned the Waipoco boundary, and at times acquiesced in it. In 1604, when the English under Leigh attempted to found a colony on the Waipoco, and crossed to the east bank of that river, the Spanish (who were by then the overlords of Portugal) informed the English that this land belonged to 'our vassal, Portugal', and joined with the Portuguese to eject the English.[4] Probably this Waipoco boundary explains the existence of the three non-Iberian colonies (or ex-colonies) on South American soil – French, Dutch and British Guiana. Portugal made no claims west of the Waipoco. Spain was never really interested beyond the Orinoco. Raleigh's expedition of 1595 first drew attention to this neglected pocket,

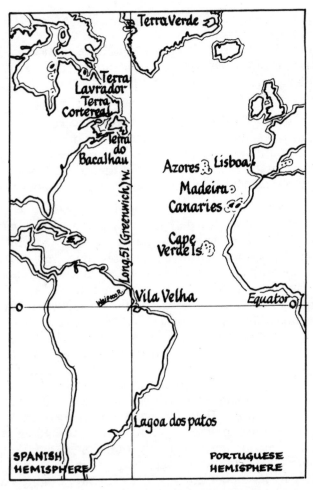

Fig. 4.1   THE LINE OF DEMARCATION IN THE ATLANTIC

and eventually the three northern nations gained footholds in this no-man's-land, as can still be seen on the map today.

It was the same on the southern boundary. Spain never physically interfered with the Lagoa dos Patos boundary. Indeed, in the Colonia War of 1777, when the Portuguese–Brazilians came to the assistance of their compatriots who had strayed over the Line to form a 'Colonia' across the river from Buenos Aires, it was the Spanish who demanded the

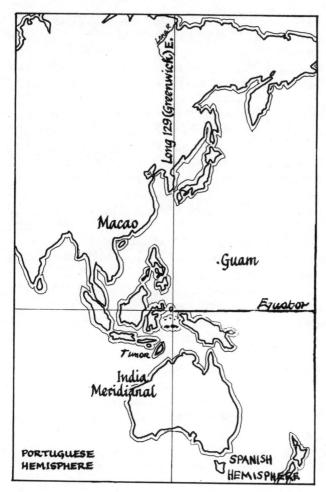

Fig. 4.2   THE LINE OF DEMARCATION IN THE PACIFIC

return to the Lagoa dos Patos boundary. And so this Line of Demarcation, unilaterally fixed by Portugal and never really challenged in South America by the Spanish (despite verbal attacks against it from time to time), has to be accepted as the de facto Line of Demarcation, whether it strictly accords with the provisions of the Treaty of Tordesillas or not.

At this point in the story it is natural to ask the question – how did the Portuguese purport to locate the 51st meridian, when they had no chronometer or other instrument for fixing longitude at sea? The fact that they did so fix it is indisputable, and modern maps testify to that fact. Just how it was done is not recorded, but can be deduced from the knowledge of Portuguese navigation methods, already outlined in Chapter 2.

First, they had the method of right-angled sailing. Santo Antão in the Cape Verde Islands is in the Altura or latitude of 17° N. Vila Velha is in latitude 3°N, making a difference of 14° between them. By right-angled sailing, the ship would first sail due south fourteen degrees, until by Altura Instrument it picked up the latitude of Vila Velha in Lat. 3°N. There a right-angled turn would be made, and the ship would run due west along that parallel until contact was made with the Brazilian coast. But this method only barely improved on the suggestion made in the Treaty: it involved sailing south and then west, instead of west and then south. Perhaps it did introduce an improved instrumental method of checking the distance at the end of the first leg, but it still required guesswork dead-reckoning on the more important westing.

But the Portuguese were by then evolving their more sophisticated technique, summarized in Chapter 2 as the fixing of position by 'the intersection of Bearing Sailed and Latitude Observed'. This purported to provide a technique for measuring the westing without recourse to dead-reckoning at all. Why sail south 14° and then west, when it is possible to sail diagonally and still know where you are? And what is more, why use the guesswork of dead-reckoning when the whole measurement can be made instrumentally, by compass and Altura?

Because of the extraordinary importance of this method of calculation in our later considerations, when we will be examining the longitudes of the Portuguese maps of Australia, the reader is asked to give careful attention to this piece of navigation, from Santo Antão to what is today Vila Velha, as a good illustration of how it works in practice. Fig. 4.3 gives a map of part of the Atlantic, showing these two ports. No longitude is given, as longitude was not in the minds of those who were attending to this problem in the early sixteenth century. They were not concerned with longitude

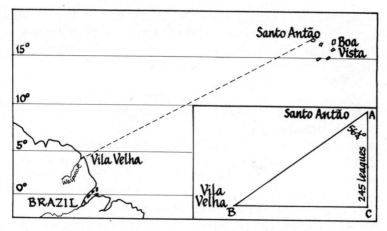

Fig. 4.3   FROM SANTO ANTÃO TO VILA VELHA

(in degrees), only with westing (in leagues) and in particular with the westing of 370 leagues prescribed by the Treaty of Tordesillas. But the figure does show the respective latitudes.

The ship left Santo Antão in Lat. 17°N, sailing south-west by west (s 56¼°w), which is the bearing of Vila Velha to the nearest of the eight sailing bearings then in use. On sighting the Brazilian coast, the ship found the latitude of the landfall (by Altura) to be Lat. 3°N. Therefore the ship had made southing of fourteen degrees, which (allowing 17½ leagues to the degree) equals 245 leagues. The triangle ABC (inset) can now be constructed with:

$$AC = 245 \text{ leagues}$$

$$\angle ACB = \text{a right-angle}$$

$$\angle BAC = 56\tfrac{1}{4}°$$

What is the length of the side BC?

Now their experience in calculating tacking and veering comes into play. As explained in Chapter 2, if they knew their bearing and their southing they could calculate their westing, by applying the table of tangents set out in the sixth column of the Marteloio Tables (Fig. 2.5). The appropriate figure for sw by w is 1.50. Multiplying 245 leagues by 1.50 gives 367½ leagues – 367½ leagues west of the Cape Verde Islands, which in anybody's language is close enough to the Tordesillas formula of 370 leagues west of the Cape Verde Islands. So that was the Line of Demarcation. They put their marker at the point so found, and in due course their frontier post of Vila Velha was set up there.

The location of the Line at this exact point is not accurate by modern standards because the allowance of $17\frac{1}{2}$ leagues to the Equatorial degree is not quite accurate, because Santo Antão is not quite N $56\frac{1}{4}$ E of Vila Velha, and because (as we shall see) the whole of this mathematical formula is wrong, upset by the curving of the loxodrome.[5] But the first two are only slight, and the third is not severe in latitudes so close to the Equator, and the result is really very good – far better than the wild gueses that the Spaniards were making, or were to make in the future. The Vila Velha line, that is the 51st meridian, must therefore be accepted as the Line of Demarcation, and the course of this meridian across the globe can now be traced.

After leaving the northern Brazilian coast at the Waipoco, the Line runs north through empty sea, leaving the Cape Verde Islands and the Azores on the Portuguese side, the West Indies, Florida and the whole of the North American coast on the Spanish side (Fig. 4.1). It then just misses Newfoundland. João II had fought to keep the Fishing Banks on the Portuguese side, and he had succeeded. If he had also tried to include the valuable Newfoundland and Nova Scotian ports, he must have made a miscalculation. For decades the Portuguese maps of the North Atlantic made the Canadian coast droop too far to the east, with Newfoundland depicted well on the Portuguese side, bravely flying the Portuguese flag and thereon named 'Stockfish-land' or 'Cortereal-land' in Portuguese tradition. The Reinel of 1535 is a good example. The Portuguese would dearly have liked to have obtained St John's Harbour – even today it is a key port in Portuguese fishing. It was during this period that the fisher folk from Viana do Castelo founded the first European settlement on North American soil, at Ingonish in Nova Scotia.[6] But once the meridians of longitude were properly located, it became clear that Newfoundland and Nova Scotia were not within the Portuguese hemisphere, and Portuguese interest in those parts dwindled. Greenland was theoretically Portuguese – most of Greenland is on the east side of the 51st meridian – and there was some activity in exploring the Greenland and Labrador coasts. Labrador takes it name from João Fernandes Lavrador, and it was in these exercises that the two sons of João Vaz Cortereal lost their lives. Portugal continued to fish the Fishing Banks from her bases in the Azores, but her energies in exploring and discovering were soon switched to the other side of the world.

Beyond Greenland the 51st meridian reaches the North Pole. It then becomes the anti-meridian of 129° east of Greenwich ('The Great Meridian'), which is the continuation of the Line of Demarcation on the Asiatic and Pacific side of the world. The Treaty of Tordesillas does not expressly state that the Line was to run right round the world – indeed the words 'from north to south' imply the opposite. But the 'other side' of the world was not known when the Treaty was drawn up; and except when it was politically expedient for one party to make a hair-splitting objection on this point, it was the common understanding that there must be a Line of Demarcation in the east, as otherwise it would be meaningless to have one in the west. This analysis therefore proceeds on the basis that there is a Line of Demarcation in the east, and that it is the 129th meridian, the Great Meridian which the Portuguese upheld and the Spaniards disputed.

The 129th runs south from the North Pole and crosses the Asiatic continent at the mouth of the Lena River, in Siberia. Further south it runs between Korea and Japan, just skirting Nagasaki. It then crosses the wider area of ocean, flanked on one side by the Portuguese colony of Macao and on the other by the ex-Spanish colony of Guam. Further south again, it passes between Halmahera (formerly Gilolo) and New Guinea. Here we are in the Moluccas, the fabulous Spice Islands, with the sixteenth-century Portuguese bases of Ternate and Tidore just inside the Line; and just across the Line is New Guinea, which was apparently only once visited by the Portuguese, when Governor Meneses was wrecked there. And next it bisects the island of Ceram (see Fig. 4.2).

Then comes the sharpest knife-edge of all, with the Line passing between Amboina (Long. 128°E) and Banda (Long.

130°E). Amboina, on the Portuguese side, became the Portuguese capital, or administrative centre, for the Moluccas. Banda, on the other side, was never occupied by the Portuguese, in spite of its proximity and its great wealth. The Portuguese traded there, but they never had any pretensions to it. They fought the Spaniards when they attempted to enter Halmahera, but they tolerated them in Banda. When the Dutch came, they had to fight for Amboina, but they entered Banda without opposition. The difference in the Portuguese attitude to these two equally wealthy islands is so marked that it can be said for certain that the 129th was for them the boundary.

Next it passes Timor, of which much more will be said later. The very name 'Timor' in the Malay language means 'the East Point', as distinct from Timorlaut – 'beyond the East Point' – which is the name given to the group of islands just the other side of the Line. The Great Meridian then skirts Australia's Bathurst and Melville Islands, leaving them on the Spanish side; and then it crosses the Australian coastline in Joseph Bonaparte Gulf, and becomes the present Western Australian boundary.

Just as the Spanish disputed the Portuguese Line of Demarcation in the Atlantic, so they disputed it in the Pacific, especially when Magellan's voyage of 1522 showed Spain that the priceless Spice Islands were very close to this boundary – close enough for genuine dispute – and that the ownership of these islands depended upon the meticulous calculation of its true location. But here Spain found herself in a cleft stick. Irrespective of where the Line of Demarcation is located, it is incontrovertible that Spain and Portugal were each entitled to exactly one hundred and eighty degrees of the earth's circumference. As the wealthy Spice Islands were much more to be coveted than dreary Brazilian jungle, Spain's ungenerous location of the Brazilian boundary rebounded, and became a positive liability. This is self-evident, yet it is a point that is almost invariably neglected in modern discussions of this subject. But this argument was clearly understood and relied on by the Portuguese at the time. Osorio, the Bishop of Silves, writing about 1571, gives expression to this exact point:[7] '*Por cujo meio ficava licito* (*visto que tem* 360 *graus o globo*) *tomar cada um* 180 *para descobrir ou conquistar.*'

So the further east the line is drawn in Brazil, the further east it must be drawn in the East Indies. If Spain insisted on the Spanish Claim line in Brazil (Long. 45°w), then it would automatically be pushed back to Long. 135°E on the Indonesian–Australian side. On the other hand, if Spain claimed the Spice Islands as far west as the Philippines (say Long. 120°E), then Portugal could justifiably claim Newfoundland, Montevideo and Buenos Aires, all of which are on the eastern side of Long 60°w. The moral of this is that you cannot have it both ways: but in spite of this, there was one stage when Spain was claiming from Singapore to near São Paulo – a total of 217 degrees.

At the Junta of Badajoz, which was called to discuss this very question, this point was apparently made.[8] Spain offered Portugal a greater share in Brazil in return for a greater share in the Spice Islands. But in the early sixteenth century Portugal was unaware of the silver and other riches which Brazil was to pour out in such profusion in later centuries: at the time Brazil was only valued as a convenient port of call on the voyage to India. So Portugal refused to budge from the Line of Demarcation which she had drawn in both hemispheres.

The year 1522 was a kind of plateau, or watershed, between two phases of the dispute over the Line. Before this date, both nations had been jockeying for more territory in South America. After this date, the focus of the dispute dramatically switched to the east. Magellan's surviving ship arrived back in Spain, bringing reports of the riches of the Moluccas and the advice, erroneous though it may have been, that these islands were on the Spanish side of the Line. After that, cool consideration of the geographical data could not be expected, when the fabulous profits of the Spice Islands were at stake. Violent disputes broke out, and the Line was to be argued about, fought over and eventually amended.

But in 1522 all of this was still in the future, and it was this moment of pause that concerns us in this study: for it was in 1522 that the Portuguese voyage of discovery down the east coast of Australia was made, and the impetus for this voyage was this very question of the location of the Great Meridian.

Chapter 5

TIMOR

I N the year 1976 the Portuguese flag was lowered in Timor
for the last time. From 1516 to 1976, four hundred and
sixty years in all, Portugal had maintained a colony in that
island, probably the longest that any European country has
ever maintained an overseas colony, anywhere, in continuous
occupation. Records of this kind do not matter much in
themselves. But this unexpected record highlights an important and little-recognised fact – that for four hundred and
sixty years there was a continuous, organised Portuguese
settlement in this island just off the shoulder of Australia,
with only two hundred and eighty-five miles of water separat-
ing it from the Australian coast. John Barrow,[1] the great
administrative secretary of the British Admiralty, wrote:
'From the neighbouring island of Timor, it is but a step to the
northern part of New Holland'; and when Australia was
rediscovered by the Dutch and the British, it was not (as so
many visualize it) a mysterious continent incredibly far from
the nearest haunts of civilised men: it was instead, in Barrow's
words, 'but a step' from an established Portuguese colony.
When Cook sailed up the east coast, the Portuguese settlers
had already been in Timor for two hundred and fifty years –
longer than the British have been in Australia at the date of
writing this book. Even when the first Dutch sighting was
made in 1606, the Portuguese had already been there for
ninety years.[2]

A glance at a modern map shows that, until 1976, the island
of Timor was divided into three parts: the main Portuguese
province (East Timor), the Portuguese enclave to the west
(Ocussi), and the Indonesian end of the island (South Timor).
The little island of Solor, across the water and almost opposite
Ocussi, should also be noted. The initial Portuguese colony
consisting of Solor plus Ocussi, was founded about 1516.
Later, there was Portuguese penetration of South Timor, and
later again of East Timor. Then in the seventeenth century
Solor and South Timor were captured by the Dutch, leaving

only East Timor plus Ocussi in Portuguese hands. The phrase 'the Portuguese colony of Timor' therefore means different things at different times, but the one constant is Ocussi, in the beginning Portuguese, and for four hundred and sixty years continuously Portuguese, until its final integration into Indonesia in 1976.

The administrative centre was first Solor,[3] then Lifou (in Ocussi) and finally Dili (in East Timor). The boundaries were finally settled in the Dutch–Portuguese war of 1911–12. Few people in Australia are aware that, as late as 1912, a war between two European powers was in progress in an island so close to their shores. And the expression 'so close to their shores' is here deliberately repeated, and it will be repeated again and again in this study, for this fact is central to the argument here presented: the distance from Cape Bougainville, on the hump of Western Australia's Kimberley Coast, to the south point of Timor is so very short that the Portuguese discovery of this off-shore island is, to all intents and purposes, the discovery of Australia, just as Columbus's sighting of Watling Island is accepted as the Columbian discovery of America; and even if this is not conceded, the immediately following Portuguese settlement of the island, ninety years before the first Dutch sighting, made it inevitable that the Portuguese would be the first Europeans to view the mainland itself.

For it is not feasible to suggest that any colony could so subsist, such a short distance from the Australian mainland, for *ninety years* without some discovery of the Australian coast being made. Possibly a backward people, with no initiative and no maritime skill, could remain horizon-bound for so many years: for example, the Australian aborigines lived on the Kimberley coast for centuries without discovering Timor. But the Portuguese were not a backward people. On the contrary, as we have seen, in the sixteenth century they were actuated by a zeal for exploration and discoveries of an intensity never before or since experienced by any nation. They had the ships, the navigators and the expertise that enabled them to sail twenty thousand miles from Lisbon to Timor and back again, and therefore they were quite capable of sailing the extra 285 miles to the Australian coast.

And the personal urge to explore was not lacking. Every Portuguese youth, every young sailor, cherished the dream that one day he too would return to Restelo, feted by a grateful people as yet another hero-discoverer, like da Gama to find an ornate tomb in the Jeronimos, or to be extolled in another epic like *The Lusiads*.

Let us take some comparable examples. Haiti is three or four hundred miles off the coast of North America. Columbus discovered it in 1492, and it was colonised by Spain shortly afterwards. Would it have been remotely possible for Spain to have maintained her colony there for ninety years – shuttling back and forth from Haiti to Spain, engaging in fishing and coast-wise sailing, and otherwise normally moving about in the area – would it have been possible for Spain to engage in these activities for ninety years without discovering the American mainland? Would it have been possible for England to have established a colony in Tasmania in 1516, again maintaining it and servicing it for ninety years, without sighting the Australian coast? The answer to these questions must be No. And in like manner, it is not possible to believe that the Portuguese, the greatest discovering nation in the history of the world, could have lived for three generations in Timor without the urge, the drive, or the ability, to check over the geography of its own Timor Sea and the land in its immediate vicinity.

The Portuguese *must* have sighted and partly explored Australia, at least the Western Australian coast, in the ninety years before the coming of the Dutch. The only problems are why the records and relics of such penetration are so sparse, why the results of such visits are so little known, why the very suggestion of Portuguese discovery of Australia receives so little credence. These are the questions which will be probed in the succeeding pages.

At the end of Chapter 1 we saw Vasco da Gama landing on the Calicut Coast. Portugal almost immediately acquired Goa, and under Affonso de Albuquerque Goa quickly rose to the status of a great metropolis, the colonial capital of the Orient. The Treaty of Tordesillas had just awarded Portugal the whole hemisphere from the Atlantic to the China Sea; and the natural desire of King Manoel in Lisbon and of Albuquerque in Goa was to explore and examine, to mark and to hold, the immense realm which the Treaty had placed into their hands.

The Emporium of the East was then Malacca, to which the Chinese, the Cochin-Chinese and the Malays all brought their produce and their riches. Portugal's first action was to extend her realm to Malacca, and this was achieved by Albuquerque, after hard fighting, in 1511. At Malacca the Portuguese had access to the spices which they craved, but at a price; for the lion's share of the profits still went to those traders, the Chinese in particular, who bartered for the spices in the islands where they were produced, and who then sold them to the Portuguese on advantageous terms. For the Portuguese, the ideal was to reach the source of the supply in their own ships, and it appeared that this source was in the islands to the east, called the Moluccas. Whether the Moluccas when found would turn out to be on Portugal's side of the Great Meridian was in the lap of the gods. The only way to find out was to go and see.

These eastern Indonesian islands were not entirely unknown to Europeans. Marco Polo had heard .of their wealth, and had left some reports of them. One of the greatest roamers of all time, Ludovico di Varthema, a native of Bologna, had been in this area just before the Portuguese arrival in the East. In 1505, travelling in native coastal craft, he had travelled to Ceylon, Pegu (in Burma), Sumatra and the Moluccas – and incidentally had heard of the large continent to the south, perhaps giving the Portuguese their earliest authentic news of the existence of Australia. When the Portuguese arrived in the East, Varthema joined them, and his invaluable information guided them in their forays further and further eastward. And of course in Malacca itself the Portuguese were in direct touch with the traders coming in from Ternate, Tidore and Amboina – names of magic and mystery until then, but soon to become commonplace words in Portuguese colonial administration – and so they were not forced to rely on Varthema or other Europeans who had been in or near that area.

As a result, in 1512 King Manoel sent out a royal order to Albuquerque, directing him to send out an expedition to explore the remainder of the Portuguese hemisphere right up to the Line of Demarcation, hoping and expecting to find that the coveted Spice Islands were on the Portuguese side of the line. This order naturally implied that the Line must be located and charted; and in normal Portuguese practice, indeed in accordance with the requirements of the Treaty itself, this would be followed up by planting a fort or 'tower' or other settlement on the nearest convenient piece of land, in order to mark the boundary, and to guard it against the expected Spanish incursion from the east. The expedition was also to indulge in what trading it could, thus opening up trading links with such islands as were on the Portuguese side, and to establish relations with the rulers of the lands discovered, as the basis for a desired Portuguese monopoly in their commodities.

This was a big order, but Albuquerque fulfilled the order in a big way. For a leader he chose António de Abreu, the almost legendary hero of the siege of Malacca. Portuguese history books[4] love to tell the story of his attack on a strongly-fortified Malay bridge, to which he directed his ship through a hail of bullets, and was himself seriously wounded. Dinis Fernandes de Melo endeavoured to take him to the river bank for surgical attention; but the wounded de Abreu refused to leave the ship, uttering the words: 'Though I have neither strength to fight, nor voice to command, I have still life to keep me at my post.' Lafitau says that his selection for the command of the Moluccas expedition was a reward for his services at Malacca.[5] By contrast with his second-in-command Serrão, Abreu was a fine and loyal Portuguese captain, conscientiously doing his duty, achieving deeds which ought to be remembered, especially in Australia. In every way except its subsequent political history, Timor belongs to the geographical area of Australia – as has been said, as surely as Haiti and Cuba belong to the geographical area of America; and if this is conceded, then Abreu is the Columbus of Australia. And if this is not conceded, at least he must be acclaimed as the undisputed discoverer of the Pacific Ocean. Abreu entered the Pacific in the Moluccas area in 1512: it was not until 1513 that Balboa, from his peak in Darien, looked down upon the waters of the same ocean. António de Abreu, the discoverer of the Pacific, never returned to Portugal to the reward that should have been his. He died at the Azores on the way home.

Albuquerque was not so fortunate in his choice of second-in-command. This post was given to Francisco Serrão, a cousin of Ferdinand Magellan, a man whose future flirtations with Spain were most dubious, and whose insidious influence on Magellan altered the course of world history. The chronicler Argensola reports that Magellan himself sailed on this voyage,[6] and that may well be so. Certainly Magellan himself always implied that he had. The fact that João de Barros, the official chronicler in Lisbon, does not mention him on this voyage, is not very significant, as it would not be normal to record the names of junior officers in the official chronicle. The point is of some importance, for if Magellan did not accompany Abreu on this voyage, then he (Magellan) was not, in his physical person, the first circumnavigator of the globe. For the purposes of this chapter, it is more important to note that Portugal's ace cartographer of the time, Francisco Rodrigues, was sent on this voyage, presumably because the surveying to be done was so delicate and so important, involving the location of the Line and the future ownership of the fabulous Moluccas. His record, *The Book of Francisco Rodrigues*, is still extant.

And Albuquerque treated them handsomely in ships, men and equipment. He gave them three caravels – the *Sabaia*, the *Santa Catarina* and one other – a first-class flotilla by any standards. The chronicler Galvão noted this feature, and wrote in admiration: 'Not more vessels or men went to discover New Spain with Columbus, nor with Vasco da Gama to India. Nor in comparison with these is Molucca less wealthy, nor ought to be held in less esteem.'[7] The reader should remember this comment, and note this evaluation, so that when later he reads of the allotment of three caravels to the flotilla sent south to discover Australia he will recognise it as a flotilla of world class, ranking in importance and sailing-power with the named expeditions of Columbus, da Gama and António de Abreu.

It is fortunate for us that Francisco Rodrigues sailed on this voyage, for from him we have derived better maps than usual, and we know more of the details of this voyage of 1512 than we do of many other voyages of that century. In addition to recording the places actually visited, Rodrigues obtained information about other islands from local seamen, showing these on his chart[8] in Javanese cartographical style, and thus giving the world its first comprehensive map of the Indonesian Archipelago. It remained the basis for knowledge of this area for ten years or more, until superseded by the *Carta Anonima Portuguesa*, which becomes important in this story later. But for the moment Rodrigues' chart holds our interest in its delineation of Abreu's course on this epoch-making voyage. A sketch is given in Fig. 5.1.

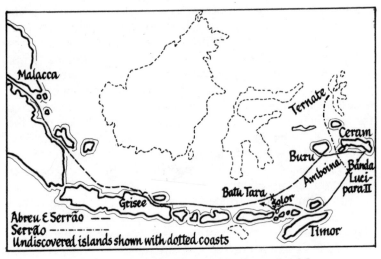

Fig. 5.1   THE VOYAGE OF ABREU AND SERRÃO

The fleet sailed[9] between Sumatra and Singapore, down the Banka Strait, and called at Grisee (not far from Surabaja) where they landed. It is interesting to note that Grisee became Portugal's main port of call in Java – it was not until Dutch days that Sunda (Djakarta) and Surabaja came into their own – and that Grisee is marked on the Dauphin Map. Then they sailed further east, and Serrão's ship was lost at Sapudi Island, and the crew (including Serrão) were jammed into the two surviving vessels. They sighted Batu Tara and Gunong Api; then moving north, away from the Lesser Sundas, they landed at Buru and Amboina. Here they were in the heart of the fabulous Moluccas; and Amboina was to become Portugal's administrative centre in this sector.

They then sailed along the south coast of Ceram (probably named after Serrão), where they landed again. We know that the Great Meridian crosses the island of Ceram – indeed, it is the only place in the whole area where a land observation of the meridian can today be made. Abreu and Rodrigues, for no recorded reason, made a landing at Gule Gule, and it is a fair guess that it was to enable Rodrigues to set up his equipment on shore, as Vasco da Gama had done at St Helena Bay, to pinpoint his Altura with the large land-based instruments, to establish True North and true local time by the gnomon method already explained, and to calculate his position as well as he could.

They crossed the Great Meridian to Banda,[10] where they bought a junk to replace Serrão's wrecked ship; and the three ships (with Serrão in charge of the junk) sailed southward, southing down the Line, indicating that they were surveying the boundary and would have liked to follow the Line as far as sea passage allowed. If they had done so, they would have passed the East Point of Timor, and would have made landfall on the Australian coast in Joseph Bonaparte Gulf. But the evil genius of this cruise was Serrão. Once again the ship under his command was wrecked, this time in the Lucipara Islands. For reasons which we can only guess. Serrão did not continue the voyage, but made his way to Ternate, where he was warmly welcomed. Perhaps he was lucky: for in that island there was a long-standing prophecy that one day a 'Man of Iron' would arrive and lead the people to prosperity and power. When Serrão came ashore in his suit of armour, he was hailed as the fulfilment of the prophecy, and treated with appropriate deference. He entered the Sultan's service, married a native woman, and lived there for the rest of his life. This may have been part of the Portuguese plan to establish a presence in some island close to the Line (Ternate is only one degree west of the Great Meridian), but this is not certain. Serrão, having wrecked two ships, was undoubtedly in disgrace with his commander, so that if someone had to be selected to be left behind it might well be that the finger was pointed at him. On the other hand, weightier considerations were then straining his loyalty. He had formed the opinion, probably at Buru, that Rodrigues was then already beyond the Line of Demarcation, and perhaps even then he was planning in his mind to sell this secret to Spain.

But further still, Serrão perhaps had an inkling that there was more in this area than just Spice Islands, valuable though they were. His manuscript is in the University of Barcelona, and has been inspected by Jaime Cortesão;[11] in it Serrão mentioned that Amboinese pilots had told him that south of Ceram there is a large country which extends to the South Pole. If the Malayan embroidery was added to this story, no doubt this southern land was linked with legends of gold. From this point onwards the name 'The Isles of Gold' appears and reappears in contemporary chronicles, and sparked off the earliest Portuguese probes to the south, particularly the voyages of Diogo Pacheco. Through Magellan, this story seeped through to the Spanish as well; and both the story of the land and the story of the gold had bearing on the Spanish probes of Mendaña and Queiros to find the continent.

With Serrão left behind, Abreu and Rodrigues turned south-west, coasting along the interlocked group of islands, Wettar, Timor, Alor and Solor, 'all so close together as to appear like one entire mainland'.[12] Timor was sighted and marked on the chart, but the landing was made at Solor. In their inability to distinguish the separate islands, the whole of the Lesser Sunda area was thought of as one territory, and this landing at Solor was the genesis of the Solor–Timor colony. José Martinho says that certain men were landed from Abreu's ship at Solor, to form the beginning of the Solor–Timor colony.[13] This is not unlikely, as the Portuguese had an inhuman habit of carrying *desgrados* (convicts) on their ships of discovery, heartlessly unloading them and leaving them behind to fend for themselves in places such as this. It is known that of the one hundred and twenty who sailed with Abreu, only eighty returned: thirty died on the voyage, and ten remained in the islands. Some four or five were left with Serrão in the Moluccas. That still leaves five or six, and the most likely place for these to be offloaded is Solor; but this is conjecture, and it is not certain that Martinho is correct in his assertion. At least by the next year the Solor settlement was established, and it became the principal Portuguese staging-point in the Lesser Sundas.

The exact date of the first landing on Timor Island itself is not known; but clearly once the Portuguese were esconced in Solor Island, from which the mountains of Timor Island can be seen, it would not be long before a visit was made. Its special attraction was the sandalwood, and maybe sandalwood cutters made visits to the island before any permanent settlement was made there. The first mention[14] of Timor, apart from its presence in Rodrigues' map, is in a letter dated 6 January 1514 from Rui de Brito, addressed to King Manoel, referring to ships which had departed for Java and Timor. In 1516 Duarte Barbosa described the island.[15] Magellan's surviving ship passed and made landing on the island in 1522, and Pigafetta noted some evidence that the Portuguese had been there. One of the indications, unhappily, was the European disease of syphilis, already known to the Timorese as 'the Portuguese disease'.[16] The general belief is that the Portuguese founded their Timor colony at Ocussi in 1516; and the writer was present in Timor in 1966 when the 450th birthday was being celebrated.

At the risk of unduly labouring the point, the extraordinarily early colonisation of this Portuguese island, so close to the mainland, is again called to notice. This means that at all material times in the subsequent discovery, exploration and colonisation of Australia, there has been this outpost of European civilisation in being, just off the shoulder of the Kimberleys. Australia is always thought of as a remote land, its remoteness inevitably delaying its discovery, hindering its exploration. This is true. But its remoteness was not ten thousand miles remote from Rotterdam or London; it was less than 300 miles remote from the nearest outpost of European establishment, in Timor. And this fact was not secret, theoretical or immaterial. All early navigators undoubtedly underlined in red ink on their charts those havens of refreshment on that island, both Portuguese and (later) Dutch. Dampier called at Lifou (in Ocussi), and it is instructive to see in his Journal the casualness with which he decided that, as he was there, he might as well make a short side-trip to that coast 'over there'. That undoubtedly parallels the casualness with which the local Portuguese similarly made a jaunt across to the continental coast when they felt like it, so casually that usually it would not even be reported. Cook's first touch of civilisation, after leaving the New South Wales coast, was not the mainland of Timor but the adjacent Portuguese-speaking island of Sawu. Bligh headed for Timor, and made it in an open boat. Flinders called there. Freycinet called there. When George Grey was commencing his exploration of the Kimberleys, he casually sent the *Lynher* across to Timor to do some shopping.[17] When the English founded a colony at Port Essington,[18] immediate contacts ensued between that colony and the Portuguese colony in Timor, like neighbours chatting across the back fence. The English even slipped across to Dili to get the London newspapers.

One historical curiosity may be mentioned. When Japan occupied Timor in the Second World War, it was often said that this enemy-held territory was the closest that any enemy had come to Australia. But as far back as Elizabeth's War of the Spanish Armada there was hostile territory there, in Timor; for Portugal was involuntarily sucked in on the Spanish side, and for sixty years Timor was technically under the flag of Spain. In Drake's voyage of circumnavigation he passed between Australia and Timor, rather warily avoiding perception by the enemy who might be lurking in their base on that island. No one can tell how close Drake came to sighting Australia; and as it was Drake who had blown up Henry's Fortaleza at Sagres, no one can tell what the Portuguese might have done to him if they had caught him.

The earliest settlers in Timor, the da Costas and the Hornays, inter-married with the native women; and after four and a half centuries there are da Costas and Hornays not only half-caste and quarter-caste and octoroon, but often completely reverted to the stock of their maternal ancestors. This produced the so-called 'Black Portuguese', who so surprisingly opted for Portuguese rule right through the Spanish captivity of 1580–1640, and right through the Japanese captivity of 1942–1945, and who are the backbone of the 'Fretlin' or anti-Indonesian opposition today. This inter-mixture of races also led the Portuguese towards Australia. For ninety years the Portuguese lived with these people, inter-married with them, learnt their language and all their secrets: so that whatever secret knowledge of Australia was possessed by the

Timorese automatically became available to the Portuguese
as well.

The Timorese are not great sailors and are not great
travellers. But the facts of life compelled them to be fishermen, and the fishing calendar of the Timorese, then as now,
sends the fishermen in proper season to the off-shore islands
of Australia, if not to the mainland itself. The Timorese
seemed, and still seem, afraid of the mainland, perhaps
because the Kimberley aborigines are warlike, physically
powerful, and were at that time cannibals:[19] and there are no
fish to be caught on land anyway. But the islands between
Timor and Australia, closer and closer to Australia, were
their natural fishing grounds.

Fig. 5.2 shows the islands that lie between Timor and
Australia. Those nearer Timor – Roti and Sawu – are as close
to Australia as Timor itself. When Cook put in at Sawu,
Banks was rather surprised to find Portuguese-speaking
people on what was by then a Dutch-owned island, but he
discovered that the Portuguese had been there almost from
their first coming to those seas.[20] Cook's Journal (19 September 1770) records that he had a man on board who could
interpret Portuguese for him. This would be Manoel Pereira,
the Portuguese who was added to the *Endeavour*'s comple-
ment in Rio de Janeiro, to replace Peter Flower who was
drowned there.[21] Manoel Pereira was the first Portuguese to
sail the east coast of Australia since the discoverers of Portugal's Golden Age.

Closer to Australia the islands become unattractive, almost
awash at high tide, uninhabited and uninhabitable. Most of
them (Cartier, Ashmore and Seringapatam Islands) were
owned by Britain (not Australia) until the mid–twentieth
century, when they were transferred to Australia and became
the Australian Territory of Ashmore and Cartier Islands. The
chief duty of the Commonwealth department administering
these islands today is to shoo off the Timorese who still
descend upon them, in due season, for their traditional fishing. From the sketch-map it can be seen that island-hopping
from one island to the next entailed only short distances, and
even for primitive native sailing craft the stepping-stones
guide and guard the natural approach to the Kimberley coast.

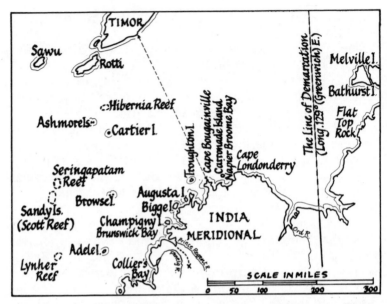

Fig. 5.2   THE STEPPING-STONES TO AUSTRALIA. Distances: Timor to Cape Bougainville (direct) 285 miles; Timor to Rotti, 20 m; Rotti to Hibernia Reef 50 m; Hibernia Reef to Ashmore Island 50 m; Ashmore Island to Cartier Island 35 m; Cartier Island to Browse Island 110 m; Browse Island to Champigny Island 90 m; Champigny Island to Mainland 25 m. The route of George Grey is shown by dotted line to Wandjina Paintings (x).

Cape Londonderry was the south coast, the contra-coast. Timorese knowledge of the Australian continent cannot be doubted, and this knowledge undoubtedly was handed on to the Portuguese.

Unfortunately, the admixture of races in the island has caused some writers to try to differentiate between those discoveries that were Portuguese and those that were Timorese. If a European-style ship, officered by Portuguese, but with a native crew, made a discovery, that presumably would be a 'Portuguese' discovery. If a native craft, wholly native manned, and without Portuguese control, made a similar discovery, that would (perhaps with some logic) be counted not as a Portuguese discovery but as a purely native discovery. But it is not clear what happened in between – if there was just one European on the native craft; or if a crew of half-caste, quarter-caste and octoroon Hornays and da Costas took out a vessel of European style. The whole thing seems to be a pointless distinction: but much denial of Portuguese discovery comes from writers such as Professor G. Arnold Wood,[22] who continually argue that such and such was probably not a 'Portuguese' discovery but something of which they had gained knowledge from the voyaging of their native people.

As an example, in 1946 Dr Mota Alves discovered a Portuguese map[23] in the National Library in Rio de Janeiro (Fig. 6.1). It is dated 1602, and it shows by a dotted line the track of a voyage south from Timor to the approximate position of Brunswick and Collier's Bays. The map derives from Manoel Godinho de Erédia, it is authentic and genuine, and its 1602 date is itself four years before the first Dutch sighting. But the pointless argument immediately starts – it must not be inferred that it was a Portuguese voyage, for it might have been a voyage of natives of Flores, or natives of Timor, or of some other island. Therefore (the argument appears to run), the Dutch sighting of 1606 is still the first 'European' sighting, for anything Portuguese might only be 'native'. This hair-splitting is particularly rife in anything that pertains to Erédia.

The only documentation of an incontestably white Portuguese to make the crossing from Timor to Australia is Francisco Resende,[24] who after taking on a cargo of sandalwood at Timor was blown by a storm many leagues to the south-east. Calculating his distance and his bearing, his landfall was probably the western side of the tip of Cape York Peninsula. But for these Timor-based passages, actual details of actual passages are not really important. Whether we know the names of the mariners or not, whether the voyages were made by white Portuguese, by black Portuguese, by Luso–Timorese, by half-castes, quarter-castes or full-blooded natives, the contacts were still made.

Professor Andrew Sharp,[25] who is not willing to make much concession to the Portuguese, when writing in a different context sees 'no difficulty' in the theory that the Norsemen discovered Greenland, for he points out with impeccable logic that it was inevitable that they must do so, once they reached Iceland only 200 miles away. The same logic must apply to the inevitability of the crossing from Timor to Australia. This is the core of the argument presented here: the Portuguese discovery of Australia was inevitable once the Timor colony, so close to the Australian coast, came into being. It is impossible to suppose that the Portuguese, being the people that they were, could have lived for three generations in Timor without discovering Australia, only 285 miles away. When we think of Captain Bligh making the crossing in an open boat, it is not hard to see that a Magellan or an Abreu or a Sequeira would be able to do the same, and more, in the comfort and convenience of a properly-equipped caravel. We could not predicate the British settling in Darwin, and occupying it for ninety years, without discovering Timor; or the British occupying Timor for ninety years without discovering Darwin. And therefore, we could not imagine the Portuguese, either, occupying Timor for ninety years without discovering Australia. The years available were so many, and their base in Timor was so close.

Chapter 6

INDIA MERIDIONAL

ONE overwhelming reason pointing to the probability, the certainty, of Portuguese probes from the islands towards the Australian coast is that the whole of the present State of Western Australia, known to the Portuguese as 'India Meridional' (the South Indies, as distinct from the East Indies), is on their side of the Great Meridian. Portugal made a fetish of the minute and thorough examination of every speck of land,[1] every island however small, in her hemisphere; and there is no reason to believe that the Australian sector alone would be neglected.

In the Atlantic, not only was the Brazil coast thoroughly examined, but isolated islands such as Fernão da Noronha and Tristão da Cunha were discovered by the Portuguese, received Portuguese names, and found their way on to Portuguese maps. Greenland did not seem attractive, but as it was in the Portuguese hemisphere it had to be investigated: the two ill-fated sons of João Cortereal gave their lives in this thankless quest. And in the Indian Ocean, the sea was crisscrossed by Portuguese navigators with a meticulousness not again encountered until Cook combed the Pacific in the eighteenth century, and the American Wilkes in the nineteenth. There is barely an atoll in the Indian Ocean that did not come under Portuguese scrutiny – the Comoros, the Laccadives, the Maldives, the Nicobars, and all the rest of them. The remote island of Diogo Garcia (at the time of writing, in the news relative to an American naval base there) advertises its Portuguese origin by its name. In the Dauphin and other maps there is an island with the size, shape and position that appear to coincide with the sub-Antarctic island of Kerguelen, an identification made two hundred years ago by no less an authority than Alexander Dalrymple.[2]

And in the north there is the same insistent demand to inspect every inch of coast on their side of the Great Meridian. Mendes Pinto pioneered the China coast to Nanking and Peking and on to Korea, where trading contact was made with

Japan. And to show that Portugal even postulated a Portuguese Siberia, which had to be examined, there is the tradition (alas, not well documented) of David Melgueiro's voyage through the Bering Straits and along the Siberian coast, to find the Great Meridian again at the mouth of the Lena River.

This activity, of course, is only common sense. Even an unpromising coast needed to be looked at, for there was always the chance that it might yield gold or other riches. Where wealth was found, a procession of Portuguese ships then followed Vasco de Gama to India, or António de Abreu to the Moluccas. Where wealth was not found, in Greenland or Siberia or Western Australia, no further investigation was called for.

Even if the Portuguese had believed that only empty sea covered the area which Australia occupies, they almost certainly would still have visited just to make sure. But in this case they did know and believe that there was land there. Ever since classical times there had been some theory of a 'Great South Land', a counterbalancing continent more akin to the modern continent of Antarctica than to Australia; and some account of this belief will be given later. Ptolemy had conceived the Indian Ocean as a lake, with a land arm stretching down from the Malay Peninsula, through where Australia is now known to stand, and around in a southern sweep to join South Africa (see Fig. 10.1). Vasco de Gama knocked a hole into this lake south of the Cape of Good Hope, and Abreu and Mendes Pinto knocked another hole into the China Sea; but instead of abandoning the conception altogether, the Ptolemaic mapmakers (and there were many editions of Ptolemy in the fifteenth and sixteenth centuries) left the remnant of this hypothetical connecting arm as a supposed continent, sweeping in a semicircle from the Australian area to below Africa. The obvious and easy place to look for this supposed continent was in the modern Australian sector.

And in addition, the travels of Marco Polo had set up the legend of a rich and populous continent called Locac in this general area. It was this name of 'Locac' which, by a succession of printer's errors, degenerated to 'Beach', and appeared ghost-like on so many maps in the subsequent centuries, from

Martim Behaim to Mercator, and even further. And it was always with the connotation that it was a land of gold. '*Beach provincia Aurifera*', Mercator wrote on his map. 'The Isles of Gold', others said.

Actually Marco Polo knew nothing and had heard nothing of Australia,[3] and his 'Locac' is only Siam. Locac is near Chamba, and by re-tracing his steps backwards we can determine that Chamba is Indo-China. He mentions Ceylon, which we know and can identify: so commencing from there, and traversing his route in reverse – the voyage of 1000 miles more or less east of Ceylon takes us to the Andaman (Angamanain) Islands, thence 150 miles south to Sumatra (Java the Less), thence 100 miles north-west to Singapore (Pentam) and Malaya (Maluar), and finally a considerable distance north to Chamba (Indo-China). A 'Locac' in that area cannot possibly be Australia; but because of a clerical error in Marco Polo's narrative, men thought that Marco Polo had meant that the great and rich country of Locac, full of gold, spices and all other treasures, was *south of Java*, and there was endless speculation about this Continent of Gold that was to be found in the south. It was even given a name – Jave-la-Grande.

Now Java and Sumatra, when visited and explored, reversed the sizes that Marco Polo had attributed to them. In relation to Java proper, Sumatra would be 'the Greater', not Marco Polo's 'Java the Less'; and it was Sumatra that at times assumed the name of Jave-la-Grande. Hence whenever a subsequent traveller (Nicolo, for example) speaks about the great, rich island of Jave-la-Grande (meaning Sumatra), men's minds immediately transferred its being to the imaginary Jave-la-Grande of Australia. Java the Great, Java the Less, Pentam, Maluar, Locac, Beach – all of these Poloesque names were bandied about for hundreds of years. Medieval maps are full of them. Inaccurate and misleading though they were, they turned men's minds to think of Australia; and they provided one more motive for Portuguese investigation of the area where Locac and Jave-la-Grande were supposed to exist.

The Muslim traveller, El Edrisi, was also known to the Portuguese through their Moorish connection. He had news of a large country, south of Borneo, said to be uninhabited by

man and populated only by large birds. This is only a traveller's tale, an unconfirmed rumour; but it does curiously fit in
with the sparseness of the Australian aborigine population,
and with the plentifulness and size of the large non-flying
birds known as emus. And it is significant, perhaps,
that the word 'emu' (ema) is an Arabic word, which
entered the English language through the Portuguese.[4]
But with stories like El Edrisi's it is not necessary to
disentangle fact and fiction. Even if stories such as these
are only rumours, they too pointed Portugal's attention
towards Australia.

The Italian Varthema had heard Amboinese rumours of a
Javanese voyage to some great island in the south, an incredible distance away. But as Amboina and Banda are not very
far from Australia, these great distances, plus the extreme
changes of climate reported, make interpretation difficult. As
we know that the Javanese, who were advanced navigators,
had sailed as far as Madagascar, and possibly to the Crozet
and Prince Edward Islands beyond, it is suspected that Varthema's story refers to voyages in that direction. But again it
does not matter. It was the existence of the rumour, not its
accuracy, that acted as a spur.

With these legends, rumours and garbled reports known to
the Portuguese, it would be incredible if they did not venture
into the area of this fabled continent at least once, to have a
look. And these rumours were still further strengthened by
Malayan tradition. The previous chapter concentrated on
Timor. But the arguments there adduced – the proximity to
Australia, the close bond between Portuguese master and
native subject, the likelihood of native contacts with
Australia – all these arguments also apply, with only less
force, to the other Portuguese islands in the Malayan and
Moluccan sectors. After all, Amboina is only a step from
Arnhem-land, Ende and Larantuca in Flores are not far
away; Macassar and Malacca were further away, but the
much greater maritime skills of the Macassarese and Malac-
cans brought them, too, within reach of the Australian mainland. And in these places, too, the cooperation and marrying
between European and native brought further knowledge of
Australia to Portuguese ears.

Malay, particularly Macassarese, voyaging to Australia was of long standing, starting long before the first coming of the white men. The attraction was the trepang or sea-slug, that repulsive-looking product of the sea, so highly prized in Chinese markets. Manoel Godinho de Erédia says that the trepang-fishing in Australian waters had been going on for six hundred years, with a lengthy break in the middle. Malay seamanship was of a high standard, as Varthema's story indicates, and there was no physical bar on their coming whenever they desired. In recent years research led by Professor Mulvaney of Canberra and Mr I. M. Crawford of Perth has uncovered strong confirmation of Malay contacts with the north coast of Australia. It is not the purpose of this book to examine this evidence in any detail – that is another branch of the story of pre-Cook contacts with Australia, concerning which the specialists are writing their own accounts. But briefly it can be said that the signs include the presence of the imported Javanese tamarind tree, the construction and use of dugout canoes, native knowledge of alcohol and betelnut, and other importations into their culture. Archaeological excavation has turned up Asiatic artifacts, and evidence of Asian sojourns. Aboriginal paintings include representations of Malayan trepang smoke-houses. There are some Malay words in their language, and legends about the coming of strangers are woven into their folklore. If the Australian aborigines knew the Malays, then the Malays knew the Australian aborigines, and through the Malays this knowledge was passed on to the Portuguese.

And Malayan visitation of the northern coasts is corroborated by no less an authority than the great Australian explorer, Matthew Flinders. In 1803, while he was circumnavigating Australia, he entered Caledon Bay, near the north-western entrance to the Gulf of Carpentaria, and there he met with natives who knew of fire-arms and of axes, and had seen oared boats. Shortly afterwards, in what is now Malay Roads, he encountered six Malay proas, under the command of a short, elderly man named Pobassoo.[5] Flinders's cook could speak the Malay language, and conversation was possible. Pobassoo said that there were sixty proas on the coast, altogether carrying one thousand men, and belonging to the Rajah of Boni. They had departed from Macassar two months before, and their route had been Macassar-Timorlaut-Australia. Pobassoo himself had made four or five voyages, stretching back over twenty years. So Pobassoo himself had been walking on Australian soil before Captain Phillip landed in Botany Bay.

Twenty years later the English attempted to form settlements on the northern coasts, in Melville Island and later at Port Essington. Major Campbell, the English commander there, wrote:[6]

'[The Malays] expressed much surprise on being told that the English were going to settle in Port Essington; they said that the Macassarese had used it as a fishing port for many years, giving it the name of Limboo Moutiara, and that the English certainly had no business there.'

And Campbell wrote to McLeay:

'I understand from Timor that the Macassarese proas resort to the north-west coast of New Holland annually, about the months of October and November. They keep a numerous fleet, and rendezvous about Port Essington.'

This proprietorial attitude on the part of the Malays to the trepang fisheries is not what would be expected of interlopers who had followed the white man into new-found parts. It looks more like the easy acceptance of traditional rights, in keeping with long-standing Malay utilisation of the coast, the white man being regarded as the interloper.

This Malay knowledge of Australia – at least Malay rumours about Australia – receives some mention in contemporary Portuguese chronicles. The best illustration is the story of Diogo Pacheco as related by João de Barros.[7] He confirms that there were widespread reports (*grandes informacões*) in India about a marvellous Isle of Gold, about a thousand miles south-east of Sumatra: and this would be approximately the North-West Cape of Western Australia. So persistent were these rumours that Governor Lopes sent out Diogo Pacheco and Francisco de Sequeira, in two ships, to search for this land. Pacheco reached Pacem, on the west coast of Sumatra, and sailed south down the west coast towards the open Indian Ocean. He reached a point 'in the realm of King Daya', on the south-western corner of the island, apparently being the first Portuguese to reach that area, where he and his party were received by the local inhabitants with great suspicion. They had some wares to barter with the locals, and were paid in gold – only a little gold, and that not freely given.

When they inquired about the origin of this gold, the natives were very noncommittal. Probably it had been mined locally, and they were trying to hide that fact from the Portuguese, for fear that such an attraction might lead to Portuguese annexation of their country. The story that they told to the Portuguese was that, far across the sea to the south-east, there is an island, peopled by black people, who have gold. To get there involves a very perilous voyage through reefs and shoals; and often of the ships that set out, only one in four return. The black people barter their gold on the water's edge, and will not allow the strangers to travel inland to see their habitations or the source of their gold. Therefore, nothing is known of the interior. If Diogo Pacheco would care to sail off to the south-east, he could see all of this for himself.

It is not clear whether the Sumatrans were telling him this from their real knowledge, or from genuine legend; or whether they were inventing the story for his benefit, hoping to get rid of him in this way. Pacheco chose to believe the story, and tried to find the Isle of Gold: if he had been successful, he would have reached Western Australia in the vicinity of Shark's Bay. But he was dogged by misfortune. On his first voyage, one of his ships was wrecked, and all of the crew (except one man) was drowned. He was forced to return to Malacca, but his story of the gold was received with such enthusiasm that he was sent out again, again equipped with two ships. This time both of the ships came to grief, and Pacheco himself lost his life. De Barros tells us: 'he was the first of the Portuguese to lose his life in the quest for the Isle of Gold.'[8] Armando Cortesão points out that if he was 'the first', then there must have been others later, who also tried and perished.

Knowledge of Australia is also shown in later writings by Portuguese voyagers or chroniclers, although as we shall see later such disclosures were officially discouraged, and mainly appeared when some Portuguese defected to a foreign power. One such was João Affonse, a Portuguese pilot of distinction, who defected to Dieppe and took the name of Jean Alfonse. He probably sailed with Sequeira in his traverse of North Australian waters in 1525, for he refers to the large Ilha dos homens brancos, one hundred and fifty leagues south-east of the Moluccas, which must be Sequeira's island of that name. He later sailed with the Frenchman Parmentier to Sumatra in 1529, and probably he had been recruited to France for that purpose. Again later, he sailed with Roberval to Canada in 1541.

In 1544 he wrote, and in 1559 he published, a book in the French language called *Voyages Aventureux*,[9] in which he described a southern continent, commencing in the Antarctic regions and rising to tropical latitudes south and south-east of 'Orphir', which is either Timor or Flores. He will be discussed later in connection with Sequeira, and in connection with the Dieppe Maps. For the moment he is mentioned to show that the Portuguese had knowledge of the existence of Australia, and therefore any suggestion that they could have dwelt in Timor for nine decades without making any attempt to reach it is palpably absurd.

Gabriel Rebelo,[10] writing in 1569, gives the same kind of picture of a great southern continent, sloping up from the Straits of Magellan on the east, and dipping below the Cape of Good Hope on the west, but rising to or about to Lat. 10°s in the present position of Australia. He too had lived in the Moluccas, and reflects local Portuguese knowledge of the area; he too seemed to have knowledge of Sequeira's voyaging, and refers to the Homens Brancos mentioned by Jean Alfonse. But for present purposes he is of less importance than Alfonse, for by 1569 this Portuguese conception of the existence and shape of Australia had found its way into the international maps of Mercator and his colleagues, and Spaniards such as Mendaña and Frenchmen such as Poplinière were already probing towards it. The reader should remember that all of this is still several decades before the first Dutch sighting in 1606, which most people accept as the first European knowledge of Australia.

At the end of the sixteenth century, an educated half-Portuguese, half-Macassarese, named Manoel Godinho de Erédia[11] produced a series of books, pamphlets and maps in Malacca, overwhelmingly confirming that the Portuguese had interest in Australia, legends about Australia, and some firm knowledge about Australia in the closing years of the century, still some years before the first Dutch sighting. One of his pamphlets, the unpublished *Tratado Ophirico* in the British Museum, states categorically (and correctly) that Java is between latitudes 6° and 8°, and that India Meridional is in Lat. 16°s. But his most famous book, and for our purposes the most important, was published in Malacca under the title of 'The Declaration of Malacca', and containing one chapter entitled 'India Meridional'. The title itself shows that he is writing about Western Australia, as do the contents of the chapter.[12]

Erédia himself later organized an expedition for the exploration of Australia – the controversial 'Nuca Antara' expedition – which probably never sailed. This story will be told in Chapter 25 for the bearing that it has on the apostasy of R. H. Major, and that alleged voyage need not detain us further at this moment. But in his book Erédia tells of other voyages in the direction of Australia. In preparation for his Nuca Antara expedition, he had read and collected all records and reports, including some rather fanciful Malayan legends and rumours, concerning the land that he was about to visit; and evidence, though confused evidence, suggesting visits to the mainland can be spelled out in his book. Because of his obscurity, historians tend to play down the value of his evidence altogether.

But one voyage to an island on the south coast of Timor, if not made by Erédia then certainly made by Erédia's colleagues, received dramatic confirmation when in 1946 Dr Mota Alves discovered the Portuguese map which has already been mentioned. It derives from Erédia, and was found in the National Library in Rio de Janeiro. R. H. Major[13] has explained to us that 'the south coast of Timor' does not mean the coast which girds Timor on the south, but rather the 'opposite coast', the 'contra-coast' – *Ilha como situada na costa fronteira ou contra-costa de Timor, que propriamente se chama Costa de Sul.*

Erédia's colleagues made this voyage to an island on the coast opposite to, across the water from, the south coast of Timor. Those colleagues were certainly not white Portuguese naval officers, all of whom would then have been in home waters, under Spanish command, forming part of that 'invincible' Spanish Armada which so disastrously attacked England in Elizabeth's reign. But, like Erédia himself, those colleagues would have been half-Portuguese, or quarter-Portuguese, or some other blend of Luso-Malayan. That crew, on Erédia's uncontradicted testimony, sailed to and reached the Kimberley Coast in 1599 or 1600; and that Portuguese discovery of Australia cannot be wiped off as

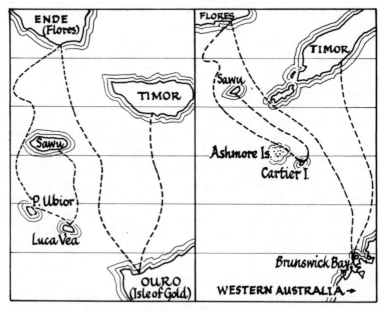

Fig. 6.1 THE MOTA ALVES MAP. The map on the left was discovered by Dr Mota Alves and is compared with a modern map (on right). Luca Vea identifies with Cartier Island, and The Isle of Gold (Ouro) with the Brunswick Bay area of Western Australia.

non-Portuguese merely because those who sailed were not one hundred percent white.

The Mota Alves map is analysed in Fig. 6.1. It is dated 1602, and shows by a dotted line the track of a voyage south from Timor, calling at what can be identified as the Collier's Bay-Brunswick Bay area of Western Australia, circling back to Flores (Ende), then continuing back past Cartier Island (which can be identified) to Sawu Island (which is named). Here we have first-hand evidence of a Portuguese landing on the Australian coast. Here we have an actual map, with an actual track marked, and a calculable point of landfall.

And corroboration of the fact that this area was known to and was visited by the Portuguese comes from still another source. Brunswick Bay and Collier's Bay are side by side. In 1838 the English explorer George Grey was exploring in this area. By coincidence, Grey was himself Lisbon-born, as his mother had travelled with his father during Wellington's Peninsula Campaign, and George Grey was born in Lisbon after his father fell at Badajoz. Grey had a distinguished career in Australasian history – explorer, Governor of South Australia, Governor of New Zealand, and finally an elder statesman of the conferences in which Australian Federation was born.

Grey's find can best be described in his own words:[14]

'On looking over some bushes I suddenly saw from one of them a most extraordinary large figure peering down on me. Upon examination, it proved to be a drawing at the entrance to a cave, which on entering proved to contain, besides, many remarkable paintings.'

This was up-stream, about twenty miles from the point where the Glenelg river debouches into Collier's Bay. Grey had come overland from Brunswick Bay, and was not sure in which direction the Glenelg led; but he was so intrigued by these paintings that he paused to investigate. As an Englishman who then knew nothing of Australia (Grey's expedition had come direct from England, without touching at either Sydney or Perth), Grey was first probably amazed that the unpromising natives of those parts – whom Dampier had so unflatteringly compared with the Hodmadods of

Monomatapa, to the locals' disadvantage – should be able to paint at all. This judgment would have been wholly astray, for we know now that Australian aborigines have talents in painting of the highest class, as the masterpieces of Albert Namatjira and his disciples testify; but at that date neither Grey nor anyone else in Australia had any inkling of this unexpected phenomenon. Secondly, on further investigation, Grey was amazed at what was portrayed in the paintings arrayed before him. To his mind, at least, they presented clear proof of aboriginal contact with other Europeans before the arrival of his expedition, which was believed to be the very first to penetrate into that area.

Australian aboriginal painting can be starkly realistic – hunting scenes, figures of running animals, and so on. On the other hand, it can be abstract and symbolic, infused with religious significance, and rooted in the folklore of their 'Dream-time'. The first of the paintings seen by Grey was of this latter type; and the name 'Wandjina' which he bestowed upon it has given a name to all aboriginal paintings of similar motif throughout the continent. He entered the cave, and described what he saw:

'On [the] sloping roof, the principal figure which I have alluded to was drawn; in order to produce the greater effect, the rock about it was painted black, and the figure itself coloured with the most vivid red and white. It thus appeared to stand out from the rock; and I was certainly rather surprised at the moment that I first saw this gigantic head and upper part of a body bending over and staring grimly down at me . . . . Its head was encircled by bright red rays, something like the rays which one sees proceeding from the sun when depicted on the sign-board of a public house; inside of this came a broad stripe of very brilliant red, which was coped by lines of white; but both inside and outside of this red space were narrow stripes of a still deeper red, intended probably to mark its boundaries; the face was painted vividly white, and the eyes black, being however surrounded by red and yellow lines; the body, hands and arms were outlined in red – the body being curiously painted with red stripes and bars.'

The general effect of this Wandjina painting is similar to that of a medieval portrayal of a saint or other religious figure, complete with halo, medallion, draped garments with sleeves and armbands. Its style is almost Byzantine, and it is hard to see how naked aborigines could so conceive a draped Euopean-styled figure, unless they had seen some such European figure. The fact that the face is white (though, in aboriginal style, mouthless) adds further to this suggestion. This assumes that the Portuguese sailors carried a Catholic processional effigy with them – which seems unlikely. Yet Magellan had a carved image, which he left behind at Cebu,[15] and which the natives 'held in great veneration' for years. If the Spaniards did so, the Portuguese could have done so too. Certainly an effigy of this kind springs to mind, and would have served as a good model for the finished painting. One similar suggestion is that the ship may have carried a carved figurehead in this likeness. Whatever was the model or the inspiration, the actual painting is in Wandjina mystical mood, aboriginal in conception, but seemingly incorporating some knowledge of European (or at least non-aboriginal) dress. Grey immediately thought of European contacts, though this one painting, on its own, would hardly be conclusive on this point.

But in another cave he found a realistic (as distinct from symbolic) representation of a man, which he took to be a priest in cassock and cowl:[16]

'In another cave . . . the principal painting was the figure of a man, ten feet six inches in height, clothed from the chin downwards in a red garment which reached to the wrists and ankles; beyond this red dress the feet and hands protruded, but were badly executed.'

Actually, these badly executed feet are tolerably well executed sandals or shoes. Grey rather fancifully likens this painting to Ezekiel's 'Men pourtrayed on the wall, the images of the Chaldeans pourtrayed with vermilion'.[17] But this is too fanciful: the painting is more like the homely portrait of a medieval friar, such as we find in an edition of Chaucer. And it is not unlikely, indeed it would have accorded with custom, for some man in holy orders to have accompanied the Portuguese mariners on an expedition. This second discovery heightened Grey's belief that he was in an area which had known some European visitation.

Then he came across the most surprising find of all: a distinctly European head, and face, carved on a sandstone

Fig. 6.2   Illustration 'The Sandstone Head' from George Grey: *Journals of two expeditions of Discovery in North-Western Australia*. Reproduction by courtesy of South Australian Libraries Board.

rock. Grey's own sketch of this is given in Fig. 6.2, and he wrote:[18]

> 'I was moving on, when we observed the profile of a human face and head, cut out in a sandstone rock which fronted the cave; this rock was so hard, that to have removed such a

large portion of it with no better tool than a knife and hatchet made of stone, such as the Australian natives generally possess, would have been a work of very great labour. The head was two feet in length, and sixteen inches in breadth at the lower part; the depth of the profile increased gradually from the edges, where it was nothing, to the centre where it was an inch and a half; the ear was rather badly placed, but otherwise the whole of the work was good, and far superior to what a savage race could be supposed capable of executing. The only proof of antiquity that it bore about it was that all the edges of the cutting were rounded and perfectly smooth, much more so than they could have been from any other cause than by exposure to atmospheric influences.'

So, in the Brunswick Bay area, almost the closest point of the mainland to the known Portuguese base at Timor, and in an area which by the evidence of Erédia was in their thoughts, and by the evidence of Dr Mota Alves's map had been visited by some one, we find: (i) a European head carved in the sandstone (Grey thought with some non-indigenous tools); (ii) a figure, not patently European in features, but apparently European in dress, which Grey took to be a priest; and (iii) the more traditional aboriginal paintings, the Wandjinas, here influenced by the mouldings of European robes. The many pieces fit together, and probably George Grey's interpretation was right.

Another indication of Portuguese penetration was discovered in Napier Broome Bay, right on the northern hump of the Kimberleys, in 1916.[19] In July of that year, HMS *Encounter* (on loan to the Royal Australian Navy and sailing as HMAS *Encounter*), under the command of Captain C. Cumberlege RN, while on routine wartime patrol along the north-west coast, entered Napier Broome Bay and made landing on a small unnamed island near the entrance to the Bay, now named Carronade Island. The Australian Navy gives the exact position of this island at Lat. 14°s, Long. 126° 40′E. This siting may be important.

Two members of the landing party, Commander C. W. Stevens RAN, and Surgeon-Lieutenant W. Roberts RAN, walked to the top of the island, and there found two bronze cannon (see Plate I), six feet apart, projecting perpendicularly from the sand. They looked as though they had been set in the ground for some surveying or position-marking purpose, though such purpose can only be conjectured. A large number of the ship's crew, equipped with shovels and no doubt urged on by visions of buried treasure, dug up and sifted practically the whole of the area. The only other object found during the digging operations was a small portion of a brass-bound chest.

One of the cannon is stamped with the Portuguese crown and the Rosa da Santa Maria – the little wild rose that Gil Eannes had brought back from beyond Cape Bojador, and which became the badge or trademark of the Portuguese discoverers in their Golden Age. Rubbings of the insignia were sent to Lisbon, where it was indisputably verified that the cannon are Portuguese, identified by the Crown and Rose. The gun-marks indicate that both cannon were forged in Seville, Spain, from which Portugal and other nations commonly purchased armaments at the time; and the probable date of manufacture was the late fifteenth or early sixteenth century.

It is tempting to try to identify this island, which is on the Australian coast absolutely due south of Timor, with the voyages of which Erédia wrote, the 'island on the coast opposite Timor which is called the South Coast'. But unless the Portuguese of Erédia's day carried very antiquated guns, this is not probable. The age of the cannon links more with Sequeira in 1525, or some other voyage of that period. The year 1525 is contemporary with the Treaty of Saragossa, when the Line of Demarcation was shifted to 17 degrees east of the meridian of the Moluccas – not 17 degrees beyond the old Tordesillas line, but 17 degrees beyond the 127th meridian, which was the meridian of the Moluccas. In the Moluccas area itself, this starting point was self-evident; but in lands to the south, first the 127th had to be located as the point from which to measure; and Carronade Island sits astride this meridian. So this may explain not only why the cannon came to be on the island, but why they were set up in that noteworthy manner as leading-marks.

The cannon distinguished by the Crown and Rose is now in Garden Island Naval Base, Sydney, where it is displayed as a showpiece outside the Commandant's Office. The other cannon, without the markings, is on loan to the Maritime Museum, Fremantle, Western Australia. It is good that they are preserved and expertly maintained in these two repositories; but the author has often voiced the opinion that it would be more fitting to house these two cannon in the Australian National Library, Canberra, which is Australia's greatest repository of historical material. There they would be honoured more fittingly, and displayed to all, as the most tangible extant link with the first European discovery of Australia.

Chapter 7

THE CARTOGRAPHICAL SPIES

THESE relics and records of Portuguese penetration of the western coast do not surprise us; indeed, the only surprise is that they are so few. Probably the Portuguese attitude to India Meridional can be likened to the Australian attitude to the Australian Antarctic Territory: it is 'ours', it is 'there', it has been visited, there have been sporadic settlements for research and survey, there would be grave opposition if any foreign power tried to muscle in on it; but, as against that, the Australian man-in-the-street does not think of it as very valuable or very useful – indeed, he does not think about it very much at all. When maps of Australia are drawn, the Antarctic Territory is left off altogether. Few Australians could, from memory, draw any kind of a map of it; and even on official maps where it is indicated (for example, on weather maps), the outline looks more like a vague wavy line doodled across the bottom of the page rather than any outline drawn with cartographical accuracy. And if some such map happened to veer twenty degrees or so too far east, or too far west, few people would have enough knowledge or interest to notice it or to remark on it.

And if Portuguese relics and records on the Western Australian coast are few enough, on the Northern Territory coast they are almost nonexistent. It is true that when Captain Phillip Parker King was exploring in Melville Island in 1818 he came across some aborigines who knew some words of Portuguese,[1] but this is probably an echo of Portuguese slave-raiding in the eighteenth century rather than of Portuguese exploration in the sixteenth. Similarly, the blond native whom Captain Stokes noticed when he put in to Port Essington Harbour[2] would not have been a descendant of sixteenth-century Portuguese, but possibly the product of some Portuguese or Malay contact of more recent times.

When England formed her settlement at Port Essington in 1838, one of those attached to the settlement was George Windsor Earl, traveller, author and interpreter. He knew

Timor – both Portuguese and Dutch – very well, and found that, at least in recent decades, there had been a good deal of voyaging between the island and the mainland. The Dutch, for example, had come across in 1705 for considerable exploring around the Darwin region, and the Portuguese at other times and in other places. This does not prove very much, for by 1838 Australia was open to the world, and even by 1705 was well advertised to the world: it does at least again underline the facility with which a voyage from Timor to the mainland could be made. But in Timor Earl found some direct evidence that there had been slave-raiding on the Australian coast, especially in Melville Island, before the English came to Botany Bay.

And this seems to be obliquely confirmed by Captain King. Apparently he did not speak the Portuguese language and could not understand what the Melville Islanders were saying – if, indeed, their Portuguese was capable of being understood at all. But one scrap of conversation that he did record seems significant. Coming in in a boat, they saw an old and ugly woman on the shore, who was doing her best to entice them to land, whether in friendly invitation or as a decoy for hidden warriors Captain King did not know. He writes:

'On pulling towards the woman, who, by the way, could not have been selected by them either for her youth or beauty, she frequently repeated the words "Ven aca, Ven aca", accompanied with an invitation to land . . .'

Now 'Ven aca', as Captain King renders it, is clearly the Portuguese imperative '*Venha-ca*'. And in an island subject to raids from the slavers, no words would be more remembered, no words would be more ominous or more dreaded than those two words, *Venha-ca*! Come here!

This lesser contact with the northern coast can be easily explained. As soon as a ship left Timor, sailing east, it immediately crossed the 129th meridian, and thereafter was trespassing in Spanish waters. This naturally diluted their enthusiasm and diminished their incentives. There was no future in finding new lands on the Spanish side of the Line, for any wealth found (gold, for example, or spices) would inevitably belong to Spain, and in due course would be exploited by Spain. The Portuguese were a practical people, and this practical consideration weighed heavy with them. If lines are drawn on a map of the world marking all known Portuguese voyages, the seas in her half of the world are almost obliterated under the web of crossed lines, while the other half of the world, the Spanish half, remains almost virgin white. For example, the Portuguese showed not the slightest interest in New Guinea, even though it was so close to the Moluccas. The half-hearted expedition of Sequeira[3] in 1525 brought some suggestion of its coasts to the charts. In 1526 Jorge de Meneses was blown off his course and stranded in Western New Guinea (or it may have been Waigeio Island); he returned to Tidore as soon as he could, and the only result of his adventure was his bestowing of the name of Os Papuas on the fuzzy-headed natives (a name which still lingers in New Guinea), and the caption *'Hic hibernavit G. de Meneses'* on some of the charts of the day.

But more importantly, the Portuguese were deterred by the Treaty of Tordesillas. The Treaty contained explicit provisions forbidding trespassing across the Line into the territory of the other nation, and to be caught in the act would put the Treaty itself in jeopardy. As the weaker military power of the two, Portugal relied on the sanctity of the Treaty, and upheld it in every way. When the Spanish wrongly (at any rate in Portugal's eyes) occupied part of Gilolo in 1524, Portugal had no option but to fight in defending her rights under the Treaty: the same Governor Jorge de Meneses drove them out. But so long as the Spanish kept to their side of the Line, Portugal took care not to provoke them. Private voyages across the Line were discouraged; and official probes, while not unknown, were kept as secret as possible. In Africa Portugal proudly marked each discovery with a *padrão*, a commemorative stone cross; in eastern Australia her voyagers carefully covered up all traces of their visits, and silently stole away.

When the Dutch made their first probe into the East Indies in 1595, their leader, Frederick Houtman, had on board certain Portuguese maps which had been clandestinely obtained in Lisbon. The Dutch had never been in those seas before, and Houtman's journal shows how carefully he was tracing his path across the unfamiliar seas with the help of these maps – sighting a named landmark here, anxiously watching out for some marked shoal there. We do not know just what maps he had, but this is immaterial: but at least one must have had some detail of the coast of India Meridional. For on a subsequent voyage in 1619, when presumably he still had the same maps, Houtman sighted a group of islands off the coast where the city of Geraldton, Western Australia, stands today – and he named them 'Abrolhos'. Today they show on modern maps as 'Houtman's Abrolhos', and have become a well-known Western Australian tourist resort.

Now *Abra-olhos* is a Portuguese word, or rather two words (*Abra Olhos* – Open your eyes! Look out! Look sharp!). There must be significance in this use by a Dutch captain of this idiomatic Portuguese expression, and the most likely is that the islands had already been discovered by the Portuguese and were so named on the Portuguese map, which he had. Yet even this rather obvious deduction is questioned by those who argue against Portuguese discovery, and their argument runs something like this. There are only two Portuguese names on a modern map of Australia – the Abrolhos in Western Australia, and Pedra Branca in Tasmania. The latter was discovered by Abel Tasman, and he tells us in his Journal that he gave the island this name because it resembled the rock of that name outside Macao.[4] On analogy with this, it can be argued[5] that the Abrolhos were actually discovered by Houtman, but that, like Tasman, he named them from resemblance to some other islands elsewhere which bore that name. The argument seems an unnecessary extension. Incidentally Tasman himself was carrying Portuguese charts, quite probably obtained as clandestinely as those on Houtman's ship. 'We have found the same in longitude and latitude according to the charts of the Portuguese,' he writes in one place;[6] and then again: 'It could be the land of New Guinea, according to the charts of the Portuguese.'

Why Frederick Houtman had to steal his maps springs partly from the Portuguese character, and partly from the situation in which they found themselves. The Portuguese

have always been a secretive people, morbidly suspicious
of foreigners; and they figured that the best way to keep
foreigners out of their New World was to tell them nothing, to
encourage them not at all, and above all never to show them
the maps and charts needed to get there. King Manoel I
elevated this into a policy of State, by decreeing in 1508 that
all Portuguese navigators engaged in voyages beyond the
Cape of Good Hope must, on return to Lisbon, immediately
hand over to the Maritime Archivist in the Casa da India all
maps, charts, logbooks and journals, on pain of death. This
was the famous Politica do Sigilo, or Policia de Segrêdo, or (in
English) The Policy of Secrecy.

Admiral S. E. Morison and others have discounted the
Politica do Sigilo, arguing that the mere locking-up of charts
could not achieve any useful security, when the sailors themselves chattered in quayside public houses and sailed in
foreign service, and were available to any cartographer who
wished to pump them for information. It is true that such
security measures could not be one hundred percent effective,
and we shall see later that in fact they were not. Yet even
England, as late as 1760, was relying on the same methods.
Cook's Instructions[7] included a Policy of Secrecy clause:

'. . . taking care before you leave the vessel to demand from
the officers and petty officers the log-books and journals
they may have kept, and to seal them up for our inspection,
and enjoining them, and the whole crew, not to divulge
where they had been.'

Pursuant to these instructions, Cook collected all journals
from his men on Sunday, 30 September 1770; and the
London Evening Post (quoted by Professor J. C. Beaglehole)[8]
reports that immediately on the arrival of the Endeavour, the
Admiralty officers seized all of these documents.

And as evidence that the Politica do Sigilo did at times
achieve its desired result, notwithstanding the quayside chat-
ter, it is possible to point to St Helena.[9] It was discovered by
João da Nova Castella in 1502, and was used by the Portuguese as a staging-post on the route to India. It is not a
distant island, and it lies in the middle of the frequented

Atlantic seaway. Yet so effective was the Politica do Sigilo that for eighty years it was not available to outside nations. If this could be achieved in the busy Atlantic, how much more easily could the Portuguese keep secret their discoveries on the other side of the world.

The Politica do Sigilo not only worked against foreigners, but against the Portuguese people themselves. Jaime Cortesão quotes the wording of the Secrecy Oath which was administered to the officials who handled the maps, and this appears to prohibit equally disclosure of maritime secrets to strangers and disclosure to nationals: '*Lhes deu el-rei juramente no lenho da Vera Cruz e sobre o Livro dos Evangelhos, que guardassem todo aquele segredo.*'[10]

This is understandable. Until about 1520 the East was the monopoly of the Portuguese Crown against Portuguese private traders. The Casa da India and the policy of secrecy were both set up to defend the Crown's monopoly against interlopers. This gave rise to two classes of Portuguese cartography: (a) maps available to the public, and (b) maps officially held, guarded jealously in the Casa da India, and attracting severe penalties for breach of secrecy.[11]

How successfully the Casa da India clamped down on Portuguese publication is shown by a survey of extant Portuguese maps. No one doubts for one moment that Cão, Dias and the others were the great discoverers of the African coast in the fifteenth century, but only one or two Portuguese charts from this century have survived. For much of our information we have to look to contemporary Italian and especially Venetian cartographers whose maps draw upon Portuguese information – whether stolen or otherwise illegally obtained we can only guess. For example, Cão's very great voyages of 1482–4 are only known to us from the Venetian map entitled *Ginea Portugalexe*, now in the British Museum. Every scholar in this field owes an immense debt to Armando Cortesão and Teixeira da Mota for their Herculean efforts in collecting, from all over the world, the Portuguese maps relating to the Great Discoveries. It is noteworthy how few are direct Portuguese publications, and how few are now housed in Portuguese libraries. Practically all leaked out to, or were pirated by, other nations; but they are all now at home together again between the covers of their great *Portugaliae Monumenta Cartografica.*

Cortesão[12] remarks many times that there is a curious gap in Portuguese cartography between 1525 and 1545. During that period – and it is the period of the great boundary disputes with Spain – security must have been especially strict. Few maps of any kind show Portuguese discoveries during those years. This gap does not only affect the cartography of Australia, even though this book is primarily concerned with this facet. In those years the Portuguese were very active in the north-west Atlantic (Newfoundland and Canada) and in the East Indies (Java, Borneo, Celebes, as well as the Moluccas and Timor), and in the China Sea to the north. All of these areas suffer because of the thorough suppression of Portuguese materials in those two decades. W. F. Ganong,[13] the expert on Canada, and E. C. Abendanon,[14] the expert on the East Indian sector, both find in their fields what this book will find in the Australian sector – that the only foreign cartographers who broke the security cordon of the 1530s were the French cartographers of Dieppe, and that the Dieppe Maps are the only sources of information concerning Portuguese voyaging in the lost decades.

It is also possible that Portuguese discoveries did slow down during that period. King Manoel, who died in 1521, managed to keep the Oriental Trade as a royal monopoly. During that time, the whole of the activity in the East, including voyages of discovery, was ordered by a government department housed in the Casa da India. The King sent the expeditions to the East. He financed them from royal resources, and aimed to take the profits. He also appointed the commanders, and gave detailed orders. Only under this system could a long, expensive and elaborate voyage be sent to a faraway coast. The private traders, when they succeeded to this royal monopoly, no doubt travelled long distances, and at times sighted new lands or pioneered new routes. But exploration for the sake of exploration has to be State inspired and State financed. It is probably fortunate that the most important expedition to Australia happened to occur when it did, in the very last years of the State-inspired voyaging, just before Portuguese voyages of this type ceased for ever.

The Casa da India e Mina, to give it its full name, was therefore a combination of a government administrative department, an office and warehouse for the King's private trading activities, and a marine office for the coordination and control of shipping. The whole establishment was housed in a former Royal Palace in the Paço do Ribeiro on the banks of the Tejo, close to where the Cais de Sodré railway station stands today. The map-room, into which all maps and charts were funnelled, was in the basement. As the sole repository in the world of the records of Portugal's maritime exploits in the east, it must have collected a wonderful collection of early Australiana. All of our research problems would be solved if we could walk into that storehouse today. But that is one wish that will never be fulfilled.

At 9.30 a.m. on Saturday, 1 November 1755, the Holy Day of All Saints, Lisbon revealed her beauty in that garment of distant calm which she wears so superbly on such occasions. Most of her people were at church. Down by the river the Casa da India, its neighbour the Palace of the Cortereals, and its next neighbour the residence of the King in the Terreiro do Paço, shared in the peace of the holiday morning. Suddenly there was heard an approaching roar, which we of the twentieth century would liken to the roar of an armada of jet aeroplanes. Walls trembled, there were affrighted screams from those who recognised the portent: then, for a few moments there was a temporary pause. Then came the shock, the chaos, the agony and the confusion of the most terrible earthquake to afflict any European capital in historical times. In two minutes the palaces on the waterfront, the churches on the higher ground, the commercial buildings in the Baixa – all, without distinguishing between patrician and plebeian, wavered and fell. Along the north bank of the Tagus the horror was at its worst. It was here, at the Cais de Pedra, that eye-witnesses recounted how the earth opened, and the buildings fell in, and the earth closed over them again. This is an exaggeration; but it is symptomatic of the destruction that seemed to be occurring all along that ill-fated waterfront, where, among the other buildings about to die, stood the Casa da India.[15]

Again there was a short pause, and then the third shock struck. The day turned into night as the dust rose to the sky.

Flames from every overturned candle roared upward through the shattered woodwork. And 45 minutes later the waters of the Sea of Straw, which had receded with the shock-wave of the earthquake, now returned from the ocean in a torrent which tore away the remnants of the ruined city. And this, too, struck with its most devastating force along the doomed river squares.

Thirty thousand people died in this holocaust, many of them under the fallen masonry of the churches in which they had been praying. The libraries, the archives, the maritime records, the art treasures, the cultural patrimony of the whole of the Portuguese race, all of these died with Lisbon; and perhaps, of all places in Lisbon, the Casa da India was the worst casualty, the most desolating annihilation. The irreplaceable maps and charts that were bought with the lifeblood of Prince Henry's galaxy of heroes are now nothing but dust and rubble underneath the cobblestones of the Ribeira dos Naus.

Today the ruins of the Carmo, perched high above the Rossio, look down upon the beautiful city of modern Lisbon. Pombal's town-planners, Pombal's architects, Pombal's builders, replaced the ruined city with a new city, even fairer than before. But there were some things that even Pombal could not replace. The Casa da India and its treasures were gone beyond recall. If there were references to these charts and voyages in the other libraries of Lisbon, these too vanished in the Earthquake, and the Fire, and the tidal wave. What little was saved suffered further devastation shortly afterwards, in the fires and the looting of the French invasion in the Napoleonic Wars. To Armando Cortesão and his co-workers in modern Lisbon, the hardest blow to bear in the unhappy history of his country is this impoverishment of the nation's documentary patrimony. With great feeling he writes:[16]

'There are still several obscure points in the history of the Portuguese discoverers which unfortunately cannot be elucidated satisfactorily in our archives and libraries, in spite of the cluster of researchers and scholars who, particularly in the last fifty years, have dedicated their efforts and unbiased criticism to this really national task. The sixty years of Spanish occupation, the Lisbon Earthquake of 1755 and the appalling fire which then destroyed the Casa da India with its invaluable treasures, and the French invaders, were calamities which, in one way or another, impoverished our documentary patrimony.'

But in spite of these catastrophes, we do have a few clues as to what went on in the Casa da India before its destruction. In the sixteenth century all nations in Europe were curious to know what the Portuguese were up to, and it has been explained before how a good deal of information concerning the discoveries made by the Portuguese leaked to other countries, especially Venice, and came to be published in foreign maps. Much of this was legal and above-board. Portuguese sailors, with some records of their voyaging, were engaged by other powers. Nationals of other countries – Columbus is a good example – sought Portuguese service and then sold its secrets. Some non-secret Portuguese maps, actually published in Lisbon, were copied abroad; and when the Portuguese edition perished in the Earthquake, the copies in the other countries could be brought forward to replace them.

But other maps were obtained from Lisbon clandestinely, illegally and dishonestly.[17] We have already heard how the Dutchman, Frederick Houtman, qualified himself to lead the Dutch to the Indies by cartographical spying and stealing in Lisbon. At one stage he was thrown into jail for this activity. The Dutch also sent their ace cartographer, J. H. Linschoten, to Lisbon and Goa to collect maps and information. He was not interested in Australia, but his great work, the *Itinerio*, is a mine of information on the East Indies, and is the document on which the subsequent empire of the Netherlands East Indies was founded.

Another method of cartographical espionage was for some foreign agent, often attached to a foreign embassy, to bribe a working Portuguese mapmaker to provide information surreptitiously. The Italian Duke of Ferrara sent his representative, Ernesto Cantino, to Lisbon, where he paid the enormous sum of twelve golden ducats to an unknown Portuguese mapmaker for the beautiful and historic Cantino Map, now the pride and joy of some Italian museum. One important Portuguese cartographer who was open to such bribes was Jorge Reinel. When the outside world was thirsting for the first maps of the Spice Islands area, where Portugal was by then well established, a German named Konrad Peutinger[18] sent his undercover men to Lisbon to acquire maps by whatever means they could, and directly or indirectly Peutinger seems to be involved in the escape of most known Spice Islands maps of this period. One of them is the unsigned Reinel of 1519 – unsigned to avoid detection – now in Munich. Another is the immensely important Penrose Chart, now in America – traceable to Peutinger, not proveably connected with Reinel. And the third was the *Carta Anonima Portuguesa*, which will play a large part in the later chapters of this book, a copy of which Peutinger (or someone like Peutinger) acquired after it had left Portugal by another channel.

But the most important of these spies was French, or (more accurately) Norman, from Dieppe. Dieppe in Normandy had always been an important port, but it had declined in the Middle Ages, and in the early sixteenth century was experiencing a sudden and dramatic new birth. Dieppois mariners began to roam the world. Her sailors became the first interlopers into Portugal's Brazil, ultimately leading to the establishment of the French colony of Guiana on the west bank of the Waipoco. Her fishermen intruded into Portugal's Fishing Banks, ultimately superseding them there. Cartier was from Dieppe, and his voyages to the St Lawrence led to the foundation of French Canada. Parmentier and others voyaged east, reaching as far as Sumatra.

And like the Portuguese of one hundred years before, they saw that this progress could only be founded upon systematic research, collation of material, and educational training in the sciences of hydrography and cartography. They set up in Dieppe, or at Arcques just outside of Dieppe, a navigational research station not unlike that which Prince Henry had established at Sagres. There Pierre Desceliers, 'Priest, Mathematician and Cartographer', taught the most promising of the young mariners the arts of the sea, especially the science of sea-instruments and the art of chart-making.[19] Even foreigners were attracted to the school by its great reputation, and one of them was a Scotsman, John Rose, or Jean Rotz, of whom much more will be said later. Because of the influence of Desceliers's School, the exciting spirit of adventure and exploring that permeated the city, and the congregation of cosmopolitan seafarers in the streets, Dieppe became a magnet for the sea-roamers, an inspiration in the world of cartography. As Admiral S. E. Morison said: 'They obtained their data fresh at the quayside from master pilots such as Cartier, and produced charts equal to those of the Portuguese for accuracy and beauty.'

And like all others at that time, they had no compunction about picking the brains of others. Renegades such as Jean Alfonse joined their ranks. Information was picked up at foreign ports, which pre-eminently meant the port of Lisbon. Agents were planted in foreign countries, Portugal inevitably included. Dieppe was the best-organised cartographical centre in the world, with the best Intelligence Service of the age. And when the security curtain of the Casa da India was cracked, and the two most secret of all Portuguese maps were smuggled out of the country, it is of no surprise to find that the feat was achieved by this superb French organisation.

One of these was a map of the world, synthesising all of Portugal's maritime knowledge up to that date, including valuable material in the north-west Atlantic (Newfoundland, Nova Scotia etc), Brazil, and other areas; but above all, in its Spice Islands sector, disclosing the most up-to-date detail of the East Indian islands ever published to the outside world up to that date. It is known as the *Carta Anonima Portuguesa,* and is housed in the Library at Wolfenbüttel, in West Germany, today.

The other was a map of Australia. It was published in Dieppe, included in the map of the world which we know as the Dauphin Map.

PART TWO

'Old-time charts bespeak some knowledge'

Chapter 8

THE DAUPHIN MAP

THE next five or six chapters of this book will be devoted to this remarkable map, and first the reader is asked to familiarise himself with its outline and its details, to facilitate the close study which is to follow. The Dauphin is a map of the world, displaying all of the continents, and there will be some limited examination of it in this role; but as this has already been exhaustively treated by Professor Harrisse,[1] and as its Asian and American features, interesting though they are, are not nearly as important in this study as its Australian feature, the emphasis will be mainly on the Australian sector of the Map.

A photograph of the Australian sector of this Map, taken directly from the original in the British Museum, is provided in Plate IV; and in the interests of clarity, a line drawing of the same sector, slightly simplified, is provided in Fig. 8.1. The reader has already seen the outline of the Dauphin's continent in Fig. 0.1; but here the area is enlarged, and the adjoining islands – Timor, Java, Sumatra and so on – also appear. It is repeated that the Dauphin was not constructed on Mercator's Projection, or on any other projection with which the reader is familiar; and therefore when the reader looks at the uncorrected Dauphin for the first time he should not be unduly perturbed about the apparent elongation of the east coast, or some of the other features which at first appear to be distortions: when it is redrawn on Mercator's Projection (Fig. 0.2) its resemblance to a modern Australia is greatly enhanced. The explanation of this transposition will be given in a later chapter. For the moment, the reader need only glance at Fig. 0.2, concentrating his attention on the original outlines.

But even when the Dauphin Map is viewed in its original projection – and after all, sixteenth-century maps have to be viewed in the form in which their cartographers drew them – it is still, by sixteenth-century standards, a very good map, a very good representation of the real shape of Australia. It

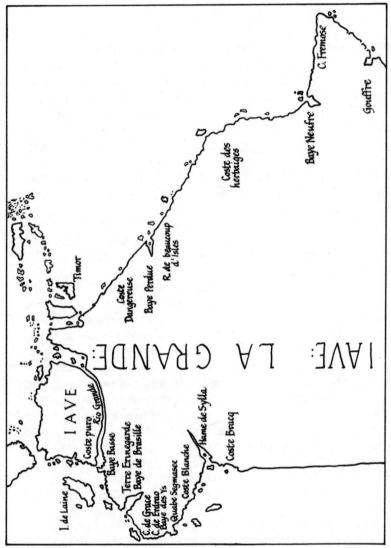

Fig. 8.1 PART OF THE DAUPHIN MAP.

must be remembered that the mapping of a previously unknown continent, or large island, takes time. A surveying genius like Cook could sail up an unknown coast, like the east coast of Australia, and immediately produce a creditable chart. But Cook was a genius, and an exception. Lesser mortals produce only the vaguest outlines on their first traverse, leaving it to their successors to evolve better outlines bit by bit. It took five centuries of constant charting before the island of Great Britain attained a recognisable shape. J. R. McClymont, speaking to the Royal Society of Tasmania, and using the island of Tasmania as his illustration, puts this very well:[2]

'If you and I, never having seen a map of Tasmania and unaware of its insular character, were cast there, one on its east coast, the other on its west, and jotted down what outlines we saw – and if those sketches were to fall into the hands of some mapmaker on the other side of the world to be elaborated into a map, and placed in a proper position relative to the other countries of the globe –: we may safely conclude that our hypothetical map of Tasmania would be no better than Jave-la-Grande.'

And further, we must remember that the Dauphin was produced in the sixteenth century. Cook was operating a quarter of a millenium later, when the techniques of marine surveying were vastly improved. Cook himself says: 'Navigators formerly wanted many of the helps towards keeping an accurate Journal which the present Age is possessed of' (*Journal*, 7 September 1770). The only instrumental 'helps' that the mariners had in the sixteenth century were a compass much less efficient than a modern Boy Scout's compass, and an astrolabe (or quadrant) far, far inferior to the precision-built sextants which even a weekend yachtsman possesses today.

And they had no instrumental means of establishing longitude. As a result, the east-west distances on all sixteenth-century maps are miscalculated, usually exaggerated, so that every continent or other feature looks 'thicker' than it really is. On the Dieppe Maps themselves (see the 'Royal', Plate V) the Caspian Sea is always shown with its east–west measurements exceeding its north–south measurements, so that it always looks like an egg lying on its side rather than an egg standing upright. As we shall see later, the method that they used for calculating longitude was defective, and itself produced this east–west exaggeration. Therefore if, on the Dauphin Map viewed on its original projection before transposition, Arnhem-land looks too bulky, or if the New South Wales coast veers too far east, it should not be thought that these coasts were being drawn from guesswork or from imagination. With proper understanding of the projections, these apparent distortions can be explained, so that they are no longer distortions at all. In Plate V is given a photograph of Desceliers' 'Royal' world map of 1546, on which are portrayed not only Australia, but the other five continents as well. His map of Australia has its defects. Yet if one compares the shapes of his North America and South America with the shape of Australia in the Dauphin, it will be seen that in that era the world did not possess American maps strikingly better than the map of Australia that appears in the Dauphin. Searching back for American maps of the same date as the Dauphin, the nearest in date is that of Sebastian Munster. The grotesque distortion of his North America and his South America – we might even add, his Africa – is so gross that the Dauphin's Australia appears a model of cartographic accuracy in comparison. A similar point is made by Professor J. A. Williamson when he says:[3]

'Its [i.e. the Dauphin's] eastern and western coasts bear a greater resemblance to the correct outline than do the coasts of the Americas in La Cosa's Spanish Map of 1500, which embodies the result of numerous voyages of discovery.'

On these considerations, and by these standards, the Dauphin Map of Australia is therefore a very good map, a very good map indeed.

And it must be noted too that the Dauphin is a world map, and in the historical geography of the world it is a world map of the highest cartographical importance. It is not some historical curiosity of limited interest in speculation about Australia. Forgetting its Australian sector altogether, its Asian and above all its American sectors are of overwhelming importance in the history of cartography. The east coast of the United States, including New York Harbour, was first explored by the renegade Portuguese discoverer Estevão Gomes: his discoveries are shown for what is believed to be the first time on the Dauphin Map. In the early sixteenth century, as we have seen in earlier chapters, the Portuguese were particularly active in two sectors, the East Indies and the Canadian coast. The Portuguese Policy of Secrecy prevented the revelation of their activities in either of these sectors, and the leakage to Dieppe, revealed in the Dauphin Map, has provided the cartographers of the world with their major clues about the Portuguese discoveries in those two sectors. E. C. Abendanon, the historian of East Indian exploration, makes the Dieppe Maps his main quarry of information in piecing together their discoveries in the East Indian islands. The French expert Henry Harrisse, the American Admiral S. E. Morison, the Canadian scholars H. P. Biggar and W. F. Ganong, lean heavily, almost exclusively, on these same Dieppe Maps in their dissection of the progressive unveiling of the Canadian coast. The reader is urged to read the works of these authorities,[4] to gain the necessary respect for and confidence in the Dieppe Maps. The Dauphin is a major world map, of major cartographical importance, by any standards; and the uninformed allegation made by Professor Scott that it is probably a 'hoax' is about as silly a suggestion as any that could be made.

The confidence that Henry Harrisse shows in the Dieppe portrayal of Australia is especially noteworthy. The early cartographical history of America poses one great puzzle. Columbus on his first voyage sighted only the offshore islands of Cuba, Haiti and the Bahamas, and it was not until years later that the NorthAmerican mainland became known. Yet in the intervening years several maps appeared which arguably show secret knowledge of the mainland. This is paralleled in Australian cartography – the Portuguese discovered the offshore islands of Timor, Solor etc, the official sighting of the mainland was much later, and yet in the interim certain

maps (the Dieppe Maps) disclose a knowledge of the mainland that was never publicly admitted. The parallel is obvious.

It is therefore tempting – irresistible, indeed – to point to
the American parallel as one further argument to establish
the plausibility of the Dieppe Maps. But Henry Harrisse
argues from the opposite end. He accepts as proven the secret
knowledge of the Australian continent (as evidenced by the
Dieppe Maps), and uses the Australian experience as the
argument to bolster the American hypothesis. He writes:[5]

'The general belief among geographers of the first quarter
of the sixteenth century was that to the north-west of Cuba
there existed a continental region, which had already been
explored, named and delineated by Spanish or Portuguese
navigators before the year 1502.

This may at first sight appear quite surprising: but it is
well to recollect that the history of geography affords other
instances of the kind; and, in a cartographical point of view,
quite as important.

Let us take Australia.

In the Lusitano–French maps of the world which originated in the year 1542 with Dieppe cosmographers, such as
Pierre Desceliers and his school, there is a continental
configuration which of late has greatly exercised the historians of maritime discovery . . . South of the well-known
island of Java, and separated by a strait, these mappamundi
exhibit an extensive continent, stretching southward, and
the north coast of which is dotted with numerous designa-
tions of dangerous coasts, rivers and landing-places.

That region, called then Jave-la-Grande . . . stands, historically speaking, relative to the Sunda Archipelago, precisely in the same position as the north-western continent
in the Cantino chart stands as regards the West Indies. No
historian, no documents of the sixteenth century, mention
the existence of such an Austral continent. We also see it
disappear from subsequent maps, until long afterwards,
when the region looms up again, but this time as an alleged
discovery accomplished recently by Dutch navigators.

That continental land, nevertheless, so far from being
imaginary or an invention of cartographers, was nothing

else than Australia, now justly considered by competent judges as having been discovered, visited and named by unknown Portuguese mariners – whose maps furnished the cartographical data used in the Dieppe charts, sixty or seventy years before the Dutch first sighted the shores of that extensive country.

Suppose that Henry Harrisse were here propounding some pet theory of his own, leading up to that unqualified final conclusion – *It was nothing else than Australia* – then because of his prestige and erudition we would have to treat his finding with respect. But here (it seems to the author) his reading has even greater weight, for he is here not propounding a pet theory, not riding a personal hobby-horse – for his interest is in American discovery, not in Australian discovery. He is indeed pressing his own theory about pre-knowledge of the American mainland. And to prove his point, he casually cites the fully-evidenced parallel – the pre-knowledge of the Australian mainland, demonstrated by the Dieppe Maps. Here the Dieppe Maps are in the most distinguished company.

The provenance of the Dauphin Map, too, is distinguished. We know that it was ordered by King Francis I of France, as a gift to his son the Dauphin, later Henry II. How it came to England we do not know, but when we next hear of it, it is owned by Edward Harley, Earl of Oxford, one of the principal Lords of the Admiralty in the early eighteenth century. Because of its association first with the Dauphin and then with Harley it is today known by two names – 'the Dauphin' (which name is used consistently throughout this book), and 'the Harleian'. In S. E. Morison's great book *The European Discovery of America*, for instance, it is referred to under the latter name. On Harley's death in 1724 it was stolen by one of his servants, and being stolen goods was hidden or not publicly disclosed for the next few decades. Dr Solander came to hear of it; and it was acquired by Sir Joseph Banks, the young scientist who sailed in the *Endeavour* with Captain Cook, and who later became the 'father' of the young Australian colony and the acknowledged expert on all

Australian affairs. His interest in this map, his ownership of it, and the importance that he placed upon it, are all significant considerations. This last is evidenced by the fact that in 1790 he presented it to the British Museum, to ensure that this great historical treasure would be safeguarded for the nation in perpetuity.

The map,[6] in the British Museum, is on rollers, $8'2'' \times 3'11''$, beautifully executed and coloured, and lavishly embellished. It is emblazoned with the Arms of the King of France, and of the Dauphin. These Arms help in fixing its date. The heraldic device in the Arms of France was changed in 1536; and as the map is emblazoned with the old Arms, it must have been completed before that date. On the other hand, the American sector includes data from Verrazano's expedition of 1529, and the Canadian sector data from Jacques Cartier's first expedition of 1534, and possibly some from his second expedition of 1536. These termini narrow the date so well that 1536 appears to be the certain date of publication.

However, Henry Harrisse disagrees with this reasoning.[7] In his opinion the place in Canada named 'Tutonaguy' on the Dauphin Map links with Cartier's Third Voyage, which therefore dates the Dauphin Map 1542 or thereabouts. He dismisses the evidence of the change in the Arms as heraldic ignorance on the part of the cartographer – he would be an expert on maps, but no expert on heraldry. That kind of mistake does happen, and has happened elsewhere: in the most famous imaginative painting of *Captain Cook's Raising of the Flag at Botany Bay*, the painting is marred by its portrayal of the Union Jack with three crossed crosses, whereas in 1770 the Union Flag had only two. It seems to the author that as the map was being produced for presentation to the Dauphin, the Crown Prince of France, care would have been taken on such a point, and the evidence of the heraldry at least balances against the evidence of the place named Tutonaguy. But even if the Harrisse date is correct, it makes little difference to the argument presented in this book, though in that case the Dauphin would be the fourth of the Dieppe Maps in date (ranking after Desliens and the two Rotz charts) and not the first. Indeed, it would assist the argument, for it would make it even more certain that the Dauphin antedates the *Carta Anonima Portuguesa* (see next chapter).

The Dauphin Map is unsigned, which makes it uncertain whether it was drawn by Desceliers himself, for Desceliers always signed his maps. It is undoubtedly the product of his establishment, and was produced either by him or under his supervision. The opportunity, the occasion and the execution point to his authorship: after all, the establishment would not often be commissioned by a King, and it seems unlikely that Desceliers would delegate this royal command to an assistant or an apprentice. The Map shows some of his traits – Desceliers lacked the meticulousness, even the integrity, of Rotz and Desliens, and innovations like the Antarctic Extension and the Rio Grande Canal smack more of Desceliers than of any of his known colleagues. A pointed comparison between the Rio Grande Canal on the Australian sector of the Dauphin Map and the St Helene Canal on the North Carolina sector of the same map will be made later. Conjecturally, though with no positive proof, the authorship of the Dauphin Map is ascribed to Pierre Desceliers.

The Dauphin Map is of the portolan type, in portolan style, but it is not a real portolan. Portolans were mariners' charts, practical charts for use at sea. Common portolans were not artistically executed on parchment, as is the Dauphin; common portolans were drawn in black and white, on paper, and these paper charts were soon torn, discoloured, lost or destroyed. Maps like the Dauphin take their substance from portolans, but in execution they are far more elaborate. They are drawn or painted in durable inks and paints on the parchment, profusely adorned, beautifully lettered, artistically illustrated, and intended to adorn the walls of the libraries or studies of noblemen.[8] The Dauphin Map, as was said, was prepared for and presented to the Dauphin of France. The third of the Dieppe Maps, that of Jean Rotz, was presented to Henry VIII of England, and from his palace found its way to the Royal Collection now in the British Museum. Because these maps were expensive, artistic, properly housed and properly looked after, they survived in aristocratic libraries long after the flimsy sea charts disappeared.

But even these expensive, ornate and substantial wall-maps were not immune from the ravages of time, and even they have only survived in small numbers, or in single impressions. Raymond Lister explains that they were too large for glazing, and whether they were rolled up or stored in cupboards or simply left on the wall, they eventually became cracked and torn, or simply rotted away. We cannot imagine that five Dieppe cartographers – Desceliers, Rotz, Vallard, Le Testu and Desliens – in the whole of their working lives produced less than a dozen single maps between the five of them. The rest of their work, undoubtedly voluminous, has gone. As we only know half a century of Portuguese cartography by the minute amount that leaked to other countries, and as we only know sixty years of Dieppe cartography by the handful of maps that have survived, we must realise that the Policy of Secrecy and the Lisbon Earthquake between them have distilled a once great output to a fraction of one percent of what once existed. The fact that, after this distillation, we have left nine or ten maps, all agreeing with each other with such fidelity, is in itself a proof of the authenticity and provenance of the Dieppe Maps.

It can be established that the Dauphin Map, and the other Dieppe Maps which followed it, are of Portuguese origin, subsequently handled and rehandled by the Norman French, by the linguistic evidence of the geographical place-names on the maps. These names are a curious mixture of Portuguese, faulty Portuguese, and French. A lengthy review of this linguistic evidence will not be attempted here, for it is difficult for an English-speaking person (whether author or reader) to appreciate the nuances of spelling, vocabulary and usage involved in the analysis; it would be like expecting a foreigner to pick up lapses such as 'New South Whales' or 'Wale-Bone Beach' on an English map. Perhaps this was best expressed in the lecture of Professor José Maria Rodrigues,[9] when he said:

'Only we, the Portuguese, have the ability to throw light on the evidenciary force of this or that word, or this or that abbreviation, occurring in the geographical names on the map: and I can say that we alone can do this work, and it must be done.'

Many scholars, among them Armando Cortesão, Jaime Cortesão, Quirinal da Fonseca and Gago Coutinho, have subjected the maps to minute linguistic examination, and this has established beyond doubt the Portuguese origin of the maps.

Very little purpose would be served by reproducing this evidence in any detail, as to Portuguese-speaking readers the evidence is self-evident, and to those who do not know the Portuguese language it would be tedious. It is sufficient to say that all modern scholars, whether Portuguese, French or otherwise (Professor Scott always excluded), agree on this finding; and in short form the weight of the evidence can best be given in this concise summary of the findings of Gago Coutinho:[10]

1 There are numerous, very numerous, pure Portuguese place-names which point to the Portuguese origin. He quotes words such as Terra Anegada (land covered with water), Terra Alta, C. de Flores, and many others.

2 He notes many lapses from good Portuguese, mistakes in copying or unintended Gallicisations. He cites:
  (a) some Portuguese words which have not been properly copied, the errors sometimes varying from map to map – e.g., C. de Fremose, C. Frimose. Actually this should be Cabo Fremoso, Cape Beautiful.
  (b) The word Ilha (island) appears in many garbled forms – Illa, Isla, Ila, Yᵉ.
  (c) some words have been completely Gallicised – e.g. Molucques for Moluccas.
  These point to hasty copying by someone not thoroughly conversant with the Portuguese language – probably the spy himself, who might not have had the time or the privacy for much careful copying.

3 Finally, there are pure French words – e.g. Jave-la-Grande. These were probably inserted after the map arrived in Dieppe, by the Dieppe editors themselves.

These linguistic findings have led to the widely-held theory that a Frenchman, speaking Portuguese but not very good Portuguese, somehow infiltrated into the Casa da India, perhaps as a draftsman or filing clerk; and that as opportunity arose he copied or memorised secret materials as they came to his notice. Because of hasty copying (the theory runs) he made mistakes both in the outlines and in the place-names; and, lacking the language instinct of a native-born Portuguese, he did not have the ability to correct these mistakes, or to avoid them, and at times he even lapsed into French forms. After the pirated material reached Dieppe, it was handled by the French-speaking cartographers themselves, who did not have the knowledge to correct the garbled forms, and who sometimes introduced new French names on their own initiative.

This theory seems to have some weaknesses. A spy with such poor command of the Portuguese language would hardly commend himself for a high-security job in the Casa da India, which seems to destroy the need for a 'Portuguese-speaking Frenchman'. More likely some Portuguese clerk employed in the Casa da India, or some Portuguese cartographer with access to its secrets, was bribed, and the secret material brought to some real French spy (perhaps in the French embassy) for hasty copying; and that is where the errors occurred, with the cartographers in Dieppe finally adding their own French words. This would be in line with what is known in other cases. We have heard how Ernesto Cantino bribed an official with twelve golden ducats. We know how cartographers such as Gaspar Viegas and Jorge Reinel went over to foreign service, or sold their maps to Konrad Peutinger and Frederick Houtman. On a grander plane, we can point to the conduct of Christopher Columbus and Ferdinand Magellan. Men in this category would have had much better opportunities for sabotage than some terrified little French filing clerk in the Casa da India.

One suspect often mentioned is the Portuguese Bishop of Viseu,[11] a high official who got into political trouble at this time, and fled the country with 'certain documents of importance'. We do not know what these documents were, but it does not seem likely that the Bishop would have had access to the Casa da India; and if he did, it seems improbable that he would have chosen to abscond with only these little-known maps, the importance of which he would barely have realised. But around 1529, when Portugal was negotiating the Treaty of Saragossa with Spain, these maps would have been of great political importance, and their disclosure to Spain might have wrecked the delicate negotiations which led up to that Treaty. These are political considerations, to which the Bishop might have been privy, and on which he might have been aiming to capitalise. The weakness in this theory is that the secret map did not finish up in Spain, but in France.

For that reason, another suspect is one who did have connections with France – João Affonso (or Jean Alfonse)[12] who has been mentioned in a previous chapter. He had been a Portuguese pilot in eastern waters, and probably had sailed with Sequeira. His book, *Voyages Aventureux*, was published in 1559, though probably written about 1544, and in it he describes a southern continent, its coasts corresponding almost point by point with the Australia of the Dauphin Map. But the interpretation of this is a matter of date, the old question of which came first, the chicken or the egg? It seems more probable that at the time of writing his book Affonso had seen the Dauphin Map, and was describing it, rather than that Desceliers had read the book and was drafting from it.

Further, it does not seem possible that the Dauphin Map could have come from the chart or from the personal knowledge of one navigator, for it embraces six or seven thousand miles of Australian coast, the whole of the west, north and east coasts – far beyond the capacity of one navigator to have visited in one voyage. On the other hand, it must have come from the Casa da India, for it was the business of the Casa da India to bring together the records of several voyages and to map them in one composite chart.

That the Casa da India prototype map was a composite chart can be seen quite clearly, for it is made up of different cartographical styles. It is probable, as later discussion will show, that it is a composite of (i) a north-west coast put together from frequent but unrelated visits from nearby Timor; (ii) a north coast which has disappeared under Java and Sumbawa, and therefore is no longer relevant; and (iii) a long east coast, which could not be anything other than one single, continuous voyage.

The west coast is firm, detailed cartography, with incisive forms. It may not always be right, but it purports to show the exact shape of each bay, cape or island. Sometimes this is very successful: take for instance, King's Sound, with its two 'ears' where the Fitzroy and May Rivers debouch into it. The draftsmen (for it is assumed that there were several) give the impression that they sailed inshore, skirted each cape and entered each bay. This is consistent with a series of single, separate visitors from Timor, each of whom saw and charted his own small section of the coast.

The east coast, on the other hand, looks like a freehand outline. The coast is mainly just a wavy line, with the wiggles in it representing no actual capes or bays, but conventionally representing a coast which is presumed to be indented. In a few places – Repulse Bay, Port Phillip Bay, and a few other places – there is distinctive detail; but mainly the detail is missing or lost. Perhaps the primary chart was sketched from a ship moving along the coast, well out to sea; perhaps the secondary chart was copied, without care, from a primary chart of greater surveying value. Whatever is the reason, the east coast of the Dauphin Map is in strikingly different cartographical style from the west coast; and the total map is a composite of two or more voyages – one for certain down the east coast, others (probably several) making up the west coast.

The nexus between the two is the Gulf of Capentaria, and the treatment of the Gulf varies in the different maps of the Dieppe School. In Jean Rotz it is very narrow, almost insignificant. In Desliens (see Plate VIII) it is wider, but still not wide enough. Later, when de Jode corrected it, it takes on a strong resemblance to the modern Gulf. This supports the above argument that the Dauphin and the other Dieppe Maps which followed it depict a combination of more than one chart which had no clear nexus in the Gulf area, thus leaving room for each cartographical editor to judge for himself how wide or how narrow the Gulf ought to be. If only Desliens had made his Gulf of Carpentaria a little bit wider and a little bit deeper, his whole map would look very much more like the correct shape of the continent.

And this theory is supported by the lack of place-names in the Gulf of Carpentaria region. The place-names on the Dauphin Map conform with the normal portolan convention.

They are printed in, always on the inland side (so as not to interfere with the legibility of the coast), at right-angles to the coast, the lettering of the words parallel to each other, reading clockwise around each island or continent. The French cartographers, particularly, were somewhat cavalier with place-names. Where the map was getting cluttered, they cheerfully left out a few names; and where the names on a coast were rather sparse, they were not above inventing a name or two to improve the balance and symmetry of the map, even though the coast in question had never been visited. Therefore a name or two on a coast does not necessarily prove a visit to that coast. On the other hand, the absence of all names on a coast is strong evidence that that coast had never been visited. On all of the Dieppe Maps, the Gulf of Carpentaria area is devoid of place-names, and that adds to the evidence that the interior of the Gulf had never been penetrated by the navigators, and that the nexus shown on the maps is wholly the invention of the cartographers.

The north coast, from Cape York to Darwin, contains a thick succession of place-names; but these are all Javanese place-names taken directly from the *Carta Anonima Portuguesa*, plus a few French additions, such as 'R. des Cobras', which Desceliers apparently threw in for local colour. These north-coast names will be mentioned again when the *Carta Anonima Portuguesa* is under discussion, but they do not belong to Australian historical geography, and do not concern us here.

Once these Javanese north-coast names are eliminated, there are not very many place-names left on the Dauphin Map. Most of them can be listed here, in anti-clockwise order, from far south-east to far south-west:

East Coast
    Gouffre
    C. de Fremose
    Baye Neufre
    Coste des Herbaiges
    R. de beaucoup d'isles
    Baye perdue
    Coste dangereuse

West Coast
> Coste puro
> Baye bassa
> Baye de Brasille
> Terre Ennegarde
> C. de Grace
> C. de Erdrao
> Baye des ys
> Quabe segmesse
> Coste blanche
> Hame de Sylla
> Coste bracq.

Considering the enormous length of the Australian coast, these names are portioned out most frugally. On the west coast, closest to Timor, the names are more plentiful, although even there only eleven names occur in one thousand miles of coast; on the east coast the allotment is even more frugal – only seven names in nearly three thousand miles. This makes nonsense of Professor Scott's claim that the mapmaker drew a serrated coast, did not like the look of so much emptiness, and so 'attributed names to the teeth of the saw, as though they were real capes'; for there are innumerable serrations on the map which are not named. On the east coast, particularly, it would seem that the navigator sailed down the coast, away from land, only coming inshore at those places where the chart takes on more detail and usually a place-name. All of the 18 named localities are identifiable with distinctive features on the modern coast, the most famous (and the most controversial) being the equation of 'Coste des Herbiages' with 'Botany Bay',[13] where the two names are similar in meaning.

As was the custom with noblemen's decorative maps at that time, most of the Dieppe Maps are adorned with artistic embellishments. There are monkeys and other exotic animals, mythical beasts, houses, people, scenes from village life, and so on: none of it with any relevance to Australia. The only exception is Desliens. This embellishment is an art form of the day, understood not to have any geographic relevance. The result is something like the colourful tourist posters for popular tourist resorts, a basic map adorned with bikini girls, smirking fishermen, courting couples and frolicking children.

Professor Wood[14] and Professor Scott[15] ridicule the monkeys and the exotic flora and fauna: they argue that as these are not typically Australian, the map could not be intended to represent Australia. This argument is myopic. The embellishment is an art form, injected by the Dieppe artists – nothing to do with the Portuguese mariners who drew the basic map, nothing to do with the continent that the map represents. Extant contemporary maps, even the Dieppe Maps themselves, invest (say) the continent of Africa with the same kind of irrelevant embellishment – and clearly Africa had already been discovered, and its coasts fully explored.

This embellishment of maps continued as a somewhat incongruous art form, particularly in France, right through to the eighteenth century. This description of the decorations of the French cartographer Charles Herbert Jaillot speaks for itself:[16]

'Decoratively, Jaillot's maps reached a level that has never since been surpassed. To take one instance, his map of Palestine of 1691 has a cartouche, the lower part formed of two cornucopias overflowing with fruit and leaves. The upper part is a decorative representation of the Garden of Eden. The tree of knowledge complete with entwined serpents, is at the apex, and Adam and Eve stand on either side, naked but for fig-leaves. Eve is pointing at the tree. Around Adam and Eve are grouped beasts of the Garden – elephant, camel, lion and peacock. Such a bare description gives little idea of the baroque magnificence of the work.'

This is French practice a hundred years or so after the Dauphin Map, but the art of the Dieppe mapmakers was of the same mould. They were producing attractive, artistic, colourful adornments for the walls of stately homes; and the artwork was not intended to have or expected to have any relationship to the geographical contents of the map which served as its base.

But the last of the Dieppe Maps, the Desliens of 1566, strips away most of this irrelevant embellishment and returns to something more like the mariners' portolan which came from the Casa da India. Without the ornament and the irrelevancy, it is more practical and more austere. By 1565 the mariners of Dieppe were sailing far afield, and this map may have been made for some gentleman mariner, actually to be taken to sea. And the only adornment with which Desliens enhances his map consists of Portuguese flags flying over the Australian mainland.

After its inclusion in the Dauphin, the Casa da India prototype map (that is, the original chart actually obtained in Lisbon) passed into the stock-in-trade, or the cartographical files, of the Dieppe cartographers. Over the next few decades, as the different Dieppe cartographers produced atlases, maps of the world, etc, they drew upon the resources of these files for the most up-to-date material available in the different sectors of the world; and in the Australian sector they were obliged to copy and recopy this map, because it was not only the most up-to-date, but in fact was the only information then available.

In consequence, we see the same map reappearing in a number of major works over a period of 33 years, those according strictly with the Casa da India prototype, and qualifying for inclusion under the generic title of 'the Dieppe Maps' being:

> Dauphin 1536
> Jean Rotz 1542
> Desceliers 1546–50–53
> Vallard 1547
> Le Testu 1556
> Desliens 1541, 1563, 1566.

Others (e.g. Sebastian Cabot's map of 1544) also derive from the Dauphin, and in degenerating forms the tradition passes down through De Jode, Wytfliet, Mercator and Ortelius. There is also another direct derivative, a Portuguese plani-sphere made by Bartolomeu Velho in Lisbon in 1561, and owned by Baron de Rio Branco. This is of importance, for it proves that the Dieppe Maps were publicly known in Portugal itself in that century, quite apart from the original still kept in its top-secret drawer in the Casa da India.

These later editions all derive from the Dauphin, or rather the Dauphin and all later editions clearly derive from the same source. There is basic agreement between all of them, but there are variations. In those days there was no photographic copying machine; and when hand copies were made it is inevitable that a cape would be left out here, a second bay inserted there. It is hoped that some day someone will publish a Variorum Edition of all of the Dieppe Maps, enabling a synoptic evaluation to be made. It would probably produce some interesting results, but it would be too technical to be attempted here.

However, what is *left out* in one or more of the maps is usually significant. If the Casa da India prototype was available in a drawer at the Dieppe establishment, each successive copyist would tend to respect it as original source material, while feeling free to add to it in accordance with his own theories and inclination. The next copyist would again tend to be faithful to the original material, while discounting his predecessor's additions or variations, yet at the same time making some other additions or variations of his own. We have seen how the Gulf of Carpentaria, which was blank on the Casa da India prototype, varies from map to map in this way. In the discussion of the Dieppe Maps in the chapters which follow, the principal examination will be of the Dauphin; but where the variations, additions or omissions on the successive maps appear to have significance, these later maps will be drawn into the discussion.

Chapter 9

JAVA

THE Dauphin is a map of the world, containing all of the continents and all of the oceans, although the full width of the Pacific is foreshortened, and of the 360 degrees of the earth's circumference only about 290 degrees are represented. We have already heard how Desceliers obtained the data for his Australian sector – from the Casa da India through the channels suggested. On the American side, he had access to some exciting new materials – he knew Verranzano's chart, he was obtaining Cartier's details from the Dieppois Cartier himself. But on the Indian Ocean side, the excellent representation that he gives of Madagascar, India, Ceylon, Sumatra and so on must have come from some source, and until recently it was not known from where. In 1939 Armando Cortesão found the answer – a Portuguese map of 1533, known as the *Carta Anonima Portuguesa*,[1] a copy of which turned up in the Herzog August Bibliotek at Wolfenbüttel in West Germany. A portion of this chart is shown in the line drawing in Fig. 9.1.

The importance of this map is the excellence of its delineation of the islands of the East Indies. Desceliers copied these island by island, point by point, with the greatest fidelity. As the Dauphin Map has been known for two hundred years, while the *Carta Anonima Portuguesa* has only been rediscovered recently, for many years the Dauphin itself was the world's best evidence of the contents of this lost map, although another copy was made by Gutiérriz in 1551, which copy is now in the Österreichische National-Bibliotek in Vienna.

As there may be some readers who are not wholly familiar with the East Indian islands, a line drawing of the modern map is given in Fig. 9.2, for comparison with the *Carta Anonima*. The most important feature to note is the large landlocked sea, sometimes known as the Indonesian Mediterranean, on which is shown a dotted line to track the Portuguese fairway in the sixteenth century. This inland sea is

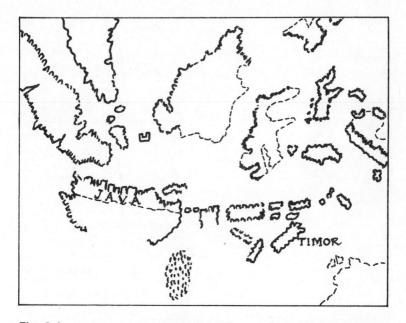

Fig. 9.1 THE CARTA ANONIMA PORTUGUESA. The Carta Anonima utilises the older cartographic conventions, with bays shown as semi-circles, capes shown as arrows, and islands as rectangles. These coasts are shown in black on the above map and existing land-shapes (including Australia) are indicated by broken lines. Note particularly the shape of Java, and the open south coasts of Java and Sumbawa.

about the size and something of the same shape as the European Mediterranean, and the population on its shores is comparable.

Unlike the Dutch in the next century, who always approached from the south, making their first landfall on the south coast of Java, the Portuguese always entered from the west. Their route from Lisbon was around the Cape of Good Hope, across to Goa, then to Malacca, then down the inland sea. After their first period of trial-and-error exploring, they settled down to the fixed track (shown by the dotted line) from Malacca, touching at Grisee in Java, and on to the islands of spice and the islands of sandalwood. They were, indeed,

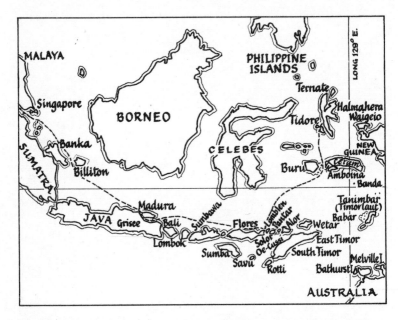

Fig. 9.2   THE EAST INDIES. The line of Demarcation (long. 129°E) is shown on the right of the map. The Portuguese Fairway is shown by dotted line.

following the track which Abreu had pioneered. In anticipation it should be noted how this route misses the south coast of Java altogether.

The inland sea divides the East Indian islands into two rows (see Fig. 9.2). The southern row consists first of the Greater Sunda islands – Sumatra and Java – then three smaller islands in Madura, Bali and Lombok, and next Sumbawa. Then follow the Lesser Sunda islands, where Portugal was particularly active – Flores, Sumba, Timor and many others. In the northern chain are the very large islands of Borneo, Celebes and others; and at the far eastern end of this chain are the Moluccas or Spice Islands, of which Ceram, Buru and Halmahera (then known as Gilolo) are the largest, but the small spice-rich islands of Amboina, Ternate, Tidore and Banda were the most important. Finally, the Indonesian islands tail off into the islands of the Arafura Sea, immediately north of

Australia – Timorlaut, Aroe, Kei and others. Most of these come into this story, in one way or another.

In the first half of the sixteenth century, this area was a close Portuguese preserve. In that period the central area (which can conveniently be called the 'Java-Sumbawa area') was never visited by any other nation at all. The Spanish under Magellan, Loaysia and Saavedra, arriving from the east, had seen something of the eastern end of the chain. Parmentier of Dieppe, in 1529, had reached Sumatra, and had seen something of the western end. Apart from these, no one except the Portuguese entered the area before 1550; and therefore every map, without exception, which describes coasts in the Java–Sumbawa area must have come from Portuguese sources. And because of the Politica do Sigilo, what maps of this area we do have must have escaped from Portugal clandestinely. Cortesão says: 'At a time when only the Portuguese possessed that knowledge, and therefore could make such charts, foreigners were only too eager to obtain this precious information.'[2]

The foreigners received their first taste of this precious information through two charts which have already been mentioned – the Rodrigues, charting the voyage of Abreu and Serrão; and the unsigned Reinel of 1517, which Konrad Peutinger had smuggled out of the country. Both of these were early, before there had been much exploring, and before Portugal's triumphant spice trade had generated the envy of all other nations in Europe. By the 1530s the foreign eagerness for 'this precious information' was at its height, and a concerted effort was made to burgle Portugal's secrets. Out of this, three maps escaped to the outside world – the Penrose, the Viegas, and the Carta Anonima Portuguesa.

The Penrose was another of Peutinger's captures. It is approximately dated 1535, and is now in the Penrose Collection in Pennsylvania. It is anonymous, not in Reinel's calligraphy, but containing the kind of information which is found in his charts: it may have been copied by someone else from his material. Gaspar Viegas was a renegade Portuguese mapmaker who went over to Spanish service, and his two charts, both dated 1537, are in Florence, in different libraries. They will be discussed later, in connection with the explorations of

Gomes de Sequeira. The *Carta Anonima Portuguesa*, in Wolfenbüttel, has already been mentioned. It is of some importance to fix the chronological order of these three maps, with only one of them (Viegas, 1537) dated with certainty.

When maps are not dated, their dates can be inferred from internal evidence. Where they contain reference to some known and dated voyage, that, of course, fixes one date. Where a series of maps shows a progressive unfolding of geographical information, that helps to put them in chronological order. For example, where one map of Borneo shows only the west coast, another in addition the north and south coasts, and another all four coasts, the sequence is fairly obvious.

With these three maps, both of these methods can be seen. The 1537 Viegas charts show geographical developments beyond the Penrose, which causes Cortesão and most other experts to date the Penrose 1535. For example, the Penrose does not show the results of Sequeira's voyage, whereas the Viegas charts do. Conversely, the Penrose shows geographical developments beyond those on the *Carta Anonima*. It shows a north coast of New Guinea, it shows all four coasts of Borneo, and it shows Timor in the curious triangular shape which was to be the standard outline of Timor for some years to come. All of these indicate that the *Carta Anonima* is still earlier, about 1533. An argument used against this inference is the appearance on the *Carta Anonima* of an island near the Seychelles called 'Corpo Santo', which seems to be copied from Viegas: it is equally possible that Viegas copied this from the *Carta Anonima Portuguesa*, or that both took it from some common source.

The *Carta Anonima Portuguesa* is, then, the earliest of the three maps which show advanced delineation of the Java–Sumbawa area, and it precedes the Dauphin in date. As its name indicates, it is unsigned, though attempts have been made to identify it as the work of Lopo Homem. Lopo Homem was the official Portuguese cartographer of the time, the only one who had access to the official secrets of the Casa da India. He too worked in Spain for a while, but no suggestion of dishonesty has ever attached to his name, and (unlike the others) he was able to return to Portugal and take up his work again. The outline of the *Carta Anonima*, and the information contained in it, both suggest his work; but, as Cortesão points out, the lettering on the map is not his. An illicit copy of a genuine Lopo Homem chart, made by some cartographical spy, and therefore containing Homem's outline but the spy's lettering, seems the obvious solution.

Now the Dauphin Map and the *Carta Anonima Portuguesa*, when placed side by side, are practically identical, except that the Australian sector appears only on the Dauphin, and not on the *Carta Anonima*. One is clearly a direct copy of the other; and as we have shown that the Dauphin is the later in date, it would appear that Desceliers had the *Carta Anonima* before him, perhaps surreptitiously obtained from Homem's own office in the Casa da India by Descelier's cartographical spy.

Now the *Carta Anonima Portuguesa*, like practically all Portuguese maps of that century, shows Java and Sumbawa with only north coasts (or north, east and west coasts), but with the south coast blank. Because the Portuguese ships sailed from Malacca along the north coast of Java on their way to Timor and the Spice Islands, they had no reason to sail along the south coast, and it seems that they actually did not. João de Barros categorically states that the Portuguese had not explored it.[3] His successor, Diogo do Couto, repeats that the south coasts of Java are little known.[4] And this is borne out by their maps. Rodrigues, charting Abreu's first voyage, does show some of the Java south coast, but the two sections that he shows are really only returns of the east and west coasts, leaving the critical central section of the south coast still uncompleted, a trick which the *Carta Anonima Portuguesa* copies. Reinel in 1519 shows a completed south coast, probably guessing it, for in the next year he shows this same coast as a dotted line on his map, indicating that its exact geography was uncertain. The Penrose shows an open coast, as do Diogo Ribeiro and others. Indeed, it is hard to find any map of the time with the Java south coast fully closed.[5]

So Desceliers had before him a map of the East Indies area showing Sumatra (on the west) complete, and the Lesser Sundas (Flores and Timor, on the east) complete, but the two large central islands of Java and Sumbawa with their south coasts blank. He then received from his spy in Lisbon the Casa da India map of Australia, with no other islands showing on the map except Timor, and with Timor either not named or labelled so illegibly that Desceliers took the lettering to read 'Laine'. There were, of course, no meridians of longitude marked on it, and no other landmarks, such as New Guinea, to indicate its relative position.

Desceliers therefore had no means of knowing where this great new continent fitted in. Should he put it south of Ceylon, or south of Java, or south of the Moluccas, or out in the middle of the Pacific Ocean? He had no means of knowing. He could only approach the problem like a man trying to solve a jigsaw puzzle. How he found his solution is shown diagrammatically in Fig. 9.3.

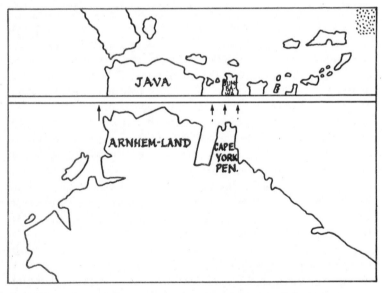

Fig. 9.3 DESCELIERS' JIGSAW. Arnhem-land is fitted into Java, and Cape York peninsula into Sumbawa. (Diagram only.)

If the non-Australian reader examines the shape of the north coast of the continent (the Australian reader would know this already), he will be struck by the boldness of its two geometrical shapes. Arnhem-land, the 'top-end' of the Northern Territory, is almost a square. Cape York is a slender peninsula, ending in a rounded peak. And in between is the Gulf of Carpentaria. If all readers now examine the *Carta Anonima Portuguesa* they will see a Java shaped like three sides of a square, but with no south coast; and a Sumbawa like a peak, also with no south coast; and an aperture in between, which we know to be a strait, but which could quite easily be a gulf. To the east of Sumbawa is the cluster of the Lesser Sunda Islands – Flores, Sumba and Timor.

So when the jigsaw-playing Desceliers saw the square top of Java on the one map and the square top of Arnhem-land on the other, he fitted them together. And it also happened that the peaked top of Cape York more or less fitted into the peaked top of Sumbawa Island, although the triple projections of Sumbawa crown Cape York in unfamiliar fashion; and probably he had to crush the Gulf of Carpentaria which he found on the Casa da India prototype to its smaller width in order to accord with the lesser mileage from Java to Sumbawa. Bali and Lombok then became islands in the Gulf of Carpentaria; and Flores, Sumba and Timor turned up incongruously in the Coral Sea (Fig. 9.3).

If only his guess had been right, we would today be praising Desceliers for his ingenuity. As it is, it was a brave piece of cartographical deduction, but unfortunately it was wrong. This is the gravest error in the Dauphin Map, and it is this error, more than anything else, that has provided ammunition for those trying to shoot down the credibility of the Dieppe Maps. The analysis given here should be carefully studied. When it is considered in this light, it is hard to see how Desceliers could have come to any other conclusion.

Mistakes of this kind are not uncommon in composite charts of former centuries, for until the grid of latitude and longitude was perfected, there could never be any certainty as to how one map adjoined or fitted into another. L. C. Wroth gives a thorough analysis of the distortions and false relations which occurred and continue to occur in composite maps, almost invariably caused by ignorance of longitude.[6] One good example can be seen in the *Suite de Neptun Francois* map,[7] showing two large islands north of Australia, separated by fifteen degrees of longitude, one labelled 'Terra da Pop-ous', the other labelled 'Nouvelle Guinee'. We know, of course, that they are the same island. But because the carto-graphical editor was combining two different charts, with two different sets of names, and two different sets of longitude (or worse still, no longitude at all), it was almost inevitable that this error would occur.

It is again repeated that these same Dieppe Maps, under almost identical circumstances, are the foundation maps in the study of early Canadian cartography. In that area too the Portuguese were the pioneer explorers; in that area too, because of the Politica do Sigilo and the Lisbon Earthquake, all original maps have been lost; so in that area too the Dauphin and the other Dieppe Maps have supplied the necessary evidence, evidence which has been meticulously studied by the Canadian historians W. F. Ganong and H. P. Biggar. On the North American coast, as on the Australian coasts, the Dieppe Maps afford a combination of superlative cartography and occasional unfortunate errors – of which the Java–Sumbawa transposition which is recorded in this chap-ter is one example. Because it is the same series of Dieppe Maps that Canadians and Australians are both studying, and because the problems with both are similar, it is of interest to read the comments of the leading Canadian expounder of these maps. W. F. Ganong writes:[8]

'For these cartographical quirks, no great blame should attach to the mapmakers [in Dieppe] who, if allowances be made of the limitations of their times, were as competent in their profession as are their greatest successors today. Geographically myopic as the first explorers often were, even blinder were the cartographers at home, who had to piece together and reconcile, without the slightest means of testing their conclusions, the diverse records and maps that explorers brought back. It is no wonder they so often tried to make place for all the possibilities, thus entailing the duplication, anachronisms, vestigial survivals and other anomalies, all further warped by their own prepossessions, which so greatly perplex later students.'

To this Canadian benediction, we can only add a heartfelt Australian 'Amen'. Everything that Professor Ganong has said, both in criticism and in extenuation, applies just as much to the Australian side of Desceliers' map as it does to the Canadian side. It has always seemed to the present author to be a fantastic coincidence that Canada and Australia, so parallel and so comparable in so many ways, should be linked so curiously by this sixteenth-century Portuguese map. Some of the elements that Professor Ganong here isolated we have already seen working, understandably and predictably working, in Desceliers. We now pass to what Professor Ganong would call one of his 'prepossessions'.

The Dauphin's Australian continent is divided into two parts by a narrow channel, labelled 'Rio Grande', running from the Gulf of Carpentaria to Joseph Bonaparte Gulf, converting Arnhem-land into an island. Arnhem-land on the Dauphin Map is named 'Java', and the rest of the continent, south of the Rio Grande, is named 'Jave-la-Grande'. The name 'Jave-la-Grande' derives from Marco Polo; and Desceliers' use of that name derives from his prepossession, Europe's prepossession, with the conviction that if a new continent were discovered in the south it assuredly would be the one adumbrated by Marco Polo.

Actually, Marco Polo never said anything of the kind. In Chapter 6 it was explained that this was a misconception, arising from an error in Marco Polo's book, where he was intending to speak of a great land (Siam) south of Chamba, and accidentally wrote 'south of Java' by mistake. But the legend persisted, and produced the utter confusion which is always associated with that uncertain, variable and often quite unintelligible term, 'Jave-la-Grande'.

Before the arrival of the Portuguese in the East, the only two East Indian islands known, or well-known, in Europe were Java and Sumatra. Java was always 'Java', but the name for Sumatra varied: sometimes it was called Taprobané, sometimes Sumatra, sometimes Big Java (Jave-la-Grande). This is understandable and quite logical, for the two islands are homogeneous, linked by race, trade and religion, and peopled by people generically known as 'Javanese'. If the dichotomy of 'Little Java' (Java) and 'Big Java' (Sumatra) had been retained, much of the later confusion could have been avoided.

But Sumatra had the two other names here mentioned, both widely used, and so 'Big Java' ceased to apply to it. When the still larger island of Borneo became known, it seemed a likely claimant for the title, and on some maps it appears as 'Jave-la-Grande'. To confuse things even more, when Sumbawa (which is smaller than Java) became known, some people called it 'Little Java', thus turning Java itself into Jave-la-Grande.

It was Marco Polo who made the name fashionable in Europe, but he created a new confusion. He visited Sumatra (see Chapter 6), which he found was a very large island. He did not visit Java proper, but he heard such wondrous reports about its enormous population, it affluence and its importance, that he imagined it to be larger still. So he took Sumatra to be the lesser of the two (as it is indeed lesser in population and in importance), and it was *Sumatra* that Marco Polo called Java-the-less. And unfortunately, as his clerical error had made it appear that the great land of Locac was south of Java, the disembodied name of Jave-la-Grande attached itself to this mythical continent.

And so the Marco Polo legend fixed two things in men's minds – (a) that there was a large land south of Java, and (b) that it was called Jave-la-Grande. These successive changes are set out compendiously in the following table, and by the time of Desceliers he was moving out of confusion No. 5 into Confusion No. 6:

	Java Minor or Java-the-less (sometimes just 'Java')	Java Major or Greater Java or Jave-la-Grande
1	Marco Polo's Sumatra	Marco Polo's Java
2	Marco Polo's Java	Marco Polo's Locac
3	Java	Sumatra
4	Java	Borneo
5	Sumbawa	Java
6	Java	Australia

It is not surprising that Desceliers made this deduction, By legend, there was such a place as Jave-la-Grande. Each of the earlier candidates numbered 1 to 5 had by now been eliminated. His Lisbon spy provided him with this secret map of a great new continent – so this must be Jave-la-Grande! The fact that he shifted it too far west and fastened it on to Java Island is at most a corollary. Even if Desceliers had understood its correct geographical location and had mapped it in its true position, south-east of Timor, he still would have thought that this was solving the mystery of Jave-la–Grande.

Jave-la-Grande is not a Portuguese word, nor is it a Portuguese conception. The form in which it appears on the Dauphin Map is, of course, French. When Jean Rotz produced his English edition, while he retained all other place names whether Portuguese, French or native, he regarded this one name as editorial, and displayed it in English translation – The Greate Londe of Java. If it had originated in Lisbon, it might have been Grão-Java or Java-maior. But the Portuguese were not given to Marco Poloesque romancing: Beach and Locac, Pentam and Maluar, and above all Jave-la-Grande, never appear on their maps, no matter how much these same names were later added to the same maps by foreign editors. When Portuguese thoughts turned to the southern continent, they thought in terms of India Meridional or The Isles of Gold. It was Desceliers who wrote 'Jave-la-Grande' on this map, not the navigators who explored the coasts or the Lisbon mapmaker who compiled it in the Casa da India.

And in the same way, it was the error of Desceliers that transposed the continent to its wrong position, south of Java, and not the ignorance of the Portuguese. It may be true that they had not actually coasted along the south coast of Java; it may be that they had not, as yet, circumnavigated Java; but nevertheless, they knew that it was an island, they knew that it had a south coast, they knew that it was only one or two hundred miles in north–south measurement. On maps such as that of Francisco Rodrigues and on the *Carta Anonima Portuguesa* itself, the east and west coasts return at both ends, leaving the eye to imagine the (unexplored) south coast which connected the two. They never claimed, as others did, that

Java was of continental size. They knew that Java did not stretch south to join on to the Antarctic continent, even if there was an Antarctic continent. When we find that in some of the Dieppe Maps this joinder is made, it is again an idea not Portuguese but Dieppois.

That the Indonesian Archipelago of the *Carta Anonima Portuguesa* accords with the Indonesian Archipelago of the Dauphin Map can be seen by comparing them island by island, and coast by coast. Above all, Java accords with Arnhem-land, and Sumbawa accords with Cape York. Put in another way, when the Dieppe cartographer was drawing what appears on the map as Arnhem-land, he was copying straight from the *Carta Anonima*'s outline of Java, and the same with Cape York and Sumbawa. Even the place-names on the two coasts are identical, except where the Dieppe cartographers added 'R. des Cobras' or similar French embroideries to achieve some local colour, or to give delicious thrills to their noble clients. The following tables list a few of the correspondences:

I Java (overlaying Arnhem-land)					
Carta Anonima	Dauphin	Rotz	Royal	Desc. 1550	Modern
Curubaja	Curabaia	Sirubina	Catabaia	Carabaia	Surabaja
Graci	Agacim	Agizim	Agacim	Agadim	Grisee
Japara	Jappara	Japar	Japara	Jaypara	Japara
—	Jaua	Jave	Jana	Java	Java
Cumpne	Simba	Sunda	Cumda	Cunda	Jakarta

II Sumbawa (overlaying Cape York)					
Carta Anonima	Dauphin	Rotz	Royal	Desc. 1550	Modern
C. Anuape	G. Annape	Gumape	Guimape	Guanape	Gunong Api
Cibuba	Symbana	Sinbana	Simbawa	Simbaua	Sumbawa
Modan	Medan	Modan	Medam	Medom	Medan

There is no fusion of the Australian and Indonesian coasts; there is no compromise of their respective place-names. The coasts and the place-names are pure Java, pure Sumbawa; and whatever Australian capes and bays and place-names had shown on the Casa da India prototype were discarded, and disappeared for ever.

Between Java and Sumbawa there are three islands – Madura (slightly to the north), Bali and Lombok. Madura is shown, and named. Bali and Lombok are shown as islands in the Gulf of Carpentaria, in their correct positions relative to Java (Arnhem-land) and Sumbawa (Cape York), but smaller than in reality, and given the names of Baralia (apparently a variant of, or misprint for, Bali) and Antare (Adonara, the old name for Lombok). George Collingridge deciphered these words on the Dauphin as Anda na Barca, which he took to be some kind of representation of the Portuguese phrase *Não andam barcos*, No boats go here.[9] As it is true that in those days no boats did go into the Gulf of Carpentaria, Collingridge and many of his successors hailed this as very significant historical information about the Gulf – when all the time the words are only two Javanese place-names.

On the Dauphin Map, to the east of Sumbawa, and therefore to the east of the wrongly-positioned Cape York, is the cluster of the Lesser Sunda Islands – Flores, Sumba and Timor, Sumba is not well drawn, for the same reason that the south coast of Java is not correct – the Portuguese always came into the Lesser Sunda group from the north-west, and found no occasion to investigate the south coast of Sumba, or other southern islands. Flores is quite distinguishable, and its place-names include Ende (which was its old name, and also the name of a Portuguese fort built on that island) and C. des Flores. Timor is named 'Tymor', although some of the later Dieppe Maps also show 'Tidor', confusing it with Tidore, which is in the Moluccas, further north. This in itself is good evidence of confused Dieppois editing, for no Portuguese would be ignorant of the difference between the two major Portuguese posts of Timor and Tidore, notwithstanding some similarity in the spelling of their names.

Far up to the north-east are some shoals marked "Papuos', marking the western end of New Guinea, which Meneses had seen. Relative to the location of Timor, it is in its correct position. No other indication of New Guinea is given, for while Sequeira had sailed along the south-west coast of that island before the Dauphin Map was published, apparently the pirated copy left Lisbon before the results of this voyage were known. It must have missed this new information only by a few months, for this coast shows on the Viegas charts.

The configuration of the Indonesian islands in the Dieppe Maps is exceptionally good, for it is faithfully copied from the *Carta Anonima Portuguesa*, which, however it was smuggled out of Lisbon, is an accurate, efficient and authentic portrayal of that area, by far the best available anywhere in the world at the date of its release. The Casa da India prototype map of Australia (that is, the map from which the pirated copy was taken) came from the same repository, and we are entitled to envisage that it was equally as accurate, efficient and authentic as its sister map, the *Carta Anonima*. Unfortunately that authenticity suffered damage – not irreparable damage, but some damage – when the Dieppe cartographical editor made his two mistakes: first, he located the continent in the wrong place, attaching it to Java and Sumbawa; and secondly, he tainted it with the suspicion which necessarily attaches to everything that is connected with that elusive, illusory, fly-away land which masquerades under the title of Jave-la-Grande.

Chapter 10

THE ANTARCTIC EXTENSION

A LL discovery of unknown areas, and all charting of discoveries, must proceed on the basis of one or the other of the two great opposing doctrines – the doctrine of the Assumption of Land, or the doctrine of the Assumption of Sea. There is no way in which a cartographer can show an area which is neither land nor sea; so he must start with the assumption that the whole of his area is vacant sea, filling in islands and coasts as he comes to them; or else he must assume that it is land, filling in bays and channels as he sees them, and in those places where he sees only open sea pushing back the frontier of the assumed land to an imaginary coast beyond his visual horizon.

Today we take it for granted that all explorers would assume sea, and we probably find it hard to comprehend the alternative doctrine: but a good illustration is the area of frozen land north of Canada, where the successive Arctic explorers nosed out channels and sounds and bays. Where they found some open water, they charted it as an interruption to the Assumed Land. Where they saw no water, they assumed that the land extended all the way to the North Pole.

The two greatest men mentioned in this book – Prince Henry at the beginning, Captain Cook at the end – were both zealous upholders of the Assumption of Sea, and in this Henry was years in advance of his time. Perhaps his environment had something to do with it: on his lonely peninsula at Sagres he lived in a world of sea, his thin corridor of land puny and insignificant beside its vastness. At Sagres one feels that the sea is boundless to the horizon, and beyond the horizon. One finds it hard to conceive that that immensity of sea could ever find a termination on a continental shore. No doubt there are islands, but one feels that of necessity they would be small and far between. This emotion is mirrored in the Portuguese maps of the fifteenth and sixteenth centuries. They seem to consist largely of empty pages of ocean; what islands were found seem to be drawn small and tend to look insignificant.

What coasts were sighted are charted only as far as they were seen, with unseen coasts left blank – as witness the south coasts of Java and Sumbawa which were discussed in the last chapter. It was not the Portuguese style to fill up maps with imaginary continents, for their philosophy was the Assumption of Sea, and their practical purpose was the guidance of mariners. This in itself is a strong argument in support of the validity of the Dieppe Maps, for unlike certain other nations Portugal was not given to dreaming up imaginary continents.

Conversely, there were other men in the world whose environment differed from that of Prince Henry and attracted them instead to the doctrine of the Assumption of Land. Ptolemy of Alexandria (circa AD 100) was one of these. To him the Earth (or the habitable Earth) was essentially land, and any unknown parts were assumed to be *land*. Certainly, this earthy world was studded with lakes, some large, such as the Black Sea and the Red Sea and the Caspian Sea, and two of them – the Mediterranean Sea and the Indian Sea – larger still, but still lakes. Sea lakes, perhaps, but not oceans. The only ocean was the Atlantic, on the edge, where the habitable world came to an end. Ptolemy's instinct in mapping was to take a fresh parchment and make the initial assumption that the whole of its surface represented land. Then from this he subtracted, by mapping in all known seas, and all half-known seas to the limit of reported information, but not beyond. Any area beyond knowledge, any area that had not been seen or reported or rumoured or hinted at, therefore, had to be treated as land.

It is important to watch how this approach conditioned Ptolemy's delineation of his Indian Sea, what we shall call the Indian Ocean. His best information told him of the northern coasts of Arabia, Persia and India, islands like Ceylon and Sumatra, an East African coast which extended to about Lat. 30°s before knowledge petered out, and a vague Far Eastern area which had to be assumed to be land, because no one had ever said that it was not.

So he drew his Indian Ocean in that form, making it a landlocked lake. The only comparable sea that anyone knew was the Mediterranean, so when he had to visualise a shape for it he visualised a shape something like that of the Mediter-

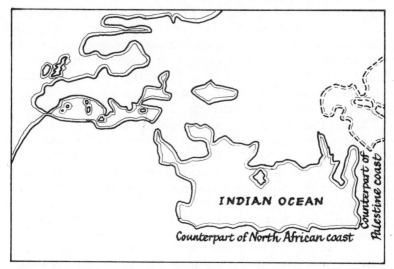

Fig. 10.1 THE PTOLEMAIC CONCEPTION based on the Basle edition of Ptolemy, 1551. Until da Gama and Magellan, Columbus's American discoveries were supposed to fit in where shown by dotted line. The 'Palestine Coast' was then equated to the west (Peruvian) coast of South America.

ranean. This is illustrated in Fig. 10.1. As can be seen, nature made the north coast of the Indian Ocean something like the north coast of the Mediterranean – a narrow entrance at Aden (Gibraltar), the square Arabian Peninsula (Spain), the Indian Peninsula with a large island at its foot (Italy and Sicily), the Malay Peninsula beyond (the Balkans), and a shadowy China Sea which no doubt corresponded with the Black Sea. Then when he came to the completely unknown east and south coasts which by the Assumption of Land he was forced to conjecture, he used the analogy of the Mediterranean's geography, and invented a 'Palestine Coast' in the east and a long 'North African Coast' in the south, bringing him back to his point of commencement. This analogous 'North African Coast', in about Lat. 30°s, joining on to Kenya and Ethiopia and thus shutting off water connection with the Atlantic, is the genesis of the myth of Terra Australis Incognita. In Ptolemy this coast is so far north (about Lat. 30°s) that it is strange to refer to it as the north coast of an 'Antarctic' continent, but that is what it is. Generations of seamen would sail along that supposed coast, never sighting it, but never abandoning the idea of it; by force of the doctrine of the Assumption of Land, each voyage drove it further and further south, until Cook reduced its sorry remnant to the icy waste the other wide of Lat. 60°s which today we know as the modern continent of Antarctica.

The Portuguese, giving no credence to the doctrine of the Assumption of Land, refused to make the Ptolemaic assumption.[1] Prince Henry refused to believe that there was a land barrier at the bottom of Africa which would prevent access to the Indian Ocean. The Portuguese did not think that Africa extended very far south at all, and when they found the coast veering east, beyond the bulge of Africa, they assumed that they would now find open sea all the way to India. In this they were disappointed, for after the Gulf of Guinea the coast turned south again; but at last their faith was rewarded when Bartolomeu Dias rounded the Cape. Beyond that point the Portuguese again Assumed Sea, and hypothetical Antarctic continents did not enter into their philosophy.

But other nations, especially France and Germany, were of the opposite school, disciples of Ptolemy. They were not confounded when da Gama revealed that there was a sea connection from the Atlantic to the Ptolemaic Lake, south of Africa, nor when Magellan revealed another entrance, south of the Americas. That was all in the game of the Assumption of Land: that merely pushed the Assumed Land back beyond the range of the explorer's field of vision, and the Ptolemaics went on happily continuing to assume land, and to chart it on their maps, beyond that horizon. Alexander Dalrymple continued with this game until Cook's second voyage.

Resulting from this, the Ptolemaic maps emanating from France and Germany – and there were many, many editions of Ptolemy in the fifteenth and sixteenth centuries – displayed thick swathes of land (beginning to be referred to as Terra Australis) extending right across the Southern Hemisphere, enveloping the South Pole in a huge continent which, if it had been real, would have been the largest landmass on earth. These maps differed from one another in two notable respects: first, in some maps the supposed southern continent obtruded into more northerly latitudes than in others; and secondly, in some the supposed coasts were restrained and sober, while in some they blossomed into the most fanciful convolutions.

On the first of these two points, it will be remembered that the coast which Ptolemy drew across the bottom of the Indian Ocean (the analogous 'North African Coast', it was called) was placed where the current maritime knowledge ceased, then about Lat. 30°s. Vasco da Gama rounded the Cape in Lat. 35°s, and as the Ptolemaics assumed that there was land just beyond his field of vision, they assumed a Terra Australis coast in (say) Lat. 40°s. In 1507 or thereabouts, João de Lisboa, financed by Nuño Manoel and Cristovão de Haro, on a secret mission to the southern point of Brazil and beyond, reported having discovered a strait through South America (it was probably the La Plata estuary) in Lat. 40°s, providing another supposed 'coast' for Terra Australis in much the same latitude.[2] João de Lisboa did not claim to have actually entered the Pacific. He reported that he had found a deep and long channel at Lat. 40°s, and that he had sailed up it for two days without finding its end, and that finally he was forced to return to the Atlantic. From our knowledge, we can see that it was almost certainly the wide La Plata estuary, but at the time of its discovery it seemed that it was the long-awaited passage through to the Pacific and the Spice Islands. As will be seen later, it was a report that greatly influenced the thinking of Magellan, and led to his subsequent voyage.

The story of this secret voyage escaped from Portugal probably through the duplicity of de Haro and the machinations of the ubiquitous Peutinger, and was printed in Augsburg, in Germany, by Ernst Oglin under the title of *Copia der Newen Zeytung auss Presill-Landt* [Brazil Land]. This little book was not rediscovered until the twentieth century, but in its own time it fell into the hands of the German cartographer Johannes Schöner, whose globe of 1515 shows this 'strait' dividing South America near the present site of Buenos Aires, and with Patagonia on the southern bank of this channel swelling out to form a huge Antarctic continent which stretches right across the Pacific to the present International Date Line. It must have been a recollection of this map that caused Tasman so confidently to identify his New Zealand with Staten Land, joining them together into an Antarctic continent remarkably like Schöner's. It was this Terra Australis of Schöner's that was the genesis of that will-of-the-wisp continent that dissipated the energies of explorers for the next 250 years; and it was to this continent that, ultimately, the Dieppe Maps came to be attached.

With one alleged Antarctic coast just south of Buenos Aires, and another alleged Antarctic coast more or less south of Cape Town, it was natural that they should be connected by a line along their common latitude, producing a pseudo-Ptolemaic coast across the bottom of the world. When Magellan finally made his entry into the Pacific it was in a much higher latitude, pushing the supposed Antarctic coast further south at that point; and successive Portuguese roundings of the Cape in progressively higher latitudes pushed the entry further south at that point as well. This dip at both ends produced a kind of 'plateau' effect, as can be seen in the 1529 map of Franciscus Monachus, which is delineated on square projection in Fig. 10.2. Monachus was honest in his cartography. By the doctrine of the Assumption of Land, plus the ideas of Ptolemy and Schöner, he accepted that there was land there, or at least that there should be land there; but he did not pretend that he had any first-hand knowledge about the actual configuration of its coasts, and so he marked it in simply and diagrammatically with geometrical straight lines. He virtually says: 'I am drawing a rhomboid shape to show where there has been no exploration. If there is a southern continent, then it must be inside this rhomboid.'

This Monachus map, or at least this Monachus conception, was available to the cartographer of the Dauphin, who in the Dauphin Map pays lip-service to the same theory. He does not pretend to know of any details of the coast of the supposed Antarctic continent, but accepts that there is land there. The bottom of the page on which the Dauphin Map is drawn can be thought of as the plateau-like top of a Monachus South Land; and so the Dauphin Map joins the southern terminus of the east coast of Australia to the bottom of the page by two conventional scallops. And as Australia on

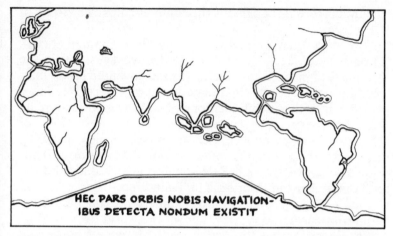

HEC PARS ORBIS NOBIS NAVIGATION-
IBUS DETECTA NONDUM EXISTIT

Fig. 10.2 FRANCISCUS MONACHUS, 1529 (re-drawn on Mercator's Projection). The Southern Continent, marked 'not yet explored', is indicated by formal straight lines. Entrances are shown below Africa (da Gama) and South America (Magellan). Asia and North America are joined in Ptolemaic fashion, and the 'Panama Canal' is fictitious. Note the surprisingly good outlines of the East Indies, including New Guinea.

the west coast terminated so much further away from the bottom of the page, this west coast was run down to the bottom of the page by a conventional, featureless perpendicular straight line, deliberately unreal. This is comparable with the Monachus implication.

Schöner, too, was forced to make modifications. As Magellan's Strait turned out to be twenty degrees further south than João de Lisboa's supposed strait, Schöner's second globe was forced to dip his ocean further south, achieving something of the same plateau effect that we saw in Monachus. But he was less honest than Monachus, and he retained – even exaggerated – the fancy gulfs and bulges, capes and bays, with which he had decorated his first globe. His revised globe is now lost, but can be inferred from his gores of 1523,[3] and from his globe of 1533, both of which are still extant. His Pacific consists of a great gulf off the coast of Chile, then a great hump in mid-Pacific, then another great gulf near the International Date Line, then another hump in what is today the Indian Ocean, and finally the continent dips away south of Capetown.

The next to handle this was the Paris mathematician, Oronce Finé. He was not interested in voyages, but in the geometry of projections; and in 1531 he invented his double-cordiform projection, a mathematical masterpiece. Needing a world map with which to demonstrate his new projection, he took Schöner's globe (presumably the now-lost globe of 1523) and transposed all of Schöner's land-shapes, including his Antarctic continent, onto his double-cordiform. Thus Finé also shows the mid-Pacific hump near Tahiti, and the polar gulf near the International Date Line.

Finé's disciple was Gerard Kramer, the talented Low Countries cartographer now known the world over as Mercator, whose famous Projection made his name a household word. Being interested in projections, he looked up to Oronce Finé as a master, and in 1538 experimented with his own double-cordiform map of the world; and because he had the Finé double-cordiform before him, he also substantially followed the Schöner–Finé land-forms, including the Schöner–Finé southern continent, which appeared thereon. It is necessary to distinguish carefully between this Mercator world map (his double-cordiform of 1538), and his later and more famous world map, on the Mercator Projection, of 1569. We are here concerned with the earlier world map; and the reader is asked to watch carefully the progressive interaction of Desceliers and Mercator. The following table is significant:

1522+	Casa da India prototype
1536	Dauphin Map
1538	Mercator's double-cordiform
1546	Desceliers' Royal
1569	Mercator's Projection.

Mercator's world map of 1538, like Finé's constructed on the elaborate double-cordiform projection, is almost a copy of Finé's, except that Mercator thought that Finé's southern continent protruded too far north, and so he dropped its north coast to about Lat. 50°s, retaining the polar gulf near the International Date Line, and retaining a modified hump in mid-Pacific, south of Tahiti, to be a beacon for Dalrymple and a nuisance for Cook in the years to come. Mercator's coast, is about Lat. 50°s, is shown in Fig. 10.3. On the western side of the polar gulf there is a triangular projection which should be noted, for it later fused with the Cape Fremose of the Dieppe Maps.

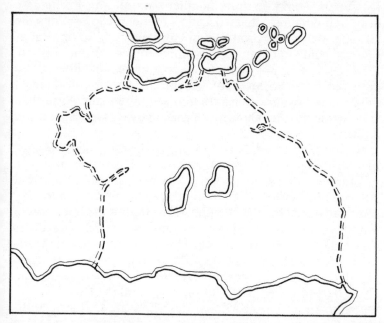

Fig. 10.3 MERCATOR'S DOUBLE-CORDIFORM, 1538 (transposed to Mercator's later projection). This shows the Antarctic Continent, with a triangular projection equating with Cape Fremose of the Dieppe maps. The Dauphin is indicated by dotted line.

Though Mercator's double-cordiform postdated the Dauphin, it is clear that, at the time, Mercator was ignorant of the work of his predecessor and draws nothing from it. It is quite different in Mercator's later and greater world map of 1569, where he discards his Finéan beliefs and instead adopts a southern continent which derives from Dieppe. But this knowledge was in the future, and was not available to him in 1538. And first it was Desceliers' turn to draw upon Mercator. This was in the fifth of the Dieppe Maps (consideration of the three intervening maps of Rotz and of Desliens being postponed for the moment), known as the 'Royal', by Desceliers, in 1546.

The Royal is ten years later than the Dauphin, and in the interim there had been explorations and cartographical development, both Portuguese and non-Portuguese. Desceliers would be quite familiar with all non-Portuguese developments in that decade – French explorations in Canada, new maps produced in Germany, and so on. But as his spy did not pirate anything further from Lisbon, Desceliers was not able to keep abreast of Portuguese developments. So his 1546 Royal chart shows nothing of Portuguese voyages such as that of Sequeira in the Australian area, while he does show new French voyages in Canada and elsewhere.

And in that decade, in 1544, Jean Alfonse (João Affonso) had written his *Voyages Aventureux*.[4] This book has been mentioned before, in Chapter 8, where it was found that Alfonse and his book were both too late to have provided any source material for the Dauphin of 1536; but the book was in time to have influenced the new material which Desceliers inserted in the Royal of 1546. However, as *Voyages Aventureux* was not actually published until 1559, it is again possible that he followed Desceliers, rather than that Desceliers followed him. But the book and the Royal do link together. In his book, Alfonse describes the southern continent as starting at Tierra del Fuego, rising to a promontory in the vicinity of Flores (which is the next island to Sumbawa, the Cape York of the Dieppe Maps) and then dropping away again to pass south of the Cape of Good Hope. It may be that from this Desceliers' Royal took the idea that Jave-la-Grande, which in the Dauphin ran inconclusively to the bottom of the page, should be identified with the southern continent in the way that Alfonse described, and therefore identified with Mercator's Antarctic coast as well.

So, influenced by Alfonse's book and by Mercator's chart, Desceliers again had to start playing at jigsaws. In 1536 he had played jigsaw when he fitted together Arnhem-land and Java, Cape York and Sumbawa. Here he does so again, bringing the southern coast of Australia and Mercator's

Antarctic coast into a fit. It is not quite as obvious as with Java and Sumbawa, for rather he brings the two coasts to touch each other, rather than to fuse; but in one area there is actual fusion, where the triangular projection marked as Cape Fremose on the Dauphin Map finds congruence with the triangular projection which Mercator expressed in his polar gulf. The result is that the map of Australia, which in the Dauphin is isolated (apart from the halfhearted lines which run down to the bottom of the page), is now sitting comfortably on what was Mercator's southern continent. Australia in fact becomes and is shown as a large peninsula or promontory of an enlarged Antarctica. To the eye, it seems precariously and unnaturally perched there, and even to Desceliers it must have seemed an unnatural joinder. The Royal is in the John Rylands Library, Manchester; there is an excellent facsimile in the Australian National Library, Canberra; and a good reduced photograph can be seen in Tooley and Bricker.[5] In all of these there is the feeling that the parts have been soldered together as an afterthought, not forged together in the map's original fabrication. To the eye, it looks like a paler Australian continent sitting on top of the Antarctic mainland. This is clearly visible in Tooley and Bricker's reproduction.

The joinder of the west coast to Antarctica has one puzzling feature. In reality, the lower Western Australian coast turns at Cape Leeuwin, in Lat. 35°s, and then trends east-north-east towards the Great Australian Bight. On the Dauphin there is notable correspondence in this area: the Dauphin similarly turns at the equivalent of Cape Leeuwin, and trends east-north-east up the Hame de Sylla. But instead of terminating there (Rotz), or joining from there to the Antarctic (Desceliers), the coast returns, with detailed cartography, to form a long, thin gulf. And this is given the Germanic name of Hame (Habn or Hafen) de Sylla (Silla, or Ceylon) – a linguistic surprise on a Luso-French map.

At the beginning of Portuguese cartography, the prestigious Dr Martim Behaim[6] was brought over from Nuremberg (in Germany) to instruct the Portuguese in globe-making; and in Lisbon he produced a globe of great authority. Magellan, for example, placed great faith in it. Behaim's globe is Ptolemaic in conception, with an elongated Malay Peninsula which dips far down into the southern hemisphere, its west coast virtually coinciding in trend and position with the south-west coast of Western Australia; and off the end of his Malay Peninsula Behaim wrongly sited a misplaced Ceylon (Silla), separated from the Malay mainland by a thin, east-north-east waterway which he named Egtis Silla. In some way that feature got imported into the Dauphin Map, probably in the Casa da India before the map left Portugal; and when Desceliers joined the west coast to the Antarctic continent this gulf of Hame de Sylla was retained, and is so retained on all of the Dieppe Maps.

Desceliers did not doubt that the Australian section of his map, as taken from the Casa da India prototype, represented the real charting of a real voyage. But at the same time he must have realised that the Antarctica to which he was joining it was only conjectural; so on the Royal he wrote, across the bottom of the map in a position which can only be referable to the Antarctic sector, the words 'The Southern Land, which was not been discovered at all'. It does not point to the Australian sector, and cannot mean that the Australian sector had 'not been discovered at all'. It is the same as if a genuine map of Canada of (say) the year 1700 had written across its Arctic Territories the words 'the Northern Lands which have not yet been explored'. Yet those critics who snatch at everything in their desire to deny the authenticity of the Dieppe Maps have used these words on Desceliers' Royal as an argument in their favour.

And it must be remembered that it was Desceliers, not the Portuguese, who created this Antarctic Extension, who joined Australia on to the Antarctic continent – whether impliedly as in the Dauphin, or expressly as in the Royal. It would have been Portuguese practice not to assume that the Australian coasts ran down to join the Antarctic continent, if indeed such an Antarctic continent existed; but to chart only the coasts which they had seen, leaving the bottoms of the east and west coasts dangling, just as they did with Java and Sumbawa in the *Carta Anonima Portuguesa*. And this is evidenced by the most famous of the Dieppe cartographers, Jean Rotz.

Jean Rotz was internationally the most celebrated of the Dieppe cartographers, for in addition to being a mapmaker he was a mathematician and geographer in his own right. More will be said of him in a later chapter.[7] There are two Rotz maps, both dated 1542, conveniently called 'the Rotz Plane Chart' and 'the Rotz Circular Chart' – the third and fourth of the Dieppe series, and necessarily earlier than the Desceliers Royal which has just been discussed. We are here concerned with the Rotz Circular Chart, the map of 1542 drawn on a circular projection (Plate VI). Its outline conforms with the Dauphin, but all illustrations, even place-names, are entirely eliminated, leaving just the clear, bald outline. Because of this uncluttered clarity, most people can 'see' Australia in it better than in the other maps, although the outline has its limitations, with an insignificant Gulf of Carpentaria, a stunted Cape York, and an unduly-emphasised Rio Grande running across Arnhem-land from Gulf to western sea.

But its most important feature is that, like its conjectured Portuguese original, it is attached to no hypothetical land to the south. The west coast is left dangling in about Lat. 35°s, and the east coast is left dangling in about Lat. 50°s. When the actual geography of the coast is examined in a later chapter, it will be found that this latter is coterminous with Warrnambool: and this establishes that the Casa da India prototype also terminated at Warrnambool, that this was the furthest point reached by the explorers, and was the point at which they turned back, and that the extensions to the south which appear in Desceliers and some of the other Dieppe cartographers came from sources other than Lisbon. And when fortified by this clue from Rotz, we can re-examine the other Dieppe Maps and see that they too show evidence that the real coast terminates there. The Dauphin joins Warrnambool to the bottom of the page by two hypothetical scallops sloping to the left: the Royal joins Warrnambool to the Antarctic continent by hypothetical scallops sloping to the right, with a distinct break in the coast at the point of junction. We are grateful to Rotz for giving us this one map uncluttered with Antarctic Extensions; we accept from him the evidence that the Portuguese maps stopped at the points mentioned; and, in many ways, we have no obligation to consider these Antarctic Extensions at all.

Rotz, in his second map, follows the Dauphin in attaching the coasts to the bottom of the page; and some of the later Dieppe cartographers followed the Royal in attaching them to an elaborate Antarctic continent. The urge to do this came from what Charles Barrett[8] called 'the pernicious contemporary fashion of leaving no loose ends of land unjoined to adjacent coasts'. When the Dieppe cartographers could not join the loose ends to adjacent coasts, they at least ran them to the edge of the page; and this 'pernicious fashion' in cartography persisted right down to Cook's day. We can see how annoyed Cook was with charts which gratuitously joined distant coasts:[9] Vaugondy, for example, who joined Queiros's New Hebrides to the Australian mainland; or Tasman, who, harking back to Schöner, joined New Zealand to Tierra del Fuego.

The French particularly loved to join up isolated islands into articulated land-masses. The extreme manifestation of this Assumption of Land can be seen in Jaillot's Australian map of 1689,[10] where Australia, Tasmania, New Zealand, New Hebrides and New Guinea are all joined together in an octopus-like cartographical monstrosity. Another illustration is the Dieppe Map of Guillaume Le Testu, one of the last of the Dieppe cartographers, who not only followed the Royal in joining Australia to a vast Antarctic continent, but resurrected the dream continent of Oronce Finé. So all-pervading is Le Testu's southern continent that Australia appears just as one of many Antarctic promontories, sharing with four or five other bulging Antarctic promontories which extend right around the globe.

It was Cook who led us, in time, to the new school of cartography, where only that which is actually viewed and surveyed is shown on the chart. In other words, Cook reverted to the teachings of Prince Henry the Navigator: to the sounder doctrine of the Assumption of Sea.

Chapter 11

THE LISBON MAPMAKERS

HAVING disposed of the spurious Antarctic Extension, we are left with those parts of the Dauphin's coasts which do represent the real coasts of Australia, and these coasts must next be considered cartographically. We cannot compare the shape of the Dauphin Map's Australia with the shape of the modern Australia, unless we can place them side by side *on the same projection*; and we cannot understand the projection on which the Dauphin is drawn unless we know something of the principles and methods and techniques used in chart- and mapmaking in the sixteenth century.

The two expressions 'chart-making' and 'mapmaking' are used deliberately, and should be kept distinct, for charts and maps were quite different things. The chart (*carta de marear*) was made and used by the seaman at sea. It did not pretend to be an elaborate map. It was just his seagoing guide, with his distances (estimated or observed), directions (read from the compass, with the traverses corrected by the Marteloio Tables), and, where the ship was close to land, an eye-sketch of what coast could be seen. These eye-sketch details are particularly suspect, as the mariners had no training in or facilities for inshore marine surveying. James Cook recognised this when he wrote:[1]

'Navigators formerly wanted many of the helps towards keeping an accurate Journal which the present age is possessed of: it is not they [i.e. the mariners] that are wholly to blame for the faultiness of their charts, but the compilers [i.e. the cartographers, the mapmakers] and publishers who publish to the world the rude sketches of the navigators as accurate surveys without telling what authority they have.'

To us, the most serious limitation in these old charts is the utter lack of longitude. Longitude at sea could not be known, or even guessed at. While latitude could be marked in degrees (observed by their Altura Instruments, astrolabe or quadrant), easting could be given only in distance, and not converted to degrees.

Sometimes the professional cartographers actually sailed in ships, producing charts of some sophistication on board ship. When some special mapping was needed, the government might attach a leading cartographer to the voyage, as when Francisco Rodrigues sailed with Abreu and Serrão in the quest for the Moluccas and the Great Meridian. But mostly the actual charting at sea was left to the more humble class of mariner-navigator – men of little education, who could add and subtract, multiply and divide, do sums in simple proportion and apply the tables which they found in their Marteloio. They produced charts by jotting down the raw, unadjusted observations of direction, distance and latitude. They did not attempt nor did they have the skill to attempt, the adjustment of their charts to any sophisticated mathematical projection, and therefore they could not etch in the different meridians of longitude.

On return to port, the mariner's chart and data (*enformacões* – 'informations' – as Pedro Nunes calls them) would find their way to the office of the cartographer, whose job it was to interpret the charts, fit them together, and adjust them for inclusion on terrestrial globes; and from these globes to transpose them to locality maps, continental maps, and eventually to atlases and maps of the world.

How they actually found their way to the cartographers' offices is uncertain. Admiral S. E. Morison writes:[2]

'Nobody [knows] how the maps were made. Did the cartographer call on individual discoverers and explorers, record what they said, and borrow their charts? Did he simply depict his own notion of the relation, dub in names of bays and promontories told to him, or even make them up?'

As to Admiral Morison's first question, the Politica do Sigilo, as we know, required all *enformacões* to be lodged in the Casa da India; and it would seem that Lopo Homem and other approved cartographers worked from there. As to his second question, there is no simple answer. If we are to interpret the finished maps as they left the office of the cartographer, we must try to establish what alterations and adjustments the cartographer habitually made in the course of his craft.

W. P. Ganong, writing of the problems in early Canadian cartography says:[3]

> 'The original [Portuguese] Maps are all lost; but the surviving compilations [i.e. the Dieppe Maps] show that they were based on eye-sketches, magnetic compass bearings, estimated distances, crudely observed latitude and dead-reckoning longitude. The defects of these methods entailed anomalies which the cartographers had to reconcile as best they could; and it is no wonder that such maps are so often inconsistent, erroneous and unintelligible, and a sore trouble to those who now attempt to interpret them.'

The cartographer, receiving these charts from the mariners, would know how these charts had been compiled and constructed. That is, the cartographers accepted the given latitudes and east-west distances as correct, and then transferred these latitudes and east-west distances to their terrestrial globes. Terrestrial globes, from their nature, establish longitude; and so next the cartographers were able to retranspose from the terrestrial globe to whatever projection they intended to use – the square projection at first, Mercator's after it had evolved, or a double-cordiform or other specialised projection if it suited their purposes to use it.

In Chapter 2 we learnt of the two Portuguese revolutions in finding position at sea. It will be remembered that in the fifteenth century the Portuguese mariners had added the astrolabe and quadrant to their equipment, and to make use of this new-found skill in finding Altura (latitude) they evolved the system of right-angled sailing – running down the meridian until the required latitude was reached, and then easting by dead-reckoning. Using this system, let us imagine some hypothetical Portuguese navigator of the fifteenth century, ideally able to sail on a due south course (and then due east) without deviation, uncannily able to fix his latitude by Altura, and miraculously able to measure his easting to the last inch. This paragon of navigational virtues is charting the west coast of Africa, sailing out of Terceira (in the Azores) and southing down the meridian in which Terceira is found, and easting as selected latitudes are reached. A diagram is given in Fig. 11.1 entitled 'Right-angled sailing'.

First he sails south down the meridian that he is using (in this case the meridian of Terceira) until he reaches (say) Lat. 5°s. There he turns to the left, at right-angles, and sails east until he sights the coast of Africa at the point where Cabinda now stands, and by dead-reckoning notes the distance travelled as 680 leagues. He pricks this on his chart, and returns to

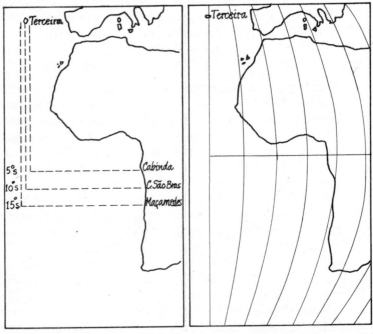

Fig. 11.1
RIGHT-ANGLED SAILING

Fig. 11.2
AFRICA ON SANSON-FLAMSTEED
PROJECTION

Terceira. He then repeats the process, this time turning when his Altura Instruments tell him that he is at Lat. 10°s, and this time he makes his landfall at Cape São Bras, reckoning his easting at 690 leagues. On the next voyage he makes his turn at Lat. 15°s, and runs in 660 leagues to Moçamedes. This monotonous procedure is repeated until he reaches the Cape of Good Hope. Then, by joining together all the landfalls, each at its correct scale distance from the Prime Meridian, he has produced a map of the west coast of Africa, as shown in Fig. 11.1.

Now if all of his Alturas and reckoned distances are correct, the result must be a mathematically perfect map of the coast. But it is not a map of Africa on any projection to which the reader is accustomed. As is indicated in the figure, the bottom of Africa slopes substantially to the west, or seems to do so to eyes that are accustomed to look at the continent of Africa on Mercator's Projection. This is not Mercator's Projection, and it is not the formal 'square' projection which preceded Mercator. To use a technical term from the science of cartography, it is the Sanson–Flamsteed Projection; to use the corresponding technical term from trigonometry, it is a sinusoidal projection. So we have the extraordinary phenomenon of a poorly-educated Portuguese mariner, totally ignorant of trigonometry, producing the highly sophisticated Sanson–Flamsteed sinusoidal projection, three hundred years before Messrs Sanson and Flamsteed were born! The explanation is that the mariner *unwittingly* produced that result. It was produced not by his conscious effort, but as the automatic result of the 'right-angled' method of sailing and charting (explained in Fig. 11.1) which he was using.

The Sanson-Flamsteed Projection[4] is based upon the fact that all parallels of latitude are circles, with the Equator (Lat. 0°) the largest, and with the subsequent circles of latitude progressively diminishing in length (i.e. in circumference) until at 90°, at each Pole, the circle vanishes altogether. If these circles are straightened out, as they must be straightened out on a flat map, their lengths still progressively diminish from the Equator to the Poles, and this diminution in length is in exact proportion to the cosine of the angle of latitude for that particular parallel. For those who are interested, this cosine ratio is proved in Fig. 11.3, and the method of constructing the graticule of the Sanson-Flamsteed Projection is set out under the diagram of the Projection itself in Fig. 12.6. Those who are not interested in the mathematical theory are still invited to look at the shape of the Projection as shown in Fig. 11.2 and to look at the illustrative map of Africa drawn on it, which is the same shape as that unwittingly

The cosine of the latitude

That the departures of latitude diminish in proportion to the cosine of the angle of latitude

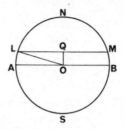

Let ALNMBS be a plane section cut through the earth from pole (N) to pole (S) and passing through the centre of the earth (O). AB is an equatorial diameter, bisected by O. L is a point on the earth's surface in latitude θ so that $\angle AOL = \theta°$, and LQM is the diameter of the small circle in latitude θ, with diameter LM bisected by Q. Join OQ, which is the polar axis at right-angles to both diameters.

Proof: Because LQ and AO are parallel,

$$\angle AOL = \angle OLQ = \theta°$$

In $\triangle LQO$,

$\angle LQO$ is a right angle,

$\angle OLQ = \theta°$

$$\therefore \quad \frac{LQ}{LO} = \cos \theta$$

But LO = AO (radii)

$$\therefore \quad \frac{LQ}{AO} = \cos \theta$$

$$\therefore \quad \frac{\text{circumference of circle with radius LQ}}{\text{circumference of circle with radius AO}} = \cos \theta$$

$$\therefore \quad \frac{\text{circumference in Lat. } \theta}{\text{equatorial circumference}} = \cos \theta$$

and each degree of longitude in Lat. θ in proportion to each degree of longitude at the equator $= \cos \theta =$ the cosine of the angle of latitude.

Fig. 11.3 THE COSINE OF THE LATITUDE.

produced by our fifteenth-century navigator in Fig. 11.1. The first person to notice that the Portuguese charts were unwittingly adopting this sinusoidal projection was Dr Pedro Nunes. Whether anyone (other than Dr Nunes) understood this or appreciated the point does not matter. These were in fact the charts that the mariners were bringing back from their voyages, strangely sloping though they were. And if these were the charts of the mariners, by what right did the Lisbon cartographers alter these charts, and by what methods did they do so?

The Lisbon mapmakers themselves were not highly-trained mathematicians; indeed, like the navigators, they stumbled upon their mathematical solutions, almost by accident. The learned mathematicians of the day were the astronomers, who appeared to the unlettered men of the day 'simply as magnicians', as Eva Taylor has said.[5] They lived in their ivory-tower observatories, peering through instruments of unbelievable complexity, juggling with mathematical computations worthy of a Senior Wrangler today. Above all, they could foretell the coming of a comet or the imminence of an eclipse with awe-inspiring accuracy. Probably they traded on these esoteric powers to clothe themselves with still greater reputations as seers and mystics, for from early times astronomer and astrologer have been hard to separate. They were aloof beings, not given to sharing their erudite secrets even among themselves; and they only grudgingly handed down their celestial knowledge to the more mundane cartographers who were wrestling with the navigational problems of the terrestrial globe.

One of the aims of Henry the Navigator's crusade was to interest some of these august beings in the problems of the ocean which interested him; and it was Henry who at least opened the door a little. For these astronomers had real, hard-core knowledge of the higher mathematics, exactly what the newborn science of oceanology needed. Working on the upturned sphere of the heavens, analysing the sky on the graticule of celestial latitude and longitude which they had mastered, calculating the complex interlacing circles and parabolas and ellipses of astral orbits, they evolved the working tool of spherical trigonometry to a point little, if at all, inferior to the spherical trigonometry in use today. Portugal in particular forged ahead in this field, for her unique contact with Arab (Moorish) culture on the one hand, and her coterie of Jewish scholars on the other, brought to Portugal and through Portugal to the Western world much of the mathematical pre-eminence which until then Arab and Jew had monopolised.

By the sixteenth century there emerged a new class – the professional or academic mathematician, not primarily interested in astrology and astronomy. Their knowledge was drawn from the mathematics of the astronomers, but it was professionally used in other fields, such as university teaching or (later) government service. Examples of these are Oronce Finé, professor of mathematics at Paris,[6] and Pedro Nunes, royal mathematician at Lisbon. These were the men who, for the first time since classical days, got to grips with the problems of hydrography – the tasks of inventing projections, the conundrums of the curving and diverging meridians of longitude, and the unsuspected and astounding waywardness of the loxodrome. And here again, their abilities must be judged great, even by modern standards. One has only to look at the ingenious, scientific and elaborate double-cordiform projection of Oronce Finé (later copied by Mercator) to appreciate their high technical ability and deep scientific knowledge. And in later chapters much more will be said of Portugal's own Pedro Nunes.

Next in rank were the hydrographers, cartographers, mapmakers – call them what you will. In this study the word 'mapmakers' will be used. These were the professional mapmakers, of whom the Lisbon mapmakers were the most famous; and as these men of Lisbon's Golden Age will appear and reappear in these pages, it is desirable that the reader be reminded of their names here – Pedro and Jorge Reinel, Lopo Homen, Diogo Ribeiro, Gaspar Viegas, João de Castro, Diogo Homem, Sebastião Lopes, Fernão Vaz Dourado, Bartolomeu Lasso and Luis Teixeira. Their reputation was Europe-wide and many were lured to Spain and other countries by princely emoluments.[7] The memorial of these great Lisbon mapmakers is that magnificent set of books the *Portugaliae Monumenta Cartografica*,[8] compiled by Armando Cortesão and Teixeira da Mota, the nation's tribute to Prince Henry the Navigator on his five-hundredth anniversary.

The chief tool of trade of the mapmakers was the terrestrial globe – often large, seven feet in height on occasions. Some of these globes, commencing with that of Martim Behaim, have come down to us. The mapmaker's first duty, after receiving a chart from a mariner, was to inscribe the outline onto a globe. They had a cunning method of coating the globe with paper, prefabricated printed segments of paper being available for pasting together in a prearranged order, covering the wooden globe without undue bulging or creasing, so that a new virgin-white global surface was available for each new job. First they would have to study the chart in order to understand it, having regard to the projection on which it had been constructed, or the implied construction which the mariner's method of charting would produce, noting the evidences of latitude (there would be no longitude shown on the charts), devising a scale of leagues if one was not already provided, reducing figured distances to a common scale, and quite frequently ironing out patent anomalies and correcting observable mistakes. Work of this kind was a very valuable, but thankless, service: where the mapmaker's guess was good, he got little thanks; when he went wrong he personally and his profession as a whole came under fire. Pedro Nunes, for instance, was willing to damn them at the drop of a hat.

Then with the *enformacões* under control, the mapmaker next transcribed the outline to his fresh, clean globe. On the chart being copied, there would be no longitude, except in so far as accuracy in east-west distances implied longitude. But once the outlines were inked in on the globe, longitude attached immediately; for a globe is a geometrical sphere, clearly divisible into 360 segments, and that is all that longitude is. And because a globe is naturally curved, the meridians on the surface of that globe were naturally and correctly curved, naturally diverging, naturally trigonometrically spaced. In this way, for the first time, meridians of longitude crept into the maps.

But because large globes are not easy to store or to carry, or even to refer to, it was next necessary to find some way of transposing these global maps (including the meridians which were now an integral part of them) to a flat piece of parchment or paper: in other words, it was necessary to invent some projection which would enable these three-dimensional global maps to be transposed to a two-dimensional plane chart which could be taken to sea or stored or referred to on an ordinary desk. It may have been considered as an academic problem, but in the event it was solved in a practical and simple way.

It has been explained that the wooden globe was pasted over with a kind of paper skin. When a global map had served its purpose, the paper skin was cut off the wooden globe, at first to be burnt. But if the paper skin was cut off with some care, it would fall to the floor with the outlines of the land-forms still visible and still usable – indeed, very nearly in the two–dimensional state that was required. And so a technique was developed for removing the 'skin' in a systematic way, so that it could be converted to a two-dimensional map with the least possible distortion. The uniform segments of paper which were cut off under this system were called 'gores'; and the 'gores' method of transposition has a long and honoured place in the history of cartography.

The technique was as follows. Taking a pair of scissors, the mapmaker first punched holes in the paper skin, at the North Pole and the South Pole, and then cut the skin, from Pole to Pole, along every thirtieth meridian of longitude (e.g. along meridians 30°, 60°, 90°, etc). This procedure produced twelve canoe-shaped segments, called 'gores', which were then laid side by side on a large sheet of grey paper (Fig. 11.4). The white gores touched each other at the Equator, but away from the Equator were separated by triangular-shaped interruptions (called 'dislocations') through which the blank grey paper could be seen. The parallels of latitude, and the outlines of the land-forms, showed as discontinuous lines on the white gores; but the mapmaker then linked the loose ends of the parallels by filling in straight lines across the grey dislocations, and vamped in freehand links to join the broken coast lines. The gores and the dislocations, taken together, then formed a large rectangular map of the world, its width equal to the length of the original Equator, as it had appeared on the wooden globe.

But while the Equator retained its original length, this mechanical operation had the effect of lengthening every other line of latitude, according to the amount of grey dislocation that was added to the original white gore. As the amount of dislocation is small near the Equator, but increases away from it – increasing quite rapidly in the higher latitudes – it is clear that the expansion bears some relationship to the latitude in which that expansion occurs. Actually, this expansion is in exact proportion to the secant* of the angle of latitude in which it is found, and today we could and do produce the same transposition by trigonometrical computation, without resorting to scissors and paste at all. The Lisbon mapmakers did the opposite: without knowledge of trigonometry, without understanding of the secant tables, they unwittingly produced the same result by the mechanical process here outlined.

This 'gores' method would indeed produce a mathematically impeccable secant expansion if it were possible to slice off an extremely large number of gores. If, instead of dislocating along every thirtieth meridian (making twelve gores) it had been possible to dislocate along every meridian (making 360 gores) or better still if it had been possible to dislocate along an infinite number of meridians (making an infinite number of gores), then this mechanical process would have produced the true projection, with every item on it bearing its proper percentage of the required expansion. But because only twelve gores were cut, there was a 'jerk' at each point of dislocation. In the higher latitudes, this 'jerk' is very perceptible, and leads to some gross distortion.

The Dauphin Map was undoubtedly laid out in gores in this way, but of course we do not know just where the dislocations were cut. By trial and error we can test out various dislocations, some of which magnify the distortions, some of which diminish them. In cartography, as in law, the principle *ut res magis valeat quam pereat* must be a good principle; and so in Fig. 11.4 the Dauphin Map is laid out in the gores which make the greatest sense. From this exercise two important results flow.

Where a globe is cut into twelve gores, each gore is necessarily 30 degrees of longitude in width – nearly 2000 miles.

* See Fig. 11.3. The secant $= \dfrac{1}{\text{cosine}}$.

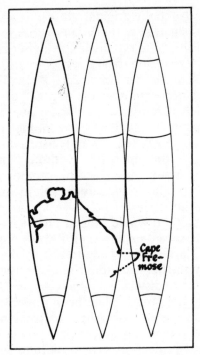

Fig. 11.4 THE DAUPHIN LAID OUT IN GORES. Note how the conjectured Dislocation creates the spout-like protuberance of Cape Fremose.

Any geographical feature on the centre-line of that gore is correctly located, but towards the edges of the gore distortion occurs. A coast running down the left-hand side of a gore unnaturally veers to the east. A coast running down the right-hand side of the gore veers to the west. It therefore is probable that (as shown in the figure) the west coast of the continent found itself on the left-hand edge of one gore, and the east coast of the continent found itself on the left-hand edge of the next gore: then the dislocation of gores causes both coasts to veer to the east, which is what they do on the Dauphin Map.

A second type of distortion appears, especially in high latitudes, where the dislocation cuts across the tip of a cape or peninsula. If the tip of an insignificant peninsula, such as Cape Howe, is cut off, the mapmaker has to link it to its mainland by east-west link lines across the dislocation, producing the spout-like protuberance which is illustrated by Cape Fremose in the figure. This shape is so characteristic of dislocation that Cape Fremose was almost certainly produced by this process. Cape Fremose is not readily identifiable with any known feature of the Australian coast, and no satisfactory explanation of this odd feature has ever previously been given. The author believes that this deduction from its shape, coupled with the trend of the west and east coasts of the continent, justifies the assumption that the gores were in fact dislocated at the meridians suggested in the figure. If this is so, then the operation of the gores process of transposition meets all of the requirements, and satisfactorily explains the mystery of Cape Fremose.

By this gores process was born the Portuguese *Projecção Quadrada*, the familiar rectangular projection, with the lines of latitude parallel and equidistant, and the meridians of longitude also parallel and equidistant. By this mechanical process of scissors and paste, the mapmakers transposed the mariners' charts to their terrestrial globes, and then again transposed them from the terrestrial globes to the *Projecção Quadrada*. And the effect of this mechanical process was to expand the east-west width of each land-form in proportion to the secant of the latitude in which that land-form was found.

It should then have been possible for the mapmakers to have obtained secant tables from the mathematicians, to enable them to dispense with the laborious scissors-and-paste work here described; but for some reason – force of habit, perhaps – few of them did. The actual mechanical procedure of transposition of gores continued until late in the century. The gore-papers were printed and numbered to facilitate the pasting and cutting. Mercator himself invented an improved method, with two circular 'caps' to take care of the Polar regions, and the gores themselves dislocated only down to Lat. 75°. It is for this reason that the polar regions show on the Mercator world maps as small circular inserts in the corners of the parchment.

This mechanical method of transposition may seem strange and primitive to us, but we must remember that we are here watching the science of cartography and the science of map-projection being born. The gores system does seem primitive. But when this seemingly primitive method was examined by mathematicians, it was found to be not only effective but, amazingly, based upon sound mathematical principles. Within the finite limitations here mentioned (twelve gores, instead of an infinite number of gores), the system used here was the best available until the invention of the calculus. It is rather amazing to realise that sixteenth-century mapmakers who knew only how to wield scissors and slap on paste were, unwittingly, multiplying their latitudes by the secant of the angle, and transposing from sphere to plane-table in accordance with the modern rules of trigonometry.

But however accurately they transposed, their finished maps could be no better than the original mariners' charts upon which they were based. It will be found later that these charts were in themselves imperfect, for at that stage they were unable to distinguish between the straight line and the curve of the loxodrome. In strict right-angled sailing, this error did not occur. So long as the line of constant bearing is due south ($\angle 0°$) or due east ($\angle 90°$), there is no difference between the straight line and the loxodrome. By some miraculous accident, the Portuguese had hit upon right-angled sailing, the one and only method which avoids this bedevilling problem altogether; and if they had been able to stick to this method, their later loxodromic problems would never have arisen. But the day on which the Portuguese navigators forgot their right-angled sailing, the day on which they started cutting corners, on that day their navigation began to fall into error, the error which we know as Erration. In this chapter it has been demonstrated that, to this point, the *Projecção Quadrada* was mathematically soundly based – unwittingly perhaps, accidentally perhaps, but nevertheless soundly based on the secant of the latitude. But once their navigators fell into this error, their mapping too fell into error and degenerated into the *Projecção Errada*, which must now be discussed.

Chapter 12

LOXODROMES AND ERRATION

U NTIL 1537 Portuguese longitudes were calculated on a mathematical misconception, and charts before that date are accordingly distorted. In that year the great Portuguese mathematician Pedro Nunes published his two great essays, 'The Treatise on the errors in chart-making' and 'The Treatise in defence of the marine chart'.[1] These two works are of overwhelming importance in the development of Portuguese navigation, in the history of cartography, and in the history of the world. In all textbooks on the history of navigation, modern navigation starts with the discovery of the loxodrome, revealed to the world by Nunes in these works. But those who have written textbooks on loxodromes have not been interested in the history of the discovery of Australia; and those who have written about the Dieppe Maps have apparently not been aware of Pedro Nunes. The lucubrations of Professors Wood[2] and Scott,[3] who for decades thundered that they 'could see no resemblance between the Dieppe Maps and the real shape of Australia',[4] are rendered valueless in the face of their ignorance of the breakthrough that Nunes made in the mathematics of navigation. An attempt will therefore be made here, it is believed for the first time, to bring these two subjects together.

Pedro Nunes (1492–1577) was Portugal's greatest mathematician. He was a Jew, at first a teacher (Prince Luis of Portugal was one of his pupils), and later Professor of Mathematics at Coimbra University, and Hydrographer-General in government service. Because of his position, he exercised more influence on the development of the science of navigation than any other man of his time, uniquely combining in his own person theoretical mathematics and practical navigation, which included a voyage to India.[5] He was one of the first to study magnetic deviation, and invented the ingenious shadow-instrument, a kind of sun-dial mounted on the card of a magnetic compass, which read True North once a day by the sun's shadow, and thus adjusted the card from magnetic north to True North. He was the first to demonstrate clearly the divergence of the meridians, and invented another ingenious machine – actually a sixteenth-century computer – which mechanically read off the cosine values of the different angles, thus giving the lengths of the various departures of longitude merely by turning a handle. To facilitate more accurate reading of instruments, he invented the Nonius, which is nothing other than the Vernier Scale, reinvented by the Frenchman Vernier 150 years later. But his great and abiding work was in the field of the loxodrome, with which his name is forever linked.

A loxodrome (sometimes called a rhumb-line) is a line of constant bearing: that is, it is a line drawn on the surface of a globe which cuts every meridian of longitude at the same angle. As an illustration, a ship travelling on a constant south-east course (s45°e) crosses every meridian at the angle of forty-five degrees. And because the earth is spherical, because the meridians are not parallel but run together at the Poles, and because the compass-needle, pointing as it does all the time to the North Magnetic Pole, keeps adjusting itself to the changing position as the ship makes easting – and for other reasons of greater mathematical complexity – this loxodrome or line of constant bearing does not describe a straight line, but an unexpected, unanticipated and almost unbelievable *spiral curve.*

Among the readers of this book there will be some who have already met with the loxodromes, who understand them, and who are no longer surprised about them. There will be some readers with such mathematical insight that they will accept and understand the loxodromes now, even if they have not had occasion to grapple with them before. But the vast majority of readers will meet with them here for the first time; and, like the author when he first met with them, will find them paradoxical, and think them almost unbelievable. In our everyday lives we travel over such a minute segment of the earth's surface that the curvature of the earth does not affect us; in our everyday maps (town maps and the like), the curve of the earth can be and is ignored. We then instinctively expect global maps to obey the same geometrical rules as our small local maps, and we are surprised because they do not.

Certainly this was the geographical mistake made by the early Portuguese.

Let us start with a simple illustration. A man owns a square field (Fig. 12.1) marked ABCD, its northern or top boundary

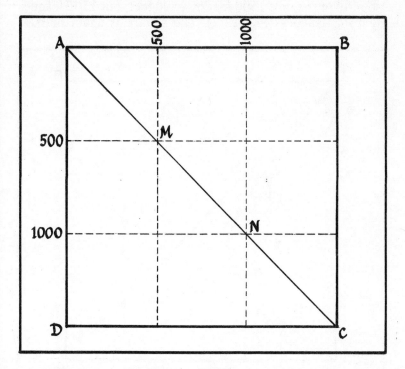

Fig. 12.1   THE SQUARE FIELD

AB 1500 feet in length, its western or side boundary AD also 1500 feet in length. For convenience, the intermediate distances at 500′ and 1000′ are also marked in, junctioning at M and N. The farmer desires to walk across his field in a south-east direction, commencing at the point A: that is, he desires to walk on the loxodrome, or line of constant bearing, of 45°. Clearly, he walks along the diagonal AC. At M, when he is 500 feet south of his top boundary, he is clearly also 500 feet east of his side boundary; at N, when he is 1000 feet south of his top boundary, he is also 1000 feet east of his side boundary. At 1500 feet south, he reaches the corner C, which is also 1500 feet east. This is how we expect a loxodrome to behave; and in a small field, that is how it does behave.

But suppose, instead, that a ship wishes to traverse a great 'square' of sea, not 1500 feet by 1500 feet, but 1500 leagues by 1500 leagues (Fig. 12.2). The square is again marked

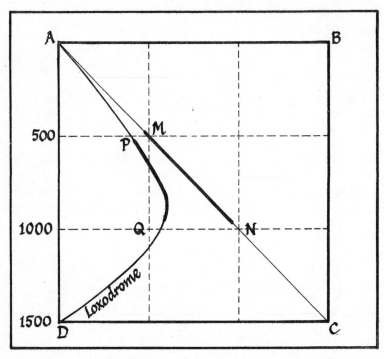

Fig. 12.2 THE OCEAN SQUARE

ABCD, the 500 and 1000 league lines are again marked, and the diagonal AMNC is again drawn, as in the farmer's field. Like the farmer, the ship wishes to start on the Equator* at A, and proceed south-east on the loxodrome or line of constant bearing of 45°. The facts are exactly the same as those in the farmer's field, and our first thought must be that the ship will

---

* Because all eastern ports of departure – Goa, Malacca, Ternate etc – are on or close to the Equator, this is assumed. Some adjustment is required in other cases.

pass down the diagonal, passing through M and N and finally arriving at the corner C. Certainly before Pedro Nunes that is how the Portuguese visualised the track of a ship at sea.

On second thoughts, we might concede that the ship would not exactly follow the diagonal AC. After all, the earth is curved, and the ship's track would probably curve to some extent. We would not be surprised if the ship's track veered away from the diagonal in a gentle curve, missing the corner C by a hundred leagues or so. But we instinctively conceive the track as substantially diagonal, substantially 'looking south-easterly', more or less following the line AC and finishing up at least relatively close to the rational and sensible destination at C. If that is what we conceive, we are in for a shattering surprise.

The actual track of the ship, on this undeviating south-east course, is shown in Fig. 12.2 by the almost unbelievable line APQD. The track starts off at A in an unmistakable south-east direction, and for the first third of its distance sticks very close to the diagonal. At P, where it is 500 leagues south of the Equator, it is about 450 leagues east of the side meridian, and so is not far away from the corresponding point M on the diagonal. The track so far retains the slope of about 45° which we expect for a ship on a constant south-east course.

But in the next third of the track, strange things happen. The ship's track between 500 leagues south and 1000 leagues south, swings sharply downwards. At Q, the ship is only 630 leagues east of the side meridian, whereas the corresponding point N on the diagonal is 1000 leagues east. In the latter section of the track here described, the line on the map is almost perpendicular on the page, looking like a south course rather than a diagonal south-east course. Yet the ship is still on its constant south-east bearing, crossing every meridian as it comes to it on the prescribed angle of 45 degrees.

But worse is to follow. Beyond 1000 leagues, the ship's track starts to *come back* towards the original meridian. Its ultimum, or furthest east, is approximately at point Q, 630 leagues from the prime meridian. The ship continues to travel *south-east*, yet soon is only 500, then 400, then 200 leagues from the prime meridian: and it eventually returns to the meridian from which it started, in high latitudes crossing it

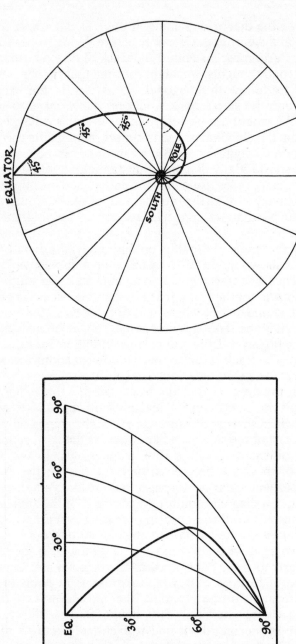

Fig. 12.4

Fig. 12.3

and recrossing it as it spirals around the Pole. In Fig. 12.2 this last third of the track appears to be travelling *south-west*, returning towards the original meridian. Yet that is not so. Assuming that the ship was steered by the most impeccable gyro-compass, adhering with absolute fidelity to its pre-scribed south-east bearing, its actual track over the surface of the ocean would be the strange spiral given in the figure; and it would inevitably finish up at the Pole.

Because the practical navigation with which we are dealing took place wholly in the navigable latitudes, say between 0° and 60°, we are not here concerned with the strange spiralling of the loxodrome in the very high latitudes. But it may briefly be mentioned here that, in the last few degrees of latitude before the Pole, the loxodrome becomes completely crazy, whizzing round the Pole in ever-decreasing spirals, and finally (perhaps one should say theoretically) reaching the Pole itself at infinity. It is a strange thought that *any* ship or aeroplane which travels from *any* point on the earth on *any* line of constant bearing (other than due east or due west) always finishes up in the same way – whizzing round and round the Pole ad infinitum.

It is not possible to explain this phenomenon to readers who are not familiar with the calculus, but an elementary explanation can be given from the materials given previously in this book. All of the illustrations used here, both the farmer's field and the ocean square, have been based upon the two ingredients of *bearing* and *distance*;[6] and as will be remembered from Chapter 11, this unwittingly produces charts on the Sanson-Flamsteed Projection.[7] In Fig. 12.3 is given a skeletal Sanson-Flamsteed Projection, only display-ing the parallels and meridians of 0°, 30°, 60°, and 90°, and

Fig. 12.3 THE SOUTH-EAST LOXODROME ON THE SANSON-FLAMSTEED PROJECTION

Fig. 12.4 THE NUNES SPIRAL. The outer circle represents the Equator, the centre of the circle is the South Pole, the straight lines are meridians of longitude, and the spiral is the south-east loxodrome, which crosses every meridian at the constant angle of 45°.

with the remarkable south-east loxodrome drawn in. In the first third of the loxodrome's track, because it is crossing meridians which are more or less perpendicular on the page, the track itself is acceptably diagonal. In the middle third of the track, because the meridians are very oblique, the track which crosses them at an angle becomes almost perpendicular to the page. The ultimum is reached just beyond Long. 60° (the 1000 leagues mark of Fig. 12.2) and thereafter the meridians become very oblique – near the Pole almost horizontal to the page – and the loxodrome which is still crossing them at 45 degrees appears to have almost reversed its original direction.

Because it uses only four meridians, this diagram is inexact and elementary. A better result can be obtained by filling in the same loxodrome on the large Sanson-Flamsteed which is given in Fig. 12.6. Pedro Nunes himself illustrated this phenomenon on à Polar Projection (Fig. 12.4), where the South Pole is in the centre of the circle, and the Equator forms the circumference. The south-east loxodrome is shown, commencing at the Equator, clearly crossing each meridian at the constant angle of 45°, and describing the spiral which (at infinity) reaches the Pole.

Now that the nature of the loxodrome is understood, how did this affect the Portuguese discoverers? Reverting to Fig. 12.2, the dotted line AMNC shows the track which the mariners thought that they were travelling – the straight line of the diagonal, similar to the diagonal in the farmer's field. When, by loxodrome, the ship was at P, the mariners thought that they were at M, and charted their position accordingly. If they discovered an island at Q, they thought it was located at N. Consequently, at all points they thought that they were *further east* than they really were; and this error, this exaggeration of easting, this distortion of charts by uniform error in longitude, is called 'Erration'.

In the centre of Fig. 12.2 a portion of the loxodrome (PQ) is emphasised in heavy black, like a reversed letter C. The corresponding section of the diagonal (MN), necessarily a straight line, is also emphasised in heavy black. We have seen that a pre-Nunes mariner, thinking that he was sailing on a constant bearing along the straight line MN, would in fact sail along the loxodromic curve PQ. He would *think* that he was sailing the straight course, he would *in fact* sail the curve.

Now let us work from the other end. Suppose that there was in existence an unexplored coast, shaped like a reversed letter C, in the position and approximately in the latitudes indicated by the curve PQ. The pre-Nunes mariner cruising along that coast would *in fact* be sailing the curve, but (by the reverse of the above reasoning) would *think* that he was sailing the straight line of the diagonal. So a coast in those latitudes which actually curved like a reversed letter C would show on his chart more like a 45° sloping straight line. If the reader now turns to Fig. 14.2 he will see that in Map I the east coast of Australia is substantially curved like a reversed letter C, and the Portuguese mariners who charted it found it in that shape; but in Map III he will see that, after allowing for their erroneous method of calculation, the coast becomes distorted, straightening out to the approximation of a 45° sloping straight line. This is the effect of Erration.

Erration is a convenient word, for it comes from the Latin root *errare*, to wander or to diverge: and Erration is the ratio of divergence which has to be applied to the pre-Nunes charts in order to correct their loxodromic distortion. At the same time, *errare* has the connotation of 'error', reminding us that this distortion is a mistake, and further reminding us that the projection upon which the pre-Nunes maps are based (the *Projecção Errada*, or the Erration Projection) is not only an unfamiliar but an erroneous projection. Lastly, while this has no etymological validity, it is a convenient mnemonic to remind us that Er-ratio-n is a *ratio*, the ratio or proportion between the true longitude which we use today and the erroneous longitude which, through miscalculation, crept into the sixteenth-century charts.

But the difficulty in dealing with Erration is that advanced mathematical processes are involved – trigonometry, spherical geometry, logarithms and calculus – and it is difficult to write in a manner which is acceptable to all readers. Some readers will have no mathematical background at all; others will be expert mathematicians; and the remainder, probably the majority, will fall in between these two extremes. It seems best to attempt to cater for these three classes separately.

Those who claim no mathematical knowledge, who are only bewildered by symbols and equations, only need to know the result and effect of the examination which is about to follow, without bothering themselves with the explanation of their basis. These readers may be satisfied to know that the false longitude in early Portuguese maps has a stable relationship to true longitude (the ratio of Erration), which varies according to the latitude; and the Erration figure for each parallel of latitude has been worked out, and can be ascertained from the adjoining table, which gives the Erration figure (ε) for each of 79 degrees of latitude. Beyond latitude 79° the distortion becomes very great; but as the Portuguese never penetrated so far south (or north) the Erration in those areas can be ignored.

These tables work in this manner. Let us suppose that an island appears on an early Portuguese chart. The latitude is correctly given as 27 degrees south of the Equator, but its

ERRATION (ε) TABLES

in respect of latitudes 0° to 79°

θ	0	1	2	3	4
0	1.0000	1.0001	1.0004	1.0009	1.0016
10	1.0103	1.0124	1.0148	1.0175	1.0203
20	1.0423	1.0469	1.0517	1.0568	1.0621
30	1.1007	1.1082	1.1162	1.1245	1.1332
40	1.1946	1.2065	1.2190	1.2321	1.2459
50	1.3433	1.3625	1.3827	1.4039	1.4263
60	1.5903	1.6238	1.6594	1.6975	1.7382
70	2.0583	2.1291	2.2068	2.2926	2.3879

θ	5	6	7	8	9
0	1.0025	1.0037	1.0050	1.0065	1.0083
10	1.0234	1.0267	1.0302	1.0340	1.0380
20	1.0678	1.0737	1.0800	1.0866	1.0934
30	1.1423	1.1518	1.1618	1.1722	1.1831
40	1.2602	1.2753	1.2911	1.3076	1.3250
50	1.4499	1.4749	1.5013	1.5293	1.5589
60	1.7819	1.8289	1.8795	1.9343	1.9937
70	2.4944	2.6143	2.7504	2.9065	3.0876

$$\varepsilon = \frac{\theta \sec \theta}{\dfrac{180}{\pi} \log_e \tan \left(\dfrac{90+\theta}{2}\right)}$$

longitude is erroneously given as 54 degrees east of the
Prime Meridian. What is the true longitude of that island?
From the above Tables it can be ascertained that in Lat. 27°
the Erration figure (ε) is 1.0800. The erroneous longitude
(54°) when divided by 1.0800 gives 50°. So the true longitude
of that island is 50° east of the Prime Meridian. In this way the
true position of every point on the Portuguese map can be
recalculated, and the map can be redrawn with these corrections. This recalculation and redrawing is called 'transposition to a different projection'. Those readers who genuinely
are not interested in mathematics can now skip the remainder
of this chapter, and turn to Fig. 0.2 to see how the Dauphin
Map looks when it is redrawn on these principles.

Secondly, for those expert mathematicians who require a
technical exposition of the equation in formal mathematical
form, the following short section is given:

The error of Erration is caused by the mistaken application of the
principles of plane geometry to phenomena which are only soluble
by spherical geometry. Let θ represent latitude and ϕ represent
longitude on a true sphere. Let ε represent the factor of error
(Erration) so that the erroneous longitude is $\varepsilon\phi$. Let β represent the
angle which the line of constant bearing from any given point on the
surface of the sphere to the primal intersection at Lat. 0° Long. 0°
makes with the meridian of Long. 0°.

Because the departure of longitude decreases in proportion to the
cosine of the angles of latitude, the length of the departure in Lat. θ°
is $\cos\theta$, or $\dfrac{1}{\sec\theta}$:

Then by plane geometry:

$$\tan\beta = \frac{\varepsilon\phi\cos\theta}{\theta} \text{ or } \frac{\varepsilon\phi}{\theta\sec\theta}$$

Now by spherical geometry:

$$\phi \text{ (in radians)} = R\tan\beta\log_e\tan\left(\frac{90+\theta}{2}\right)$$

$$\therefore \quad \phi \text{ (in degrees)} = \frac{360}{2\pi R}\times R\tan\beta\log_e\tan\left(\frac{90+\theta}{2}\right)$$

$$= \frac{180}{\pi}\times\tan\beta\log_e\tan\left(\frac{90+\theta}{2}\right)$$

So, substituting for tan β,

$$\phi = \frac{\varepsilon\phi}{\theta \sec \theta} \times \frac{180}{\pi} \cdot \log_e \tan \left(\frac{90+\theta}{2}\right)$$

$$= \varepsilon\phi \times \frac{\left(\frac{180}{\pi}\right) \log_e \tan \left(\frac{90+\theta}{2}\right)}{\theta \sec \theta}$$

And

$$\varepsilon\phi = \phi \times \frac{\theta \sec \theta}{\left(\frac{180}{\pi}\right) \cdot \log_e \tan \left(\frac{90+\theta}{2}\right)}$$

And

$$\varepsilon = \frac{\theta \sec \theta}{\left(\frac{180}{\pi}\right) \cdot \log_e \tan \left(\frac{90+\theta}{2}\right)}$$

This last equation gives the value of ε, which is expressed in tabular form in the Erration Table printed above.

The graticule of a projection in which the curved meridians of longitude conform with this equation is the *Projecção Errada*. The Projection constructed on the converse of this equation, where the longitude remains constant but the latitude varies, is Mercator's Projection.

If the non-mathematicians and the expert mathematicians have now, in their different ways, received all the information that they need, the great majority of readers in between these two extremes may be prepared to brush up their recollections of their school trigonometry, and delve into this discussion which relates how the navigators went astray, and how Pedro Nunes brought them back to the proper mathematical track.

So first, for the benefit of those who need it, a little brushing up of elementary trigonometry. First, the symbols need to be defined. Every place on the globe is fixed by its latitude and longitude; and its modern latitude is expressed by the Greek letter θ (theta), which conveniently has a short bar across it looking like a parallel of latitude. Modern longitude is represented by the Greek letter ϕ (phi), the shape of which also conveniently reminds us of a meridian of longitude. The bearing of one point from another (south-west, or as the case may be) is represented by β (beta). Erration is represented by

ε, and as this is the ratio of the erroneous Portuguese longitude to the true longitude, the erroneous Portuguese longitude is therefore $\varepsilon\phi$.

Now for a few triangles. In any right-angled triangle there is a fixed ratio between the sides, depending on the angle in the corner.

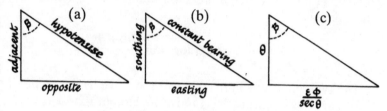

Fig. 12.5   ELEMENTARY TRIANGLES

In Fig. 12.5a the ratio of the side opposite $\angle\beta$ to the side adjacent to $\angle\beta$ is called the *tangent* of angle β, or tan β. The ratio of the hypotenuse to the adjacent side is the *secant* of angle β, or sec β. The other four relationships, which do not concern us at the moment, are sine, cosine, cotangent and co-secant. So the easting equals the southing multiplied by tan β (Fig. 12.5b).

But when this is translated from leagues into degrees, difficulty occurs. The southing (in leagues) remains in constant ratio to the latitude (in degrees), for the number of leagues in one degree of latitude is always the same, anywhere in the world. But the easting (in leagues) does not remain in this ratio to the longitude (in degrees), for the number of leagues in one degree of longitude diminishes as we move away from the equator, in inverse ratio to the secant of the latitude. So, in degrees (see Fig. 12.5c),

$$\theta° \times \tan \beta \text{ does not equal } \varepsilon\phi° \quad \text{but equals } \frac{\varepsilon\phi°}{\sec \theta}$$

and therefore:

$$\varepsilon\phi = \tan \beta \times \theta \sec \theta$$

Now this calculation would be correct if the earth were flat. The mistake made by the Portuguese was in doing these calculations according to the principles of plane (flat) geometry,[8] when they should have been applying the principles of spherical geometry, where all of the lines are curved, and not straight lines. In modern navigation, based upon modern spherical trigonometry, it is known that the longitude of any point can be calculated only by applying the following difficult equation, which is based on Napierian logarithms and the calculus:

$$\phi = \frac{180}{\pi} \times \tan \beta \, \log_e \tan \left(\frac{90+\theta}{2} \right)$$

The two equations in heavy print now give us the value of the erroneous longitude $(\varepsilon\phi)$ and of true longitude (ϕ): and as Erration (ε) is only the ratio that exists between these two, we can find the value of Erration by combining these two equations, and thus finding a new equation, thus:

$$\varepsilon = \frac{\varepsilon\phi}{\varepsilon} = \frac{\tan \beta \times \theta \sec \theta}{\left(\frac{180}{\pi} \right) \cdot \tan \beta \times \log_e \tan \left(\frac{90+\theta}{2} \right)}$$

so

$$\varepsilon = \frac{\theta \sec \theta}{\left(\frac{180}{\pi} \right) \log_e \tan \left(\frac{90+\theta}{2} \right)}$$

It will be seen that this is the same answer as is given in the paragraph (expert mathematicians, for the use of) printed in small print above, and it also accords with the Erration Tables printed in the square at the beginning of this chapter. If any reader still finds this difficult, it will be sufficient if he remembers the three basic equations:

ERRATION equals the Erroneous Longitude divided by True Longitude

$$\left(\varepsilon = \frac{\varepsilon\phi}{\phi} \right)$$

TRUE LONGITUDE equals the Erroneous Longitude divided by Erration

$$\left(\phi = \frac{\varepsilon\phi}{\varepsilon} \right)$$

THE ERRONEOUS LONGITUDE equals the True Longitude multiplied by Erration

$$(\varepsilon\phi = \varepsilon \times \phi)$$

When memorised in this form, the symbols in brackets should be self-explanatory.

To explain how the early Portuguese fell into the mathematical error which has here been analysed, we have to go back to Chapter 2. By now the reader is familiar with their system of right-angled sailing, sailing due south down the meridian, then turning east to run in to the African coast. So long as they stuck rigidly to this system, they were making no mathematical mistake. Apart from human error (incorrect compass readings, incorrect Altura, misjudged distances, or failing to steer on a constant course), the right-angled system should have produced correct longitude calculations – and, by and large, on the West African coast their calculations of their east-west position were good. This is because due south and due east are cardinal directions, not upset by the curvature of the earth. But once oblique bearings intruded – south-east sailing, for instance, or south-south-east – immense problems arose in the spherical triangles, requiring a sophisticated knowledge of higher mathematics to solve them.

We have seen how the mariners had become familiar with the tangent ratios, first in their Marteloio Tables, and later in the *Regimento do Astrolábio e do Quadrante Tables*, and gradually this knowledge encouraged them to 'cut the corners' of their right-angled courses. By their knowledge of latitude (Altura) they knew how far south they had travelled; by the compass and the traverse board, they knew their bearing; and they had tables which enabled them to calculate their easting from these two ingredients – or so they thought. Once the African coast turned substantially east in the Gulf of Guinea, there was a growing temptation to sail south-easterly instead of down the meridian, adjusting the easting from the tables. And once the mariners found themselves in the Indian Ocean, where there were no traditional or useful north-south meridians and where the monsoons and trade winds never blew north and south, but always north-east or south-east or south west, the old idea of right-angled sailing was superseded by the newer method of bearing sailing. Unfortunately, this new method was not mathematically sound, and false east-west distances calculated from the tables began to replace the truer eastings previously reckoned. This applied throughout the first quarter of the sixteenth century, which included the date of the Dauphin's prototype; and it necessarily continued until someone knowledgeable in mathematics arose to point out how the mariners had gone astray, by mathematical admonition seeking to bring them back to truer methods. This was the task of Pedro Nunes.

Pedro Nunes isolated and explained the phenomenon of the loxodromic spiral. But because logarithms and the calculus had not then been invented, it was beyond his resources to solve the equation. In 1700 the Swiss genius Jakob Bernoulli investigated and solved the logarithmic spiral, and, as is well known, he was so thrilled with his Spiral that he asked for it to be engraved on his tomb, with the words '*Eadem Mutata Resurgo*'. His tomb with this inscription can be seen today in Basle. The loxodromic spiral is merely the application of this from plane geometry to spherical geometry, and so the solution of the loxodromic spiral soon followed. The working of the equation is not given here, but it is a standard equation the solution of which is given in all textbooks on spherical trigonometry, and for the purposes of this book can be accepted in the form which has been given earlier in this chapter, namely:

$$\phi = R \cdot \tan \beta \, \log_e \tan \left(\frac{90 + \theta}{2} \right) \text{ (in radians)} \qquad \cdot$$

A projection can be constructed, with the lines of latitude straight, parallel and equidistant, but with the lines of longitude curved convex to the Prime Meridian, the curves expressing the Erration Equation. As this is the projection which the Portuguese were unwittingly using, though they thought that they were using the simple squares of the *Projecção Quadrada*, the projection constructed on the Erration equation is called the *Projecção Errada*. The characteristic of this projection is that the lines of longitude curve convexly to the Prime Meridian, widening exponentially the further they go from the Equator. The graticule of this projection is given in Fig. 12.7, together with a technical description of its method of construction. On the right-hand side of this figure, a modern map of Australia is inserted, transposed to this projection: it is immediately noticeable how this transposition resembles the shape of the Dauphin Map. Close to the Equator, the divergence of the Erration meridians from the normal perpendicular lines is not very great, and in these low latitudes the land-shapes are not greatly distorted. It is interesting to note that the East Indian islands on the Dieppe Maps obey the projection here described: because they are all near the Equator, they are not greatly distorted, but such distortion as does occur is related to the Erration curve. In high latitudes the curved meridians veer away violently, and the shapes of the southern portions of Australia accordingly appear grossly distorted.

This was noticed in 1581, in France, by F. M. Coignet, who pointed out that in high latitudes the unadjusted trigonometrical tables then in use were quite inadequate for the calculations involved, because of their failure to allow for the loxodromes. He published a set of correctives. While Coignet did not use the term, his tables were in fact Erration Tables, apparently the first to appear. The Englishman William Borough about the same time pointed out the same thing.

Mercator was a student of Nunes' loxodromes, and acknowledged his debt to him by engraving the Nunes Spirals on his globe. What is more important, the great Mercator's Projection is the direct product of the loxodromic equation which we have been considering. The fundamental basis of Mercator's Projection is that he compensates for the east-west expansion of the meridians by a corresponding expansion (waxing) of the parallels of latitude in a north-south direction, in exact proportion. Many textbooks wrongly say that because the transposition of the meridians of a globe to the meridians of a flat plane expands the meridians in the ratio of the secant of the latitude, therefore Mercator merely waxes his latitudes in the same proportion – i.e. in the ratio of the secant. This is not correct. Because the loxodrome veers away from the Prime Meridian in the loxodromic ratio ($\phi =$

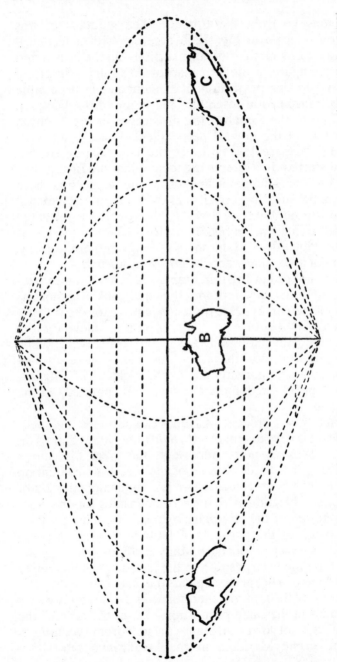

Fig. 12.6 THE SANSON-FLAMSTEED PROJECTION. Parallels of latitude are equidistant straight lines: away from the equator, departures decrease in proportion with the cosine of the angle of latitude. Note how map A resembles the shape of the Dauphin.

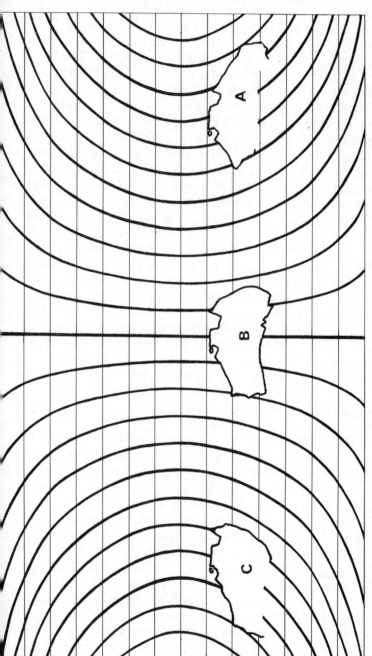

Fig. 12.7 THE PROJECÇÃO ERRADA. Parallels of latitude are equidistant straight lines: away from the Equator, departures increase in proportion with the Erration of the latitude (see Tables on page 170). Note how map A resembles the shape of the Dauphin.

$R \log_e \tan ((90 + \theta)/2)$ which we have been considering, Mercator waxes his latitudes, stretching them in a north-south direction, in accord with this loxodromic equation. The Mercator distance from the Equator to any given latitude is this exact distance: $\theta = R \log_e \tan ((90 + \theta)/2)$. It is not known by what mathematical process he arrived at this sophisticated solution. He promised that he would give a full mathematical explanation, but he never did, and it was not until the English mathematician William Wright sorted it out that we have any explanation at all. But it was a very great breakthrough in the history of navigation, and it is the direct corollary of the Nunes research on the loxodrome.

The construction of the graticule of the *Projecção Errada* enables us to transfer a modern map of Australia to this projection, subject to one further consideration: which Prime Meridian is to be selected for this exercise? This is most important, for on any curved-meridian projection the position of a land-form relative to the Prime Meridian drastically affects its shape. The three positions of Australia (A, B and C) on both the Sanson-Flamsteed (Fig. 12.6) and the *Projecção Errada* (Fig. 12.7) demonstrate this. Remember that these charts are real charts of real voyages, not concoctions of arm-chair theorists. The sixteenth-century mariner did not say 'I think that today I shall use a Sanson-Flamsteed (or a *Projecção Errada*, according to taste) basing my Prime Meridian on Long. 20° (Lisbon) w.' He would know nothing of those things. But when he departed from the port of São Vicente in the Cape Verde Islands to 'run down the southing' off the west coast of Africa, he was naturally running south down whatever meridian São Vicente is in: and that automatically became his Prime Meridian. So the Prime Meridian of the mariner's chart was not selected capriciously or advisedly: the meridian of the Port of Departure selected itself as the Prime Meridian in the construction of the chart.

Similarly, when a navigator sailing on the newer 'bearing and latitude' system was about to commence an east-bound voyage at (say) Malacca, he presumably would take a clean sheet of chart-paper, he would mark 'Malacca' near the left-hand margin of the page at its appropriate latitude and longitude, and thereafter triangle by triangle, trig. tangent by trig. tangent, he would prick his course across the sheet. Unknown to him, the error of Erration had already obtruded into his first triangle, and in constant formula cumulatively misplaced each successive triangle; and when he finally reached his 'furthest east' point, his erroneous method of calculation had him charted many leagues further east of his Port of Departure than he really was. In a later chapter we shall see that the voyage which charted the east coast of Australia commenced (or was believed to have commenced) at Malacca: and in the transpositions which follow, it is the meridian of Malacca that is adopted as the Prime Meridian.

When Australia is so transposed to the *Projecção Errada*, it takes on the shape of the Dauphin (see Fig. 14.2, Map V). Conversely, when we take the Dauphin, set it out on its *Projecção Errada*, and then transpose it to the *Projecção Quadrada*, or to Mercator's Projection, the corrected outline visibly approximates to the real shape of the continent (Fig. 0.2). There may be some readers who have found it difficult to recognize the shape of Australia in the original Dauphin, although the consensus of competent opinion is that the resemblance is too great to be ignored: but when the map is re-drawn as it has been in this figure, no one could now fail to see that this sixteenth-century map is indubitably a map of Australia, based on authentic exploration and real knowledge.

The Dauphin Map is wrong, but calculably wrong, and by calculation can be and ought to be put right. *'Do qual se segue'*, wrote Pedro Nunes, *'que os lugares ficam situados onde nam estam . . . e ficam os lugares em mais longura da que tem'*.[9] Every point on the map is in the wrong place, too far over. But understanding of the loxodromes, which he himself gave us, enables us to correct the error, and to reproduce the map on the projection which we can understand, in a shape which beyond question we can recognize.

Chapter 13

MAGNETIC SOUTH

IT appears to be a universal trait of human nature to be willing to trust instruments. Most modern motorists are blindly sure that when their speedometer says 100 kilometres per hour, they are in fact travelling at that speed; and yet, of course, their instrument may be most inaccurate in its readings. But because it is an instrument, its information has a credibility which overrides all other information. The Portuguese mariners had this blind faith in their magnetic compasses. Probably the possession of such an instrument gave them standing, and bolstered their self-esteem. With this on their ships, they felt that they were masters of the art of navigation, and any doubt cast on the precious instrument would certainly have been resented.

Yet by our standards their compasses would seem crude and untrustworthy; and it seems miraculous that the Portuguese achieved the good results they did with this embryonic instrument. Not that the compass was really new. Alexander Neckham mentions it as early as 1180,[1] although the earliest models, consisting of a needle inserted in a straw which was then floated in a basin of water, were obviously very primitive and correspondingly inaccurate and unreliable. Chapter 2 related how the instrument-makers gradually evolved better instruments, progressing from an eight-point card to the sophistication of a 32-point, or even 64-point, card. A compass with a 32-point card purported to be accurated to about twelve degrees; and under good conditions, in a still ship, and in the hands of an expert, it probably gave results as good as six degrees. The bearings followed by a sixteenth-century navigator, and those shown on a sixteenth-century chart, are therefore quite scientific and reasonably accurate – although, of course, not as accurate as present-day usage requires. Their greatest difficulty was reading the needle on a ship at sea. To read the swinging needle of a primitive instrument on a tossing ship must have called for much manual dexterity and visual accuracy on the part of the navigator; but again the knack of the experienced seadog, almost the instinct for doing the right thing, seemed to produce results of unexpectedly high quality.

On land, the compass could be checked and corrected against the True North of the sun's shadow by the gnomon method. This performance was not possible on a moving and heaving ship. Where possible, landings were made for these astronomical observations, as when Vasco da Gama landed at St Helena Bay to check his True North, his local time, and his Altura. Also, the early mariners had much knowledge of the stars; and before the compass was introduced they had learned to navigate by the stars, especially the North Star. It is true to say that, given time and good weather, the mariner could always establish his True North, with quite considerable accuracy, by one or more of these methods.

But the main use of the compass was not to establish True North but to hold bearing. The binnacle was immediately beside the helmsman. The course was laid down – south-east, or south-south-east, or as the case may be – and the helmsman's eyes never left the needle; for the holding of course, the recording of changes of course, was the very basis of their reckoning of distance and their calculation of position.[2] For this, there could be no substitute for the magnetic compass. Now if the compass were defective, or not properly adjusted, or for any other reason did not read True North, the helmsman would still be told to hold his course *according to the needle*. It was no good saying: 'Steer south-east by east. By the way, the compass is $16\frac{1}{4}$ degrees out, so take that into your calculations.' The helmsman would not have had the time or the knowledge to make adjustments of this kind. Instead of the above instruction, he would be told: 'Steer south-east a quarter east according to the needle.' It may be in fact that the needle's reading diverged $16\frac{1}{4}°$ so that in fact the ship was sailing south-east by east, but if so, only the navigator knew, while the helmsman just did what he had been told.

This need to steer by the needle meant that it was necessary to have charts which agreed with the needle, irrespective of the trueness or otherwise of the needle reading; and this became a problem when the magnetic deviation of the needle started to have effect. So that both the navigator and the helmsman could steer by the needle without having to calculate and allow for variations, charts were not drawn on True North, but on Magnetic North; and as this affected all charts, including the Dauphin, the subject must be examined here in some detail.

So long as shipping was confined to the Mediterranean, the fact that the compass needle did not point to True North was of little account. In the fifteenth and sixteenth centuries the declination of the needle, in European waters, was about 10°E. As their compasses did not read any closer than that anyway, it was barely noticeable except that in the aggregate the charts seemed to incline the one way; and on maps which extended well to the east, to Constantinople and Black Sea ports, there is always a distinct hump towards the eastern end, indicating the Magnetic North chart, as distinct from the True North. This must not be thought of as primitive or ignorant: after all, even Captain Cook drew his charts in this way.[3] It was not that the navigators did not know what they were doing, but merely that it suited them to proceed in this way.

But as soon as the Portuguese and the Spaniards began their ocean voyaging, magnetic deviation became a problem. If on a certain voyage the magnetic declination was 10°E, and it stayed at 10°E throughout the whole voyage, then no problem arose. Either the navigator ordered a course ten degrees more westerly than intended, enabling the helmsman to steer by the card; or (as sometimes they did) they could jigger the card itself to make the needle read true. This was fine so long as the magnetic declination remained constant. But when the ship was on a voyage in which the declination was changing, and often changing rapidly, during the voyage itself, something had better be done to allow for this phenomenon.

Broadly speaking, on the north–south voyage to Africa there was little variation during the voyage, but on the east–west voyage to America it was extreme. As the ship proceeded west across the Atlantic, it was found that the 10°E declination of home waters rapidly diminished, until in the Azores there was no variation at all, the needle naturally pointing to True North. Columbus is often credited with this discovery, but as the Azores Islands had been discovered long before his time, surely someone must have already compared the compass needle with the north shadow to notice how they there coincided.

But after leaving the Azores, in the one thousand miles or so between the Azores and Newfoundland, the declination quickly altered from 0° to 20°w. This is because the North Magnetic Pole is in North Canada (though not in the same place as it is now); and approaching the Magnetic Pole causes the distance between the isogonic lines to diminish, because they are there all running towards a common junction – in the same way that a set of railway lines, running from scattered outer suburbs to a central city station, get nearer together as they approach their hub. R. A. Skelton tells us[4] that in the earliest transatlantic crossings ships believed that they were running down the latitude on the outward journey, and that they were running back along the same latitude on the return voyage, and yet to their surprise were always making their return landfall on the north sea coast much further north than they had intended.

When they discovered the reason, they did not know how to provide for this deviation in their charts. The correct remedy would have been to rectify all of their compass readings to True North, and to draw all of their charts on True North. But in the first half of the sixteenth century they were still trying to provide 'Magnetic North' charts, because that is what the mariners, and especially the helmsmen, wanted. So the clumsy expedient was adopted of having two scales on the Atlantic charts, called the Oblique Latitudinal Scale, giving compass readings based on 10°E on the European side of the Atlantic, and based on 20°w on the other side. There are charts in existence with these two scales marked on them, the most famous being the Kunstmann.[5]

The Dauphin Map (which, as a world map, contains the Atlantic crossing and the North American coast) does not have an Oblique Latitudinal Scale; but it is obvious at a glance that its North American coast is tilted twenty degrees, perhaps more, to the east – i.e. it is drawn on Magnetic North, not True North. And as Desceliers applied that practice in his North American sector, there is a strong assumption that he applied it in his Australian sector too. Fortunately, there is no wild variation of the magnetic compass readings in the Australian area; but what there is, is an important element in the interpretation of the Dauphin Map.

What force compels a compass needle to point towards the north (even though it is not True North) is a mysterious question. It seems that the spinning earth generates a magnetic field: even more simply, the earth itself is a spinning magnet. Because the earth spins on its Pole-to-Pole axis, it would be easy to assume that the poles of the magnet would synchronise with the geographical poles. But for some even more mysterious reason, that is not so. The North Magnetic Pole is today in Canada, in Lat. 75°N Long. 102°W; and the South Magnetic Pole is in Antarctica, in Lat. 71°S Long. 151°E. From those last mentioned readings, it can be seen that the South Magnetic Pole is due south of the continent of Australia, which helps to explain why magnetic deviation in Australia is not extreme.

The North and South Magnetic Poles are today in the two places mentioned, but they were not always there. The two Magnetic Poles are always on the move, and appear to describe erratic circular tracks around their respective geographical poles. At least, that appears to be the case with the North Magnetic Pole (which has been studied for longer than its southern counterpart). Its course has been tracked since Elizabethan days, and in that time it has almost completely circumnativated the north geographic pole, in or about latitude 80°N, although on such an irregular course that there appears to be no system about it.

It might then be thought – and in the sixteenth century it was so thought – that there is a kind of 'magnetic latitude' and 'magnetic longitude', a systematic graticule corresponding with geographical latitude and longitude, but slightly off balance because the polarisation is different. Indeed, Jean Rotz (one of the Dieppe cartographers) advanced a theory[6] that geographical longitude could be ascertained by noting the waxing and diminishing magnetic declinations. But this theory is unsound. The compass needle is not only affected by the two strong influences of the North and South Magnetic Poles, but also by a variety of local influences (perhaps shifting metallic or magnetic belts under the surface of the earth's crust) which cause further distortions and deviations. Isogonic maps, as they are called, are published yearly, showing the magnetic changes that have occurred, and these keep the modern mariner abreast of the current deviations of the compass needle at all parts of the globe.

But in spite of the illogical meandering of the isogonic lines, if we place a series of isogonic maps before us, covering (say) two hundred years at 50-year intervals, some pattern does emerge. Largely because of the stately precession of the Magnetic Poles, there is a trend towards predictable change, and some basis for deducing what was the magnetic pattern in still earlier times. For instance, if the needle deviated at a certain place 10°E in 1950, 9°E in 1900, 8°E in 1850 and 7°E in 1800, then it is logical to deduce that it would have been 6°E in 1750 (before that place was discovered, or before any magnetic readings were made there). But that would only be an assumption. In 1760 there might have been some sudden subsidence of a metallic belt miles underground, and for all that we know the magnetic deviation at that place in 1750 might have been totally different.

This waywardness of magnetic deviation causes particular difficulty in Australia. Because regular observations only start in 1788, and because only Tasman (1643) before that kept a systematic record of his magnetic observations, there is little data but much guesswork about the magnetic variations in former centuries. Lacking documentation, we can only trust the experts who have studied the question in depth, and who have made assessments (guesses, maybe) of the probable readings, movements and changes in the centuries before observation began.

Our best first-hand observations can be gleaned from Abel Tasman, who passed along the south coast of Australia, touching at Tasmania, in 1643. In his *Journal* he meticulously noted the Variation of the magnetic compass on every day on which the necessary observations could be made.[7] His longitudes are not very reliable (no improvement in ascertaining longitude had been made in the preceding century) and as his longitudes are calculated from Tenerife, an adjustment has to be made to bring them to Greenwich readings. From Mauritius to the Great Australian Bight he records sharply-falling declination readings, from 27°w down to nil. Then in Lat. 42°s Long. 160° (Tenerife) E, which is almost on the west coast of Tasmania, he found his compass 'unstable': he was passing the point due north of, and not far from, the then South Magnetic Pole. After that, in Lat. 42°s Long. 162° (Tenerife) E the easterly declination commenced, and it rose slowly to 9°E or 10°E off the coast of New Zealand.

This gives a pattern of the isogonic lines splaying out like a fleur-de-lys (see Fig. 13.1), with the nil isogonic line close to the coast of Tasmania trending north, the west lines fanning away sharply to the west, and the east lines trending north more or less parallel to the nil line.

With this solid historical evidence to reassure us, we turn to the highly technical studies made by experts – scientific material which neither the author nor any other layman could be expected to follow; and we can do no more than rely on the experts. The first compilation was made by Hansteen in 1819, then by van Bemmeln in 1899,[8] and the present authority on the subject is Dr Takesi Yukutake of Tokyo University.[9] Collecting all available data, interpreting the movements and the trends, and interpolating their suppositions to fit in with the observed data, these experts have been able to draw up maps showing the probable isogonic lines in the earlier centuries. The Van Bemmeln is the one most relevant for our purposes.

In Fig. 13.1 is shown a map of Australia, crossed by eight lines – Van Bemmeln's 5°E and 5°w notation of declination for 1700, 1650 and 1600, and the author's conjectured lines for 1522. Van Bemmeln's calculations do not go back as far as this year.

It can be seen that the 5°E line of 1700 barely touches the east coast. In 1650 it is coterminous with the east coast. In 1600 it runs inland, parallel to the coast, from Cape Howe to the Gulf of Carpentaria. Seventy-eight years earlier, in 1522, it would be further west still – conjecturally running from Darwin to Tasmania. All declinations to the east of this would necessarily be more than 5°, rising upwards from this figure, although admittedly the gradients are not steep. From these figures, a 7° or 8° declination along the coast would appear to be a fair assumption.

On the west coast there is a distinct withdrawal of the 5°w
line over a hundred years, which withdrawal would surely
have been constant over the preceding 78 years as well. It is
fair to assume that in 1522 this isogonic line would have
missed the coast altogether, and the whole coast would have
been between the 5° and 0° lines. Probably 2° or 3° would be a
fair guess; but whatever it is, the deviation on the west coast is
too small to cause us much concern.

The figures given in the last two paragraphs should not be
regarded as very firm figures, for accuracy of this quality is not
really obtainable. The calculations are based on the van
Bemmeln charts, themselves only suppositions, and the 8°
and 2° conjectures are, at best, 'plus or minus'. Secondly, the
variations were not and are not uniform all along the continental coasts – at best the 8° and 2° are only averages for the
respective coasts. There are places – Cook's Magnetic Island,
near Townsville, and Tasman's Lat. 42°s Long. 160°
(Tenerife) E, off Tasmania – where local conditions make the
compass needle go completely haywire. And in all places, not
merely these two, readings of the wildly swinging needle
could be hopelessly astray. More modern investigation has
shown that the magnetic needle is susceptible to magnetic
influences on the ship itself: the presence of iron on board was
counteracted by Matthew Flinders by the invention of an
ingenious device, but on the Portuguese ships these influences
falsified their readings, simply because they did not know of
the fault. These and other reasons make a big question-mark
intrude into all of these calculations. But in spite of all this, the
broad evidence is that there was a trend to an east declination
on the east coast of Australia at the time, and the 8°E figure
adopted here is both realistic and conservative.

And if this assumption is adopted, the deviation of 8°E on
the east coast is significant. Much has been said in the
previous chapters about bearing. It was the all-important
element in the Portuguese method of navigation (based on
the tangent of the bearing); and in loxodromes it is fundamental, as by definition the loxodrome is the 'line of constant
bearing'. So in both calculations the hidden 8° of magnetic
deviation is a material element. And what is most important
and most significant is that it is an *east* declination. Erration

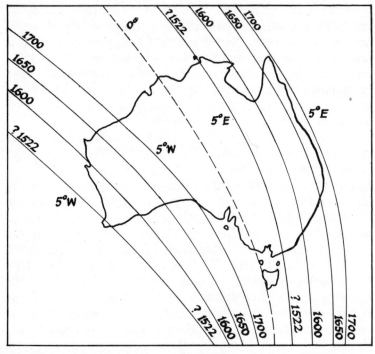

Fig. 13.1 ISOGONIC MAP (after van Bemmeln) showing van Bemmeln's Isogonic lines (5°E and 5°W) for 1700, 1650, and 1600, and the author's conjectured lines for 1522.

made the meridians curve to the east, and made the coast veer to the east. This additional 8° intensifies this trend, drawing out the Portuguese east coast still further to the east; and conversely, when the Dauphin Map is redrawn, transposed to a familiar projection, the real east coast retracts still further, and is drawn back still more identifiably to coincide with the continental shape that we know.

Unlike Erration, which leaves the parallels of latitude where they are but curves the meridians, Deviation affects both. The easiest way to alter a map which has been drawn on Magnetic North to a map on True North is simply to tilt the whole map the required number of degrees. But this is only applicable where the whole of the map is already uniformly tilted under the influence of a constant deviation. In a large area like Australia, where the conjectured deviation of the west coast was 2°w, where the north coast graduated rapidly from nil at one end to 8° or more east at the other end, and where the long east coast, while averaging 8°E, departed from this average in different sectors, no single tilting of the axis of the map can cope with all of these variations. It would be mathematically possible to take the Erration Table (see page 170) which gives the Erration ratio latitude by latitude; and to draw up an approximate and conjectured Deviation Table for the east coast, again latitude by latitude; and by combining them by the appropriate mathematical process to produce new ratios for the transpositions. The author experimented by swinging the east coast on the fulcrum of Cape York, and found that, in the northern and middle sections of the coast, the small amount of magnetic deviation did not unduly magnify the trend already set by Erration; but that in the south-east sector (roughly, the present State of Victoria) the magnetic deviation of 7° or 8°, when added to the existing Erration, was quite significant.

Because in these areas Erration and magnetic deviation trend the same way, tilting the chart to the east and requiring it to be relocated to the west, the combined effect of these two factors is very powerful. In Chapter 18, where the geography of the Victorian coast will be examined, the tilt caused by these combined factors will be calculated, and in the figure in that chapter (Fig. 18.1) the shape of the Victorian coast will be redrawn in the light of these considerations. The reader will then find that these two factors, in combination, greatly modify the land-shapes in the Dauphin Map, and that the rectified map then closely accords with the modern map of the Victorian coast.

Chapter 14

THE RIO GRANDE

I N Chapter 9 it was explained that Desceliers had before him the Portuguese map of the East Indies (the *Carta Anonima Portuguesa*) with the south coasts of Java and Sumbawa left blank, and also the map of Australia which he had obtained from the Casa da India; and, seeing the correspondence between the square top of Arnhem-land on the one map, and the square top of Java on the other, and the peaked top of Cape York on the one and the peaked top of Sumbawa on the other, he fitted the two maps together, like a man solving a jigsaw puzzle. This explanation stands. But in Chapter 9 the diagrammatic illustration[1] is too simplistic. It should be quite clear that the coast of Arnhem-land and the coast of Java did not miraculously agree in every curve and twist, nor miraculously correspond in every cape and bay and island. They did not literally coincide in area and position and latitude. The two pairs had a suggestive likeness, a resemblance that is more than a passing resemblance, an illusion of identity that was enough to mislead Desceliers into thinking that they were the same, to justify him in fitting them together. But their lesser details necessarily disagreed, and it is essential to search for clues to show where the features of the one gave way to the features of the other.

Now to start with, the north coasts on the Dieppe Maps, that is the north coast of Arnhem-land and the tip of Cape York, solely manifest the features of the north coasts of Java and Sumbawa. There is no compromise with the corresponding features of the Australian coast, whatever they were; no capes or bays taken from Arnhem-land or Cape York have intruded to disturb the correct geographical outlines of Java and Sumbawa. To such extent as the field was covered by the *Carta Anonima Portuguesa*, the *Carta Anonima* prevailed; whatever features had appeared on the Arnhem-land and Cape York coasts were wholly discarded, superseded and lost. If any place-names had appeared on those Australian coasts, they too are now lost, for we saw in Chapter 9 that on the Dauphin Map all of the place-names in those areas are wholly Javanese and Sumbawese.

The author has found the following simile useful, especially when considering Mercator and the decapitated Continent.[2] Suppose that in some police department they had a photograph in the Unknown Suspects file showing the head and torso of an unknown suspect. Detective Desceliers, while looking through John Doe's file, sees a photograph (head and face only) of John Doe, and erroneously convinces himself that John Doe and the Unknown Suspect are one and the same person. He takes the photograph out of the Unknown file, puts it in John Doe's file, and pastes John Doe's head over the other man's head, of course joining it on to the unknown man's torso and completely obliterating the unknown man's face. This, of course, represents Java–Sumbawa being stuck not on top of Arnhem-land and Cape York, but *over* Arnhem-land and Cape York, totally obliterating the Arnhem-land–Cape York features just as John Doe's head obliterated the face underneath. Detective Desceliers now has a composite of John Doe's head and the unknown man's torso. The police artist then draws in some conventional legs (the Antarctic Extension), and this triple combination is a fair representation of the triple combination in the Dauphin Map.

In the Dauphin Map there is nothing to show where these undisturbed Java–Sumbawa coasts end, and where the Australian coasts take over. But in the Rotz Plane Chart it is different. It will be remembered from Chapter 10 that two of the Dieppe Maps are by Jean Rotz: the Rotz Plane Chart and the Rotz Circular Chart. In that chapter something was said concerning the Rotz Circular, which gave the necessary evidence to show where Australia finished and the Antarctic Extension began. The Rotz Plane Chart performs something of the same service in the north.

In previous chapters Jean Rotz (John Rose, to give him his original Scottish name) has been described as a mathematician and a scholar. His 'Boke of Idrography', presented to King Henry VIII and now in the British Museum, is the most erudite publication to emerge from the Dieppe School. In the chapter on the magnetic compass, Rotz's very interesting theories on magnetic deviation were mentioned. And in the quality of his map-drawing, in his capacity as a cartographer, Rotz had an international reputation that surpasses that of his colleagues. He was a better cartographer than Desceliers – more accurate, less impetuous, more critical, more detailed, more subtle. His cartography subtly indicates the state of his knowledge and the limitations of his materials, and the degree of credence that he placed and that the reader should place, in the different parts of the map before him. Some parts of his coasts are clear, detailed forms, with bays and capes authoritatively delineated. But on both coasts there is a noticeable 'join' where Australia junctions with Java–Sumbawa. On the east coast, from the top to Princess Charlotte Bay,[3] is a stylized straight line; on the west coast, near the Western Australia–Northern Territory border there is – unusual in the sixteenth century – a dotted line, or its near equivalent.

So it would seem that the Dieppe cartographers received from their man in Lisbon a map of Australia with a north coast sufficiently resembling Java–Sumbawa, enough to invite them to fit the square top of Arnhem-land into Java, and the pointed top of Cape York into Sumbawa. But these two Australian features would not have exactly coincided with the islands' features, and they would not have exactly filled the two islands. In particular, the real north coast of Arnhem-land, being further south, would have dropped much lower on the page than the north coast of Java. In Rotz's Plane Chart there is indeed a suggestion of this – a false coast, which looks as though he marked this line as he superimposed one map on the other, and then forgot to rub it out. Whether this is the correct reading of the 'false coast' or not, the north coasts of Australia must be visualized as fitting into Java and Sumbawa, but not extending far enough north to touch or approach the real north coasts of the two islands.

Now that Australia's north coast is visualized as sitting lower on the page, it can be seen – perhaps for the first time – that the cigar-shaped island to the west of Darwin and to the north of the Kimberleys is Timor. So there are two Timors on the Dauphin Map: the cigar-shaped island just described is the Timor taken from the Casa da India prototype map of Australia; and over to the east, in its correct place relative to

Java and Sumbawa, is another Timor, the East Indian Timor taken from the *Carta Anonima Portuguesa*.

On the Dauphin Map the East Indies Timor is correctly labelled 'Timor', but the cigar-shaped Australian Timor is labelled 'Laine'. It is not known what 'Laine' means. In the Desceliers map of 1550 this word occurs many times: Timor is 'Isle de Laine'; immediately opposite on the Kimberley coast is 'P. de Laine' (whatever that means); and down in the Antarctic there are many capes marked 'P. de Laine'. The author hopes that the mention here of this minor puzzle may bring some enlightenment from some Portuguese or French linguist who happens to read it. The author candidly does not know, but if 'Laine' had some meaning like 'Unidentified' it would make sense.

If the Australian Timor (which Desceliers labelled 'Laine') had been correctly labelled 'Timor' on the map which reached Dieppe from Lisbon, the Dieppe cartographers would have had the one clue that they lacked. If they had recognised the identity of this island on the two maps, naturally that would have led them to place the continent of Australia in its correct longitudinal position. Unfortunately they did not have that clue, and accordingly Australia was placed in its wrong longitudinal position, south of Java and not south of New Guinea – not south-east of the true Timor, but south-east of a misidentified Timor erroneously called 'Laine', and therefore *south-west* of the true Timor. If this mistake had not been made, the authenticity of the Dieppe Maps would never have been called into question, and this book would have had no excuse to be written.

And this brings us to one last problem in connection with the north coast of Australia – the channel which connects the Gulf of Carpentaria with the west coast, named on the Dieppe Maps 'Rio Grande'. In the Dauphin, in Rotz and in the first Desceliers it shows clearly as a wide, navigable channel, perhaps properly to be termed a Strait. In the 1550 Desceliers it was blacked out. Collingridge fancifully noticed the two agricultural labourers in the pictorial illustration of that map, who have mattocks in their hands and appear to be filling in the channel![4] And in Desliens the channel is omitted, and becomes a mere river.

The channel, the blacking-out of the channel, and the disappearance of the channel all indicate uncertainty on the part of the Dieppe cartographers. First, they had in the back of their minds that Java is an island, and therefore ought to have a south coast. On the *Carta Anonima Portuguesa* the full south coast (Fig. 9.1) is not shown, but the returns are so pronounced that no one could doubt that a south coast is indicated. In those maps which bear labels, Arnhem-land north of the Rio Grande is labelled 'Jave' or 'The Lytel Java' (Rotz), while the large continent south of the Rio Grande is labelled 'Jave-la-Grande' or 'The Londe of Java' (Rotz): this dichotomy shows that they knew that these were two lands, not one, and they needed some sort of a channel to divide them. And above all, they knew that Magellan's *Vitoria* had sailed home south of Java, so there must be a channel there.

So they compromised, deciding that they would fit the new continent into Java and Sumbawa, as the jigsaw required; but at the same time they would still have some sort of a sea channel south of Java, to satisfy the points raised in the last paragraph. Rotz's plane chart is the clearest indication of this. The return of the south-east coast of Java (copied from the *Carta Anonima*) is retained as the north bank of the Rio Grande; the return of the south-west coast becomes a long inlet, coming in south of Darwin. Probably with a little more thought on the part of Rotz and Desceliers these two outlets could have been joined, in which case the Rio Grande would have corresponded with the true south coast of Java.

The fact that the south coasts of Java and Sumbawa are shown blank on the *Carta Anonima Portuguesa*, and on most other Portuguese maps of the sixteenth century, has been made the jumping-off point for a rather pointless argument about this coast, often referred to as the Mystery of the South Coast of Java. The only mystery is why anyone should try to make a mystery out of it. Professor Clark, for instance, ransacks Malay history to build up a kind of 'Cape Bojador' aura about it, with the wicked south coast scaring off Malays and Portuguese alike. Why it did not also scare off the Dutch is not explained.

And Professors Wood[5] and Scott[6] use this alleged Mystery of the South Coast of Java as some kind of evidence, or

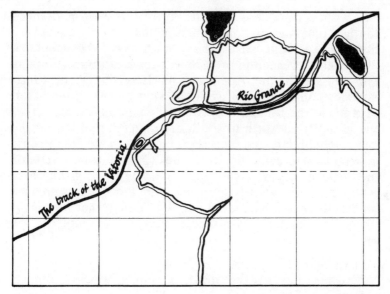

Fig. 14.1 THE RIO GRANDE. The black line is the track of the
Vitoria, as taken from the map of Battista Agnese. Desceliers
provided a waterway south of Java 'to let the *Vitoria* through'.

argument, against the authenticity of the Dieppe Maps themselves. Their argument appears to run thus: if the Portuguese
had no knowledge of the south coast of Java, as their maps
implied, then a fortiori they would have no knowledge of the
seas south of Java, and therefore they could have no knowledge of any islands (or continents) in those seas; and as the
Dieppe Maps pretended that they did have knowledge of a
large continent in those seas, therefore the Dieppe Maps are a
fake. The argument, of course, is absurd. Australia is not
south of Java; it is not an island off the south coast of Java, or
in the seas south of Java – it was wrongly drawn in this
position on the Dauphin Map because of the bad guess of
Desceliers. Australia is in fact a thousand miles further east,
south and south-east of Timor – and no one ever said that the
Portuguese were ignorant of the south coast of Timor, or of
the seas south and south-east of Timor. That is where they
discovered their new continent, not south of Java at all.

It is not correct to say that the Portuguese were ignorant of the fact that Java was an island, or that they were unaware that it had a south coast. Faria y Sousa says:[7] 'Java contains 200 leagues of longitude and 70 leagues of latitude. A mountain range like the Apennines in Italy bisects it, which impedes communication with the south coast.' Linschoten says much the same: cross-country communications across the island from north to south are difficult, and the north-coast inhabitants did not know much about south-coast geography. Actually the 70 leagues (200 miles) estimate of the thickness of Java is too great – perhaps twice as thick as it really is. The implied south coast in the *Carta Anonima* implies this extra thickness. Diogo de Couto rather amusingly likens its outline (on Portuguese maps) to the shape of a fat pig:[8]

> 'The figure of the island of Java resembles a pig, with its hind legs towards the Straits of Sunda, which are much frequented by us.
>
> The southern coast is not frequented, and its bays and ports are not known.'

Professors Wood and Scott[9] and the other mystery-mongers always try to make great capital out of the second sentence in this quotation, but how or why is not clear; for do Couto says exactly what is said here – the south coast of Java is unfrequented by the Portuguese. Full Stop.

The Portuguese knew that it was an island (a little bigger, they believed, but not much bigger, than it is in reality). They knew that it had a south coast, with open sea beyond, and that they could sail there if they wanted to. And that was the understanding of El Cano in the *Vitoria*, no doubt conveyed to him by Magellan before he died. El Cano knew that there was sea south of Java (i.e. that it was not joined to a mainland); he knew that the sea was not mysteriously impassable; and he knew that it was unfrequented. But it suited him to choose an unfrequented route, and so he took his ship home that way – Pigafetta tells us, 'for fear of the King of Portugal'.

And therefore they clearly did not hug the south coasts of Java and Sumatra, but sailed well south of them, as the well-known map of Battista Agnese shows. Describing it in terms of the Dauphin Map, the Agnese track first dips well south through the Gulf of Carpentaria area, then turns rather sharply west in about Lat. 15°s. So Rotz could not make his channel run along the line of the actual south coast of Java, when the *Vitoria* had in fact made its crossing much further south. Adopting the *Vitoria*'s track from the Agnese chart,[10] Rotz allows his Rio Grande to commence at the eastern return; but instead of running westerly to connect up with the western return of the Java coast, the Rio Grande (like the *Vitoria*) veers away from the Java coast and (following the shape on the Agnese map) emerges in Joseph Bonaparte Gulf (Fig. 14.1).

The drawing of a fictitious inland channel across an unexplored continent is, by our standards, a cartographical sin. But in the sixteenth century it was not looked at in that way. Rotz himself, in this same world map, supplied a navigable channel from the Amazon to the La Plata Estuary. Desceliers, in the Dauphin, supplied an equally imaginary channel called the St Helene River, in North Carolina. And this is of sufficient interest to warrant some explanation.

One of the navigators who came to Dieppe, attracted by its new-found maritime vigour, was the Italian Verrazano. In 1524 he made an important voyage up the North American coast, among other things naming the 'Rhode Island' which was to become one of the United States. But on the North Carolina coast he made a major geographical error.[11] Just south of Roanoke Island there is a wide, shallow arm of the sea known as Pamlico Sound, separated from the Atlantic by a row of offshore islands known as the Carolina Banks, one of which contains the celebrated Cape Hatteras. These islands are less than a mile wide, but the chain of islands from Roanoke Island to Cape Lookout appears to constitute a long isthmus, cutting off Pamlico Sound from the Atlantic altogether. Verrazano looked across this 'isthmus', saw the wide waters of Pamlico Sound disappearing beyond the horizon, and immediately decided that it must be the Pacific Ocean; and he drew a map in which the Pacific (which had already been seen by Balboa across the Panama Isthmus) bent back to approach within one mile of the Atlantic at Cape Hatteras. In other words, he mistook Pamlico Sound for the Pacific Ocean.

The Dauphin Map, in its American sector, displays the geography reported by Verrazano;[12] it shows that bent-back Pacific, approaching and almost reaching the Atlantic. But Desceliers goes one better than Verrazano: he invented a channel through the Carolina Banks, connecting the two oceans, and called it the Riv. St Helene. Desceliers has often been criticised for this unauthorised tampering with an explorer's map. He has been accused of irresponsibility, even of lack of professional integrity. Actually, though, Desceliers was not wrong. There is a channel – several channels, in fact – from the Atlantic to Pamlico Sound, and possibly some Dieppois sailor from Verrazano's ship had personally attested to seeing such a channel. There can be no lack of professional integrity in showing a channel where one in fact exists. The mistake was not in the recording of a channel, but in the prior identification of Pamlico Sound with the Pacific Ocean – a mistake for which Verrazano must take the blame, not Desceliers.

And in a similar way Desceliers was not wrong in showing a waterway from the Sumbawa area to the seas south of Sumatra, for such a waterway does exist. Not only did the *Vitoria* pass that way, but thousands of modern ships have passed that way since. Desceliers did not make a mistake in providing the channel; he made the mistake earlier, when he transposed Australia to its incorrect position, making it adjoin Java. His channel was a dimly-understood recognition that something was wrong. The Desceliers channel at Pamlico Sound, the Rotz channel through South America, the Schöner channel near Buenos Aires – all of these offend against good cartography, for the cartographer is inserting a feature which he desires to be there, not one that has been reported to him. The Rio Grande is a lie, but perhaps it is only a white lie: after all, there was a waterway of a different kind there: the *Vitoria* had traversed it, Pigafetta had recorded it, and Battista Agnese had shown it on his map.

The Rio Grande had one curious result. The Dauphin Map was known in Australia in the early days of European settlement. Flinders, for example, had a copy, and had commented on it favourably.[13] The representation of a 'strait' from the Gulf of Carpentaria to the west coast led to the belief that such a strait really existed, and some efforts were made to find

it. Ernest Favenc[14] says 'It was more than probable that this
view was originally suggested by this map [i.e. the Dauphin]
and from it sprang the current belief that an open passage
existed . . . into the Gulf of Carpentaria'.

The lowering of the north coast to conform with Arnhem-
land's coast and the provision of the *Vitoria's* track (the Rio
Grande) are the last two of the interpretative amendments
that have been engaging our attention over the last seven
chapters. As a final recapitulation, it is instructive to go
through the progressive amendments again, but this time in
reverse order – not from erroneous map to real coast, but
from real coast to erroneous map. This is attempted in
diagrammatic form in the series of maps in Fig. 14.2, and by
now this series should be self-explanatory.

   It should not be thought that all of these troublesome
amendments have to be made in order to coerce a recalcitrant
map into some kind of a resemblance to the real shape of
Australia. When no amendments at all are made, the
Dauphin is still a recognizable map of Australia, sufficient
without alteration to evidence the Portuguese discovery. But
it is valuable to examine and to understand the projection on
which it is based, the longitudinal and magnetic problems, the
explainable errors which crept in from navigator to Lisbon
map-maker, from Lisbon map-maker to French spy, from spy
to Dieppe cartographer, and even from Dieppe cartographer
to later Dieppe cartographers. When we understand these
things, we realize that it is a miracle that the Dauphin Map is
as good as it is; with the amendments which the evidence
compels, it is a still better map.

   In the elucidation of the very comparable sixteenth-
century Portuguese charts of Eastern Canada, the Canadian
and American scholars found similar problems, applied similar processes, and made similar amendments. The legitimacy
of the arguments presented in this book can be tested against
the standards set by them. The late Admiral S. E. Morison,
for example, a cartographic critic with a world-wide reputation for sober and responsible scholarship, worked on the
early maps of Newfoundland in this way. In the passage
reproduced below we see him tilting them, making magnetic

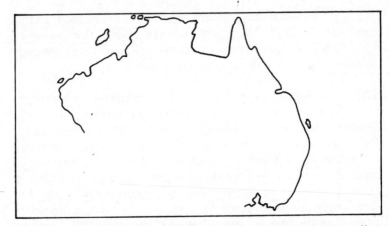

I. THE CONTINENTAL BASIS. This is a reasonably accurate outline from Abrolhos Islands to Warrnambool (the two furthest points evidencing Portuguese visits). The west coast was visited spasmodically from Timor, resulting in some errors: King's Sound and Exmouth Gulf are rolled into one, Barrow Island is too large, Timor is too close.

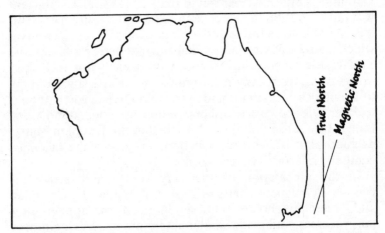

II. MAGNETIC DEVIATION. Next, the south-east coast is adjusted from true north to magnetic north. The northern and western coasts are not greatly affected (see Chapter 13).

Fig. 14.2 THE EVOLUTION OF THE DAUPHIN (continued on next page).

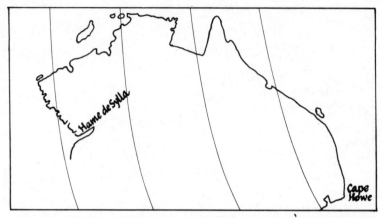

III. ERRATION. The curved meridians caused by Erration (Chapter 12), based on the Meridian of Malacca, are now drawn in, and the coast adjusted to accord. Note how Cape Howe projects towards the side of the page. On the west coast, Martim Behaim's Hame de Sylla is added to the map (see Chapter 10).

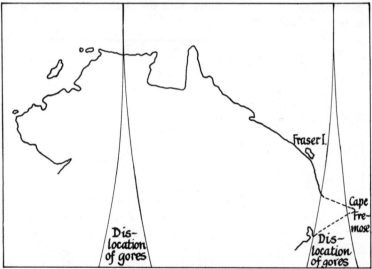

IV. THE DISLOCATION OF GORES. Assuming that the gores were dislocated in the two places shown (Chapter 11), the land-shape spreads as shown. The south coast (south of Fraser Island) dips south, and Cape Howe juts out beyond the dislocation to become Cape Fremose (Chapter 11).

Fig. 14.2 THE EVOLUTION OF THE DAUPHIN (continued).

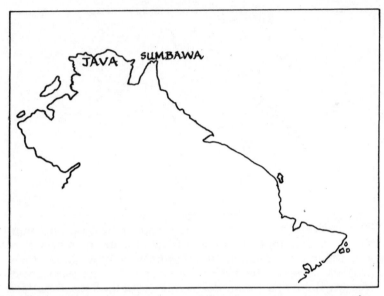

V. DESCELIERS' JIGSAW. Java and Sumbawa are now superimposed upon the north coast, and the Australian north coast entirely disappears.

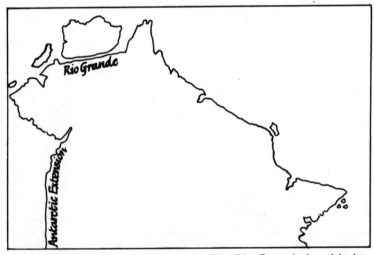

VI. THE FINAL FORM OF THE DAUPHIN. The Rio Grande is added to let the *Vitoria* through (Chapter 14). On the west coast the Antarctic Extension is shown as a perpendicular line (Chapter 10) and the east coast is joined to the bottom of the page with two scallops.

Fig. 14.2   THE EVOLUTION OF THE DAUPHIN (continued).

corrections, rectifying detail, supplying missing coasts, interpreting scallops, and so on: and opposite his paragraphs are
set out selections from the argument of this book, re-phrased
to bring out the likenesses both in the problems involved and
in the solutions applied.[15]

MORISON ON NEWFOUNDLAND

We have only cartographic evidence about what was going on
in northern waters. These
(three) early maps tell us a great
deal. Suppose we tilt a modern
map of Newfoundland about 40
degrees so that the coast
appears to run almost due north
and south, and compare it with
the delineations of the same
coast on three old maps which
took no account of compass variations. This will indicate a
gradual unfolding and correction of the coast line ...

The first is the Cantino Map-
pemonde of 1502, still preserved in the Biblioteca Estense
at Modena. The 'Terra del Rey
de Portuguall' (Newfoundland)
is placed much too far east in
order to get it on the Portuguese
side of the Line of Demarcation.
The west coast is vague, since
nobody knew anything about it.
Newfoundland is out of scale,
lengthwise, being twice as long
as Ireland and longer than Great
Britain.

The next outline is on the Pedro
Reinel Map. Here the big island
is not named, but two Portuguese flags are planted

RE-PHRASED PARALLELS

We have only cartographic evidence as to what took place on
the east Australian coast. The
seven Dieppe maps tell us a
great deal. Suppose we tilt a
modern map of Australia about
$22\frac{1}{2}°$ so that the coast runs somewhat south-easterly, and com-
pare it with the delineation of
the same coast on the seven old
maps which were drawn on
different projections and also
took no account of compass variations. This will indicate a
knowledge of the coast ...

The first is the Dauphin Map, of
1536, still preserved in the British Museum, London. Jave-la-
Grande (the continent of
Australia) is placed much too far
west – Collingridge says to get it
on the Portuguese side of the
Line. The Gulf of Carpentaria is
vague, since nobody had
entered it. Australia is out of
scale, stretching over 50 degrees
of latitude instead of 40 degrees.

Another map is that of Nicholas
Desliens. Here the big island is
not embellished, but Portuguese
flags are planted thereon. Our

thereon. Our third map is the Miller No. 1.

other maps are by Rotz, Desceliers, Vallard and Le Testu.

Note a little north of centre on the three old maps, a deep bay containing three harbours. Comparing this with the modern map, it is evidently meant for Notre Dame and White Bays rolled into one . . .

Note in the centre of the north-west coast on all of these old maps is a deep bay. When we compare this with a modern map, it is evidently meant for King's Sound and Exmouth Gulf rolled into one . . .

West and north of these capes all the early maps show the Strait of Belle Isle, but it fades out in such a way as to suggest that the Portuguese navigators supposed it to be just another fiord. And the west coast of Newfoundland is always conventionalised as a straight line, half-moon, or series of scallops, proving it to have been as yet undiscovered.

In the south-east corner all the Dieppe Maps (except Rotz) show Bass Strait closed at the end in such a way as to suggest that the Portuguese navigators supposed that there was no passage through it to the west. The hypothetical lines joining Australia to the Antarctic are always conventionalised as a straight line (in the west) or a series of scallops (in the east) providing that they did not know whether it was so connected or not.

Equally significant evidence of Portuguese supremacy on the outer Newfoundland coast are [Portuguese names] . . . found, in various spellings on all the early maps.

Equally significant evidence of Portuguese penetration of the Australian coast are Portuguese names found in various spellings on all the Dieppe Maps.

An impressive record indeed of the Portuguese impact on Newfoundland.

An impressive record indeed of the Portuguese impact on Australia.

Chapter 15

FROM ROTZ TO DESLIENS

To make for greater simplicity, most of the foregoing discussion has been illustrated by reference to the Dauphin, conjecturally by Desceliers, of 1536, although in some chapters the Rotz Plane Chart, the Rotz Circular and the Desceliers Royal held the stage. The full list of the Dieppe Maps, from the Dauphin onwards, is:

Dauphin	1536
Desliens (damaged)	1541
Rotz Plane	1542
Rotz Circular	1542
Desceliers 'Royal'	1546
Desceliers	1550
Desceliers (lost)	1553
Vallard	1547
Le Testu	1556
Desliens	1563
Desliens	1566

The third (and fourth) of these Dieppe maps are the two by Jean Rotz. Possibly in actual date of preparation they precede the Dauphin, as they contain references to Cartier's first Canadian voyage only, whereas the Dauphin contains references to his second voyage as well.[1] But even if they were prepared earlier, their publication must have been held back; the date 1542 makes them subsequent in date of publication to the Dauphin of 1536 and the first Desliens of 1541.

Jean Rotz (or John Rose) was of Scottish descent, but he went to Dieppe for his training, and to all intents and purposes became a Norman. Later he went to the Low Countries, and joined the service of Anne of Cleves, before her marriage with Henry VIII. Later again he came to England, presumably with the party of Anne of Cleves, and entered service as a hydrographer in England. His book, the 'Boke of Idrography' was produced in manuscript at this time, and was presented to Henry VIII, to whom it is dedicated. It seems reasonable to presume that it was part of Anne's wedding present to him.

The 'Boke' is dated, by Rotz himself, 1542; if it were not for that, it would undoubtedly be presumed to have an earlier date; the book is a kind of atlas, and the Rotz Plane Chart and the Rotz Circular are contained in it.

Rotz was not only a cartographer but (in J. A. Williamson's words) 'a rare combination of practical seaman and navigator, and book-learned geographer, with mathematical skill'. Among other things he was the world's leading expert on the Variation of the Magnetic Compass, and the founder of the science of geomagnetics. From this, he became deeply immersed in the study of longitude, and believed that he had found a method of fixing longitude at sea by means of magnetic variation. If the magnetic variation changes from 10°E to 9°E in (say) Long. 5°w, would not observation of the point at which the change occurred fix the longitude? It turned out that, because of the capriciousness of magnetic variation, this theory would not work. But his pioneering in this and other fields of study marks him as a man of intellectual ability far above his contemporary mapmakers.

Everyone speaks in the highest terms of his ability and his integrity. All of the Dieppe Maps are of great importance in the cartographical history of Canada, but of the Rotz Plane Chart Professor Ganong says: 'This map stands out in the cartography of Eastern Canada.' It is this high professional competence that gives point to the reliance placed on Rotz's variation of line in the examination of the Plane Chart in the previous chapter. In lesser draftsmen, unevenness of line might result from mere clumsiness in drafting: in Rotz, the variation of line appears meaningful, deliberate and (for us) highly informative and of great importance. His influence can be seen in all of the later Dieppe Maps. In pure draftsmanship his only rival among the Dieppe cartographers was Nicolas Desliens.

The Rotz Plane Chart is similar in outline to the Dauphin, but with more detail, more subtlety, more authority, more cartographical skill. It differs from the Dauphin in its treatment of the Gulf of Carpentaria, which in Rotz is so narrow and shallow as to be almost insignificant. As said before, it is believed that the Gulf was not indicated on the Casa da India prototype, leaving it to each individual cartographical editor to arrange it as he saw fit. The integrity of Rotz would not allow him to enlarge the entrance beyond what was the known scale distance from Java to Sumbawa, and so he made his Gulf very narrow.

Our earliest knowledge of Rotz comes from Admiral James Burney. Burney sailed on Cook's second and third voyages; and after his return to England became the greatest contemporary authority on voyages to the South Seas. His monumental *Chronological History of Voyages and Discoveries in the South Sea or Pacific Ocean* (London, 1803), in five volumes, became the standard work on Pacific voyaging. Because of his knowledge of navigation, his Navy rank, his personal contact with Cook and his colleagues, his own role as an explorer and his great personal reputation, Burney's judgments must carry weight far beyond those of subsequent armchair navigators such as Professor G. Arnold Wood: and Burney's considered judgment is that the Dauphin and the Rotz maps, both of which he knew, do portray Australia, and are records of authentic explorations of the Australian coasts. He wrote:[2]

'Evidences however exist which leave very little reason to doubt that it [i.e. Australia] was known at no late period of the sixteenth century.'

And again:

'The general outlines of the sea-coasts are drawn with more appearance of correctness, and the whole is executed with better judgement, than the credit which is given to that date for geographical knowledge afforded reason to expect . . . The whole is well worth description as an excellent specimen of the geography of that early period . . . with greater resemblance to that of New Holland than is to be found in the charts of many years later date. All these circumstances justify and support the opinion that the Northern and Western coasts of New Holland were known, and were the Great Java of the sixteenth century. There are likewise reasons for supposing that the eastern coast had been seen . . . . The chart and dedication of Rotz . . . are proofs that, at that early period, many voyages were undertaken; and it may be concluded, many discoveries were made, of which no account was ever published; that of some, every remembrance has died away; and the various indications that appear in the old charts, to which no clue can be found, may be the remains, and possibly the only remains, of this.'

By the time that Burney wrote, the Dauphin Map was already available to the public through the publication of Dalrymple's facsimile; but it was Burney himself who first announced to the world the existence of the Rotz charts. He probably obtained the material from Dalrymple, for in his Introduction he acknowledges his debt to Dalrymple in general terms; but Burney's announcement of the discovery of the Rotz charts does not explicitly attribute the find to Dalrymple:

'Since Mr Dalrymple published the fac-simile, a discovery has been made in the King's Library in the British Museum . . . dedicated to the King of England. At the beginning is written "This book of Idrography is made by me Johne Rotz 1542".'

If Burney is accurate in this, the Rotz charts were not found until after 1786. For that reason, Barbie du Bocage is wrong in his insinuation that the English authorities knew of them before Cook sailed, or at the most he could only have been implying that the authorities secretly knew of them before that date. This fixing of the date also renders incorrect Admiral S. E. Morison's assertion that the Rotz charts were discovered by the American Justin Winsor in 1884.

Burney, as an expert cartographer, was particularly interested in the mathematical structure of the Rotz Circular. It is not a natural projection – that is, it cannot be mechanically produced by beaming a light through a transparent globe on to a screen; it is a piece of pure mathematical theory, something of a mathematical tour-de-force. It is mentioned at some length here, to underline Rotz's striking ability, for the intellectual calibre of this man who lent his name to the Dieppe Maps is one of the strongest indications of their authenticity. Burney thought Rotz's invention of this sophisticated graticule, at so early a date, to be quite remarkable.

The Rotz Projection is based on the geometrical axiom that when any three points are known (not being three points in a straight line) it is always possible to draw one, and only one, circle to pass through all three. Rotz therefore drew his world in two hemispheres, each represented as a circle, each bisected by a horizontal straight-line Equator and a perpendicular straight-line Prime Meridian. The Equator is then divided into 180 equal units (representing 180 degrees of longitude in that hemisphere). Then for each meridian of longitude three points are known – the North Pole, the South Pole, and the appropriate Equatorial point. Each meridian is then drawn as the true arc of a true circle, passing through these three points (see Plate VI).

For latitude, the Prime Meridian is similarly divided into 180 units; and each peripheral semicircle of the hemisphere is similarly divided into 180 units. Then 180 true arcs of true circles can be drawn through the appropriate three points for each line of latitude. Thus every meridian of longitude and each line of latitude is shown as part of a true circle. Rotz's Projection has not been much used in cartography, for the representation of the world as two hemispheres is usually not convenient. But whenever we see a symbol of a terrestrial hemisphere in a badge or a trademark or an ornamentation, it is very probable that it will be the multiple-circle projection which Rotz invented. Today it is known as the 'Global Projection'. For Rotz to have invented this advanced piece of cartography in 1542 was an outstanding achievement; and Burney, himself highly qualified in this field, wrote admiringly:

'The parallels are circular and are described through equal divisions of the right circle and of the primitive circle; a method of projection which, notwithstanding its advantages for purposes of geography, has since been so much out of use, that when M. de la Hire revived it 150 years afterwards, he was supposed to be the original inventor.'

On this topic Rotz was 150 years ahead of his time, as Burney pointed out. The same might be said for the whole of Rotz's hydrography.

Because on the Rotz Circular the outline of Australia is centrally positioned, lying centrally across the Prime Meridian, the curved meridians do not help to correct the Erration error. If by chance the outline of Australia had been positioned obliquely on the right-hand side of its hemisphere, there would have been a fortuitous correction, as far as the eye is concerned. Even without this, the shape of Australia on the Rotz Circular seems to be particularly recognisable: unlike the Dauphin and the Rotz Plane, the Circular has no place-names on it, and no joinder to the bottom of the page; and this uncluttered appearance helps the eye to appreciate its recognisable approximation to the real shape of Australia. Burney could see this, and he joins with Matthew Flinders in giving the expert testimony: 'The many instances of resemblance to the present charts which are to be found in the general outline of this land, it is not easy to imagine were produced by chance.'

With reason, Professor J. A. Williamson describes him as a man who 'refuses to theorise, who leaves blank what he does not know ... [whose] work shows him to have been a cool critic of cartographic material'.[3] If, in 1542, a geographer with the reputation and experience of Jean Rotz had left a document stating that he was in possession of a Portuguese map, the genuineness of which he did not doubt, the provenance of which was known to him, the credibility of which was beyond dispute, and that this map evidenced Portuguese discovery of a great continent between the Equator and Lat. 50°s, but with uncertainty as to its longitudinal position, we would today hail that document as impeccable evidence of the secret discovery of Australia. By including that map in his book, Jean Rotz did no less.

The fifth of the Dieppe Maps is the Desceliers of 1546. This has also been mentioned previously, as it is the map which attached Australia to Mercator's Antarctic continent. It is a mappe-monde, made for King Henry II of France, and for that reason is often known as the 'Carte de Henri II' and sometimes as the 'Royal' Map. It was formerly owned by the French geographer E. F. Jomard, and later by the Earl of Crawford, and is now in the John Rylands Library, Manchester. An excellent facsimile is in the Australian National

Library, Canberra, and a reproduction is given in Plate V.

Cartographically, it is much better than the Dauphin; but, like the Dauphin, it was considered to be of uncertain author-ship. C. H. Coote, the keeper of maps at the British Museum, by accident noticed a slight thickening of the paint in one corner, near the outline of Japan, leading to the uncovering of the words 'Faictes à Arques par P.D.' and the date. In its detail, it links with the Rotz Plane Chart, suggesting either that Desceliers collaborated with Rotz, or (more probably) that he had the Rotz Plane Chart in front of him. To this, Desceliers added the Antarctic Extension, which has already been discussed; and on the bottom of the map, in the area of this Antarctic continent, there is an inscription which, when translated, says 'The Great Southern Land not yet discov-ered'. This has wrongly been claimed as a denial of the validity of the Australian sector, but that claim cannot be substantiated. The inscription refers only to Antarctica.

Most of the critics regard the Desceliers of 1546 as a splendid map of the world. Dr J. G. Kohl writes:[4]

'This map is not only one of the most brilliant, but also one of the most exact and trustworthy pictures of the world which we have in the first part of the sixteenth century. It gives accurately all that was known in 1546 . . . The author of the map must have been a well-instructed, intelligent and conscientious man.'

The map is beautifully illustrated, and its Canadian sector is of especial interest because of the portrait of Roberval addressing his soldiers on the banks of the Saguenay. When E. F. Jomard wrote of this map, it was renowned for its brilliant colours; but it has not aged well, and is now very faded. Nevertheless, it is still a beautiful specimen of the cartographer's art, and it shows out well on the dust-cover of this book.

The Desceliers of 1550[5] is very like the Vallard, which pre-dates it; but it is unique in being covered with cartouches, little squares containing geographical information about the different places. None of these cartouches throws any further light on Australia. The map was discovered in Padua in 1847, and is now in the British Museum. This is the map in which the Rio Grande channel is first drawn in and then blacked out, suggesting that it is not a feature genuinely taken from the Casa da India prototype, but inserted in the earlier Dieppe Maps for reasons which then appealed to the cartographers, but which were since discarded. There is, or was, also another Desceliers, dated 1553, once owned by Abbé Bubies of Vienna, but now apparently lost.

Nicolas Vallard produced his world map in 1547,[6] but it adds little to the others, It echoes the Rotz Plane Chart of 1542 and anticipates the Desceliers of 1550. Vallard's map is peculiar in that it is upside-down, with south at the top. This map is associated with the name of the great collector Sir Thomas Phillips, who toured Europe after the Napoleonic War, buying up and saving from destruction countless historic maps which had been disturbed when libraries and mansions were damaged during the fighting. It is now in the H. E. Huntingdon Library, San Marino, California, and it is the Dieppe Map which is best known on that side of the Atlantic. It is important linguistically, containing more Portuguese place-names than any of the other Dieppe Maps; and the strongest linguistic proofs of the Portuguese provenance of the Dieppe Maps are drawn from the evidence which Vallard presents.

If the Vallard is the most Portuguese of the Dieppe Maps, the Guillaume le Testu[7] is the most French, and also the most artistic; yet cartographically, it is the most unreliable. Le Testu's *Cosmographie Universelle* (1555) is decorated with the most evocative of pictures, calling to anyone with adventure in his blood to follow across the wondrous seas to 'far-away islands with strange-sounding names', to the lands of mystery and romance which beckoned so strongly in that century. And one of his most romantic pictures depicts a Portuguese ship, flying a Portuguese flag.

But all of this is at the expense of cartographical accuracy, unusual among the Dieppe Maps. Where the other eight or nine, from the Dauphin onwards, can be compared with each other point by point, Le Testu escapes into a free rendering away from reality. He himself warns the reader that he is depicting much from imagination; and as he incorporates fictions from older sources, especially from Oronce Finé, his work is retrograde. This is especially so in his delineation of the southern continent. It has the Finéan bulges in many places, imaginary promontories burgeoning towards the Equator wherever he has a blank space to fill in. To Le Testu, Australia is just one of these promontories, among many: and while its shape reveals it as a descendant of the Dauphin Map's Australia, its deviation into inaccuracy and free line dissociates it from the main line of the Dieppe work. As Ganong says, the artist has dominated the cartographer. The *Cosmographie Universelle* is in the Department of the Ministry of War, Paris; and in France Le Testu's work is regarded more highly than it is in English-speaking countries.

The reputation which Le Testu enjoys in his home country may be enhanced by the theory sometimes aired by French writers that, after the Portuguese probes petered out at the end of the first quarter of the sixteenth century, they were replaced by French probes in the second quarter: and that Le Testu's map enshrines information gleaned from these sources. To anyone whose eye is attuned to the Dauphin and its derivatives, Le Testu's map looks merely like a badly-drawn, carelessly executed and indeed incompetent rehash of the traditional Dieppe outline. But it is true that in one or two respects his deviations from the traditional shape may be interpreted as new information. For example, all of the other Dieppe Maps show King's Sound and Exmouth Gulf (both on the north-west coast) confused and combined – 'rolled into one', as has been said. Le Testu appears to have this sorted out, as he provides two gulfs, approximately in their right places. Does this record some unpublished French visit to the area?

To the author's mind, a minor correction of this kind does not need to be explained by postulating some massive international expedition. The coast is just opposite Timor; and over the years the Portuguese of Timor must have increased their familiarity at least a little. Some of this information might have been picked up by Le Testu.

Le Testu also has some link with the Italian engraver Paolo Forlani, but Forlani's strange map has not yet been fully investigated, and the author is unable to give any firm

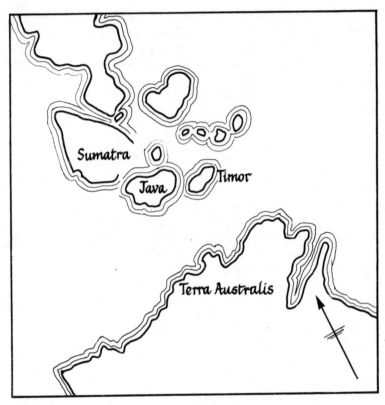

Fig. 15.1 PAOLO FORLANI 1565 (transposed to Mercator's Projection).

interpretation of it. Forlani's map of 1565 – *Universale Descrittione di tutta la terra conosciuta* (Venice) – is a remarkable and somewhat mysterious production, which on the face of it implies advancement in the exploration of Australia. An outline of it, transposed to Mercator's projection, is given in Fig. 15.1: and, as can be seen, it portrays a recognisable Australia, more correctly positioned than in any of the Dieppe Maps, though wrongly tilted off the true north-south line by many degrees. Forlani anticipates de Jode, but the full Le Testu–Forlani story (whatever it is) awaits further research. For our present purposes, the Forlani is at least one more piece of evidence that Australia was known, clearly visualised and identifiably charted decades before the first Dutch sighting in 1606.

The last Dieppe cartographer demanding our attention is Nicolas Desliens, who is just the opposite of Le Testu. Not only Le Testu, but all of the other Dieppe cartographers (except Rotz in his Circular Chart), were producing highly ornamented, beautifully painted 'picture-maps' to adorn the studies and libraries of the wealthy clients who acquired them. All of them are smothered in illustrations of native life, exciting events, fauna, flora and landscapes. But Desliens shunned these art forms altogether, using no ornamentation other than Portuguese flags flying over the Australian continent. On the other hand, his geography is impeccable. His first map (1541) is clearly drawn directly from the Casa da India prototype; even his last map, a quarter of a century later, avoids the additions which had become encrusted upon it over the intervening years, and serves up to us again an outline which gives every evidence of nautical accuracy. Because of the lack of pictures, his maps look like mariners' portolans – which, indeed, is what they are. It is conjectured that his maps may have been prepared for some person of rank who actually intended to use them at sea.

But it is in the detail of the coast that Desliens is so outstanding and astounding. Any geographer who is well acquainted with the details of the Australian coast can take any of the Dieppe Maps (except, perhaps, Le Testu) and find considerable correspondence between the detail shown and the detail observed. With Desliens, this point-by-point correspondence reaches its pinnacle. The reader is referred forward to Fig. 24.2, where the Cooktown coast of Desliens is shown beside the Cooktown coast from a modern map, and the same coast from Cook's chart: the correspondence is seen to be extremely close. In later parts of this book, when these correspondences are being traced, the author for preference will be drawing upon Desliens for the geographical detail; and this is not because of cartographical advancement over the years, for the very early Desliens of 1541 (in Dresden) is just as accurate as the Desliens of 1566 (in the National Library at Paris).

This draws our attention to the fact that Desliens is unique in surviving in more than one copy, and in more than one city. This does not apply to any of the other Dieppe Maps, and it raises the question why this is so. Why are there so few copies of the Dieppe Maps in existence? Why were the Maps not better known outside of Dieppe in their own day? The answer to these questions is the same. The Dieppe Maps were not common mariners' charts. They were works of art, high forms of creative expression, prestigious, expensive – 'picture maps', if you like, painted with the care and finesse of a great Master, and not capable of reproduction or susceptible to repetition. One does not inquire why Leonardo da Vinci painted only one copy of the *Mona Lisa*.

When Desceliers painted his 1546 'Royal' map at the order of the King of France, when Rotz produced his 'Boke of Idrography' for the King of England, it would probably have been lèse-majesté to have made additional copies for lesser beings; and as the originals went directly into a royal palace or library, there to remain for centuries, they probably would not often be seen outside of those repositories. Therefore they could not have great circulation, and they could not gain great popular reputation. One argument often raised against the Dieppe Maps is, Why were they (apparently) unknown to the great Lisbon cartographers? If the discovery of Australia was on the secret list, then of course it was not open to Lopo Homem or Vaz Dourado to break the Portuguese equivalent of the Official Secrets Act. But if Homem or Vaz Dourado obtained a copy of the Dauphin or the Rotz Plane Chart from Dieppe or from Versailles or from London, it would surely be no breach of the Politica do Sigilo to publish material that was already available in the outside world. The answer again is, that because of the character of these artistic picture-maps, they were not in circulation, and it would probably be just as hard for a Portuguese to pirate a map from the foreign king's library as it would be for a Frenchman or an Englishman to pirate one from the Casa da India.

But with Desliens it was different. His maps are beautifully executed specimens of cartography, and as maps they are very artistic; but they were maps, not paintings, not picture-maps in the Vallard and Le Testu tradition. The ordinary portolan,

PLATE I Portuguese Cannon, found at Carronade Island, Western Australia.

PLATE II The ruins at BITTANGABEE BAY, New South Wales consist of roofless walls made of local stone, rubble and seashell mortar, and might well be the remains of a 16th-century Portuguese fort. Was this the winter headquarters of Mendonça in 1524?

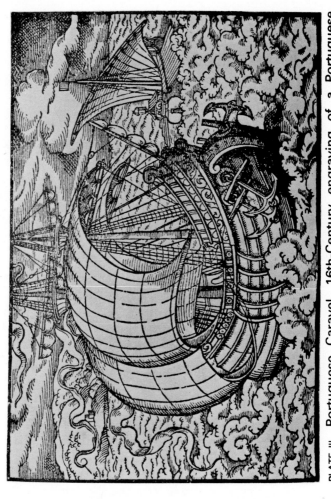

PLATE III Portuguese Caravel. 16th-Century engraving of a Portuguese Caravel, the ship in which the early explorers braved some of the most dangerous seas in the world. Reproduced by permission of the Mansell Collection, London.

PLATE IV The Dauphin Map, 1536. Part of map, showing the Australian continent. Reproduced by permission of the British Library.

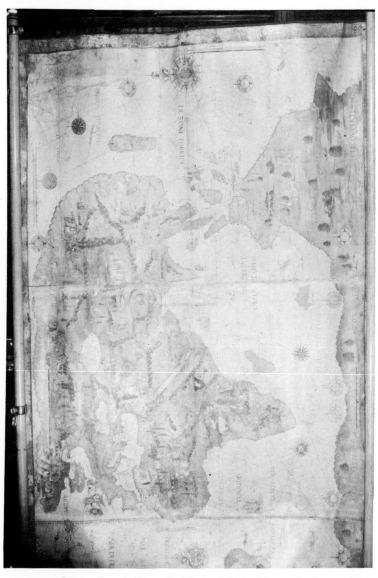

PLATE V Desceliers' 'Royal' Map, 1546. Map of the world, showing all continents, including hypothetical Antarctic continent. Reproduced by permission of the John Rylands collection, University of Manchester Library.

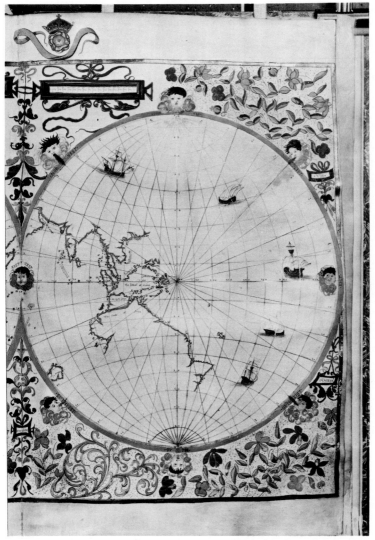

PLATE VI   Jean Rotz, Circular Chart, 1542. Asian–Australian
hemisphere. Reproduced by permission of the British Library.

SPE=
CVLVM
ORBIS
TERRÆ

ANTVERPIÆ.
Sumptibus Viduæ et Hæredū Gerardi de Iudæis

PLATE VII   De Jode's 'Kangaroo'—the title page of Cornelis
de Jode's *Speculum Orbis Terrae* (left) as it appears, and
(right) with the unidentified animal, bottom right, supplied

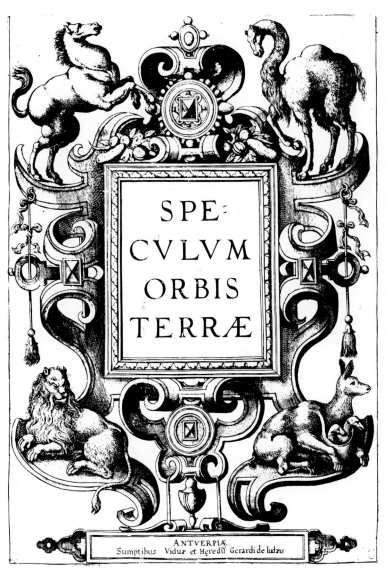

SPE-
CVLVM
ORBIS
TERRÆ

with a Kangaroo's head. Reproduced by permission
of Rijksmuseum, Nederlands Scheepvaart Museum,
Amsterdam.

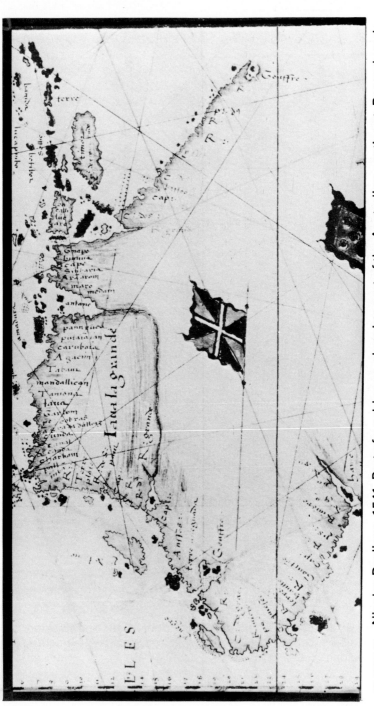

PLATE VIII Nicolas Desliens, 1541. Part of world map, showing part of the Australian continent. Reproduced by permission of the British Library.

beautiful though it is in its own way, does not pretend to the elegance and style of a Desliens; but, nevertheless, the maps of Nicolas Desliens, especially the later ones of 1563 and 1566, are near-normal portolans, and as such could be reproduced by the ordinary techniques of map-office copying, in the same way that any other portolan could be. And because his charts became the property of seagoing gentlemen (not only kings and princes) they had the chance to scatter all over the world. The presence of specimens in places as far distant apart as Paris and Dresden indicates this, and quite likely there were other copies, possibly there still are other copies, in libraries and archives elsewhere.

The span of Desliens' working life was greater than that of any other Dieppe cartographer. His first map, signed by him and dated 1541, is actually the second of the series – indeed, if Professor Harrisse is correct in postponing the date of the Dauphin because of the 'Tutonaguy' evidence, the Desliens of 1541 is actually the first. As his last maps were produced in 1563 and 1566, he is also the last.

The Desliens world map of 1541 is (or was) in the ex-Royal Library in Dresden. The library was destroyed by bombing in the Second World War, and the map in which we are interested was damaged. Fortunately, before this damage, it was painstakingly copied and published by Hantsch and Schmidt in their facsimile atlas *Kartographische Denkmäler* (Leipzig, 1903); and the reproduction in Plate VIII of this book is taken from that facsimile.

But Desliens lived into the decade of the 1560's, which witnessed an enormous increase in the availability and circulation of maps and charts, and of sailing directions and other books pertaining to them. Before 1560 maps were mainly hand-made, on awkward, large, single sheets, expensive, few in number and hard to obtain. They reached only the governing classes, the maritime classes and the very wealthy. But after 1560 the hunger for geographical knowledge was touching all educated people; and to satisfy this popular demand, maps began to be mass-produced – engraved, printed, and otherwise multiplied. The next step was to bind several maps together into what came to be known as 'atlases'. The first atlas to be so published the the *Theatrum Orbis Terrarum* of

Ortelius in 1570, and a new era in cartography was ushered in. The public began to buy maps, and for the first time maps were freely offered for sale in shops. This produced a new professional class, the professional map-sellers, including Mercator, Ortelius and de Jode. Map-sellers in the different capitals established trading channels between themselves, and in this way the international circulation of maps began.

Nicolas Desliens is a link between the old order and the new. His style lent itself to the requirements. It seems that when he became aware of the new demand, he got out his old 1541 map, and made copies – two of which are known to exist, but no doubt there were more – and his work circulated in Germany and other parts of Europe. Evidence of this influence can be traced in the output of these new commercial map-sellers. When Sebastian Cabot, pretending that he had sailed with his famous father when in fact he had not, desired to counterfeit a map to substantiate his false claim, he clearly took Desliens' map and plagiarised from it. The publication of this plagiarised map is of importance in the history of Newfoundland and in the biography of Sebastian Cabot; but to us it is only of importance in showing that Desliens was known abroad, and that he was in the mainstream of the cartographical currents of the day. And when we here produce evidence to show that Mercator had knowledge of at least one of the Dieppe Maps, the natural inference is that the one he was using was the Desliens. The dates of these two world maps – Desliens 1566, Mercator 1569 – seem to support this assumption. In the next chapter, where the influence of the Dieppe Maps on Mercator and other late sixteenth-century cartographers is traced, this assumption will be employed, and this influence which flows on in the history of cartography will be attributed to Nicolas Desliens.

Chapter 16

MERCATOR AND DE JODE

In Chapter 10 something was said of the genesis of Terra Australis Incognita. Schöner had received information about João de Lisboa's supposed strait through the middle of South America. He knew that the northern segment of the continent (north of the alleged strait) extended to the Equator; and he took it for granted that the southern segment (i.e. Patagonia, south of the alleged strait) similarly extended to the South Pole. So he prepared his globe[1] on this assumption, with two large Antarctic islands (or, more probably, one large horseshoe-shaped island) circling the globe in high latitudes. And this supposed continent was not limited to the latitudes where the continent of Antarctica really exists today, but instead it extended Equator-wards over much of its extent.

After Magellan's voyage, Schöner had to modify his conception, receding his Antarctic continent where it passed under the tip of South America and again under the Cape of Good Hope, but still permitting it to burgeon northwards in great bulges in the Pacific area. In his globe of 1523 (now lost) and the comparable globe of 1533 (still extant) his hypothetical continent, swollen to immense size, circles the globe almost as far north as the Tropic of Capricorn; and it is furbished with capes and bays of the most fanciful kind.[1] This is misleading cartography, for the fictional detail invites acceptance as real; and the failure to distinguish between that which is real and that which is fanciful confused and misled subsequent cartographers, creating doubts and disputes which have continued to irritate scholars down to the present day.

Most of the contemporary cartographers, while adopting this Schönerian continent, were more modest in their pretensions. Mapmakers such as Franciscus Monachus, Battista Agnese and Gastaldi contented themselves with a more modest Antarctic continent, not greatly in excess of the

Antarctica seen on modern maps. But Oronce Finé in his double-cordiform (*Nova et Integra universi orbis descriptio*, 1531)[2] retained all of the Schönerian excess; and his hypothetical continent, too, displays huge bulging promontories protruding from the Antarctic Circle right up to the Tropic of Capricorn. And like Schöner (whom he was copying), he muddies the truth with his fictional capes and inlets.

Mercator – in his earlier career, at least – was an admirer and follower of Oronce Finé: and he followed his master in also producing a double-cordiform in 1538,[3] quite slavishly imitating Finé, and with much of his geographical information drawn from him. But Mercator could see that Finé's great southern continent was exaggerated; he accepted the Ptolemaic idea that there must be some counterbalancing continent in the far south, but he was not willing to certify the existence of unreported land right up to the Tropic: so he dropped the coast back to the position approximately suggested by Monachus. In his double-cordiform Mercator retains the Finéan type of detail – bulges and promontories, capes and bays, in imaginative profusion – but by limiting the supposed coasts to the high latitudes of 50°s and over, he avoided the Finéan excess. It was this chart that Desceliers used as the model for his Antarctic Extension. The Desceliers of 1546 is virtually the Dauphin Map of Australia, attached to Mercator's Great South Land.

Mercator, then, in 1538 showed an entirely unobstructed rectangle of sea between the Equator and Lat. 50°s, and between Madagascar and Peru. Yet in his next world map in 1569 (the famous Mercator's Projection map) he does show a large land in the approximate area of Australia. What caused him to change his mind? In between the years 1538 and 1569 no voyage of discovery occurred which could have changed his thinking. There were no other maps in the libraries of the world (other than the Dieppe Maps) which might have come to his attention in this intervening period, that were capable of changing his thinking in this way. And yet in that period something happened which forced Mercator to abandon his 1538 beliefs, to change his mind completely, turning about to accept that after all there *is* something more than ocean in that rectangle, that there is a continental mass in the area, which we call the Australian area today.

The evidence for this can be seen in the famous Mercator's Projection world map of 1569,[4] but not quite as clearly as we would like, for a cartouche (a little square, with information printed in it) unfortunately obtrudes into the area in which we are interested; and while Mercator indicates a continent in that position, the cartouche largely hides the shape and the detail which we most particularly need to see. But happily this missing information can be supplied from another source. Gerard Mercator spent the last years of his life in sorting and arranging his great collection of maps for printing in one of the new atlases. He died before his own atlas was published. But after his death his son, Rumold Mercator, attended to its publication, and in this atlas the map in which we are interested again appears, this time without the obscuring cartouche. The cartographic evidence that is needed can be taken from Gerard Mercator's map as it appears in Rumold Mercator's atlas; and the coasts of Australia as they there appear show evidence that Mercator had knowledge of Desliens' map.[5]

By this time the island of New Guinea had been discovered, and was known to Mercator. By this time, too, Java was better known, and was seen to be an island, neither joined to Jave-la-Grande nor separated from it merely by a narrow strait. Information was available that it was New Guinea, not Java, that is separated from this southern continent by a narrow strait. And if Mercator had all of this new information in his head, and the Desliens Map in front of him on his desk, it would be as plain as daylight that Desliens's Australia (which in its turn is the Australia of the Dauphin Map, and of all the other Dieppe cartographers) was wrongly located. The jigsaw of Desceliers was about to be corrected. Mercator was about to shift it back to its rightful place on the map, thirty degrees east of its Dieppe location, away from Java, away from Beach and Locac and Pentam and Maluar, away from Marco Polo and all of the obscurantism of the Middle Ages, into the sunlit sea where it rightly belongs, and where cartographically it came to rest.

It will be remembered that the Australia of the Casa da India prototype, which was misplaced by Desceliers, originally contained a north coast – presumably an Arnhem-land and a Cape York Peninsula. When Desceliers transferred this map of Australia, his 'Jave-la-Grande', to the Java–Sumbawa area, both the coast of Arnhem-land and the coast of Cape York disappeared under the shapes of Java and Sumbawa, losing their identity and their being. Mercator, seeing only the face of Desliens' map without knowing its history, would have no clue that there was explored Australian land *under* Java and Sumbawa; he would see only the remnant of the misplaced continent adjoining Java and Sumbawa to the south, and in his efforts to transfer the continent back to its correct position he would handle only this remnant, not knowing that Arnhem-land and Cape York had been overlaid and were now invisible.[6]

Again we return to the analogy of the police photograph. The photograph of the torso and head of the unknown man was transferred by Detective Desceliers, in error, to John Doe's file, and there John Doe's head was pasted over the unknown man's head, resulting in the composite figure of John Doe's head and the unknown man's torso. Thirty years later Detective Mercator established that there had been an error – the unknown man was Richard Roe, and the photograph ought to be transferred back to Richard Roe's file. The correct procedure would have been to unpaste John Doe's head, by some chemical treatment to restore Richard Roe's obliterated face to its pristine beauty, and then to transfer the full photograph of the unknown man – both torso and head – to its new file. But Detective Mercator did not know that there was a face underneath the other face. With scissors he cut John Doe's head off Richard Roe's torso, and merely transferred the headless torso to its new file.

So, following the line of reasoning adumbrated in this parable, Mercator severed Java and Sumbawa from the Australia of Desliens' map, which had the effect of severing Arnhem-land and Cape York from the Australia which had originally appeared in the Casa da India prototype; then taking this decapitated continent, which was all that was left, he transferred it to its correct longitudinal position south of New Guinea. This is illustrated in Fig. 16.1.

Mercator's world map of 1569, notwithstanding its great importance in cartographical history, is not a mariner's but a scholar's map. It is intended to give expression to high philosophical conceptions of world geography, not to navigational problems of local reefs and harbours. It is common knowledge that it contains material drawn from literary and speculative sources, and Mercator felt free to modify detail where his wider conceptions so dictated. There is not the meticulous attention to the shape of each bay, the bearing of each cape, the direction of each coast, that we look for in Rotz and Desliens; nevertheless, the genius of Mercator enabled him to retain the essence of his basic information, improving it rather than depreciating it by his interpretative skill.

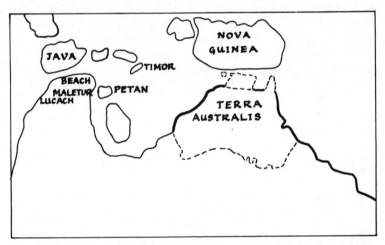

Fig. 16.1   THE DECAPITATED CONTINENT. The conception of the two Mercators, re-drawn on Mercator's Projection, is shown here with the "decapitated" sections of Arnhem-land and Cape York supplied by dotted line. The position of the continent of Australia is indicated. The Marco Polo lands of Beach, Lucach, Malatur and Petan are to the west.

In Fig. 16.1 the continental shape south of New Guinea (with an Arnhem-land and a Cape York added by dotted line) is substantially the shape of Jave-la-Grande taken from the

Dauphin Map. Admittedly the detail is taken from Mercator and not from the Dauphin, and therefore the correspondence is not perfect, but still it is quite closely approximate. If Mercator had drawn his continent in this form, then notwithstanding the minor deviations here presented there would be no doubt that he was following the Dieppe conception – probably working from Desliens. But as has been explained, while Mercator correctly shifted the continent from its incorrect Dieppe location (south of Java) to its correct location (south of New Guinea), in making this shift he moved not the whole continent, but only those parts which were not already incorporated in Java and Sumbawa. So that Java and Sumbawa could be left behind, he decapitated the continent; and only the headless remnant was transferred to its new position south of New Guinea. To us, the result seems strange. To our eyes, accustomed to the correct shape of Australia with the characteristic bold geometric forms of Arnhem-land and Cape York, Mercator's shape seems amorphous and nondescript, but when it is compared with the 'remnant' in Fig. 16.1 they appear as one and the same. And now that he had removed this troublesome continent from the erroneous position which had been assigned to it by the Dieppe cartographers, the seas south of Java suddenly became empty – as, in fact, they are. It would have been wise for Mercator to leave well alone; and if he had been a Portuguese mapmaker, wedded to the Doctrine of the Assumption of Sea, he probably would have left those seas vacant.

But Mercator had been brought up on the Ptolemaic and Marco Poloesque theories which had so obsessed his mentors Gemmius Frisius and Oronce Finé, and this sudden emptiness of the sea south of Java did not look right to him. Had not Marco Polo said that there was a great land south of Java, called Locac or Beach, with two adjacent islands called Pentam and Maluar? We have been into this in an earlier chapter, and we know that Marco Polo had not meant this at all. But this was the only reading of Marco Polo that Mercator knew, and he felt that respect for Marco Polo obliged him to put some kind of Locac, Maluar and Pentam in the seas *west* of Australia and south of Java. And this he did, inventing the shape shown by the thinner line in Fig. 16.1 as his version of the southland of Marco Polo, and labelling it with the traditional Marco Polo names.

This western peninsula is not meant by Mercator to be Australia, or any part of it; nor is it meant by Mercator to represent anything taken from Desliens, for the whole of Desliens' decapitated continent had been banished to its new position thirty degrees further east. Mercator's map, reading from west to east, from left to right, gives (a) Ceylon, south of India, (b) Marco Polo's Locac south of Java, and (c) Desliens' Australia, now decapitated, south of New Guinea.

The interpretation of Mercator expressed here is difficult to explain, and is probably different from any to which the reader is accustomed. But it is the only interpretation that fits all the known facts, and it is the one which is now patently advanced in Portugal, and which in the past was implied there. Jaime Cortesão sums it up well: 'Mercator's map is a compromise between two different sources – (a) that which relates to regions south of New Guinea, and (b) those which were *supposed to* exist south of Java.'

And this can be seen in the Portuguese cartographers. Mercator's map became internationally famous, reaching Portugal too, with the Portuguese cartographers producing charts in the Mercator tradition. One of these is the *Theatrum Mundi* (1612) of João Baptista Lavanha and Luis Teixeira, shown in outline in Fig. 16.2. Lavanha and Teixeira were so sure that Mercator was trying to present a southern continent in Dieppe tradition (but shifted to its correct position) and also a Jave-la-Grande in Dieppe tradition, that they replaced Mercator's amorphous western promontory with a recollection of the Java promontory of the Dauphin, complete even with a Rio Grande. The completed map looks like a Dauphin Map which has been cut down the middle with scissors, and then reassembled with the east and west coasts separated by an additional 1000 miles. The date of this map (1612) is after the first Dutch sighting, which reduces its importance. But as the cartographers would not have then known of the Dutch sightings, this map too is evidence of Portuguese awareness of the continent of Australia in the sixteenth century.

The influence of Mercator was very strong, and this arrangement of the land-masses was followed in almost all

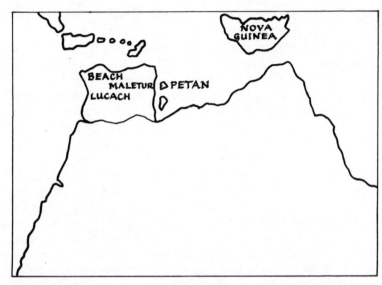

Fig. 16.2: 'THE PORTUGUESE MERCATOR' – Lavanha & Teixeira 1612. Compare the general outline with Mercator (Fig. 16.1) but compare the Beach-Lucach area with the Dauphin.

maps for the rest of the century. In Ortelius, Plancius, Hondius, the Englishman Frobisher, and most other maps, there can be seen the double hump derived from Mercator – the first, Marco Polo's mythical continent; the second, Desliens' decapitated continent. And in each successive cartographer the drafting deteriorated a little more, the outline diverged a little more, the copy became a little worse, until finally the likeness to Australia disappeared altogether. This analysis is not being given to suggest that the Dieppe Maps achieved any continuing usefulness through this progression. On the contrary, Mercator's action in grafting the useless Marco Polo hump on to the useful Portuguese–Dieppois outline only confused and mutilated the latter. Already the east coast of Australia was distorted by Erration and the south coast lost in the Antarctic Extension; with Mercator, the north coast was now decapitated, and the west coast largely hidden by its junction with the Marco Polo promontory. This left very little in Mercator, and none in his subsequent imitators.

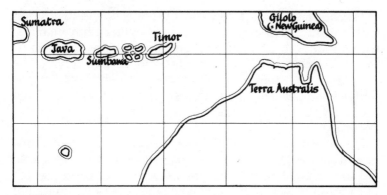

Fig. 16.3 CORNELIS DE JODE. SPECULUM ORBIS TERRAE 1593 (transposed to Mercator's Projection).

But there was one Flemish cartographer, Cornelis de Jode, who was not of the school of Mercator and Ortelius; and de Jode made the correct interpretation where Mercator failed. Cornelis de Jode and his father Gerard de Jode[7] were also professional map-sellers, in bitter commercial competition with the map-selling firm of Abraham Ortelius. At first the elder de Jode and Ortelius had been cooperating colleagues in the trade; but when the new public demand arose for mass-produced maps, both of them realised that a fortune was waiting for the bookseller who could first market a popular atlas, and the two firms became locked in a hotly-contested race for this lucrative prize. There were no holds barred. Each pirated maps from the other, each stole expert staff from the other, and each manoeuvred relentlessly to obtain scoops in cartographical material. Ortelius especially can be accused of not fighting fairly. He had important connections in government circles (which de Jode lacked), and he used these contacts to delay the issue of de Jode's Royal Licence. Through this, his own atlas was enabled to come out first. Ortelius' *Theatrum Orbis Terrarum* hit the bookstalls in 1570, and sold by the hundred. Gerard de Jode eventually got his rival atlas, the *Speculum Orbis Terrarum*, on to the counters of the bookstalls in 1578, but it was too late. Practically no copies were sold, and Gerard de Jode died a disappointed and financially ruined man.[8]

His business was carried on by his widow and his son Cornelis. In a desperate effort to retrieve the family finances, Cornelis de Jode decided to revive his father's work, presenting it in more attractive format, and adding interest by inserting some new maps, especially foreign or foreign-derived maps, which might interest the public. And one of the areas in which he sought to improve on his father was that of Australia.

Cornelis, too, knew of the shape of the Australian continent from the Dieppe Maps – again probably from Desliens. He too knew that Java and Sumbawa were islands, which must be left where they were, while the Australian continent needed to be shifted east, to a position south of New Guinea.[9] But in some manner, perhaps by instinct, perhaps by luck, de Jode saw that the *whole* of the continent needed to be shifted. In other words, he transposed Australia to its correct longitudinal position without decapitating it: and in this way he achieved the only properly interpreted and correctly placed map of Australia before the coming of the Dutch maps in the next century. Cornelis de Jode's map of Australia, transposed from his Polar circular projection to a familiar projection, is given in Fig. 16.3.

Cornelis de Jode renamed his father's atlas with the slightly different name of *Speculum Orbis Terrae*,[10] and it was ready for sale in 1593. This was the moment of destiny for the Dieppe Maps. If de Jode's atlas were accepted and acclaimed by the public, then this map of the southern hemisphere with its correct delineation of Australia would have become famous and influential all over the world, and such matters as the separation of Australia from New Guinea would have become common knowledge. On the other hand, if de Jode's atlas failed, this correct map of Australia would make no impact on the world, while the decapitated monstrosity which Ortelius was palming off on the public would continue its stultifying career. The *Speculum Orbis Terrae* again failed and with it the sixteenth century's best map of Australia sank into oblivion.

The de Jode family could not survive this second crash. Cornelis died at the age of 32. His mother was forced to sell the business, and it was bought up or taken over by the rival firm of Ortelius. So that the de Jode atlas would not compete with the booming sales of their own production, the *Speculum Orbis Terrae* was withdrawn from circulation, and the plates on which the de Jode maps were engraved were either destroyed or dispersed. Denucé says: 'This is the final phase in the suppression of a meritorious work.' He is here referring to the *Speculum Orbis Terrae* as a whole; but his words are equally applicable to the Australian map in it, to the Desliens from which he was copying, to the Dieppe Maps as a whole – for it was, too, the final phase in the saga of that meritorious work.

One noticeable feature about Desliens and the other late Dieppe Maps is their failure to advance or improve in the East Indian sector. On the Canadian side, each successive Dieppe Map records some new voyage or discovery; on the Indonesian side, nothing is added since the *Carta Anonima Portuguesa*, implying that nothing further had been explored or discovered there in a whole generation. That is not true: for the Spanish explorers Loaysia, Saavedra, Grijalva and others had steadily increased the world's knowledge of the island of New Guinea; and 'Nova Guinea' was by now a well-known geographical place-name. Yet Desliens follows the Dauphin in showing nothing newer than the 'Os Papuas' shoals of Jorge de Meneses, and no large island further south than Gilolo.

It is significant, therefore, that Cornelis de Jode's Southern Hemisphere – Map 2b in the *Speculum Orbis Terrae* – which shows Australia (Fig. 16.3) in such good shape immediately south of a large island which is undoubtedly New Guinea, should erroneously name that large island with the Portuguese–Dieppois name of 'Gilolo'. De Jode knew of New Guinea, and of the name 'New Guinea', for in Map 12 in his atlas there is an excellent and up-to-date map of that island – 'Novae Guineae forma et situs'; and he volunteers the information: 'The mariners call it "New Guinea" because its shores, position and character resemble the land of Guinea in Africa.' So when he drew his Map 2b, the Southern Hemisphere, he was not thinking of the Spanish maps of Nova Guinea, but was concentrating on some map which delineated Australia, which knew Gilolo, and yet was ignorant of 'New Guinea'. The only map in the world that would conform with all of these requirements was that of Desliens, or of his predecessors in the Dieppe School.

One strange fact remains about Cornelis de Jode and his atlas. On the title-page of the *Speculum Orbis Terrae* he represents four animals – a horse for Europe, a camel for Asia, a lion for Africa, and an animal which is not known for a continent which is not indicated. It is delineated in Plate VII, and it can be seen that it is a queer-looking animal with a head like a dinosaur. If we get rid of that head, and without altering one detail of the body substitute a different head, as shown – behold, this disorganized animal suddenly reveals that it has the characteristically bent hind legs and the drooping forearms of Australia's Kangaroo, with two little 'joeys' in its marsupial pouch! To Australians this illustration should be of great sentimental value, the world's first pictorial representation of the most typically Australian of all animals.

The best theory that can be raised to explain the scattered information about Australia that de Jode possessed is to assume that he had been in communication with some one who had been living in, or had visited, the Portuguese colony of Timor. De Jode was a great traveller, who had been as far as Rome in search of maps; and by 1580 Spain, Portugal and the Low Countries were all united under one crown, with free intercourse between them. There had been no new, large-scale exploring expedition to Australia; but anyone familiar with Timor could tell de Jode that Desliens's map was misplaced: that large continent, they would say, is not south of Java – is is south-east of Timor, south of New Guinea. And from Timorese contact with the Western Australian coast, they probably knew of the kangaroo; in any case, Timor itself has a small marsupial of that family. 'Nas planicies da costa sul tem sido vista uma variedade de marsupial que marca a transicão para a fauna australiana'.[11] The Portuguese of Timor knew too of that typically Australian bird the emu, which they had met with either on the Australian mainland or in the off-shore islands. Not only did they know the bird,[12] but they named it – for the Oxford Dictionary tells us that 'emu' is derived from their word 'ema', and is a Portuguese word. Timor also has a species of Australian wattle, which probably explains how Portugal was yellow with its bloom centuries before Captain Cook.

De Jode's atlas also contains printed material about Australia, printed on the versum of his Southern Hemisphere map, and also on the versum of his New Guinea. The former passage contains only shreds of information – the land is large, it has a variety of climates, and so on: the trite deductions made by a geographer as he ran his eye over his source-map. But the latter passage contains more precise information, and it also provides one clue about the source-map itself. Speaking of New Guinea ('this region' = New Guinea) de Jode writes:

> On the south of this region is the great tract of Terra Australia, which when explored may form the fifth part of the world, so wide and vast is it thought to be. On the east it has the Solomon Islands, on the north is the archipelago of S. Lazarus, and it begins at two or three degrees below the Equator. On the west, if it be not an island, it is joined to the Great Southern Continent.[13]

So the west coast of de Jode's source-map ambiguously indicated that 'if it be not an island it is joined to the Great Southern Continent'. This exactly accords with Desliens' map, which on the west repeats the hypothetical Antarctic Extension, that tentative, featureless, perpendicular line which is characteristic of all (except one) of the Dieppe Maps. De Jode here mentions this ambiguity, though he does not show it in this way in his own map.

De Jode's atlas, containing this map and these descriptions, only fleetingly saw the light of day. It sold only a few copies, it was quickly bought up and suppressed, and today only three copies of the book are known to exist. It is one further manifestation of the strange story of secrecy, suppression, neglect and misfortune which has dogged the Portuguese Discovery of Australia, ever since the first caravel sighted its shores.

The devolution of the Dieppe maps can be set out in tabular form, as in the following table:

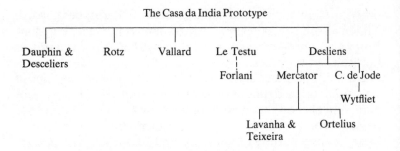

The Casa da India Prototype

From this table can be seen that de Jode had one follower; and even though he was only one, he was a mighty one, probably the greatest geographer of them all, Cornelis Wytfliet of Louvain.[14] Wytfliet is revered as one of the giants of geography, especially by the Americans, and deservedly so, for so much of their historic patrimony derives from him. Nordenskjold's famous phrase is that Wytfliet is to the geography of the New World what Ptolemy was to the geography of the ancient world; his biographer Nicholls says the same. No praise could be greater than that; but the comparison is just, for Wytfliet, like Ptolemy, was not a cartographer but a geographical compiler – a geographical encyclopedia is not too strong a term – an analyst who sifted through all the available geographical knowledge of his day, and resolved it in synthesised form. Indeed, he himself accepted the mantle of Ptolemy, entitling his monumental work *Descriptionis Ptolemaicae Augmentum*, the Supplement to Ptolemy.

It is an unexpected experience to look through this monumental work of 1595, still before the end of the sixteenth century, to find in it chapter after chapter on Florida, Yucatan, Jamaica, California, Chile, Australia . . . all packed with information beyond all expectations in so early a publication. In every other part of the world in which his information can be tested, Wytfliet has been found to be utterly reliable, with his material drawn from the best sources then available in the world. There is no reason to believe that his information concerning the Australian section should be less reliable: and in the Australian section the authority upon whom he drew was Cornelis de Jode, especially drawing upon the two passages which have been mentioned above. Wytfliet wrote:

'Terra Australis is the most southern of all lands, and it is separated from New Guinea by a narrow strait. Its shores are little known, since after one voyage and then a second voyage, that sector has been deserted, except for mariners blown thither by storms.'

Evidence of mariners blown thither by storms is not hard to find. We have already heard, in Chapter 5, of Francis Resende,[15] who was blown from Timor to the vicinity of Cape York Peninsula, and there were others. But these storm-tossed mariners are rarely of any value to us. They never knew where they had been, they never did any exploring, they never brought back any charts. Vaguely, they had sighted the Isles of Gold, or the Great South Land. Beyond that, they had nothing to report.

But by juxtaposition Wytfliet indicated that there were two voyages quite different from these; two voyages that were deliberate, intended, organised and planned, by inference government-sanctioned and government-sponsored. Preparations for voyages of this kind cannot be kept wholly secret from prying eyes. Sailors who sail on such voyages do not keep silent for ever. It may be that, at the end of such voyages, the Casa da India swallowed up the fruits of the voyages, the charts and journals and written records; but at least the chroniclers of the day should have known something of the setting out, hopefully something of the return. At least we have this to work on – Wytfliet stated unequivocally that there were two voyages, not one, not three, but two. And the clue is given to us that we must search through the Portuguese chronicles of the period, especially through the Decades of João de Barros,[16] the official chronicler, to find some hint of the two voyages to which Wytfliet refers.

. And in João de Barros we do find record of the two voyages required. One is the voyages of Gomes de Sequeira. The other is the still more important voyage of Cristovão de Mendonça.

PART THREE

'In their rivalry with Spain they kept a secret'

Chapter 17

CRISTOVÃO DE MENDONÇA

B Y 1518 the start that Portugal had gained on the Spanish was drawing to a close. Rumours were beginning to leak through concerning the preparations being made in Seville for the projected entry into the Pacific from the east. The King of Portugal was 'very angry', both with Magellan and with the Spaniards. Clearly Portugal would do everything in her power to protect her monopoly in the Spice Islands.

And in that year of 1518 King Manoel received definite news that Magellan's flotilla was about to sail. The Portuguese government took alarm. They probably now realised that, in the easy pickings which they had been making in the East during the period of their undisturbed monopoly, they had become lax in security measures, and had left themselves wide open if Spain arrived and attacked. Their shield was the Treaty of Tordesillas, but if there was dispute about the border, that might prove a weak shield or no shield at all. Belatedly, Manoel ordered the Indian Ocean coast to be fortified, and between 1519 and 1522 seven forts were erected in the East, one of them at Ternate. It was just in time, and the erection of the Ternate fort probably saved the Portuguese Empire.

Magellan sailed from San Lucar on 20 September 1519, and the Portuguese Navy was ordered out to intercept him. The Portuguese did not know by which route he was going, but according to their then geographical beliefs he had only a choice of two possible routes. One was the normal Portuguese route to the East Indies via the Cape of Good Hope. The other was, or could be, through the alleged South American straight in Lat. 40°s which João de Lisboa had found, and which later turned out to be merely the La Plata estuary. To head him off, they sent warships to those two points.

Our information about these moves comes from a rather unexpected source. It will be remembered from Chapter 5 that Magellan's cousin, the renegade Serrão, had been left behind at Ternate, with a few other Portuguese of his faction.

Over the years Serrão corresponded with Magellan – danger-ous, treasonable correspondence which was found at Ternate after his death. He drummed into Magellan the richness and importance of the Moluccas, the value that they would be to Spain, and his conviction that they were on the Spanish side of the Line of Demarcation. But Serrão was under suspicion, and as soon as the Magellan threat to the Moluccas arose, Jorge de Meneses sailed into Ternate to arrest him. He gave them the slip, but died soon afterwards, poisoned either by his own hand or by a Portuguese agent.

When, after Magellan's death, the Spanish ships under El Cano reached Ternate, one of Serrão's henchmen named Pedro Affonso de Lorosa contacted the Spaniards, pleading with them to give him passage to Europe. He could tell them how the Portuguese had reacted when they first heard that the Magellan expedition was on the way.[1] First they sent warships to the Cape of Good Hope and to Brazil. Then when news came to hand that Magellan had actually entered the Pacific, Governor Diogo Lopes of Goa was ordered to send out naval forces to engage him. But (de Lorosa said) Lopes was unable to comply satisfactorily with this order, for first he had trouble with the Arabs, having to stop to fight against them; and when he did send a large ship with two tiers of guns (de Lorosa says the captain was Francisco Faria) it became stranded in shallow water at Malacca, and could not proceed further. What had occurred since, de Lorosa did not know: but he assumed that further moves would be made against the Spaniards, and he warned them that the Portuguese 'would come from India to seek them and kill them all, for this was spoken of in India'.

So first the Portuguese tried to head Magellan off by sending naval forces to the Cape and to Brazil. The Por-tuguese would have regarded themselves as quite within their rights to shoot him down if he were detected in Portuguese waters off the Cape. Their right to accost him in the Atlantic was more questionable, as the Atlantic was not a mare clausum; but they were within their rights in sending a fleet to South Brazilian waters, and what the fleet would have done if it had sighted Magellan there would have been decided by exigency and not by law. And undoubtedly they would have been within their rights in attacking him if they had found him trespassing over the Line of Demarcation in the Spice Islands area, whether he had arrived there from the east or from the west.

De Lorosa did not have the fullest information concerning these naval preparations, but such preparations were being made. In the vital years, three (and only three) fleets reached Goa from Lisbon. The first of these was the great armada of fourteen ships under Jorge de Albuquerque (not to be confused with his more illustrious namesake, Affonso), which left Lisbon in mid-1519, before Magellan sailed. It was sent out to bolster the defences of the East, and Albuquerque was given the instruction to build the forts. On de Loroso's testimony, the fleet was first held up by the Arabs, and then delayed by the grounding of its capital ship at Malacca.

And the chronicler João de Barros[2] specially mentions that one of the captains of this armada was an officer named Cristovão (or Cristoval) de Mendonça. The word 'captain' can be used loosely as meaning the master of any ship, however small, naval or civilian. But the circumstances and the title here indicate that de Mendonça was a man of superior importance, what we would call a Royal Navy Captain, outranking our Lieutenant James Cook. And further he was a man of some birth, for de Barros tells us that his father was the son of Pedro de Mendonça, *alcayde-môr* of Mouram – a person of importance. Cristovão de Mendonça was a man of considerable prowess. There was trouble with the Malays at Pacem, and after Albuquerque had quelled that trouble and returned to Malacca 'with his ship came those of Cristoval de Mendonça, who well enabled him to resist and humiliate a proud Mir who had infested that part with oared ships'.[3]

The small second flotilla of three ships under Rafael Catanho set out at the end of the year, and the larger third flotilla under Jorge de Brito in the following year. Catanho sailed after the Magellan panic had commenced, and his force of three ships was probably the force (mentioned by de Lorosa) which was to try to cut him off at the Cape of Good Hope, proceeding on to Goa when that strategem failed. Short of men and ships and beset by these other troubles, Governor Lopes at Goa anxiously awaited Catanho's arrival and the instructions that he would bring. And these instructions when they came were – to search the Isles of Gold. That is, to search the Australian Coast.

For the moment, this chapter will interpret these instructions as meaning 'to search the Isles of Gold for Magellan', which is consistent with the war-like tactics in which they were engaged. Meneses had been ordered to search for him in Ternate, Brito (when he came) was despatched to Tidore, Faria was sent to Malacca, Albuquerque proceeded to Pacem, and so on. It was logical to expect an order to search for him in the south-east also, and this is presumably what the Royal order meant. And Lopes's response to the order confirms this understanding. He appointed the prestigious Captain Cristovão de Mendonça to lead this expedition, with Pedro Eanes[4] as his second in command, and equipped them with *three caravels*. As Galvão[5] pointed out, three caravels is a world-class flotilla: Columbus had no more, Vasco da Gama had no more, Abreu had no more, Magellan (by this time) had less. De Barros tells us of Mendonça's appointment, and promises to tell us more about it later, which he does.

But de Barros does not interpret the order 'to search the Isles of Gold' in the manner outlined here. Perhaps because he had just before been writing of Pacheco, perhaps because of the association of ideas in the words 'of gold', de Barros assumed that the order meant 'to search the Isles of Gold for gold'. When de Barros eventually does return to this subject, the third flotilla (under de Brito) had already arrived,[6] and de Barros[7] tells us that 'Jorge de Brito and Rafael Catanho and the others were all full of hope for the gold', and apparently carried away by their expectation of successful fossicking or mining or whatever it was that they intended to do, although he keeps repeating that they had a most dangerous assignment on their hands. Perhaps de Barros just misinterpreted the meaning, jumping to the wrong conclusion because of the reference to gold; perhaps, under war-time censorship, the information given to him was deliberately ambiguous, or was blue-pencilled to make it misleading. Whatever it is, it is impossible to believe that the Portuguese authorities, plagued by lack of manpower, the wreck of the large ship, Arab intransigence and Spanish threats, would choose that moment to dissipate their remaining strength in abortive search for that legendary gold which had already brought Diogo Pacheco to disaster. And if Governor Lopes had really received some such foolish order from Lisbon, and had felt compelled to obey it, he surely would have sent some civilian mariner in some lesser ships, not depriving himself of two senior naval captains and three front-line ships at this time of crisis.

So de Barros says that de Mendonça was ordered to search the Isles of Gold for gold, and logic says that he was ordered to search the Isles of Gold for Magellan. Whichever way it was, at least it is clear that he was to search the Isles of Gold. But first he had to combine with other flotillas to deal with the recalcitrant Mir at Pacem; and although Mendonça distinguished himself in this engagement, the main Portuguese force suffered losses, and the dispirited survivors eventually limped back to Pedir, joining up again with Mendonça and Catanho who were already there. By this time they had missed the monsoon, and all hands were set to work to help in the construction of Albuquerque's fort:[8] and when the wind permitted, Cristovão de Mendonça moved on to Malacca. He was now on his way – on his way to the Isles of Gold.

But where, at this time, was Magellan? Because of the split-second timing involved in the next part of this analysis here being made, it is best to set out the dates and movements in tabular form thus:

Date	Spanish	Portuguese
1519	20 Sept: Magellan sails from Spain	Albuquerque arrives at Goa
1520	28 Nov.: Magellan enters Pacific	Lopes ordered to attack Magellan
1521	24 Jan.: Magellan at Ladrones	Fighting at Pacem against Mir
	18 Mar.: Magellan at Philippines	Mendonça sails from Pedir

The Spanish dates and the Spanish movements are accurate, taken direct from Pigafetta. The Portuguese data is collated from de Barros, with less accuracy, but as well as is possible. In early 1521 Mendonça called at Pedir, travelled east to Malacca, and from there continued his journey, but with what result de Barros does not know. But if (as has been argued) he was proceeding in search of Magellan, which way would he go? This question requires some review of the state of Portuguese geographical knowledge at the time.

First, they did not know of the subcontinent of New Guinea. It is here called a 'subcontinent', for outside of Australia few people realize how large an island it is. Apart from Greenland, it is the largest island in the world. In its lateral span, it would stretch from New York to Denver. It was not until Sequeira and Meneses sighted it in 1525–1526 that the Portuguese knew of it at all, and not until Magellan's Spanish successors was its immensity made apparent. Had Mendonça known of it – while of course ignorant of the existence of Torres Strait – he might have hesitated about sailing down the long 'gulf' between it and India Meridional, risking a dead-end at Cape York. But lacking knowledge of the existence of New Guinea he would not have had this problem present in his mind; and his instinct would have been to pick up the north coast of India Meridional, and then follow it to the east, or to the east and south-east, according to the lie of the coasts.

Also Mendonça would have known from Atlantic explorers that there was land (now Patagonia) apparently stretching as far as the South Pole. From João de Lisboa he had been given to understand that there was a strait through from the Atlantic to the Pacific, in about Lat. 40°s (La Plata estuary). And from the copy of Schöner's globe in the monastery at Alcobaça he would envisage Schöner's South-land with a coast more or less encircling the globe in the latitude of João de Lisboa's strait. If these items of information were correct, it would seem that India Meridional joined up with the South American land-mass.

Now if India Meridional does so connect with Chile (give or take a few gulfs and bulges of the kind envisaged by Schöner and later by Finé) the connecting coast must slip away to the south-east. Or looking at it from the other end, João de Lisboa's strait must skirt a coast which gradually rises from Lat. 40°s, trending north-westerly, until it terminates in the Kimberleys of Western Australia. The Portuguese had received news that Magellan had entered the Pacific: therefore he must now be coasting along this Terra Australis

Incognita coast, admittedly crossing the mouths of gulfs if there were any, or skirting around promontories if there were any, but in the main moving north-westerly with the general trend of the coast, ultimately to reach the Line of Demarcation near Darwin, and from there to strike north into the Moluccas. So Mendonça, in wartime disregard of treaties, crossed the Line of Demarcation, picked up the Australian coast probably at Cape York, and planned to follow its trend east and south-east until he met with Magellan, coming in the opposite direction. It was the logical way in which to look for him.

By the time that Mendonça set out, Magellan was already in the western Pacific; but in any case he had not come by the route which has just been described. For a variety of reasons he first sailed up the west coast of South America to and beyond the Equator, where he turned west. The Humboldt Current attracted in that direction, the Roaring Forties discouraged westing in their latitude, and no doubt his sailors were glad to escape from the icy blasts of Cape Deseado for warmer climes further north. As far as Valdivia he was obeying Schöner's map, and it might have been expected that he would turn west there, where Schöner's land purported to commence its westward trend; but he did not do so. Again, when he reached within a few degrees of the Equator he might have been expected to turn west, for the Moluccas lie in that latitude; but again he did not. Instead he moved up to Lat. 10°N, made his westing from there, and sailed in that latitude spot on for the Philippines, causing some writers to conjecture that he must have prior knowledge of the Philippines, perhaps from Serrão. Whatever was his motive, he did steer for and arrive at the Philippines, with the unexpected result that eventually his ships (then under the command of El Cano) made their entry into the Spice Islands from the *north*, not from the south-east as had been expected; and Mendonça, patrolling the south-east track along which he should have come, missed him altogether.

But this is anticipating. Mendonça, sailing east across the Arafura Sea, reached Cape York Peninsula, and passed through Torres Strait, without knowing it was a strait (for he was ignorant of the land-mass of New Guinea on the other side), and thus entered the Pacific. And then he would be puzzled. At Cape York the land suddenly trends south, or south by only a trifle east – no longer trending towards the assumed coast of João de Lisboa. Still, it was an unknown coast which might soon trend to the east again, and so Mendonça had to follow it. Thus he found himself traversing the east coast of Australia, 250 years before Captain Cook, but travelling in the reverse direction.

From the Dauphin or any other Dieppe Map it is impossible to check Mendonça's track from the Line of Demarcation, across the Arafura Sea, and through Torres Strait, for the whole of the geography of the north coast of Australia has been overlaid by the geography of Java and Sumbawa, and has entirely disappeared. This was explained in the chapter on the Rio Grande, but it should be remembered here. We cannot tell what islands he saw in Torres Strait, but it can be inferred that he did not sight the coast of New Guinea. On the Dieppe Maps the only hint of New Guinea is the shoal marked 'Os Papuas' at its western end, which de Meneses discovered. There is just the possibility that Mendonça landed at Marbiak Island, for in 1878 John Douglas, the Premier of Queensland, and Mr Chester, the Magistrate at Thursday Island, found buried in the sand on that island an old-fashioned gun 'not of British manufacture', in circumstances not unlike those of the cannon at Carronade Island. The gun is preserved at Maryborough, Queensland; but many ships of many nations had passed through Torres Strait in the century prior to the finding of the gun, and connection with the Portuguese is unlikely. But if that island, or any other island, was marked on the Casa da India prototype of the chart, it disappeared and was blotted out when Desceliers superimposed Sumbawa on that area.

The *Carta Anonima* gives Sumbawa a short east coast, which junctions somewhere with Mendonça's chart, and we can only guess where it occurs. But Rotz, with his usual care, gives the sixteenth-century equivalent of a 'dotted line' – a thin, perpendicular, straight line – from the end of the Sumbawa coast to the centre of Princess Charlotte Bay, where detailed Australian cartography commences. It would seem that Mendonça came down from Cape York out of sight of land, made landfall in the middle of the bay, and had to make easting in order to round Cape Melville. Cape Melville, with Princess Charlotte Bay behind it, is a very prominent and noticeable feature of the east Australian coast, and this distinctive feature is prominent on all of the Dieppe maps, its shape and position identifying it with the utmost clarity. Cook passed it, out of sight of land; and it was not until 1815 that Captain Jeffries in the *Kangaroo* re-discovered it and placed it on English maps.

It is not wise to fall into George Collingridge's trap of trying to identify each cape and inlet all the way down the long coast. Mendonça, passing most of it well out to sea, and seeing it only as a dim coast, at times just a smudge on the horizon, filled in at times with a wavy line not intended to represent real features. But at other times his cartography is more explicit.

The explicit cartography from Princess Charlotte Bay to Repulse Bay can best be followed in the amazingly accurate drafting of Desliens. A short distance south of Cape Melville Desliens shows a land-locked harbour, where Cooktown stands today, at the mouth of the Endeavour- River (Fig. 24.2). It is shown as larger than in real life, which will receive a comment when we come to Captain Cook. From this point the Great Barrier Reef begins and Desliens shows, by a row of dots, the run of this reef. The Great Barrier Reef is a unique formation, one of the wonders of the world: the fact that Mendonça was aware of its existence and marked it with such distinctiveness on his chart, is first-class evidence, for the correct indication of an unusual feature is better evidence than is portrayal of the commonplace. And, in an evaluation with which Cook and Flinders and all subsequent navigators would wholeheartedly concur, Mendonça labelled this coast Coste Dangereux. At the correct distance from Cooktown Harbour, on the correct bearing, he shows a reef, exactly according with Endeavour Reef, where Captain Cook's vessel came to grief.

For the next section of the coast it is best to turn to Rotz, or to the Desceliers of 1550. These, and all other Dieppe Maps, next show a large island, the largest offshore island shown on the east coast. Its latitude corresponds with Fraser (also called

Great Sandy) Island; and Gago Coutinho has made considerable point of the correspondence here between chart and
reality.[9]

The next section of the coast, from the Tropic of Capricorn
to Cape Howe, is not as easy to interpret as the more
northerly coast, for two reasons. Above the Tropic, neither
Erration nor Magnetic Deviation has much effect. Further
south, both of these begin to bite increasingly, and the outline
of the map swings more and more east of true longitude.
Those readers who have by now mastered loxodromes and
Erration will have no difficulty in equating the real coast with
the chart; those who still find Erration difficult might understand this correspondence best by comparing the two coasts in
Figs. 0.1 and 0.2.

But further, this section of the coast lacks the detail of the
higher coast. Up north, the ships were travelling inside the
Barrier Reef, and would of necessity be close to land all the
while. But the Barrier Reef ceases at Heron Island; and from
that point south it would seem that Mendonça traversed the
coast further out to sea, charting the dimly-seen coast without
much detail. Collingridge has, with much ingenuity, matched
each wiggle on that chart with some real feature, but his
matching seems forced. Nevertheless, one or two of these
correspondences are usually pointed out, especially the bay
on the chart which evidently corresponds with Botany Bay. It
is not a good representation of the contours of the Bay, and
under other circumstances it might be passed over as an
insignificant detail.

But what has raised fierce controversy is the fact that this
indentation on the chart is there labelled 'Coste des Herbaiges', which might be translated as 'Botany Bay'. What is
the significance of this? Did Cook have one of the Dieppe
Maps in front of him when he was naming his bay? The reader
will have to wait until we come to the chapters on Dalrymple
and Cook before an answer to this intriguing question can be
attempted.

Chapter 18

THE GEELONG KEYS

IT is when the coast turns to the west in about Lat. 40°s (corresponding with the entrance to Bass Strait) that real difficulty occurs. It must be remembered that the *Projecção Errada* is not only a different projection, an unfamiliar projection, but it is also an erroneous projection. By the Erration formula, the curve of the coast can be brought back to its correct mathematical position; but it is not easy to preserve detail when massive transpositions take place. This applies in all transpositions, even to projections which are mathematically correct: when, say, North America is projected on a Polar Azimuthal Projection, the intellect can translate the altered form of the continental outline, but even the cartographer does not try very hard to preserve the detail of, say,

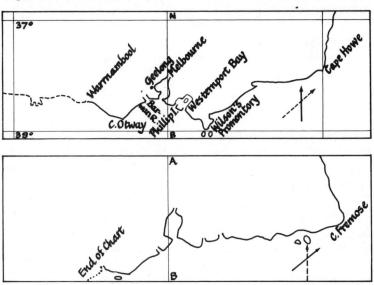

Fig. 18.1 THE BASS STRAIT AREA. The upper map shows the modern coast of Victoria. The lower map is taken from the Dauphin map, tilted as shown by the crossed north-south lines.

New York Harbour. A fortiori, any transposition creates difficulties when transposing from the erroneous Portuguese projection.

But with this word of warning, some examination is required of that part of the Dauphin Map which relates to Bass Strait and the Victorian coast. In Fig. 18.1 is shown a modern map of the Victorian coast, with the 145th meridian (NB) passing through Melbourne shown as its central north–south axis. At what angle is the corresponding axis AB required to lie on the Dauphin Map?

This is a trigonometrical calculation, which is set out in Fig. 18.2 for the benefit of those who like trigonometrical calculations. Those who do not can accept the answer that the axis NB, which is north–south on the modern map, is tilted twenty-two degrees (AB) on the Dauphin as the result of Erration. To this must be added the Magnetic Compass Deviation, which today is 10°E, but which was probably a little less in 1522, estimated in Chapter 13 to have then been about 7°E. Adding these two together,

By Erration AB is tilted	22°
By Magnetic Deviation AB is tilted	7°
Total tilt	29°

So in Fig. 18.1 the portion of the Dauphin Map which resembles the Victorian coast is shown tilted at approximately 29°, as required by this calculation. It can be seen that this brings the exaggerated, even distorted, tilt of the Dauphin Map back to a trend which is not far different from that of the true modern coast. Cape Howe then corresponds with the Cape Fremose of the Dauphin Map; and Port Phillip Bay (of which Corio Bay, upon which the city of Geelong stands, is the western arm) corresponds with Gouffre of the Dauphin. It is stressed again that pinpoint accuracy of identification must not be expected; but notwithstanding this, the Dauphin coast as redrawn in Fig. 18.1 is more recognisable than the first British charting of the same coast, made by Lieutenant Grant in 1801. The principal error is that Cape Fremose is in Lat. 44° 30′s on the Dauphin, whereas Cape

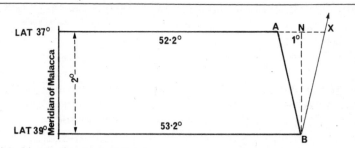

Adopting the meridian of Malacca (see p. 181 above) in Longitude 100° (Greenwich) East as the Prime Meridian, then

Point N (Shepparton) is in Lat. 37°s, Long. 45° (Malacca) E,

Point B (in Bass Str.) is in Lat. 39°s, Long. 45° (Malacca) E,

so

Transposing these two points to the *Projecção Errada* by the Erration tables (see tables on p. 170, supra):

Point A:

$$\varepsilon\phi^1 = \phi^1 \times \text{erration of Lat. } 37°$$
$$= 45° \times 1.16\dot{1}8$$
$$= 52.2° \text{ (Malacca) E}$$

Point B

$$\varepsilon\phi^2 = \phi^2 \times \text{erration of Lat. } 39°$$
$$= 45° \times 1.832$$
$$= 53.2° \text{ (Malacca) E}$$

so Difference $= 53.2 - 52.2° = 1$ degree

As BN is the true north–south meridian passing through B (i.e. is the Meridian of Melbourne), then in $\triangle$BAN

AN $= 1°$ difference in longitude (as calculated),

BN $= 2°$ difference in latitude

so

$$\tan \angle ABN = \frac{AN \times \cos 37°}{BN} = \frac{1 \times 0.7986}{2} = 0.3993$$

so

$$\angle ABN = 22° \text{ (approximately)}$$

By Erration AB is tilted (as calculated) 22°

By Magnetic Variation AB is tilted (say) 7°

Total tilt 29°

Fig. 18.2 THE TILT OF THE VICTORIAN COAST

Howe is in Lat. 37° 30', making an error of some seven degrees: but in far southern latitudes, where both Erration and Magnetic Deviation play tricks with east–west lines, the parallels suffer in accuracy, and seven degrees is a tolerable error.

When one looks at the two coasts compared in Fig. 18.1, the stretch of coast from Cape Howe to Warrnambool is quite recognisable, and the correspondence between the two coasts is too obvious to require much comment. Wilson's Promontory shows on the Dauphin as a group of islands, but that is understandable, for the Promontory looks like that when viewed from the sea. It is today joined to the mainland by an almost invisible spit of sand, and five hundred years ago it may have actually been separated by water. Further west appear two inlets, which may be the twin entrances to Westernport Bay, with Phillip Island in between. Then comes the characteristic shape of Port Phillip Bay, with its narrow entrance, with the Yarra River (where Melbourne now stands) running in from the north, and Corio Bay bulging out to the west. On emerging from Port Phillip Heads and following the coast to the west, the first inlet is the estuary of the Barwon, which shows clearly on both maps. Then the coast trends southwesterly, just the right distance, to the familiar right-angled corner at Cape Otway, veering back north-westerly to the present site of the city of Warrnambool. On the Rotz, there it stops; the Dauphin joins to the bottom of the parchment with two conventional scallops, which in the figure are represented by a dotted line. More will be said of this section of the coast later. The immediate focus of attention is Port Phillip Bay.

Port Phillip and Corio Bays were first discovered by the British in 1802, and Melbourne (at the head of Port Phillip Bay) and Geelong (at the head of Corio Bay) were first settled in 1834. Therefore, anything of European origin discovered in Geelong in 1847 could not have been more than forty-five years old, unless some other European navigator had preceded the British into Corio Bay. In 1847 Geelong was still part of the colony of New South Wales, as Victoria was not elevated to the rank of a separate colony until Separation in 1851: but already the Port Phillip District had some degree of autonomy, and was separately administered by Superintendent Charles Joseph La Trobe, who was later appointed first Governor of Victoria when Separation occurred.

Charles La Trobe was a very great man, still remembered with great esteem in the State of Victoria. He was a man of superior intellect and culture, a man of the highest integrity, a trained observer and chronicler, and (what is important for our purposes) a naturalist and amateur geologist of more than average ability. If anything, he was too refined for the rough frontier province which he was administering, and he found it very difficult to find congenial companions among the inhabitants. He did find one kindred spirit in Ronald Campbell Gunn, secretary to Sir John Franklin (the Governor of Tasmania, and a noted Arctic explorer), and in his private life a botanist and scientist of distinction – 'one of the few scientific men with whom I was then acquainted in Australia'. Another was Alexander F. Mollison, an early settler and a man of education. But La Trobe indicates that such kindred spirits were few and far between.[1]

La Trobe's capital was Melbourne, and (as the newspaper quotation hereunder shows) there then was fierce rivalry between Melbourne and Geelong. In his official capacity La Trobe made visits to Geelong and other parts of his dominions, flanked by advisors, feted by local dignitaries, and badgered by lobbyists and reporters. But at other times it was his delight to slip away from his desk in Melbourne, to travel incognito (or at least off duty) without the flanking officials, and to enjoy himself with his geological hobby far away from the cares of office.

In August 1847 he arrived in Geelong, unannounced, on a private jaunt of this kind. The fact and the date are important for our story, and it is good that they can be verified from a newspaper of 14 September 1847:[2]

'His Honour Mr La Trobe is at present on a visit to Geelong. Numerous are the speculative guesses hazarded as to his object in coming this way. The real secret is, we believe, that he has no particular business at all. He has had a little leisure time on his hands, and as in duty bound is spending a little of it in beholding with his own eyes the progress of the future capital of the province.'

Geelong was then a noted producer of lime, and it still is a noted manufacturer of cement and lime products. There is a small peninsula named Limeburners' Point, within the city limits, jutting out into Corio Bay, where in early days shafts were sunk and lime-kilns were erected, the remains of the kilns still visible until quite recently, and the area still pock-marked with the old shafts. This area was an attraction to La Trobe, for the shafts and excavations uncovered strata of shells and marine deposits which were of interest to him as a geologist; and on this off-duty excursion he naturally sought out this area to further his hobby. But on this occasion he found something more memorable than shells. By a lucky chance he was in attendance to bear witness to the discovery of the Geelong Keys, in circumstances which point to some European presence in Corio Bay long before the coming of the British, linking by implication with the Mendonça expedition of 1522.

As soon as La Trobe returned to Melbourne (23 September 1847) he hastened to pass on the exciting news to his friend Gunn in Tasmania. Not only is this letter important as on-the-spot verification of what occurred, but the flame of excitement in the letter itself shines brightly down the corridor of one hundred and thirty years. La Trobe wrote:[3]

'... I went as usually I do to see the progress of the lime works near the point about a mile below the town – and hearing that they were excavating the slope of the hill at a point where it approached the shore for the formation of a larger kiln than ordinary, I took occasion to go to this spot and get down into the excavation to see the character of the formation at this point. My attention was immediately caught by a thin layer of shells in the position I have marked on the accompanying scratch, and a little examination showed me that this inclined stratum of shells had at no very great distance of time formed the shore. The very shells of which it was mainly composed was the same as those actually edging the water below ... I was examining the shells and detaching some of them, and a cluster of wombat teeth from the seam, when the excavator followed me, and on my saying to him that this seam marked the

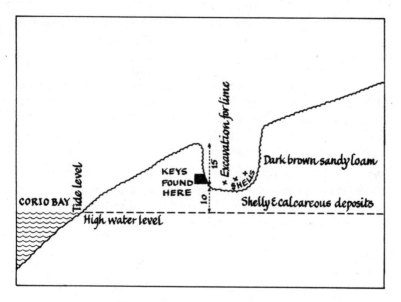

Fig. 18.3 LA TROBE'S SKETCH

position of the shore at a very ancient period, said 'Why, Sir, I picked out a bunch of five keys from that very spot yesterday' – and so he had!

Strange as it may seem, I am satisfied myself beyond a doubt that he spoke the truth. His children had been playing with and lost one of the keys, he had given away another – someone who was passing at the time he took them out – but I saw the other three – still showing the marks of the soil out of which they had been taken – and satisfied myself on . . . a material point of interest connected with the fact. Point A at which they were found is between forty and fifty feet from recent high-water mark – ten feet or thereabouts above it – and buried beneath fifteen feet of solid undisturbed soil forming the slope of the open and elevated downs behind. The keys were corroded – but the precise form and character of the wards even were distinguishable . . .

Is not this very extraordinary?'

On the day after this event his other friend, Alexander Mollison, also visited the scene of the discovery, and like La Trobe was also much excited by the find. Mollison and La Trobe retained a lifelong interest in the keys, and they corresponded with each other for many years, even after La Trobe returned to England. In 1870 Mollison made a trip to England, and called on the ageing La Trobe at Lewes in Sussex; and their conversation naturally turned to this remarkable event. As La Trobe wrote, their meeting:[4]

'...set me again thinking upon the subject which has always been of great interest to me, and can never cease to be a puzzle. I have, since my return, laid my hand upon the scratch and memorandum made at the very time and on the very spot ... The circumstance is so vividly impressed upon my memory that I really believe that I might venture to take my "Bible Oath" in reference to every detail.'

Mollison returned to Australia; and La Trobe, in Sussex, with his eyesight failing and the realisation that he did not have long to live, apparently gave consideration as to how best he might safeguard and protect the record of this experience, and decided that it would be safest in the hands of Mr Mollison. On 20 December 1870 he wrote again to Mollison, sending him the original sketch which he had made on the site, and also a long narrative covering in detail all of the facts, which (because of his failing eyesight) he had dictated to his daughter. His letter under cover of which he sent these materials to Mollison concludes with words which underline this conundrum. They are La Trobe's final comments on this question which had interested him so much:[5]

'The fact of the presence of the keys in the position where they were found must continue to furnish the same inextricable puzzle.'

So Mollison became the trustee of the records, but again there was the danger that on his death they might be lost or destroyed. Fortunately, in 1874 he mentioned the existence of La Trobe's narrative and sketch to Mr T. Rawlinson, C.E., who took a copy of them, and made them the subject of a paper delivered to the Royal Society of Victoria, and caused

the materials to be printed.[6] In that way this unique evidence
has been preserved. The people of Victoria are indebted to
the Geelong historian Mr L. J. Blake for his invaluable
researches which have again brought this material to light,
and to the Geelong Historical Society which has done so
much to raise public interest in the story.

The narrative which was dictated by La Trobe himself is so
full and complete, so vivid, and so convincing, that it seems
best to produce it in full, omitting only those geological
speculations which are not material to the story which is here
being presented. The La Trobe narrative reads:

'I believe it was either in the year 1845 or 1846, during
one of my occasional visits to Geelong, that I, understanding from Mr Addis, our Crown Lands Commisioner, that a
man, of the name of Boucher I think, who had a licence for
lime-burning on the shore half a mile or more below
Geelong, had made a new excavation for a lime-kiln, I
proposed to walk down and see it, as I thought it would give
me some further information on the geological structure of
that portion of the coast line.

'We walked over the open down, descended the abruptly
swelling banks to the seaside, a little beyond the first point
to the southward, and then proceeding along the shore,
entered the excavation from below over the rubbish which
had been thrown out.

'A labourer on the spot was sent up to the hut above, to
inform the lime-burner of our visit.

'As soon as I entered the circular excavation, which was
about twenty feet deep, my eye was immediately attracted
by the appearance of a line of calcareous matter, presenting
itself above the level of my head, and I saw at a glance that it
was composed of decayed calcareous shelly matter, the
upper line of which was thickly strewn with sea-shells of
different species, exactly similar to those which lay on the
beach, a few yards below us. Many of these were so little
altered as to be scarcely decayed, even preserving their
enamel.

'I directed my companion's attention to the fact, and to
the certainty that at no very distant period this line of

shells must have formed the beach. This stratum was so far
consolidated as to render its removal, except by the pick,
very difficult.

'I was working with my knife, to detach some of the
shells, when the lime-burner joined us. On seeing how I
was engaged, and overhearing the conversation with my
companion, he said, "I found a bunch of keys yesterday,
just where your honour is picking the shells." "Keys?" I
said. "Keys, your honour," he replied. "What can you
mean?" I enquired. "Yes, here," he said, laying his hand
just upon the shellbed. I asked him "Where are they?" "Up
at the hut, your honour," he replied. "Let me see them," I
said. He immediately left the excavation and ran up the
bank to his hut, returning a minute or two afterwards with
two keys, each about two inches in length, which he handed
to me, saying that there had been three, but that the
children had been playing with them, and he could only lay
his hand upon the two. There could be no question but that
they were keys, very little, if any way corroded with rust,
very similar to those of the present day, except that they
were a little longer in the shank, and the wards smaller than
is now usual. The latter were not only distinguishable but
were partially filled and encrusted with the calcareous
matter upon which they had lain. They were just of the
description still used for a box or trunk, or seaman's chest,
and I should judge from the form that they were not more
than a hundred or one hundred and fifty years old at most.
The position in which they were found gave me the impression of their having been dropped on the beach at the time
when the shellbed formed the shore line.

'I am thus circumstantial, in order to convey to the mind
the feeling of certainty that I have entertained from the
first, that there could be no doubt as to the fact that these
three keys (probably only originally tied together) were
found at the time and in the position I have stated.

'I immediately took a rough measurement of the over-
laying soil, which consisted of a compact bed of dark brown
sandy loam, tinged with iron, underlying a thin layer of
vegetable mould. This overlay was about 15 feet in thickness, and the height of the old shelly beach above the

present high water mark about ten feet, and the distance from the actual shore being about 40 feet inland. I was very careful to see that the sloping down of the land above showed no marks of a land slip, or wombat holes, or springs, or any interstices through which the keys might have reached the position in which they were found. In fact, I came away thoroughly convinced that none such had existed, but that at the time the keys were deposited the matrix was an open beach, forming the then shore line. (*He then enters upon geological speculation concerning possible changes in the level of the waters of Port Phillip and Corio Bays. K. G. McI.*)

'The two keys in question were long in my possession, and the original pencil memorandum and sketch (but unfortunately not the precise date) still remain so.

The circumstances of the finding were of course well known among my friends, and if I remember right, were the subject of a correspondence with my friend Ronald Gunn, one of the few scientific men with whom I was then acquainted in Australia. I have an idea that the keys were given to the Mechanics' Institute, which unfortunately received from me before it went to the bad, many objects of interest which are now seemingly lost. I do not recollect that there was any mention of the finding of the keys at the time in the Melbourne papers, but think it possible that as it excited some curiosity among a few at the time, some mention may have been made in the Geelong paper, then conducted by Mr Harrison.

My only companion at the time was, as I have said, Mr Commissioner Addis, now unfortunately no more.'

This report is so full that little comment is needed. The pencilled sketch which La Trobe made at the scene of the discovery has been found among the La Trobe papers by Mr L. J. Blake (see Fig. 18.3). This sketch clarifies his geological descriptions. The top of the excavation is 25 feet above sea-level. From sea-level to ten feet above sea-level there is a layer of compressed sea-shells so consolidated that they could only be loosened by a pick, yet in a surprisingly good state of preservation. La Trobe's first question was how this shelly composition, which normally would not be above sea-level, had risen ten feet above sea-level, and his long digression (omitted above) examines this problem. It does not concern us here.

The keys, then, were dropped on, or close to, the top of this shelly compound, i.e. about ten feet above sea-level. If Cristovão de Mendonça dropped the keys in 1522, then in that year the shoreline must have been ten feet above sea-level, consisting wholly of consolidated shell, with a little humus on top of it. Since the date on which the keys were so dropped, fifteen feet of dark brown sandy loam has descended upon the site, covering the shells and the keys to that depth, with finally some vegetable mould on top of the loam. In that area there is no tide, and no wind accumulation; the overburden could only build up by water-borne detritus from the hill above. How long it would take to overlay fifteen feet is a matter of debate. La Trobe conjectured 100 to 150 years, but that is far too short. But Rawlinson's estimate is longer:

> 'The question naturally arises as to where the keys could have come from originally, or by what means could they have been lodged in such a locality at so remote a period as to allow of so great an accumulation above them as described, namely fifteen feet. I do not see any alternative but to extend the period for from 200 to a little over 300 years back. The discovery of the lost keys on the old Corio Beach is full of suggestions as to their possible history, and that of their adventurous owners.'

Perhaps Rawlinson's estimate is only a guess, although he was a civil engineer and knowledgeable in such matters. But it is an interesting and significant guess; for the 'little over 300 years' subtracted from 1847, the year of the finding, takes us back to the date of 1522: and if that is accepted, then Rawlinson has answered his own question, for with that coincidence of dates the 'adventurous owners' of the keys could be none other than Cristovão de Mendonça and his colleagues.

When Rawlinson's estimate is linked with the cartographical evidence of the shapes of the bays on the Dieppe Maps, the likelihood is much stronger. Port Phillip is a closed bay, almost a hidden bay. When the first British explorer, Grant, passed its entrance, he failed to notice it at all, so narrow and hidden is the opening. It could not be seen and roughly charted from a caravel sighting the opening from out at sea. To draw the outline of the bay as well as it is drawn on the Dauphin Map, it would be necessary to enter the bay and make quite thorough-going examination of it. Port Phillip is a very large bay – in places on one shore the opposite shore cannot be seen. The correspondence of the shape of the Dauphin's Gouffre with the shape of the bay is quite remarkable. And therefore the Dieppe maps indicate that Mendonça did enter the bay; and the keys indicate that some European explorer entered the same bay in or about the same century. The possibility of coincidental duplication – that is, of two separate visitors, unknown to each other, being involved – is most unlikely.

It is a pity that the keys themselves have been lost, and cannot now be examined. La Trobe's narrative tells us that the children lost one, one was given to a passer-by, and three passed into La Trobe's possession. He did not mention, and apparently had forgotten, that he gave the third key to Ronald Gunn, evidenced by a letter to Gunn, dated 7 April 1848, which also evidences La Trobe's continued excitement about the whole matter:

> 'My dear Gunn – I have secured one of the keys for you. I have repeatedly visited the locality again, and am unshaken and unshakeable in my story . . . .'[7]

The fourth and fifth keys were given to the Mechanics' Institute, and were lost when that institution went bankrupt. Probably even if the keys could be found, they could only be identified as common European keys, not especially identifiable as Portuguese. The hiatus is the total lack of Portuguese content in La Trobe's evidence, and for that reason the Geelong keys only minimally corroborate the cartographical evidence.

Because the mystery of the Geelong Keys holds and always has held such interest for Australians, the evidence is produced here in full, notwithstanding this hiatus. The prestige, qualifications, and integrity of the chief witness, Charles Joseph La Trobe, give the materials a special weight, and he himself was obviously convinced that there had been some European ship in the bay in a preceding century. The Dieppe Maps indicate Portuguese voyaging in this exact area, including a recognisable chart of Port Phillip and Corio Bays. There is room for inference: and the reader has been given the full source material to enable him to judge for himself.

Chapter 19

THE MAHOGANY SHIP

A N D so, after losing his keys at Limeburners' Point, Cristovão de Mendonça sailed out of Corio Bay, through Port Phillip Heads, sighted the mouth of the Barwon (see Fig. 18.1), skirted past Loutit Bay, and rounded the characteristic right-angled corner at Cape Otway, heading west. Cape Otway is a formidable headland of rock, facing across to Cape Wickham on King Island, the two forming the twin pillars of the western entrance to Bass Strait. In early days the whole of this area was notorious as the graveyard of wrecked ships.

Beyond the portals of Bass Strait the mighty Southern Ocean begins, stretching in unbroken sea fifteen thousand miles west to the Patagonian coast of South America, the longest unbroken stretch of water in the world. To the south, the ocean extends to the Antarctic Circle, and the frozen land beyond. The long rollers surge in from South America; the formidable westerly winds blow continuously from their birthplace on the Antarctic continent. And the coast which stretches west from Cape Otway, usually known as the Warrnambool coast, takes the shock of these on its dreaded lee shore.

A hundred miles west of Cape Otway, in the vicinity of the present city of Warrnambool, Cristovão de Mendonça turned back, as evidenced by the termination of his chart at that point. It is true that the Dauphin Map makes two indeterminate scallops here, joining the Warrnambool coast to the bottom of the page; and as seen in the chapter on the Antarctic Extension, some of the Dieppe Maps go further and join the Warrnambool coast to a Terra Australis Incognita which then runs all the way to Cape Horn. But Rotz joins the coast to nothing: in Rotz the coast finishes at Warrnambool, and in the other Dieppe Maps what is demonstrably the real coast finishes there likewise, though hypothetically continued either to the bottom of the page or to the imagined Great South Land. And that is where Cristovão de Mendonça turned back.

It cannot be assumed that he turned back merely because the winds and currents were against him. It is true that they would present a difficulty, but not an impossibility. A hundred years later the Dutchman Pieter Nuyts made his return journey westward across the Great Australian Bight, apparently without bother; and Cristovão de Mendonça himself clearly faced and overcame the same westerly winds and currents on his subsequent return journey to Portugal, 'round the dreadful cape Speranza'. The fact that he could cope with these same conditions south of Africa proves that he could have coped with the same conditions south of Australia.

And that same westerly swell must have indicated to him that there was open ocean almost certainly connecting with the Indian Ocean. An armchair geographer in Dieppe might fill in a closed coast just to the west of his then position; the navigator himself, on the deck of his ship, would know that those rollers came from no closed coast, but from thousands of miles of open sea. George Bass, the English discoverer of Bass Strait, under similar conditions, rightly inferred insularity from the westerly swell, and there is no reason to believe that an experienced navigator like Mendonça would not make the same inference. So, sensing the insularity of Australia, he would be encouraged to go on. He would know that by continuing to sail west he would be taking the shortest route home. If scurvy or shortage of provisions or any similar cause troubled him at that point, it could better be remedied by going further than by going back.

And moreover, even after making allowances for Erration and other navigational error, Mendonça must have known that he was now moving out of Spanish territory, back towards the Line of Demarcation. In modern geographical terms, he would meet the Line again at Eucla, where the Western Australian boundary intersects the Great Australian Bight. At Warrnambool he was a mere thousand miles away from it. Once at the Line, he would be exploring Portugal's own India Meridional, and the thought must have occurred to him that if attractive country were found there, as it is to be found at Albany and Perth, he might return home as the discoverer of a new Brazil. And yet he turned back.

So the last remaining inference available is that he turned back there because he was compelled to do so. Perhaps some catastrophe, such as a great storm, drove him back. Perhaps his ships were damaged, perhaps one was actually sunk. All of this may seem to be pointless conjecture, except for one startling piece of evidence. There, at Warrnambool, the point at which Mendonça's chart terminates, was found the wreckage of a ship which tallies with a Portuguese caravel.

In the year 1836, when the colony of Victoria was only two years old, three sealers from Launceston named Gibbs, Wilson and Smith were plying their trade off the Warrnambool coast, and took their boat into the mouth of the Hopkins River. There the boat overturned, and Smith was drowned. There was then no habitation at Warrnambool, but they knew of a sealers' depot at the Moyne River (now Port Fairy), sixteen miles away: so the two survivors set out to walk along the beach to reach this goal. Their course (see Fig. 19.1) led along the edge of the sandhills, keeping the sandhills on their right, with reasonably easy progress along the flat beach. About one third of the way to the Moyne River, they reached the lagoon where the Merri River attempts to enter the sea, spreading out in swamps and quicksands. This forced them to veer inland a little, climbing the first row of sandhills. And there, in the hollow between that row and the next, they saw what remained of the wreck of an ancient ship. They were the first men to see and report the fabled 'Mahogany Ship'. What is significant for the purposes of this book is that they may have been looking upon the remains of one of Cristovão de Mendonça's caravels, lost there at that point where Rotz's coast comes to an end, where it was assumed that the commander turned back, three hundred and fourteen years before.

On their arrival at the Moyne River depot they reported this sighting to Captain Mills, a sealer who had put into that harbour, and who later became a resident of the town of Port Fairy when it rose on that site. Captain Mills was interested in the report of the old wreck, but immediately was much more concerned about the loss of the sealing boat (in which he had a financial interest); and at the first opportunity he and his brother Charles Mills set out for the mouth of the Hopkins

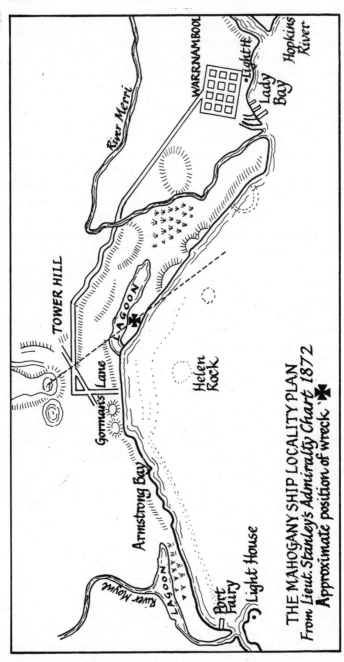

THE MAHOGANY SHIP LOCALITY PLAN
From Lieut. Stanley's Admiralty Chart 1872
Approximate position of wreck '✠'

Fig. 19.1   THE LOCATION OF THE MAHOGANY SHIP

River in two whaleboats for the purposes of salvaging it. No doubt they had some intention of visiting the ancient wreck on the way home, but difficulties prevented this. The whaleboat in charge of Charles Mills was itself overturned in the Hopkins River, and the men in the boat narrowly escaped drowning. The boats were damaged, and much of their equipment was lost. It was necessary for the party to beach all three boats, and for four days they had to remain on the shore. Then a strong westerly wind blew up, and they were faced with the back-breaking task of rowing the heavy boats back to Port Fairy, against the wind. In the circumstances it is no wonder that they then made no inspection of the ancient wreck that had been reported to them.

One of the crew of the Mills whaleboat was a boy of sixteen named Hugh Donnelly, and it is from him that the above facts were elicited. His story was given by word of mouth to the Warrnambool historian, Richard Osburne:[1]

'Mr Hugh Donnelly, now a selector at Lang, near Panmure, was one of the whalers actively engaged at Port Fairy in the 40's, and he has kindly supplied us with some exceedingly interesting notes of the early days . . . [here Osburne sets out the story substantially as above]'

The story was therefore directly reported to a responsible historian by an eye-witness of the events. Even better, Mr Osburne is able to corroborate the most important part of the story from his personal experience: he can recount having seen the ancient wreck in the hummocks between Belfast (Port Fairy) and Warrnambool in 1847 and 1848 – closer to Warrnambool than to Port Fairy, and 'to the west of the big hummock which was supposed to fill Warrnambool Bay with drift sand'. This fits in with the geographical facts of the area.

Hugh Donnelly himself lived to a great age. He retained a lifelong interest in the Mahogany Ship, and visited it from time to time. He was still alive, aged about seventy, when Joseph Archibald made his systematic re-examination of the available evidence in 1890, and the reports of Archibald's interviews with the old man, and holograph letters to Archibald from Donnelly himself, are extant in the Archibald

Manuscripts[2] in the Mitchell Library. This first-hand evidence is too strong to be disregarded.

The Mills Brothers, too, eventually visited the Mahogany Ship, and left some account of it. Captain John Mills became Harbour Master at Belfast (which was the first name for Port Fairy), and no doubt it was part of his official duties to be familiar with wrecks and similar phenomena in his area. For certain he visited the wreck twice between 1843 and 1847. He gave this information to Mr J. A. Lynam, the Postmaster at Belfast, and in due course Lynam's evidence was preserved by Archibald. The biography of Captain Mills has been written by his daughter, Olive Mills,[3] who records these latter visits. Curiously she makes no mention of the Hopkins River disaster; but she was writing from her own personal memory, and perhaps that first act in the drama was too early for her to have taken note.

It was probably Captain Mills who was responsible for the wreck being dubbed 'The Mahogany Ship'. He commented on the hardness and the redness of the remaining timbers, and recorded that when he tried to cut a splinter of timber with his clasp knife, the knife glanced off like glancing off iron. The hardness and redness of the wood, on which all witnesses agree, accord with the characteristics of Portuguese oak, from which the hulls of the caravels were constructed. The durability of this oak accounts for the preservation of the ribs and outside planks, whereas the soft Leiria pine of which the decks and spars were constructed had long since disintegrated. Captain Mills is also of special importance in the positioning of the wreck; and his observations have been the basis for most of the calculations used by later search parties. The passage has often been quoted:

> 'Well to the eastward of Gorman's Lane – proceed eastward along the beach till you bring the point of land on which the old iron church stood in line with the highest point of Tower Hill Island: the wreck would be about in a straight line with those objects, well in the hummocks.'

Stronger evidence comes from Captain John Mason, who saw it in 1846. The best account is in his own letter:[4]

'Riding along the beach from Port Fairy to Warrnambool in the summer of 1846, my attention was attracted to the hull of a vessel embedded high and dry in the hummocks, far above the reach of the tide. It appears to have been that of a vessel of about 100 tons burden, and from its bleached and weather-beaten appearance must have been there very many years. The spars and decks were gone, and the hull full of drift sand. The timber of which she was built had the appearance of either mahogany or cedar. The fact of the vessel being in that position was well known to whalers in 1841, when the first whaling station was formed in that neighbourhood, and the oldest natives when they were questioned stated that their knowledge of it extended from their earliest recollection.'

Captain Mason estimated the size of the ship at about 100 tons and 'she struck me as a vessel of a model altogether unfamiliar, and at variance in some respects with the rules of ship-building as far as we know them'. Joseph Archibald, many years later, examined the Captain closely on these points. In a letter to Archibald on 3 September 1890 Mason wrote:[5]

'It was situated high up in the hummocks, in a hollow formed by the action of the wind . . . at least two chains from the surf. The only portion remaining was the hull, full of sand, partially buried, and the centre portion of the deck planning. As regards the nationality of the wreck, I do not profess to be a judge, but if the ships depicted in the celebrated picture "A long-forgotten expedition" published in the London Art Union some years since are correctly represented as being either of a Spanish or Portuguese build, then I should say the wreck in question is connected with neither; the high ornamented prow and the deep shear common to ships of those nations in the 15th and 16th centuries were here entirely absent; her general appearance bespoke a very slight acquaintance of the builder with marine architecture, and resembled more the outlines of our local lighters, though of greater dimensions.'

This passage confirms, rather than denies, the likeness of the wreck to a Portuguese caravel. The Art Union reference is to an oil painting by Mr J. C. Curtis, showing a stately galleon allegedly gliding out of Lisbon Harbour, and painted solely from the painter's imagination, based upon ornamental galleons of a later era. Cristovão de Mendonça's ship would accord much more with the lines of a Port Fairy blubber lighter than with a stately Spanish galleon. Indeed, the nearest approach to a sixteenth-century caravel on the waters today is the humble Alcochete fishing boat, with its lateen sail.

What is more important is that Captain Mason, a man used to ships, did not recognise the wreck as of modern marine architecture. If he thought the wreck of 'antique design', a build which 'bespoke ignorance' of the art of shipbuilding as he knew it, then the Mahogany Ship at least pre-dated the coming of the British to Australia. Captain Mason's knowledge would carry back to the ships of the era of Cook's *Endeavour*. What he regarded as 'antique' would pre-date Cook or Marion de Fresne. At least Mason establishes that the Mahogany Ship is a genuine pre-British relic, and he was perhaps the first to turn his mind explicitly to this possibility. And if it is a pre-British wreck, that phenomenon is most readily explicable in terms of the Portuguese voyaging which has been the subject of this book.

In 1860 Mrs T. C. Manifold (then an unmarried girl) was riding along the beach, and alighted from her horse near the wreck, and spent some time in examining it. Her story has been researched by the Australian poet G. G. McCrae[6] while Mrs Manifold was still alive, and is evidenced by letters from her daughter-in-law Mrs Walter Manifold, and from Mr James McDonnell of Warrnambool. Mrs Manifold senior still had recollection of the wreck which she had seen as a girl, and describes what she saw most convincingly. Only a portion of the stern was then showing above the sand. Like all others who had seen it, she was surprised at how far it was from the water's edge. And as all others agree, the bow was pointing towards Port Fairy.

All of these facts are so consistently corroborated by everything else that has been reported, that her evidence, above all others, must be respected. She was a woman of high family, of good education, of reputation and integrity. Notwithstanding these attributes, she would almost certainly be unaware of technical details of Portuguese marine architecture in the sixteenth century: and the concluding passage in her report contains a curious and at the same time most convincing reference to this very subject.

The word 'caravel', or 'carvel', as can be read in any dictionary, means a ship with planks meeting flush at the seams, instead of overlapping as in a clinker-built boat. The wreck of one of Mendonça's caravels should show flush planks in this design. It is probably this unusual feature which led Mills and Mason to feel that the design was unusual, antique, not in accord with the rules of modern boatbuilding. And it is to this peculiarity that Mrs Manifold pointed when she said: 'The sides, or bulwarks, [were] after the fashion of a panelled door, with mouldings (as in a door) stout and strong.'

Nothing could describe a Portuguese caravel better.

Altogether 27 different people are on record as having seen the wreck between the first finding in 1836 and its final disappearance in 1880. The 27 have been listed by McCrae, and to delve into the minutiae of the evidence of each one would require a new book as thick as this present one. Some of these later ones have little to say – they saw the wreck, and that is all. Others are more interesting. A carpenter named Saul, while erecting a council fence on the wasteland near the wreck, had it under surveillance for some weeks while he was engaged on the job. A policeman named Funnell claimed to have seen the wreck from the top of Tower Hill – a claim which was at the time ridiculed: but modern-day tests have shown that an object placed in the sand-dunes in the supposed position of the wreck can in fact be seen from the top of Tower Hill, provided that the viewer knows which way to look. But except on the question of position (of interest to those who are trying to uncover the wreck) these others add little to what has already been recorded. Perhaps the very last witness, Mr H. C. Donnelly of Smeaton (no relation to Hugh Donnelly), is most informative. In a letter to Archibald dated 19 April 1880 and in another letter to Mr T. H. Osborne, he confirms what is by now the familiar picture – dark wood (like mahogany), rough and weather-worn, standing a foot and a half above the sand, undoubtedly the ribs of a ship of about 100 tons burden, undoubtedly an ancient ship; and curiously high, about thirty feet indeed, above the level of the sea. As Mr Donnelly was an engineer and surveyor, these estimates have special value. Mr Donnelly was the last person to see her. In 1890 an exceptional storm greatly disturbed all of the sandhills in the area, and the normal seasonal reappearances of the wreck ceased.

These appearances and reappearances of the wreck require some explanation. During the forty years following its first sighting, the wreck was seen occasionally, but not continuously. Because of the swamp land caused by the Merri River, the coastal land between Port Fairy and Warrnambool is rarely crossed, even today. The modern highway between the two towns runs very much inland from the coast. In colonial days, a track called the 'Hummocks Road', suitable for horse-riding, ran on the inland side of the dunes, with the horses obliged to ford the Merri River. But because the wreck lay in the hollow between the two rows of dunes, it was not visible from the Hummocks Road. For the same reason, it was not visible from the beach or from the sea; and few people travelled along the beach, either from Warrnambool or from Port Fairy, because from either town the beach leads to the dead-end where the swamps and quicksands join the sea. The wreck therefore lay, and still lies, in an invisible, somewhat inaccessible and unattractive area, only findable by those who stumbled upon it by accident, or who deliberately set out, with good directions, for the purpose of finding it. In early colonial days there were not many of the latter type.

These sand-dunes (sandhills, they are called in Australia) are a characteristic of most Australian coasts – quite large and high, usually in a double row with a large and deep sand-valley in between. When left in their natural state they unexpectedly become covered with native grasses. It is a botanical mystery how anything can grow on these Sahara-like dunes, with no soil and no water; but the native grasses do grow, clinging on in a fragile existence. Stabilised by these grasses, the sandhills become permanent, steadily increasing in size ('creeping' is the Australian term) as the wind blows in more sand.

With the coming of the white man, livestock was intro-euced, in particular sheep and rabbits. All along the Victorian coast they ate the natural grasses with which the sandhills were covered, upsetting the delicate balance of nature, and removing the binding which stabilised the sand at steeper than the angle of rest. This is a well-known phenomenon, which has been recorded and checked elsewhere. The wreck, lying at the bottom of a steep valley between the sandhills, was substantially buried in sand when first sighted – only portions of its timbers obtruding. Once the grasses were removed, the sand slipped downwards, filling in the valley and covering the wreck. But the grass never recovered. The loose sand at times blew away in high winds, at times built up again. Over a period of years the 'plus' of the creep outweighs the 'minus', so that while for some time the wreck was intermittently visible, it was inevitable that it would eventually permanently disappear.

So while there were several thousand inhabitants in the area in colonial days, it is not surprising that only a comparative handful of them actually saw the wreck, or are on record as having seen it. When infrequent observers did visit the spot, sometimes they saw nothing. The infrequency of the appearances, and of the visits, together produced the infrequent sightings. Mr H. C. Donnelly was the last person to see the wreck, in 1880. Since then, despite several searches, it has not been seen by anyone.

One puzzling feature of the wreck is its height above sea-level – 'high up in the hummocks', they all say, with Mr Surveyor Donnelly fixing it as thirty feet up. If the wreck was in the saddle between the sandhills, this must be true; and this would be a factor in its unique state of preservation. Other wrecks on the Victorian coast lie on the beach, at high-water mark. Over the decades they are reached and pummelled by waves at the spring tides, or in storms, and as a result they deteriorate. The Mahogany Ship could not have weathered this treatment for three hundred years. But high up in the sandhills it was out of reach of the sea. Because the high sandhills are permanently dry, there was no moisture to rot the wood; and as is known from aboriginal relics (boomerangs and so forth) found in sandhills, the sand has a petrifying effect, preserving the wood but rendering it brittle, and hard like stone. Some of those who saw the Mahogany Ship, particularly Captain Mills, testify to this condition.

But how did this ship, or any ship, reach a position so high in the sandhills? The coast there is not rising – if anything, it is sinking; so it was not lifted by upheaval of the earth. Blown sand cannot lift a wreck, it can only cover it. The only suggestion that can be made is that it was lifted to its present position, high in the sandhills, by a tidal wave. Whenever there is submarine disturbance in Antarctica, a tidal wave rolls in towards the Australian south coast, and such disturbances have been experienced even in this century. If some such freak wave lifted Mendonça's three ships, carrying one to its doom in the sandhills, and terrifying the others into turning back on their traces, a solution can be envisaged which satisfies all requirements.

In the years that have followed there have been some attempts to find the wreck. In 1872 Lieutenant Stanley, a government marine surveyor, was sent to chart Warrnambool Harbour, and to locate various wrecks (including John Batman's *Enterprise*, which was lost there). The Mahogany Ship, being on land, did not come directly within his terms of reference, but he may have listened to local stories about the wreck. At any rate, on one of the Stanley charts there is a symbol to mark the reputed position, and a dotted line to indicate Captain Mills's sighting line. The map has no evidentiary value, and it adds nothing to what we already know from Mills; and indeed we do not know whether these details were added to the chart by Stanley or by a contemporary. But this near-contemporary map has the charm of age, and has served as a 'Bible' for most of those who have since searched for the wreck, and as a matter of interest it is reproduced in Fig. 19.1.

With this map, coupled with such clues as can be obtained from the written reports, the Mayor of Warrnambool made a search for the ship in 1890, and the Public Works Department in about 1900. More recently, much more scientific exploration has been put in hand by Mr Ian McKiggan, with the help of sophisticated instruments made available by the Department of the Army. Mr McKiggan's researches are encouraging, bringing up some decomposed timber, and indicating a body of opaque matter in approximately the charted area, and at approximately the expected level. At the time of writing, the only articles recovered close to the site, possibly from the wreck, are a bronze spike and an iron latch (both in the Warrnambool Museum), and an interesting but unexplained piece of timber in the Australian National Library, Canberra, bearing the inscription 'Warrnambool, Mahogany Ship'.

The quantum of the evidence points conclusively to the fact that there was such a wreck, it was seen by 27 known witnesses, its existence was common knowledge throughout colonial days, its position is reasonably well-known, its description is consistent throughout the various reports, and the mode of its interment under the sands is quite understandable to those who have seen the site, and who know Australian sandhills. To this, the author of this book has added two more facts – the site is at the point where the Rotz coast stops, and where Mendonça presumably turned back; and the description – especially Mrs Manifold's – are consistent with the description of a Portugal caravel of that century. Nevertheless, readers in other countries may wonder why the records are not more complete. Why, for example, were there no headlines in the newspapers of the day, no university teams to examine it immediately after the first sighting, no government moves to house it in a museum? Why are the reports that do exist so myth-like, so embedded in folk-lore, instead of being recorded in prosaic entries in newspapers and public records?

To explain this it must be understood that the Warrnambool coast in 1836 was frontier land, new and primitive frontier land. Melbourne and Geelong were only two years old. Warrnambool did not exist. Port Fairy was a rough, primitive depot where whalers and sealers took shelter. There was no town, no administration, no civilisation. There were no libraries, no newspapers, no historical societies. There were none of the amenities and adjuncts to civilisation which we take for granted today: so that if some event of historical importance occurred, such as the sighting of a Portuguese wreck, the miracle is that it came to be recorded at all.

But these frontier days passed. The discovery of gold at Ballarat and Bendigo snapped the province of Victoria from its frontier primitiveness to sophisticated urbanism within one generation. Melbourne and Geelong grew into big cities. Warrnambool, founded in 1846, by 1886 had a newspaper (the *Warrnambool Standard*), a museum (Joseph Archibald, curator), and other organs of culture; and it was from these, particularly from Mr Archibald, that the impetus came to rescue the threads of local history, including (and especially) the story of the Mahogany Ship.

The first impetus came from Melbourne. On Saturday, 15 November 1884, a journalist named Julian Thomas, writing under the nom-de-plume of 'The Vagabond' in the Melbourne *Argus*, announced to the world – and in this context 'the world' means the colonial world of Melbourne and the colony of Victoria – that the Mahogany Ship existed. Except for Captain Mason's letter to the same paper eight years before (which letter apparently created little interest) 'The Vagabond's' article was really Melbourne's introduction to this story, and is the springboard from which a considerable and ever-increasing literature on the subject has been launched over the succeeding 92 years. Because of this historical importance, and because of its interest per se, the article is worth quoting at some length here:[7]

'Australia has no Columbus to claim the honour of first discovery. As it is unknown who first sighted and landed on the shores of Terra Australis, so it is unkown who was the first white man to plant his foot on Victorian soil. Was it Guillaume le Testu of Provence? – or some long-forgotten Portuguese or Spanish navigator, one of whom claims to have discovered a great south land, which he called 'Luca Antara', containing many populous cities and towns, abounding in gold, and with inhabitants addicted to cockfighting? But those ancient mariners, good brave sailormen though they were, had lively imaginations. Queiros "the Portingall", who discovered the New Hebrides, described those islands as an earthly paradise, peopled by different coloured races, from white to black, and full of gold, silver and pearls. His account of the Tierra Australis del Espiritu Santo, discovered in 1606, did not, however, make the rulers and peoples of Portugal and Spain anxious to annex or emigrate thither. Neither did the flowery reports of the unknown early Portuguese mariners, "who, on or before the year 1531" appear to have first discovered Australia, have for a long time any effect. To the Portuguese or Spaniards even before Guillaume le Testu I give the honour of the first discovery of Australia and Victoria. Their names have passed into oblivion – they never returned to tell the tale. Lying buried in the sand-hummocks between Belfast and Warrnambool is the hull of a vessel of a long-forgotten Australian expedition. It is built of Spanish mahogany. Greybeards have recently related to me how in their youth they played around this wreck, how they cut pieces of the rare hardwood out of it, and endeavoured to dig down into the keel for the coins which tradition states were always embedded in the timbers of Portuguese and Spanish vessels. Now it is all buried in the sands which at this point are slowly but surely changing the whole face of the country. The Unknown Dead who manned this vessel, and who, like Balboa, might have claimed our waters "For Rome! For Leon! For Castile!" I believe were the first navigators who saw our shores. After them, till the commencement of this century, "the long wash of Australasian seas" on our southern coast were never gazed upon by civilised men.'

This was the message – with only slight modification, still the message of the present book. And the man who received the message with the greatest enthusiasm was Joseph Archibald, the curator of the Warrnambool Museum. The collection and collation of material about the Mahogany Ship became his life work. Fortunately for him, most of those who had participated in the original sightings were still alive, although getting old. Mr Archibald interviewed them where possible and took statements from them; or interviewed their children or relatives when the original witness was already dead. For this reason, most of the evidence which he took was somewhat 'stale', testifying to events which had taken place many years before, and therefore open to the suspicion of distortion or embroidery through lapse of time. But the circumstance of the uncultured frontier, followed a generation later by the more cultured city, offers sufficient excuse; and the students of the Mahogany Ship are unusually fortunate in having this mass of first-hand (even though stale) source material in the Archibald Manuscripts in the Mitchell Library.

Apart from collecting documentary evidence and oral testimony, he also made careful observations in situ, especially in relation to the 'creep' of the sandhills; and his calculations produced an interesting result. He would have been unaware of the critical date of 1522 required for the Mendonça theory which is propounded in this book. Yet when he took out his figures, his answer was that the distance from the reputed position of the wreck to the sea would have required an aggregate accumulation of three hundred years up to the date of the first sighting. And that brings us to the third decade of the sixteenth century, the exact period in which Cristovão de Mendonça was off the Warrnambool coast – and at the exact spot where, according to the Rotz chart, some event occurred which caused him to turn back.

Chapter 20

WRECKS AND RUINS

So Cristovão de Mendonça turned back at Warrnambool, returning to his base by the route that he had come. But few navigators who have tangled with the Barrier Reef Coast – Cook and Flinders not excepted – show any great longing to tangle with it again; and Mendonça had already placed the ominous label 'Dangerous Coast' on that part of his chart. It is therefore reasonable to assume that, on his return voyage, he would sail up the central Tasman, well away from the forbidding coast, until it was time to turn westward through the Torres Straits again. And if he followed this plan, he might or might not have fallen in with the islands that lie east of Australia.

In this area on the Dauphin Map there are two islands, bearing the names Ilha de Saill and Ilha de Magna. The larger of these islands corresponds with the large island of New Caledonia, now a French possession; and it is an attractive hypothesis to assume that Mendonça sighted that island. The two islands show on all of the Dieppe Maps except Desliens; and their omission by the accurate and methodical Desliens is a strong suggestion that they were not on the Casa da India prototype, and therefore should be rejected or highly suspected, now. Professor Andrew Sharp supports this dismissal, pointing out that the name 'Saill' may be a corruption of Ceylon, and the name 'Magna' may be corruption of Andaman, both of these names appearing fleetingly on other charts of the period.[1] R. H. Major propounded a similar theory, that Saill and Magna represent the two islands of New Zealand,[2] but that theory has the same defects as the New Caledonia theory, without the geographical correspondence which New Caledonia appears to have. It seems safer to assume that Saill and Magna are two flyaway islands which were given chart room by the earlier Dieppe cartographers.

In 1807 the French geographer de la Rochette produced an interesting theory to explain the Dauphin's great swing to the east in southern latitudes. He postulated that the Cape

Fremose area is a representation of the east coast of New
Zealand, fitted on as shown diagrammatically in Fig. 20.1. In
this figure Australia and New Zealand are both set in their
true longitudes, and that portion of the Dauphin Map which
runs south from Cape Fremose to the bottom of the page is
equated with the east coasts of the two New Zealand islands.
It must be admitted that there is a correspondence in length,
configuration, bearing and longitude.

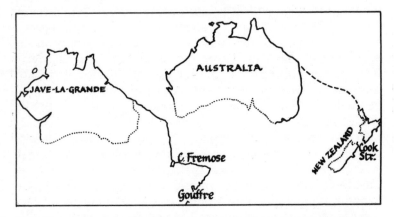

Fig. 20.1   DE LA ROCHETTE'S THEORY. This theory identifies the
Cape Fremose area of the Dauphin (upper map) with the east
coast of New Zealand (lower map). The suggested link from
Repulse Bay in Queensland to the North Cape of New Zealand
is shown by dotted line.

In 1817, when the British government was taking its first
interest in New Zealand, shortly to become a British colony,
someone in the Admiralty Office in London was apparently
asked to make a report, and the current English maps of that
area were checked against de la Rochette's version. There is
extant today in the Public Record office, in London, an
Admiralty chart of New Zealand,[3] with an 1817 annotation
stating that New Zealand had been discovered by Tasman in
1642, but that the eastern coast was known to the Portuguese
in 1550 (sic). The large harbour below Cape Fremose on the
Dauphin Map is labelled 'Gouffre'; and so the Admiralty
clerk added, against Cook Strait, the caption 'Gulf of the

Portuguese'. This is clear evidence of an Admiralty handling of the Dauphin, or one of the Dieppe Maps, as late as 1817.

The author does not subscribe to de la Rochette's theory, and finds two arguments against it. First, de la Rochette clearly did not know of Pedro Nunes and his loxodromes. When the Erration correction is applied, the east coast of the Dauphin swings back into Australian longitudes, and does not obtrude into New Zealand longitudes at all. De la Rochette was attributing to the Portuguese pioneers a greater exactness in the fixing of longitude than they did in fact possess. Secondly, while the eye can easily run a line from Repulse Bay in Queensland to the north cape of New Zealand, shown by a dotted line in Fig. 20.1, it is not likely that Desceliers would have hypothesised so long a coast, complete with explicit bays and capes and place-names, and certainly it would have been out of character for the Portuguese to invent a fictitious coast in this manner.

Nevertheless, Cristovão de Mendonça may have sailed near the New Zealand coast. Miss Robyn Jenkin, in her interesting book *New Zealand Mysteries*, tells of the ancient wreck uncovered in a great storm at Ruapuke Beach, near Raglan, on the west coast of New Zealand, in 1877.[4] The evidence is rather flimsy; yet the existence of a wreck at that spot, corresponding with the 1877 story, is undoubted, for it has been uncovered again from time to time right into this century. It was inspected by an official of the Dominion Museum in 1902, although he was not convinced of its antiquity. C. G. Hunt, who sifted the evidence very thoroughly, decided that it is the relic of some ship (perhaps the *Schomberg*) that was wrecked subsequent to the founding of Sydney in 1788.[5] The report of those who saw it in 1877 says that it was built of teak, with diagonal planking, and attached to it was a metal plate bearing characters in the Tamil language. It is tempting to dismiss this story out of hand, as some garbled version of the Mahogany Ship legend that had found its way from Warrnambool to the other side of the Tasman. If this were all, the Ruapuke Wreck could be brushed aside. But because of two other much better pieces of evidence which seem to connect with it, it becomes a possibility that this wreck is the remains of a second of Cristovão de Mendonça's caravels.

The first is the evidence of the Tamil Bell, which is in the Dominion Museum, Wellington, bequeathed to it by no less a personage than Bishop William Colenso,[6] and labelled with an inscription in Colenso's own handwriting to the effect that it had been found by him in 1836 in the hands of some Maoris, who had assured him that it had been in their hands for several generations. It is a bronze bell, with part of the lip broken; and around the rim is an inscription in writing which has been identified as the Tamil script of Southern India, the region of Goa.

Now it must be understood that Portuguese vessels sailing out of Goa in the sixteenth century carried a few Portuguese officers and a predominantly Indian crew of Goanese – 'lascars', as they have been called, who have continued as first-class seamen throughout the centuries. As the ships called at Java, sometimes Javanese were added to the crew. Duarte Barbosa, writing about the Moluccas in 1518, said:[7]

> 'Hither every year come ships from Malacca and Java ... [carrying] metal bells from Java, as large as a great basin, which they hang up by the rim; in the middle they have a handle, and they strike them with some object to make them sound.'

In his *History of Java*, Sir Stamford Raffles described Hindu bells, dating back to the pre-Muslim (i.e. pre-1478) days in Java; and the engravings which he supplied are remarkably like the New Zealand bell. So the finding of this bell in New Zealand is not evidence of the coming of an Indian or Javanese ship, but of a Portuguese ship with its normal lascar crew.

The most eminent scholar to offer his comments on the bell was John Crawfurd, FRS, who read a paper on the subject to the Ethnological Society of London in 1867.[8] He was an expert on such subjects, and he himself owned a somewhat similar artifact. His conclusion is: 'I am satisfied that the relic is a Hindu Sacrificial Bell, such as the Brahmins are wont to use in the performance of the rituals of their religion.' Crawfurd's hypothesis is that the bell is Javanese. He was familiar with the modern Javanese language, but had to confess that he could not recognise the characters in the inscription. The closest parallel that he could find was the inscription on a 1489 coin from Bantam. But it is not surprising that he could not recognise the lettering, for more modern scholarship has proved that the lettering is not Javanese but Tamil, a South Indian language. The inscription has since been examined by Tamil scholars, but somewhat inconclusively. It appears that the script and the wording are not modern Tamil, and some say not good Tamil at all. Professor Vivanathan of India has fixed its age at 400–500 years: so this professor's estimate, Crawfurd's guess and the Bantam coin are all in close proximity to the date of Cristovão de Mendonça.

Crawfurd also made the guess that the bell came from Asia to New Zealand via the Pacific islands. This is because the Maoris themselves came to New Zealand from Asia, in far distant ages, via Samoa and perhaps Hawaii, in more recent times. Because Crawfurd knew that their language, their culture and their customs arrived by this circuitous route, he jumped to the conclusion that their bell did also. In this, he must be wrong.

Even more interesting is the story of the Wellington Helmet. In 1906 the top half of a medieval helmet was dredged out of the harbour at Petone, a Wellington suburb. It was sent to armorial experts in Europe for identification, and was pronounced to belong to the sixteenth century. One interesting expert commentary was published in *The Connoisseur*, later in the same year.[9] The unnamed experts who wrote the article said that they:

'. . . recognise the skull-piece of a European helmet and have no difficulty in assigning it to the spacious times of Good Queen Bess . . . it is quite clear that the skull-piece belonged to a "close-helmet" of the sixteenth century. The large hole on the side was for the rivet on which the vizor and the bevor worked. The smaller holes on the edges were for the attachment of the lining, probably more or less padded for the comfort of the wearer. The surface is evidently deeply pitted by long exposure . . . . It points to the probability of some European ship having been there in the sixteenth century. Think of the tale of daring and romantic adventure we have lost in not having the records of that voyage. What brave explorer of the unknown, what storm-driven navigator far away from a friendly port on an uncharted ocean, left this evidence of struggle and disaster in the Antipodes.'

These experts say that the corrosion observed was equal to four or five centuries of corrosion on land, but clearly the metal could not have been in the sea for that length of time. This point has been taken against the helmet. Professor Andrew Sharp, for example, suggests that some Spanish or Portuguese immigrant may have brought his ancestor's helmet with him; and after tiring of it had thrown it into the harbour. More likely it had been in Maori hands for centuries (like the Tamil Bell) and from their hands had fallen into the water in more recent years. The date accords with the Mendonça period, and it may well be that a second of Mendonça's caravels – perhaps the Ruapuke wreck – came to grief off the New Zealand coast, and that this is all that remains of the armour of the officer on board. It could not have been Mendonça himself, for he returns to history later: so perhaps it was his lieutenant, Pedro Eanes, whose name we know, who lost his ship, his helmet and his life on that distant New Zealand shore.

The helmet, together with a cannon-ball that was found near by, is in the Dominion Museum, Wellington, labelled 'Spanish Helmet'. This is predictable, for both in Australia and New Zealand there seems to be an instinct to label every ancient relic 'Spanish' – never 'Portuguese'. A rather amusing illustration of this was the excitement caused in Port Fairy when the 'Spanish Sword' was dredged up from the River Moyne in 1878. All of the experts were busy pointing out the characteristics of size, shape and design which irrefutably identified it as a Spanish sword of the seventeenth century – until it was positively identified as the property of a Tasmanian sea captain, who had accidentally dropped it overboard. Until the author started to raise interest in the possibility of Portuguese voyages, the word 'Portuguese' was seldom heard, and theories about Portuguese penetration were always discounted. Even the Portuguese cannon from Carronade Island, with its distinguishing Portuguese Crown and

Rose, stands in Garden Island under a label reading 'Spanish cannon found by HMAS *Encounter*'.

Why this should be so is hard to explain. In Australian imaginative fiction, ancient wrecks on the east coast are always 'Spanish' and on the west coast they are always 'Dutch' – never 'Portuguese'. Henry Kingsley, for example, in the *Recollections of Geoffrey Hamlyn*,[10] wrote:

'Said the Doctor "Down the coast here, under a hopeless black basaltic cliff, is to be found the wreck of a very, very old ship now covered with coral and seaweed. I waited down there for a spring tide to examine her, but could determine nothing, save that she was very old, whether Dutch or Spanish I know not." '

That is probably because the stories of the Spanish voyages of Mendaña and Queiros are quite well known, whereas Portuguese voyages – even the major voyage of António de Abreu, which came much closer to Australia than Mendaña ever did – are quite unknown. The fame of Queiros, in particular, was extended by Cardinal Moran,[11] the Catholic Archbishop of Sydney, who traced his track from the authoritative accounts – the Arias Memorial, the Torres Letter and the Queiros Memorial of 1617, and extracted the description of the Bay of St Philip and St James, where Queiros founded his New Jerusalem. In his attempt to identify this bay (which actually is in the New Hebrides), Cardinal Moran convinced himself that the description fitted the geographical detail of Port Curtis, in Queensland, where the city of Gladstone stands today. He wrote:

'All these details fit in admirably with Port Curtis on the Queensland coast . . . . The trend of the land from east to west, the row of islands in front of the harbour, the large Curtis Island at the distance of a few miles, all correspond to the harbour of the Holy Cross in which de Queiros cast anchor.'

So convinced was Cardinal Moran, that a cairn (since demolished) was erected at Barney Point to record this fact. For years, following Cardinal Moran, the Catholic schools in Australia taught that Queiros was the discoverer of

Australia;[12] and through that the idea of Spanish landings on
the coast came to be given some acceptance.

And even more explicitly, two Spanish ships which were
lost in the Pacific seem to leap to the popular mind whenever
an ancient wreck on the Australian coast is mentioned. It is
when we come to these ships, particularly the *Santa Ysabel*,
that we pass beyond the fringe of historical investigation into
irresponsible folklore.

It will be remembered that after the Treaty of Saragossa
Spain mounted three expeditions in search of the Australian
continent, the first two commanded by Mendaña. In the
second of these, in 1595, Mendaña sailed with three large
ships and a frigate. One of the large ships, the *Santa Ysabel*,
was in charge of Lope de Vega, brother-in-law of Mendaña,
and de Vega's wife Mariana was with him. In the vicinity of
Bora Bora the *Santa Ysabel* disappeared. Sir Clements
Markham[13] has given his opinion that the *Santa Ysabel* was
most unseaworthy, and almost certainly sank immediately;
and some relics later found on the island of Taumaka probably link with this disaster. A second of Mendaña's ships, the
Santa Catarina, was lost later, somewhere in the Caroline
Islands, when the remnant of the expedition under Queiros
was heading for the Philippines. Certain relics of this ship
have been found at Truk. Therefore neither of the two
vanished ships was ever anywhere near Australia.

Just why these two ships are continually brought forward as
the probable originals for vessels wrecked on the Australian
coast is not clear, but it is presumably because these ships
were lost 'in the Pacific', in the appropriate century; and as
very few other European ships entered the Pacific at all
during those years, the wreck 'must' be the *Santa Ysabel* or
the *Santa Catarina*. But the Pacific is a big place. It is as far
from Bora Bora to Melbourne as it is from London to
Vancouver, or from London to St Paul's Rocks off the coast of
Brazil. When ships are wrecked on St Paul's Rocks they do
not habitually wash up in the English Channel. And if it is
postulated that the *Santa Ysabel*, or the *Santa Catarina* (or
both of them) sailed off under her own volition, either lost or
captive after mutiny, it is hard to know why those steering her
would head for an unknown and dangerous continent. Yet the

Santa Catarina, the *Santa Ysabel*, and the commander Lope de Vega, crop up repeatedly in conjectures about early Australian maritime history.

Now it must be remembered that Australia commenced as a convict colony. Many convicts absconded from their places of work, and fled into the bush. There was nowhere for them to go, and so the best that they could do was to find some hidden cave or beach where they could eke out a precarious and usually short existence before death overtook them. The classic example of this is the escaped convict William Buckley, who escaped from the abortive Collins settlement at Sorrento in 1803 and lived as a 'wild man' for 33 years before the new settlement at Geelong brought him back to civilisation in 1836. But many other escaped convicts tried this and were not so fortunate. In consequence, when many years later legitimate settlers, believing that they were pasturing their flocks in hitherto unexplored country, came to some cove which showed signs of previous occupation – some letters scatched on a rock, an implement or two, a few coins – it always seemed easier to assume some romantic wreck of a Spanish or other ship in distant ages, rather than to assume an unromantic and lonely death of some escaped convict in more modern times.

The same applied to the sealers. The first international influx of strangers to Australia came with the sealing ships, especially American, which swarmed to the south-east as soon as the news of new sealing grounds reached their owners. Kangaroo Island (SA) was first inhabited by American sealers, as the name of its American River indicates. George Bass, the undisputed English discoverer of the strait which bears his name, found a pair of trousers nailed to a tree, no doubt as a distress signal, at what is now Trousers Point. These sealers were of necessity secretive, for their profits depended upon keeping secret any new colony of seals that they had found. So shipwrecked sealers also added mystery to these unfrequented coasts; and the discovery of the remains of a sealer's camp, or the evidence of a sealer's disaster, almost invariably became another 'Spanish' mystery.

Three very doubtful categories of supporting evidence are then usually forthcoming. At the site of the convict's den or the sealer's camp it was not uncommon to find a few Spanish coins. Probably it was the finding of these that so often turned the finder's mind to some 'Spanish' mystery. But in the early days of New South Wales the Spanish dollar was the currency of the country. No coins were sent out by England with Governor Phillip: there seemed to be some vague thought that convicts would not need money. And as the Spanish dollar was the international token of barter in the east, it found its way into Australia, and became Australian currency as well. So the few Spanish coins, exotic though they may have seemed to the finders half a century later, were just commonplace coins at the date at which they were lost.

Secondly, evidence is always forthcoming concerning 'white aborigines' who were seen in the vicinity – or were alleged to have been seen by grandfather some decades further back. It seems to be assumed that the first thing that shipwrecked Spanish sailors would do would be to mate with the aboriginal women. It is much more likely that they would have been speared before that stage was reached. On the north-west coast there is much evidence, which the anthropologists accept, of crossing with Malay and Timorese strains.[14] But on the east coast there is no firm evidence of such miscegenation, other than the fanciful belief that some natives 'looked whiter' than others. No skull with the necessary European characteristics has ever been found. Robert Langdon has collected this kind of evidence over a large area of the Pacific,[15] but its validity is open to question. And similarly doubtful is the opinion of James Lyner, the Port Fairy postmaster at the time of the sighting of the Mahogany Ship, who recalled a native girl thus: 'Her colour, her hair, the general contour of her countenance, particularly her profile, all suggested some foreign strain.'

Thirdly, evidence from aboriginal folklore is most suspect. The aboriginal Dream-time, that is, the period before living memory, is mysterious, symbolic, religious and not very factual; and as the early police magistrates found to their sorrow, an aboriginal witness answering questions will always say what he thinks will please the questioner, not what he knows to be true. So questioning the aborigines about historical relics is not very rewarding, and it is best to discount information such as:

> 'The Yangery Tribe [who lived in the Mahogany Ship area]
> had a legend of the coming of the "yellow-men" among
> them; numerous people had noticed and commented on
> the difference in colour and facial contour of some of the
> coastal blacks.'[16]

And, similarly, strange wrecks in unexpected places tend to
be explained as antique foreign wrecks rather than more
plausible local wrecks. If an explorer, exploring in virgin
country in (say) North Queensland in 1820, found some
strange wreck, he would tend to forget that already there had
been half a century of intermittent sailing along those coasts
since Captain Cook traversed them in 1770. Thus when John
Oxley, in the *Mermaid*, was exploring Port Douglas in 1823, it
was no doubt a surprise to him to find the wreck of a ship; yet
that ship could quite probably have ended its life there well
within the period of European occupation. Similar reasoning
can probably explain away the mysterious wreck at Stradbroke Island, which appears intermittently above the sand-
dunes.

Just as the pre-Cook history of Australia is littered with
Spanish coins, white aborigines, rock-carvings and wrecked
ships, so pre-Columbian America has its researchers stum-
bling over the same things. America has its valid prehistory of
legitimate inquiry in the Norse and other voyages, just as
Australia has its valid prehistory in the Portuguese and Dutch
sightings of the sixteenth and seventeenth centuries. But from
there the American trails lead downwards, through folklore,
to unsupported tradition, to wild surmise, to the lunatic fringe
of fraud, hoax and forgery. This grey area includes the
mystical arrivals of Irishmen under St Brendan, and Welshmen under Madoc,[17] the Kensington Stone suspected of
fraud, the wild decoding of the Dighton Rock,[18] and in our
own day the Vinland Map of disputed validity. Perhaps the
Dighton Rock could be here explained, by way of illustration.

Near Pawntucket in Massachusetts, on the bank of a river
which opens into Narangansett Bay, there is a rock covered
with carvings. They seem to be the initials and dates and crude
drawings with which vandals habitually disfigure rocks, and

99 per cent of the inscriptions on the rock are obviously of this class. In 1920 Professor E. B. Delabarre went over the inscriptions with a magnifying glass, and among the hundreds of letters and figures found one date '1511' and one abbreviation 'M.CORT', and also three thin-footed crosses resembling the symbol of Henry the Navigator's organisation, the Order of Christ. These various finds are not close together on the rock; and if they are placed in position on a blank photograph of the rock, their placing seems most haphazard. Yet Dr Delabarre has woven these few facts into a mighty theory that Miguel Cortereal, who set out from Lisbon in 1502 and was never seen again, sailed up this river and stayed there for nine years, at the end of which time he engraved his initials and the year 1511 and three crosses on the rock; but unfortunately generations of vandals followed his example, and with their initials and dates made the whole rock very untidy. It was this theory that drew from the late Admiral Morison his famous broadside of sarcastic wit ('It has fallen to my lot to read some of the most tiresome historical literature in existence ... etc.').[19] And Dighton Rocks are not confined to America: Australia's equivalent of the Dighton Rock is at Point Piper, in Sydney.

Lawrence Hargrave was a great man. Among other things, he was one of the world's pioneers in aviation, experimenting with heavier-than-air flight before Wilbur Wright, and earning his niche in history in this field. But on the subject of Spanish voyages he had his blind spot. Immediately below his residence on Point Piper there are rocks, in which two ring-bolts have been sunk. It is assumed that they were put there by the servants of his predecessor to facilitate the mooring of boats; but Hargrave convinced himself that they were relics of some ancient Spanish visitation.[20] On the rocks also are scrawled many initials and dates (as on the Dighton Rock); and some miles away at Bondi is another rock with more inscriptions. Hargrave selected one small batch of these, quite unintelligible and almost indecipherable, which in his reconstruction could be:

B A L N
Z A I H

He works out that z a means Ysabel (Y-ZA-BEL) and b a stands for another ship, the *Santa Barbara*. From this he was able to deduce the story that this other ship, the *Santa Barbara* (it is not clear where it came from), found the *Santa Ysabel* in Sydney and that together they sank ringbolts at Point Piper and carved their signatures at Bondi, and then sailed north. The *Santa Barbara* (so his theory runs) was lost at Facing Island, and the *Santa Ysabel* at Prince of Wales Island, where (so Hargrave alleges) a skeleton was found beside a golden goblet. Lawrence Hargrave typed out all of these revelations in a thick screed which ultimately found its way to the Mitchell Library, where it is now, indexed under Lope de Vega.[21]

Facing Island, which sits athwart the entrance to Port Curtis, where the city of Gladstone now stands, has always been a favoured place for flyaway wrecks and insoluble mysteries. Cardinal Moran's erroneous theory about Port Curtis has already been mentioned. The 'Spanish Wreck' at Facing Island seems to have originated with the naturalist J. B. Jukes,[22] who made some strange finds and queer observations there; it was nurtured by the missionary advocacy of Lawrence Hargrave, and then given wide currency by the story-writer E. J. Brady,[23] whose work of fiction *The King's Caravan* draws upon the local legends. At this distance it is very hard to disentangle fact and fiction, but Facing Island has always been noted for fiction rather than fact. Among the claims are the existence of an extensive clearing at South Trees Point, two wells lined with timbers not native to Australia, a building erected of teak, a smooth stone marked with crosses, a rock-carving of a man's head (with the date 1600), a load of gold that was hijacked on its way to the British Museum, and much more. In 1911, thoroughly confident that all of these stories would be substantiated, Lawrence Hargrave petitioned the Queensland government to make an official inspection and investigation. This was done, but the findings of the investigators were wholly negative. The report – together with Hargrave's bitter and disappointed comments on it – is still in existence in the Dixson Library, Sydney, and a perusal of it extinguishes for ever the stories and the theories in which Lawrence Hargrave had such strong belief.[24]

Equally ludicrous, it was thought at the time, was the supposed 'Spanish Ruin' at Bittangabee Bay, near Eden, on the south Coast of New South Wales. In March 1967 the remains of Queiros's City of New Jerusalem were found at Big Bay in the New Hebrides, consisting mainly of a roofless wall, made of local stone, rubble and seashell mortar, but with some tooling at the windows in the form of embrasures. It answered exactly to the description of the building recorded by the chronicler Fray Munilla, who was one of the party at New Jerusalem: 'They collected ballast [heavy stones] and built a stockade, fortifying it with sturdy stakes, and a rampart with its embrasures.' The publicity which this find evoked in 1967 led to the recollection of a mysterious ruined 'blockhouse', made similarly of rough stones, rubble and crushed seashell, at Bittangabee Bay, the appearance of the ruin being surprisingly like the find at New Jerusalem. Again aborigines in the area were reported to show white strains, and there were the usual reports of Spanish coins and other articles being found in the vicinity,[25] but these can be discounted for the reasons advanced earlier in this chapter. As it seemed that there never had been any Spanish expedition at any time near that coast (Hargrave and his wandering Spanish ships always excepted), the 'Spanish' theory died down, and it became accepted that some anonymous sealer or whaler must have built the blockhouse in the early days.

But the substantial ruins, still in existence at Bittangabee Bay, make this explanation untenable. They consist of a square platform, perhaps 100 feet by 100 feet, surrounded by jumbled heaps of large rocks, which apparently once stood as a heavy wall on the perimeter of the platform, the rocks merely resting upon each other without mortar or cement or other binding. In the middle of the platform are the foundations and part of the walls of the so-called blockhouse, with the stones (again large stones) roughly tooled, and firmly mortared with seashell mortar. The shells in the mortar can be easily seen.

Two considerations emerge. The first is the enormous amount of labour that must have been expended in collecting, transporting, working and erecting these large stones, especially the huge piles of large stones comprised in the fallen outer walls. Such labour would have been completely beyond the capacity of a shipwrecked sailor, or a runaway convict, or a group of sealers, in early colonial days. But such work would have been possible if carried out by, say, the whole of a ship's company. It is hard to understand why a ship's company would decide to fatigue itself in such back-breaking work, but a strange foreign ship wintering in a strange foreign land might feel that it needed such security against unknown and unseen native inhabitants. And it was normal for sixteenth-century Portuguese to make a fort.

Secondly, the primitiveness of the construction of the ruined building – broken stones, seashell mortar, rough tooling – all of these things seem out of place in Bittangabee Bay, however appropriate they might have been in the wilderness of Queiros's New Jerusalem. Bittangabee Bay is just south of Twofold Bay, part of the elaborate new colony which the empire-builder Benjamin Boyd founded in 1842.[26] The Boyd colony was not primitive. It was London-based and London-financed. All necessary equipment and supplies were brought in by sea from London, or from Sydney (which by 1842 was a well-established town), and such things as rock walls and seashell mortar were just not in fashion there. Boydtown had brickmaking facilities, and imported its mortar: the church and other buildings which are the remains of Boydtown are quite different architecture from that of the blockhouse ruins.

Local legends, not supported by any documentation, aver that the ruins in fact pre-date the establishment of Boydtown, and attribute their first finding to the Imlay brothers, some years before Benjamin Boyd first came to Twofold Bay. There are several versions of the story of the finding, but all insist that the Imlays noted a large and fully-matured tree growing inside the ruined blockhouse. From this it has been inferred that the building had been in ruins for at least a generation; that it therefore pre-dates the first colonization of New South Wales. But even if the Imlay story is true – and it probably is – the tree and the deduction drawn from the tree add very little to what we know or can assume already. But it does seem that someone was at Bittangabee Bay before both

Imlay and Boyd, and that someone had manpower at his disposal at least equal to that of a ship's crew. (See Plate II.)

It is not wise to fall into the Dighton Rock trap of reading significance into letters and figures which may have been carved much later by tourists or vandals. Fortunately, because of the secluded site, the ruins have not attracted vandals, and there are practically no carvings on them. But on the front face of the blockhouse is the bold date 15?4. The third figure is hard to decipher, and all figures are old enough to be weathered and heavily overlaid with moss. If the third figure could be a 2 (although candidly it does not look much like a 2), we would be back at the approximate date of Cristovão de Mendonça.

The principal argument advanced against the suggested antiquity of these ruins is that there never were any European ships down the coast before Cook's days, so the ruins must have some more mundane explanation. But as this book now reveals that Portuguese passed down that coast, these ruins are worth reconsidering. Cristovão de Mendonça would not have completed his round voyage in one year, and therefore he must have wintered somewhere. Magellan in like circumstances and in like latitude, wintered at St Julian's Bay in Patagonia, leaving enough evidence of his stay to be identifiable by Drake seventy years later. The possibility that Bittangabee Bay was the winter quarters of Mendonça deserves the attention of those who are sufficiently knowledgeable in the evaluation and dating of ancient ruins, with the hope that this mystery can be cleared up.

So Cristovão de Mendonça left his traces, tenuous and fleeting though they be, on the shores of Australia and New Zealand, corroborating the much firmer evidence of the Dieppe Maps. One of his caravels was surely lost at Warrnambool, the second perhaps somewhere off the New Zealand coast. But the third must have got home to Malacca, and Goa, and Lisbon. Costa y Sousa has a brief note to say that Mendonça made another voyage to Goa later; and we finally hear of him as the Governor of Ormuz, presumably for services rendered. When João Vaz Cortereal discovered Stockfish-land – which could be America – he was rewarded with the governorship of Terceira in the Azores: it would be

nice to think that the discoverer of Australia was rewarded in
the same way.

.

Chapter 21
GOMES DE SEQUEIRA

In Chapter 7 it was explained that, in times of political equilibrium, it was to Portugal's advantage to refrain from trespassing across the Line of Demarcation, and that it would only be in abnormal circumstances, or for special reasons, that this policy would be reversed. In times of peace they voyaged and discovered to extend trade and to save souls, not to explore for the sake of exploring. The Pope and the Treaty of Tordesillas had marked the boundary for these Portuguese activities, and there was no profit in attempting to pursue them beyond the boundary: indeed, there was obvious detriment in doing so, for crossing the Line was a stipulated breach of the Treaty, a breach which might result in the abrogation of the whole Treaty. For Portugal, this would never do.

But exceptional circumstances bend policies, and we have seen how the open hostilities of 1522 led to Mendonça's sortie across the Line. He was not sent for trade or for religious conversions, but to fight; he was not deterred from crossing the Line by the usual considerations of trespass, for in this year of open hostilities the Treaty was in the melting-pot in any case. After Magellan's last surviving ship had limped back home, and Loaysia was effectively bottled up in Gilolo, these circumstances resolved themselves, and for a few years there were no more sorties across the Line. But by 1525 another change had occurred in the political arena, and again an exploring expedition was sent east, dictated by the special circumstances. This brings us to Gomes de Sequeira.

Spain's pressure on the Spice Islands was Portugal's constant anxiety. When Magellan's men came, Portugal tried to head them off; when Loaysia's men came, she tried to fight them off; at the Junta of Badajoz, she tried to argue them off: but all to no avail. After the failure of the Junta of Badajoz, Spain announced that her patience was exhausted, and gave orders for an invasion of the Moluccas.

But Portugal had one strength left – money. While Spain was bankrupting herself in foreign wars, Portugal, at peace, was piling up the profits of her Spice Islands monopoly, and apparently was beginning to think that it would be better to part with some of this capital, rather than let the whole of the revenue-producing islands be taken from her by force. As things were, the Spice Islands could never be safe while the Spanish threat was so close. Even if the Spanish accepted Long. 129° (Greenwich) E as the true Line of Demarcation – which they did not – they were still too close for comfort, for the Moluccas are perilously close to this line. For example, Spain might establish a post in New Guinea, or Waigeio Island, or even in Australia's Arnhem-land, which was just across the way. Jaime Cortesão puts it:[1]

'They feared that Australia could be a base for Spanish operations capable of impairing the security of the Portuguese dominions. This gave special point to the Policy of Secrecy, for it prolonged the period before that might occur.'

Worse still, Spain might illegally establish posts on the Portuguese side of the Line, as later she did in the Philippines. Spain, leading from strength, was even beginning to ride rough-shod over the Treaty of Tordesillas itself. Among the documents known as the *Gavetas Antigas* in the Torre de Tombé in Lisbon are some important papers relative to an inquiry held in Portugal in August 1523 to counter the Spanish claim that Spain was entitled to the Moluccas by virtue of Magellan's discoveries, even if they were on the wrong side of the Tordesillas Line. The Portuguese desperately collected together their evidence to show that, even on this argument, Abreu's discoveries had given prior rights to the Portuguese.

So to the King of Portugal it seemed that it would be good business to make a deal with Spain. It would cost a lot of money, but it would be worth it. Not only would the 129th meridian be confirmed as the boundary, but Portugal might be able to purchase a wide, defendable buffer-zone further east – even if she did not colonise it herself, that would prevent Spain from breathing down her neck from some post in Waigeio or Banda or Australia. And here we have the first germ of Portugal's plan to purchase the Spanish half of Australia, to add to the half which Portugal owned already.

But if Portugal could so purchase this buffer-zone, how wide should that zone be? What lands or islands lay in that zone to the east, which so far only the Spaniards had traversed? What barriers of land, fortifiable islands, strategic capes and closable straits were available in that region? Portugal did not know, but it seemed to be time to find out. And this change in Portugal's line of thinking was the genesis of two new Portuguese exploring expeditions that marked the year 1525 – two new probes, one to the north-east, one to the south-east. These are the two voyages of Gomes de Sequeira.

The voyages of Sequeira differed from that of Mendonça in that they were exploring expeditions, in which, presumably, the commander had some discretion to wander, to follow and chart coasts, to seek geographical knowledge (at least for the purposes mentioned) and to report on what he had discovered. But like Mendonça he sailed under circumstances of secrecy, national security, and political tension. Again the main fruits of the exploration disappeared into the silence of the Casa da India. Again the information which the chroniclers could gather, or which they were allowed to publish, is scrappy, incomplete and (in Sequeira's case) conflicting. There are four sources of information about him:

João de Barros, *Asia*, Decada III Lib x cap 5;
Castanheda, Book VI cap. xxvii;
Galvão, *Tratado*, Fol 54;
Andrade, *Crónica de João III*, Pt I cap lxxxxii.

An attempt will be made to reconcile them; but as other investigators have also tried to reconcile them, but with different results. it must be admitted that no single, firm interpretation is possible.

For Sequeira's first voyage the most reliable account is found in Galvão. Sequeira commenced his voyage from Ternate, and as Galvão himself became Governor of Ternate shortly afterwards, he would be in a position to know something of what happened. He says:[2]

'In 1525 Jorge de Meneses, captain of Molucca, sent a foyst to discover land to the north, where went as captain one Diogo da Rocha, and Gomes de Sequeira for pilot who afterwards went en route for India. In 9° or 10° they found certain islands, and called them As ilhas de Gomes de Sequeira.'

This passage refers to Sequeira's first voyage, but it adumbrates the second which 'afterwards' took place. Other details appear in the other chroniclers, and by piecing them together it seems quite definite that Sequeira reached the Caroline Islands, and especially one island which he called São Tomé, in Lat. 10° N Long. 144° (Greenwich) E. There is no island there on a modern map, but Faraulep in Lat. 9° N Long. 145° (Greenwich) E seems close enough. A more tempting deduction is that this island discovered by Sequeira is Guam, so much more attractive and important, in the same longitude, but unfortunately three degrees of latitude further north.

Guam had been discovered by Magellan. He sailed west in approximately Lat. 13° N, discovering the Marianas (which he named the 'Ladrones', or the Islands of Thieves); and the section in which Guam is found he named Islas de las velas latinas ('the island of the lateen sails'), because the natives there used lateen sails on their canoes. The second Spanish expedition under Loaysia (1526) and the third under Saavedra (1527–8) both travelled south of Magellan's track, in about Lat. 9° or 10° N. If their latitudes are accurate, they would not have sighted Guam but would have sighted Faraulep. Galvão tells us that Saavedra 'sailed to the islands which had been discovered by Gomez de Sequeira ... but not knowing of this previous discovery, they call them Islas de los Reyes.'[3] Later, Lopes de Vilhalobos confirms both the Spanish and the Portuguese discoveries in this area: 'On 15th December [1542] they had sight of the islands which Diogo de Roca and Gomes de Sequeira *and* Alvaro de Saavedra had discovered.'[4] This is a very accurate cross-reference. The island which is here referred to, called by them São Tomé or its Spanish equivalent, is at the intersection of the tracks of Sequeira and Saavedra, and that would be where the modern Faraulep, in the Carolines, is situated.

Now Sequeira is the only recorded Portuguese of that decade to make a sortie into the Spanish Carolines and Marianas. Apart from Mendonça's naval expedition against Magellan (which was a hostile action in time of war, and so not controlled by the Treaty of Tordesillas), his are the only recorded Portuguese expeditions deliberately sent across the international Line of Demarcation. He was ordered to do so, and the only reason that there could be for such order was to reconnoitre the sea and the islands in anticipation of the projected conference where, hopefully, that area would be purchased by Portugal from Spain. When the meeting did take place, we can deduce what was discussed; and at that meeting any Portuguese geographical information that was brought forward must have come from Sequeira, any Spanish information from Magellan, Loaysia and Saavedra.

The one point of common knowledge to the two conferring nations was this island of São Tomé, reported by both Sequeira and Saavedra, and (in typically sixteenth-century manner) then confused with Magellan's Isla de las Velas, until they were not sure whether they were talking about two different islands – one the Isla de las Velas, the other the Isla de São Tomé – or only one called Isla de las Velas y San Thomé. This island (or these islands) played an important part in the subsequent Treaty of Saragossa.

The Treaty of Saragossa will be treated in full detail in the next chapter. It is mentioned here in anticipation, because the text of the Treaty gives data bearing on the identification of this island. It refers to two islands, north-east by east of the Moluccas, in easting $297\frac{1}{2}$ leagues (equal to seventeen

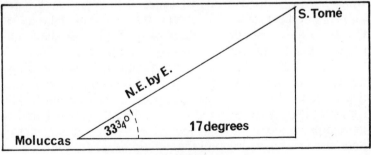

Fig. 21.1   THE SARAGOSSA LINE.

degrees) east of the meridian of the Moluccas. The latitude is not mentioned, but by resolving the triangle (Fig. 21.1) trigonometrically it can be calculated that the northing is about 11 degrees. This accords with Sequeira's island (Galvão said Lat. 10° N), rediscovered by Saavedra and confirmed by Vilhalobos, and on a modern map this is Faraulep. Magellan's Ilha de las Velas (probably Guam) is further north; so I. de Velas and I. de S. Tomé are two islands, and the Sequeira discovery can be pinpointed with accuracy.

What is more important than the identification of the island is the fact that Sequeira sailed seventeen degrees east through boundless sea, occupied by very few and very small islands – the modern name for this area, Micronesia, means 'the very small islands' – and was in a position to report to his masters that this huge buffer of open ocean could be put between Spain and Portugal's precious Spice Islands, if Portugal could arrange to have the Line pushed back the seventeen degrees which he had sailed.

Sequeira and da Rocha were back in Ternate by the middle of the year, and, as Galvão mentioned, Sequeira undertook another voyage 'en route for India' later in that same year. That does not necessarily mean that he went to India: Galvão's phrase 'na carreira da India' means 'on the India run', and any voyage west from the Moluccas would come under that description; and we find that when Sequeira did sail, he sailed for the Celebes, which is in that direction.

For the details of this second voyage we have to turn to Castanheda, another reliable chronicler. Castanheda had himself been in the East, although he wrote this account in Lisbon, no doubt from records which had been censored and edited in the delicate political situation that then pertained. He records[5] that Sequeira was ordered by the Governor of Ternate to sail for the island of Celebes. He set out from Ternate in July 1525, heading west (Galvão's 'na carreira da India'), but was carried by storms into the sea between the Straits of Magellan and the Moluccas. Checking this on a map, it must be south-east of the Moluccas, therefore south of New Guinea, and towards the north coast of Australia. Castanheda says that he was blown three hundred leagues (900 miles), and suffered great perils including the loss of the rudder. Then he discovered an island 'thirty leagues in circumference' – if it were a round island, that would make it about 28 miles in diameter; and as there are not many islands of that size in that area, it offers some clue to its identification.

João de Barros also purports to give an account of Sequeira's voyaging, but it is not clear whether he is writing of the first voyage or of the second. Like Galvão, de Barros's account takes him to the Celebes, from whence he is carried *east* by a storm, which would take him out to the Micronesian islands. For this reason, some writers (including Armando Cortesão) think that de Barros is rehashing the first voyage. But in most respects the descriptions given by de Barros correspond with those given by Castanheda in respect of the second voyage; and this seems to demand some beneficial interpretation of the word 'east', to alter his course towards the Arafura Sea. It is not hard to give this interpretation. De Barros dramatically describes their fearful adventure as they drove before the storm:[6]

> 'They did not know where they were, but ran all the time in the direction of the sunrise. They could not stop where they were; and, relying on God's mercy, they ran before the storm, keeping the wind on their stern for they could not risk any other course. In this way they ran three hundred leagues. They trusted more on God's grace than on their own navigation. So great was the panic, that one night they lost their rudder and were unable to steer . . .

In this fearful, confused and desperate flight before the storm, without compass or rudder, without the ability to navigate, without charts, it would be churlish to criticise the bearing given by them. All that they knew is that they ran 'always towards the sunrise', and that could mean almost anything from north-north-east to south-south-east. If in fact they travelled in a generally south-easterly direction, that would be near enough to 'the direction of the sunrise': it would accord with Castanheda, it would not depart too violently from de Barros.

Allowing this amount of latitude, and spelling out the scattered facts as well as is possible, the best reading is that on his second voyage Sequeira was sent south-east for the same reason that on his first voyage he was sent north-east: it was a reconnoitring mission into the Arafura Sea, to explore the islands there, to inspect the south coast of New Guinea, to cross over to or towards the Australian mainland which Mendonça had sighted, and generally to report what the area had to offer if the opportunity to purchase it turned up.

The Arafura Sea area is an unfamiliar area, even to Australians, and to assist the reader a sketch-map is given in Fig. 21.2. Drawing upon de Barros, it seems that the earlier part of Sequeira's voyage was through the island groups shown on this sketch-map, and the 28-miles-in-diameter

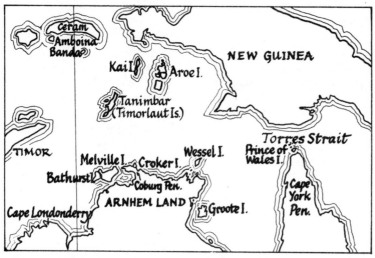

Fig. 21.2 THE ISLANDS OF THE ARAFURA SEA

island might be Tanimbar. According to de Barros, that island was inhabited by people more white in colour than black, with straight hair, and beards; but they were not Malayan, and did not know the Malayan language. All of this fits in with the inhabitants of the Timorlaut group of islands, of which Tanimbar is the largest; and none of this would fit in with the people of Australian aborigine stock who occupy the islands further south, offshore to the Australian coast. And the name given by Sequeira, Ilha dos homens brancos ('the island of pale-skins') accords. But there were *two* islands, this Ilha dos homens brancos and another which de Barros names as the Ilha de Gomez de Sequeira. And the second could be further south, and in that event off the Australian coast.

Castanheda's description, like that of de Barros, says that the inhabitants of the one island which he mentions were very light brown in colour, with long black hair. The size of the island and the colour and description of the people fit in with the Ilha dos homens brancos, and to that extent Castanheda does not contradict de Barros. But Castanheda makes no mention of the second island which is shown on the later maps. Perhaps this second island was not interesting enough to be mentioned in the journal, although large enough to be marked on the chart.

The historian Maffei, who wrote the history of India,[7] is clearly drawing on Castanheda, so that any embroideries that he adds are probably from his imagination, not from the records. But Maffei says that it was this island that was named 'Gomez Sequeira'. So if there were two islands, one pleasant and fertile and inhabited, and the other not far away but less notewrothy, then the identification forced upon us is that the latter is Australia's Croker Island, or even part of the Arnhem-land coast.

R. H. Major, on the other hand, taking the distance and bearings literally, feels that Sequeira's second island was much further east.[8] Adhering to the stated distance of 900 miles south-east of Ternate, and looking for an island large enough to fit in with a stated circumference of 90 miles (or diameter of 28 miles), Major calculated that the ship must have reached Torres Strait, but did not pass through Torres Strait – for there was apparently no difficulty in getting back – and the only island on the western edge of Torres Strait which lines up with all of these requirements is Prince of Wales Island. So he claims that this was the second island visited by Sequeira. It seems quite a good case, and Major goes even further in venturing this thought: 'Having discovered in 1525 an island so close [to Australia] we must believe that the discovery of that continent followed very soon after.'

That Sequeira did voyage at least close to the Australian north coast, discovering islands in the Arafura Sea, if not parts of the mainland itself, is confirmed by two important later maps. In these maps, the Ilhas de Gomez Sequeira, in the approximate position of Arnhem-land and its offshore islands, are shown; and when later seen on these maps by certain eminent geographers, Sequeira's cause was given a posthumous boost. For that reason, these two maps are worth considering.[9]

The first is the Riccardiana version of Gaspar Viegas's map of 1537. Viegas was Portuguese, but has crossed to the service of Spain, and therefore the information concerning the islands of Gomes de Sequeira may have been a Portuguese secret divulged by him to his new masters, and through them to the world. There are two versions of this map, in Florence in two different libraries; but the other version, the Archivo Version, is not of importance to us here. What is of importance[10] is the evidence, in the Riccardiana, that Sequeira did in fact come south-east into the Arafura Sea area, supporting Castanheda, and refuting the error or confusion that had crept into de Barros.

The Riccardiana version separates the Arafura Sea area into two parchments (or pages)[11] – Folium 8 R and Folium 9 R. On the former, which is the more westerly segment, appears one island named the island of GUOMES RIQUEIRA; on the adjoining segment is shown a lengthy coast which is undoubtedly the south-west coast of New Guinea, and to the south of that a second island with the garbled name of GOMEZBRACQ. It is not difficult to untangle this to produce 'The Island of (Homens) Bracq of Gomez (Sequeira)'.

Both in the Riccardiana Viegas and in the Gastaldi which followed it, the two most identifiable features are Banda (named in both) and Ceram (with its name mutilated in both). It seems strange that a Portuguese name – for the island takes its name from Serrão of unhappy memory – should be such a spelling problem, but 'Samborna' and 'Selamia' correspond with it in shape and position, and somewhat resemble it in pronunciation. In both are added an unnamed island, shaped like a figure eight or a dumb-bell, sited south of Ceram and east of Timor. Unavoidably one must identify this island with Tanimbar, the largest of the Timorlaut islands, and its neighbour as the nest of islands in the Aroe Group – subdivided by waterways into several islands, but then and for a century later looked upon as one large island.

But what is the third island, further to the south-east? It is hard to say, but clearly it is some island very close to the Australian mainland, if not actually the mainland itself. By strict comparison with a modern map, it should be Croker Island, the Australian island north of Darwin. Equally it could be the protuberance of the Coburg Peninsula, or Melville or Bathurst Island. Allowing a little licence to the cartographer, it could represent the Wessel Islands further east, or the Prince of Wales Island, much further east, which was favoured by Major. Either of these fits in with Castanheda's account of the course of the voyage.

G. B. Gastaldi's map of 1554 is a very famous Italian map. It gives a more familiar map of the East Indian islands – Java, Java Minor (Sumbawa), Ende (Flores), Timor and the Terra Alta island which so often shows up east of Timor. Like Viegas he shows a real but mis-spelt Ceram, a real Banda and again to the east and south-east two islands – Is de hombres blancos, and Insul de gomes desquiro.[12] As is usual in maps of that time, latitudes are shown, but not longitudes. The latitude of the latter group, in Lat. 11° s, can be read on the map. The longitude can only be estimated by a check against known islands, such as Timor; but the group appears to be in approximately Long. 132° (Greenwich) E. Adopting this latitude and estimated longitude, the Islands of Gomes de Sequeira equate comfortably with Croker Island, Melville Island and the Coburg Peninsula (see Fig. 23.1). And as the Coburg Peninsula is part of the Australian mainland, this is firm documentary evidence that Sequeira sighted the mainland, at least at that one point. If there is any reader who is still unwilling to accept all of the evidence heretofore produced in favour of Cristovão de Mendonça, then at least by Gastaldi's map that honour must next be transferred to the second of the Portuguese discoverers.

Sequeira's New Guinea coast and his 'Isle of Pale-skins' both show on the *Carta Anonima Portuguesa*, but in the Dauphin and the succeeding Dieppe Maps they are shrouded in the mass of shoals marked 'Os Papuas', and are unidentifiable. If the Casa da India prototype map of Australia contained any Sequeira detail, such detail necessarily disappeared when Desceliers transposed the coast to the Java–Sumbawa area. Sequeira's voyaging around the islands of the Arafura Sea, including Arnhem-land and possibly the Cape York Peninsula, is necessarily a north-coast investigation. In the Casa da India prototype from which the Dieppe cartographers were working, there must have been a north coast sufficiently resembling Java and Sumbawa to cause Desceliers to make his wrong guess, and yet necessarily differing in detail from the capes, bays and islands which were imported into the Dauphin's north coasts from the north coasts of Java and Sumbawa. It is possible that the Casa da India prototype did contain all of Sequeira's detail; but if so that detail was superseded and blotted out and would have disappeared when Java and Sumbawa were superimposed on top of it. If Australia's Wessel Island, for example, which superficially equates with Indonesia's Madura Island, had found its way onto the Casa da India prototype either from Sequeira or from Mendonça, it still would have disappeared under the Madura Island which shows on the Dauphin Map, leaving no trace. The Dauphin's delineation of Australia's north-west coast may incorporate some of Sequeira's charting, but it is impossible to prove this, or even to make valid conjectures. Sequeira does not support the Dauphin Map, and the Dauphin Map does not support Sequeira.

The trace of the south-west New Guinea coast, which we noted on the Viegas chart, however, has an interesting sequel. New Guinea was beyond the Line of Demarcation, and not much frequented by the Portuguese. Apart from Governor Meneses's storm-swept visit to the far north-west point of New Guinea, this voyage of Sequeira's is the only known Portuguese contact with that island, and the only known contact with the south-west coast by any nation, before Torres.

A hundred-odd years later, in 1663, when Torres had explored the eastern third of New Guinea's south coast sprinkling Spanish names as he passed, and after the Dutch had inspected the western third of the south coast similarly sprinkling Dutch names, there was in Lisbon a composite map showing these, plus a small section of connecting coast in the centre which showed Portuguese names. In the absence of any information about any other Portuguese probes in this area, the sketchy delineation of this centre-south coast may be a relic of Sequeira's second voyage.

History then repeated itself. The French sent a carto-graphical spy, J. J. de Frément d'Ablancourt, to Lisbon to obtain what maps he could. Working through the French Embassy in Lisbon, he gained access to the collection of maps which had been built up under express direction of the Portuguese Crown, including this composite map which brought to light one of Portugal's oldest secrets.[13] From d'Ablancourt these maps passed to M. d'Hallewyn, who arranged for them to be published by Pierre Mortier, and they were so published in Amsterdam in 1700, under the title of *Suite de Neptun François*. For our present considerations, the inscription which Mortier placed upon the title-page is sig-nificant:

'*Suite de Neptun François ou Atlas nouveau des cartes marines leveés par ordre exprès des Roys de Portugal et données au public par les soins de feu M. d'Ablancourt. Pierre Mortier, Amsterdam, 1700.*'

After this publication, the map was public property. Robert de Vaugondy drew upon it for his map of New Holland; and Vaugondy's map found a place in the atlas of Charles de Brosses, which Cook had with him on board the *Endeavour*. So whether Cook knew or did not know of Mendonça's voyage (through the Dauphin), he did have, at third or fourth hand, some information ultimately derived from Sequeira. He did not pick up the Portuguese names on the centre-south coast ('Abrolhos', which was discussed in Chapter 6, among them), for Cook did not distinguish between Spanish and Portuguese – it was all Spanish as far as he was concerned. But he was right in saying of this sector of the map, that the 'islands which bound this sea have been discovered and explored by different people, and at different times, and compiled and put together by others, perhaps some ages after the first discoveries were made' (*Journal*, 7 September 1770).

If we had only the cartographical evidence of Viegas and Gastaldi, plus the incidental cartographical derivatives here discussed, we would be justified in claiming Sequeira as the undisputed discoverer of Arnhem-land, and his reputation today would be greater than it is. But the accounts in the four chroniclers seem so evasive, so lacking in candour, and so inconsistent, that they detract from Sequeira's reputation rather than augmenting it. But the reader must remember that here the mapmakers had the advantage over the chroniclers. The mapmakers were foreigners, Spanish (as Viegas was by then) and Italian, and therefore not subject to the Portuguese security censorship which hogtied the Portuguese chroniclers, especially the official chronicler de Barros. And in a year of real political crisis, when the Junta of Badajoz had failed and the Spanish invasion of the Spice Islands was threatening, when delicate negotiations were in train and Portugal was particularly anxious not to offend Spain by admitting trespasses over the Line – in that political climate it is unreal to expect clarity and candour in the chronicles. On the movements of Sequeira, the chronicles are not clear and candid; on the contrary, they seem garbled, incomplete, deliberately misleading and puzzling. Like Mendonça, Sequeira was 'just looking for gold in the Isles of Gold'. Like Resende, he was 'unfortunately blown a thousand miles or so out of his course'.

And what is hardest of all to believe is the timetable that the chroniclers serve up to us. According to these reports, Sequeira reached the pleasant island, and there disembarked and for five months dallied in Arcadian surroundings, before finally deciding to start back for home. Why would a government ship dally for months on an idyllic island instead of getting on with the job? Something is being suppressed here, and it would be very interesting to know just what Sequeira was doing, and where he went. A hint of his arrival in the Northern Territory slipped out when Viegas defected to Spain. And at or about the time when Sequeira was dallying, for such an inordinate length of time, in his idyllic island, someone drew the accurate, continuous and homogeneous western coast which a few years later appeared in the Dieppe Map.

There is in these mysteries sufficient possibility to suggest that Sequeira saw more of the north and west coasts of the continent than the laconic chronicles suggest. Perhaps it was Sequeira who mapped the west coast, as Mendonça mapped the east coast. If it were, then at least Wytfliet's information that there had been two, and only two, voyages would be wholly justified. And this conclusion is assisted by the high reputation, quite out of proportion to his known achievements, that Sequeira enjoyed and still enjoys. It has been mentioned that Maffei expanded his exploits. Barbie du Bocage firmly opts for him as the discoverer of Australia. R. H. Major does the same. And in Portugal today the reputation of Gomes de Sequeira stands high.

Most Portuguese who think on this subject at all believe that the Portuguese discovered Australia, though few except the most knowledgeable could confidently name the discoverer. Among those who claim to know, Gomes de Sequeira is the name that would come to mind most readily. On the wall-maps which have been mentioned once or twice before, it is usually Sequeira's name that is written beside the ribbon which runs to Australia.

Chapter 22

THE TREATY OF SARAGOSSA

SEQUEIRA'S exploration of the Australian coast, whether great or small, was made in 1525; and therefore, in any case, it is subsequent in date to that of Cristovão de Mendonça. If Mendonça's priority is admitted, Sequeira sinks back to obscurity. There are no second prizes in exploring. Few remember that the second voyager along Tasman's track was the Frenchman Marion de Fresne, or that the next voyager up the east coast of Australia after Captain Cook (and before Captain Phillip) was the American Thomas Read.[1] In any case, Sequeira's contribution, on the barren north and north-west coasts, lessens his achievement. Dirk Hartog preceded Tasman, and Dampier preceded Cook; but the two former pale into insignificance in comparison with the latter two. And so, it seems, it must be the road to oblivion for Gomes de Sequeira.

His patent distinction is that he does figure quite prominently on the two important maps which have been mentioned. His latent distinction is that he paved the way for that stupendous deal in real estate which we know as the Treaty of Saragossa.

The opportunity came in 1529, through Spain's financial difficulties. Spain could not involve herself in the Americas, in the Orient, and in the maelstrom of European politics at the same time, without strain. Probably realising that Portugal was too well established in the East to be moved without immense cost, she saw that she should cut her losses, and the best place to cut losses was in the East.[2]

J. A. Williamson has unearthed the interesting information that the Emperor Charles V thought of selling his claim in the Moluccas (for what it was worth) to Henry VIII of England.[3] Henry called on his Spanish ambassador, Dr Edward Ley, for advice on this proposal, and Ley in his turn asked for advice from Robert Thorne. This latter report is extant ('Letter to Dr Ley'),[4] and shows that there were Englishmen already contemplating entry into the Pacific.

This idea came to nothing, and Spain again put pressure on Portugal. This was the year of crisis, when after the failure of the Junta of Badajoz the Emperor ordered fleets to be prepared for the invasion of the Spice Islands. But the heat was taken out of the crisis by some opportune royal marriages: King João III married Caterina of Castile, sister of the Emperor; and Charles V married Isabella, sister of the Portuguese King. And the Spanish Emperor let it be known that he would be susceptible to a cash offer. By the Treaty of Saragossa in 1529 a deal was made. Portugal paid the Emperor of Spain three hundred and fifty thousand ducats, and the Tordesillas boundary was adjusted.[5]

The Treaty[6] is puzzling, because neither side really laid its cards on the table, and each side proceeded from a different set of premises. Portugal firmly and consistently affirmed that the meridian of Long. 129° (Greenwich) E was the Line of Demarcation, and that all of her forts and possessions were entirely on her side of the line. By this time the Spaniards were convinced – privately, if not openly – that Portugal had correctly fixed the Brazilian boundary, even though for political purposes it was convenient to argue about this too. This is evidenced in the Spanish chroniclers. Argensola says that the line fixed by the Treaty of Tordesillas fell at the western entrance of the River Mananoa. Pigafetta says: 'The Line of Demarcation is 30° from the Meridian, and the Meridian is 3° from Cape Verde.' As Cape Verde is on, or close to, Long. 18° (Greenwich) w, the total $18 + 3 + 30 = 51$, and it will be remembered that Long. 51° (Greenwich) w is the meridian of the Waipoco River:[7] and as $180 - 51 = 129$, the Line of Demarcation in the Spice Islands sector must be Long. 129° (Greenwich) E, the line that Portugal propounded. Therefore the only dispute that could remain was where the 129th meridian actually ran on the ground (or sea); and while the uncertainty of longitude in those days admittedly could create differences of opinion lengthening into fifty or a hundred or even two hundred miles, it could not possibly have resulted in the extravagant westward placement of the line that the Spaniards propounded. Magellan and Pigafetta, straining to give Spain the most favourable boundary possible, were only able to place the Moluccas eight degrees on the Spanish side of the line. Yet at the abortive Junta of Badajoz and on similar occasions, Spain made the extravagant claim that the whole of the East Indian Archipelago, even Java and Borneo and Singapore, was on the east side of the Line. One of the Spanish representatives at Badajoz was Nuno Garcia de Toreno,[7] and the map which he prepared for the discussions there is still preserved: it shows his version of the Line just touching Singapore, a full thirty degrees away from the Portuguese boundary.

As a result, the negotiations at Saragossa ran on the unreal basis of Spain saying: 'We offer to sell you Java, Borneo, Timor and the Moluccas for 350,000 ducats,' to which Portugal's real answer should have been: 'But we own all of these already.' On the other hand, Portugal was wanting to say: 'We offer to pay you 350,000 ducats in consideration of your dropping claim to Java, Borneo, Timor and the Moluccas,' but this would have entailed loss of face in admitting that Spain *did* have some such claim, in admitting that the Tordesillas Line was not where Portugal had marked it.

One interpretation of the Treaty that resulted is that it is a face-saving compromise to solve this dilemma. Another zone, from the disputed Portuguese boundary eastwards to Long. 144° (Greenwich) E, was brought into the bargaining. Then Spain could offer to sell 'all its rights as far as this meridian' without either side having to admit where the old Tordesillas Line was, or should have been. Spain could say that she had sold from 100° to 144° for that sum; Portugal could say that she had bought from 129° to 144° for that sum; and then everybody would be happy.

And that is the form in which the Treaty of Saragossa was finally cast. The text runs:[8]

'A line must be determined from Pole to Pole, that is to say from north to south, by a semi-circle extending north-east by east nineteen degrees from Molucca, to which number of leagues correspond about seventeen degrees on the equinoctial, amounting to $297\frac{1}{2}$ leagues east of the Islands of Moluccas, allowing $17\frac{1}{2}$ to an equinoctial degree. In this north-east-by-east rhumb-line are situated the Islands of Las Velas and Santo Tomé, through which the said line and semi-circle pass. Since these islands are situated and are distant from the Moluccas the said distance, more or less, the deputies determine and agree that the said line be drawn at the said $297\frac{1}{2}$ leagues to the east, the equivalent of 19° north-east-by-east from the said islands of Moluccas as aforesaid.'

The trigonometry of this calculation is not correct, for the secant of the north-east-by-east angle ($\angle 33\frac{3}{4}°$) to the radix of 17 is 20.4, not 19; but the idea is quite clear. There is an island (islands), they said, in Lat. 11° N or thereabouts, north-east-by-east from the Moluccas, and that island (islands) can be found from these directions. That island lies on a meridian of longitude 17 degrees east of the Moluccas, and it is declared that the boundary of the new zone being purchased by Portugal is this meridian. For the price of 350,000 ducats, Portugal purchases everything up to that new line. For the remainder of this discussion, that new line will be called 'the Saragossa Line'. As the main Spice Islands, Ternate, Tidore and Amboina, were about two degrees west of the Tordesillas Line – say in Long. 127° (Greenwich) E – the Saragossa Line can be taken as Long. $127° + 17°$, or Long. 144° (Greenwich) E.

It is here that the first voyage of Gomes de Sequeira becomes significant.[9] He was the Portuguese who went out to investigate that area, and to report. His report would have said that he had sighted such and such islands, that they had such and such potentialities, that the area was of such and such strategic value: we do not know his exact findings, but it can be inferred from the subsequent Treaty that he had recommended that the Carolines and Marianas be included in the purchase. De Barros admits that his discoveries were 'the most easterly that we have achieved',[10] and the boundary must have resulted from his investigations, for the island of São Tomé (which was discussed in the consideration of his first voyage) is cited as the boundary-post in the Treaty itself.

But what of Sequeira's second voyage? Clearly his voyage to the south-east was also connected with these negotiations, but, unlike his first voyage, it is not explicitly referred to in the text of the Treaty. From Magellan and Saavedra, Spain knew as much as Portugal knew about the north-east sector – boundless sea, with only a few tiny islands, possibly with only the two tiny islands of Velas and São Tomé – and Spain could without compunction part with an area as desolate as that. But Spain had no inkling of what Portugal knew about the south-east sector. The second voyage of Sequeira[11] had brought reports of the Timorlaut and Aroe and Kei Islands, probably Wessel and Croker and Melville and Bathurst Islands, and part of the Arnhem-land coast, certainly the south-west coast of New Guinea, possibly the Torres Strait Islands, even Cape York Peninsula itself. Over and above that, Cristovão de Mendonça had brought back a chart of an immense continent stretching south from those northern borders; and unlike all other pre-Cook visitors from Jantzoon to Dampier, Mendonça had more to report than arid coasts, for at the places where he probably landed, such as Geelong and Bittangabee Bay, he saw the Australia Felix of later times. And most of this was on the Portuguese side of the new boundary which was being negotiated.

Portugal paid 350,000 ducats for something, and it is a theory seriously propounded by the Cortesão brothers[12] and others that, by withholding information about the existence of the Australian continent, she was tricking Spain into the inclusion of this in the sale. After all, there is precedent for this: for at the Treaty of Tordesillas[13] itself Portugal miraculously got the huge Brazilian slice of the American continent, something which Spain would certainly have refused if she had known of it, and something of which Portugal quite probably had advance knowledge at the time. The fact that one half of Sequeira's findings was disclosed, and the other half rigorously and deliberately suppressed, is quite significant. Even if Portugal was not deliberately angling to acquire Australia, conversely she may have been scheming to prevent Spain from hearing of these large lands to the south-east, for such knowledge might have caused Spain to increase her price, or even to discontinue negotiations altogether.

It is not true to suggest that Portugal paid 350,000 ducats just to buy Australia. The main value received for her money was the removal of the Spanish claim to the East Indies and the Spice Islands, the tacit admission that at least everything west of Long. 129° (Greenwich) E was, and always had been, Portuguese. Secondly, she bought a buffer-zone of a thousand miles of sea – probably of strategic value, even if it contained no lands at all. Thirdly, she openly obtained the Carolines and Marianas, and (by implication) the Philippines – although we shall find that later Spain took these back. On the secret list, there was New Guinea (for what it was worth), known from Meneses and Sequeira at least as a land-mass in being; and the Arafura Sea islands, two of which have been favourably reported upon by Sequeira. Further than this, it may be that the configurations of the coasts which by now were building up in the Casa da India would have suggested something of the ultimate geography of the Torres Strait area – a Gibraltar-like portal which is really the back door to the Spice Islands, and which could conveniently be fortified and closed against intruders. Jaime Cortesão puts it:[14]

> 'We conclude the geographical facts derived from Velho and Rebelo show that the Portuguese explorations were made with the deliberate intention of exploring that part of the world. And as these parts are in a geographical strategic position, they are material to the Treaty of Saragossa.'

It is significant that the boundary-line which was drawn at Saragossa (Long. 144° (Greenwich) E) is just east of Cape York, leaving the Strait and its approaches wholly on the Portuguese side. All of these things were, to Portugal, worth 350,000 ducats, even if the bonus of the Australian continent were not thrown in as well. But if, through the ignorance of Spain, this large new land was coming Portugal's way by default – well, it was not in the Portuguese character to say no to something which the gods were so liberally providing.

Cortesão's theory is not accepted by everyone, and for our purposes it does not much matter whether or not Portugal was deliberately angling to acquire the continent of Australia. The author thinks not: for Portugal's avarice was mainly commercial, and even if Mendonça and Sequeira had given a good indication of the shape and strategic position of the continent, they would scarcely have brought home glowing reports of its wealth or its trading potential. But probably Cortesão did not intend to go so far. He means more that

Portugal was angling to acquire Australia as a barrier against Spain, and Torres Strait as a defendable waterway. She had the knowledge that geography so provided; and if Spain was in ignorance of these geographical facts, then Portugal was willing to take advantage of such ignorance. For our purposes, this is not important. What is important is that the Treaty of Saragossa, and all that led up to it, is in itself strong confirmation of the fact that Portugal already had knowledge of the existence of Australia.

The signing of the Treaty of Saragossa made Portugal feel safer, and after this some of the old restrictions were modified. Cartographers now had much more access to Portuguese maps, and to this time belong the great names among the Lisbon mapmakers – the Reinels, the Homems, and Vaz Dourado.[15] During this time Spain found that her huge commitments in the Americas were absorbing all of her energies,[16] and for 13 years Portugal was left alone in the East. It was during this period that, if she had wanted it, Portugal had her golden chance to explore, annex and colonise Australia. All except a sliver along the east coast was now legally hers. In the Casa da India were the records of Mendonça and Sequeira, including the invaluable information concerning the passage through Torres Strait. Neither the Dutch nor the English were as yet posing any threat. In Timor she had a firmly established base, just a step from the Australian coast.

But Portugal, too, had overstrained her energies. Her widespread commitments elsewhere engaged all the manpower that she could spare. Greed directed most of her attentions to the wealth-providing Spice Islands, to the exclusion of all else. If Portugal indeed paid 350,000 ducats to buy Australia, she frittered away her chance to obtain any value from the purchase, for in 1542,[17] only 13 years after the signing of the Treaty of Saragossa and the acceptance of that load of ducats, Spain came back to the East. Cynically tearing up the Treaty, she arrived again in the Philippines, made attempts to settle colonies there, and in 1562 succeeded when Miguel Lopes Legaspi founded and then consolidated a colony at Cebu. It was many miles beyond the Saragossa Line – miles, indeed, on the Portuguese side of the old Tordesillas

Line: but Might is no respecter of Treaties, and Portugal had little redress. There was a Portuguese attempt to expel them from the Philippines in 1569, but it failed, and in 1571 Legaspi founded Manila.

But by then the Golden Age of the Portuguese nation was drawing to its close. On the fourth day of August 1578 it came to an abrupt end. Most objective historians place the blame for this squarely upon the unbalanced young King Sebastião. He had developed delusions of grandeur, visionary projects of extravagant ambition, delusory ideas of Portugal's wealth and strength, paranoic conceptions of his own greatness as King. In his wild dreams he saw himself as the Scourge of Islam, and embarked upon an invasion of Morocco which took sixteen thousand men across the Strait, leaving Portugal almost denuded of troops at home. He engaged the Moroccans at the battle of Alcazar-Quivir, and the whole of the Portuguese army was destroyed. The King himself lost his life there. Two years later, the Spanish invaded Portugal, and Portugal became a mere vassal of the Spanish Crown, and remained in Spanish captivity for sixty years.

Perhaps 'captivity' is a misnomer, although it is the word still used in Portugal to describe that unhappy period. It was not a total military occupation, and not a destruction of the Portuguese nation. Rather, it was a union of the two Crowns, not unlike the Union of England and Scotland after 1603. Portugal had a Spanish Governor, but retained self-government as a province. The Portuguese Empire in the East was not entirely absorbed into the Spanish Empire, although the Emperor's phrase of 'the empire upon which the sun never sets' implies it. Goa remained a metropolis in its own right, fighting the Dutch and trying to hold the Empire together, though unsuccessfully. Spain was not uncooperative in this – at times reinforcements were sent from Manila to help the hard-pressed Portuguese, and we have already heard how the Spanish helped defend the Waipoco border in Brazil.

But the union of the Crowns meant the effective end of the Treaties. Spain and its wholly-owned province could not go on arguing about theoretical boundaries, and the exact details of Tordesillas and Saragossa became blurred and forgotten. Similarly, the Politica do Sigilo lost its meaning, as it was hard for the Portuguese to keep matters secret against their Spanish overlords. Patriotic Portuguese officials tried to keep the Casa da India secrets inviolate, against the day when Portuguese discovering might flourish again: some charts and secret documents were surreptitiously removed,[18] others were hidden, none were made available except under pressure. There is no evidence that the Spanish governors ever saw the charts of Mendonça and Sequeira, or any other hard evidence of the discovery of Australia.

But at least the rumours and hearsay gossip about the Australian lands now came more freely to Spanish ears, and Spain was fired to do something positive about discovering and examining what we have called 'Spanish Australia'. Mendaña, who had been to the Solomon Islands in 1567, set out again in 1595 in search of the Great South Land, and another probe followed nine years later. In these Spanish expeditions to the South Seas, the Portuguese explorers Pedro Fernandes de Queiros and Luis Vaz de Torres played a leading part. Unlike Magellan and Estevão Gomes, who were renegades and are disowned by the Portuguese, these two still rank as Portuguese discoverers, sailing under the united flags of Spain and Portugal, and require some mention in a book devoted to Portuguese exploration in Australian waters.

De Queiros, who made two attempts to reach Australia, got no further than the Santa Cruz Islands on his first voyage, and the New Hebrides on his second. But before his documents became available it was believed by some that he had in fact made landfall in Australia, and it has been told how Archbishop Moran spread the belief that Queiros had landed at Gladstone, in North Queensland. That myth has now been exploded. It is true that Queiros landed in what are, in a sense, outlying Australian islands, but still they are more than a thousand miles away, and nowhere as near as the Portuguese were in their outlying island of Timor. Queiros belongs to the history of the Pacific, but only incidentally to the history of Australia.

Yet Pedro Fernandes de Queiros is a man who deserves a place in Australian history, and whose name ought to be revered. He consumed his life in pursuit of his dream, in advocacy of the Great South Land. Not only was he certain of its geographical existence, but he was certain of its economic potential and its future greatness. He was moved to desperation, even to tears, by officialdom's blindness to the great land which was there for the taking. Queiros is the mystical prophet of Australia. Though he never actually landed on Australian soil, his burning advocacy links him with Erédia as the first patriotic Australian. And Queiros was Portuguese. His unquestioning belief in the Great South Land was born of his juvenile dreams – 'almost from the cradle',[19] he tells us – in that distant Portuguese village in which he was born. It is interesting to note that there were such thoughts in such places in the sixteenth century, traditions about a great southern continent which were talked over at Portuguese firesides, stories treasured and repeated by the sons and grandsons of the men who had voyaged with Abreu and Mendonça and Sequeira, living legends which even the locks of the Casa da India could not suppress. The traditions which inspired Queiros were the traditions rooted in the Portuguese voyaging of the sixteenth century, traditions which still stir the Portuguese today when they gaze at the Fortaleza de Sagres or the Torre de Belém.

Queiros did not know directly of the Dieppe Maps, but he knew of the work of his Portuguese predecessors in Australian waters. Clear proof of this is given by one detail – his pre-knowledge of the existence of Torres Strait, which Cristovão de Mendonça (at least) had traversed. On one morning his pilot, Gaspar Gonsales de Leza, took the Altura and reported to Queiros that the ship was in Lat. $10\frac{1}{2}°$ s. Queiros remarked that the ship must then be in the latitude of Santa Cruz Island, but as that island was not in sight it would not be prudent to go in search of it in such weather. If the ship did so proceed to the west and happened to miss Santa Cruz Island, in that event – and the exact words of Queiros are here quoted:[20]

> '... we should come to the south side of New Guinea, where it would be a bad time of the year to make voyage, being the season of the south-west winds.'

So Queiros knew that New Guinea had a south side: and he knew that in proper season that south side could be navigated.

This pre-knowledge will be referred to again when the actual passage of the strait by Torres is under examination; but it is well to remember that Queiros, like Torres, had knowledge of the discoveries made by the Portuguese navigators before him.

And the Spanish officials who sent him out either knew of the Dieppe Maps, or of the tradition which produced them, for the instructions given to Queiros are in phraseology which links with the Dieppe Maps:[21]

> Forasmuch as I have ordered Captain Pedro Fernandes de Queiros, a Portuguese by nation, to proceed ... to discover New Guinea, Java Major and other southern lands ...

Cristovão de Mendonça had sought to find Jave-la-Grande from the west; now it was the turn of Pedro Fernandes de Queiros to try to find it from the east. The greatest tragedy in the history of discovery is that this burning seeker failed in his quest.

Torres, too, showed knowledge of the prior penetration of the strait, and therefore prior knowledge of the existence of the continent to the south of it. On 8 June 1606 the ships of de Queiros and Torres became separated under mysterious circumstances in the New Hebrides. They were returning to the Bay of St Philip and St James, Torres entering the bay first. According to de Queiros' later story, he (de Queiros) was prevented from entering by the wind, tried again and failed, and thus lost contact with Torres. Torres tells us a very different story. According to him, de Queiros entered, anchored in the most sheltered part of the bay, and then in the middle of the night slipped out again 'without making any signal'. The probable explanation is that the crew had mutinied, as Torres' colleague de Prado later learnt at Manila.[22]

Torres was therefore deserted in mid-ocean, under stress to get back to civilisation in Manila as soon and as quickly as possible: 'we had at this time nothing but bread and water; it was the height of winter, with sea, wind and ill-will against us'. In this state of emergency he sailed for home. It would have been open to him to proceed from the New Hebrides to Manila along the well-known track north of New Guinea –

indeed that was the instruction that de Queiros had given for the event of the separation of the ships. But Torres did not take this route. He chose instead to coast along the south coast of New Guinea. 'I could not weather the east point, so I coasted along to the westward under the south side'. So he chose to coast along the south side, *because he knew that New Guinea had a south side.* By electing to take this route, he advertised that he had prior knowledge that there was a water-way between Australia and New Guinea, that before entering it he knew for certain that the strait which we now call Torres Strait existed. And by this he confirms de Leza's conversation with de Queiros.

Some writers try to interpret the passage about 'weathering the east point' of New Guinea as meaning that he was not a free agent, that he was forced against his will to take that course. That argument is not sound. As can be seen from his track in Fig. 24.1 he was westing towards the 'point' of New Guinea for many hundreds of miles. At Tagula Island, at Misima Island, he had open water to the north of him – yet he kept heading westwards towards New Guinea. Perhaps he did intend to turn north at the point itself, and the argument against him apparently assumes that by bad seamanship he allowed himself to overshoot the turn, and then because of unfavourable winds he was unable to get back. That could happen, and in a sailing ship it could be a very annoying temporary obstacle. But if it had been absolutely necessary there would always have been some way around the difficulty, some way to turn back, some way to retrace steps, however circuitous. Supposing that Torres had known absolutely for certain that there was no strait to the west of him, it is not possible to believe that he would fatalistically have sailed up to the dead-end of the gulf, just because of one adverse wind at Samarai. Surely a man who had sailed half way round the world was not going irretrievably to be put off course by one difficult wind at the China Strait corner. What Torres said is that he knew that there was a passage around the north, that he also knew that there was a passage around the south, and it was immaterial to him which way he went.[23] The wind at the China Strait corner decided it for him – as it was not suitable to choose the northern track, quite happily he chose the southern track.

This view is supported by the mental reactions which Torres reveals. In the course of his voyage from the New Hebrides he discovered some new Land – Tagula Island, Jenkin's Bay, Orangerie Bay – and at each he reacted as is normal with explorers, recording them, naming them, and showing his interest in them. But when he came to the great Strait which today bears his name, he did not even mention it. He did not say 'There is a strait here! Thank God, we're saved'. He did not claim it as the solution of a great geographical puzzle, as Cook did 164 years later. He did not name it after himself. He just sailed through it without comment, treating the whole operation as commonplace.[24] Clearly Torres knew of the existence of that strait before he left the New Hebrides. Clearly he knew of the work of his Portuguese predecessors in those waters.

For Torres, too, was Portuguese.[25] It is true that his one great voyage was under the Spanish flag, but it was after the union of the two crowns, so he was not a renegade. In his person he brings to a close the Golden Age of the Portuguese Discoverers. Already the Portuguese nation was under the yoke of Spain, not to emerge again as a free nation until the mid-seventeenth century, when one of the signs of her newfound independence was the appearance of a Portuguese princess as Queen of England. In the next hundred years Portugal blossomed again as a great power, but this was her Silver Age, her wealth based upon the mines of Brazil and not upon the enterprise of her seamen. After Torres, the great Portuguese brotherhood of the sea was no more.

PART FOUR

'Something, for sure'

Chapter 23

ALEXANDER DALRYMPLE

IT was Alexander Dalrymple (1737–1808) who was primarily responsible for the renewed English interest in exploration which led to Cook's voyage in 1770; and as a by-product Dalrymple's labours also brought to light the Dauphin Map, and raised the questions of the Portuguese discovery of Australia.

Anyone who looked at Alexander Dalrymple in his earlier life would have been hard put to see explorer material in him. An official in the East India Company, his interests seemed to be limited to country houses and trade – he did not appear to be a roamer or an adventurer. As an officer in the Company he was posted to Madras, and there two events changed his life. Thereafter his single purpose in life was to explore the South Seas: in the Introduction to his book on discoveries in the South Pacific he confessed that he was 'induced to forego every wish towards objects perhaps more lucrative and was solicitous to be engaged in Discovery in the South Sea.'[1]

The first of these events was the death of William Roberts, who had lived in Manila. When his effects were sold, Dalrymple bought his books, and found himself studying the history of the Spanish Pacific. Later in his travels he acquired other Spanish maps and manuscripts; and later again, in London, he managed to purchase the Arias Memorial.[2] But this purchase of the Roberts books put him on the track which he never left for the rest of his life – interest in maps and histories of voyages, interest in the Pacific and in the alleged Great South Land. It was this that made him a hydrographer, later reaching the pinnacle of that profession when the British Admiralty made him Hydrographer (i.e. map expert) in charge of the newly-created Hydrography Department of the British Navy. And on his death his own private collection was said to total twenty thousand maps.

The second turning-point was when the East India Company put him in command of the *Cuddalore* in its voyage in search of new trade outlets in the central East Indies.

Dalrymple was not a trained navigator, either in the Navy or the Merchant Marine. But he acquitted himself well on this voyage, handled his ship and the crew admirably, and received praise from his employers for his efforts. After that he fancied himself as an explorer, and marked out the Great Unknown Southern Continent (Terra Australis Incognita) as the venue for his exploits.

It must be understood that Dalrymple's Great Southern Continent (that is the term which he himself habitually used) was *not* Australia, or New Holland, as it was then called. The reader will remember the theories about this unknown continent, and the Doctrine of the Assumption of Land, which was discussed at some length in Chapter 10.[3] The first theory was that there must be a great counterbalancing continent, as large as the Euro-Asian land-mass, covering the South Pole and filling up most of the Pacific. As each successive explorer whittled this down in size, dividing it, diminishing it, driving back a coast here and cutting off a bulge there, there was nevertheless always some residual unexplored area left in which the remnant of the unknown continent was still assumed to exist. Before Dalrymple's day, Tasman had split the supposed continuous land-mass down the middle, creating two continents – Australia (New Holland) to the west, and the Unknown Continent somewhere out in the east, presumably south of Tahiti, west of Roggeveen's track, east of Tasman's track. In other words, the triangle just described had still not been entered by anyone, and therefore it was the assumed home of the assumed continent. When Dalrymple speaks of his Great Southern Continent, he means this presumed eastern continent, not New Holland, which by then was tolerably well-known. When Dalrymple uses the word 'Australia' he does not mean our Australia (or New Holland), but one particular section of the Great Antarctic Continent, by whatever name the world called it.

Dalrymple was quite aware of the existence of New Holland – the continent already two-thirds charted by Tasman and Pieter Nuyts and others, including the Englishman Dampier – and he was not very interested in it. While he was in the East India Company's service he did sometimes make reference to New Holland, but always without interest. When he was planning his Sulu settlement, it occurred to him that the new settlement might have opportunity to trade with New Holland, if New Holland had any facilities for trade – that is, if the little-known Australian aborigines had any coconuts or other produce to barter – so he made some inquiries about it. He knew from his reading that 'geographers ascribe to the Portuguese in early times the discovery of a country in this quarter', and he sought information about the prospects of trade from the Bugis,[4] far-roaming adventurers from Macassar whose strong-arm tactics took them into contact with the outer tribes beyond the pale of civilisation. But what the Bugis had to tell him does not seem very applicable to Australia, and probably they were under the impression that Dalrymple was inquiring about New Guinea, or the Arafura Sea Islands. There Dalrymple's inquiries ended. He was not then, or at any time afterwards, really interested in our Australia (New Holland). It had already been discovered, and there would not be much glory in rediscovering it. His glory would be in the discovery of that other bigger, better, richer continent which he thought to be in the area between New Zealand and South America.

He returned to London in 1765. At this time there was a great public wave of enthusiasm for Pacific exploration. Charles de Brosses[5] and Buache tried to drum up French enthusiasm for the founding of a New France in southern seas, but France's defeat in the Seven Years War took the momentum out of this drive. When Dalrymple was in Manila,[6] he had heard of Spanish plans to send expeditions of discovery to the South Pacific, which she claimed as her mare clausum by right of Tordesillas and Saragossa. In England, the Earl of Egmont, First Lord of the Admiralty, was full of enthusiasm for British exploitation of this empty area. England had just defeated Spain in the Seven Years War, in which Manila (Spain's capital in the Pacific) had been captured, and the bottom had been knocked right out of the mare clausum claim. In 1766 John Callander wrote that it was England's duty to find out what she had won in this war.[7] The English Pacific probes which followed have something in common with the probes of Vasco de Gama and António de Abreu for Portugal, and of Magellan for Spain, following the Treaty of

Tordesillas – a rather excited rush to see what had been acquired in the lucky dip.

Dalrymple clearly set himself to enter into this activity. He joined the Royal Society, and became influential in it. He remade or courted acquaintance with people in power, and established for himself a reputation as a great authority on the former Spanish Pacific. He let it be known that he was writing a book – which he did[8] – on the voyages already made in the Pacific, stressing every shred of evidence which pointed to the existence of the Great Southern Continent. He soon had Egmont openly advocating that it would be to England's advantage to discover this great continent, and that expeditions should be mounted to do so.

Dalrymple's Great Southern Continent was not his own invention, and his arguments in its favour were no more than a re-statement of old theories. He argued again the counter-balancing theory. He produced again the 'evidence' of those who had claimed to have seen its edges. Above all, he hammered home the undeniable fact that there was there a great triangle of the earth's surface which had never been entered by anyone: no one could prove that it was sea, and so it could be assumed to be land. This was the Doctrine of the Assumption of Land, at its most potent.

In the course of collecting the material for his book he ransacked the bookshops, the libraries and the private collections of the country. His greatest known prize was the two Arias Memorials – the reports which Dr Arias presented to the King of Spain concerning the Juan Fernandez 'discovery' of land west of the coast of Chile, and concerning the Torres voyage through the strait between Australia and New Guinea. Considerably later he also unearthed the Torres letter, which he permitted James Burney to publish in Burney's book of discoveries.[9]

Dalrymple was much more interested in the first-mentioned Memorial than in the second. His burning interest was not in Australia, but in the great Unknown Continent between Chile and New Zealand. He emphasised in every way possible the 'proof' that Juan Fernandez had seen the coast of this, and he was only mildly and incidentally interested in Torres and his Strait. He did think that this Strait should be examined, as it might be a useful avenue of trade between the East India Company and the continent which he (Dalrymple) was going to discover. But he was not interested in the Australia-New Guinea area for its own sake, for demonstrably it was not, or was no longer, part of the conjectured Great Southern Continent. This was Tasman's doing. By his track from Mauritius, south of Australia, to Tasmania, then east of Australia to New Zealand and Tonga, then north of both Australia and New Guinea back to Java, Tasman had completely circumnavigated the continent without seeing any of it, but in doing so had irrevocably severed the whole of this area from the hypothetical continent to the east, and thus had removed it from the area which Dalrymple had pledged himself to discover. It was not Dalrymple's ambition to strut in London as the discoverer of Australia, not even as discoverer of the east coast of Australia; and he was not going to enthuse over anyone who did. The triumph he coveted was to be hailed as the Great Discoverer of the Great South Land.

And in the course of his systematic combing of libraries and collections he may have seen – Barbie du Bocage says he must have seen – one or more of the Dieppe Maps. The Rotz Circular and the Rotz Plane had been presented to King Henry VIII, and were extant in the Royal Papers. Eventually they found their way to the British Museum, where they can be seen in the Royal Collection today. In Dalrymple's time they were still under Palace control, but Dalrymple's influential connections were such that he was not barred from such collections. The Dauphin was in England, previously owned by Edward Harley, Earl of Oxford,[10] who like Egmont had been one of the Lords of the Admiralty, and whose information on this subject would surely be known by someone in the Admiralty Office. We shall return to this subject again, at the stage in Dalrymple's life where the question of his knowledge, or lack of knowledge, of the Dauphin Map becomes of interest. But at this stage the Dieppe Maps would not be of much importance to Dalrymple, for they were not relevant to Dalrymple's dream. The Dieppe Maps dealt with New Holland, not with the Great Southern Continent. Dalrymple knew that the Portuguese had some knowledge of New

Holland – just how much, he did not know and he did not care – but they had no knowledge at all of the Dalrymplean Southern Continent further east, so they were not of any use to him. He was writing a book, which while it was to be called *Discoveries in the Pacific* was unadulterated propaganda for his own pet continent, and the Dieppe Maps of New Holland would not have made the pages of his book, even if copies had been open on his desk. Therefore we do not know whether Dalrymple had or had not seen these Maps before his first mention of them in 1786.

Dalrymple's great chance to lead an exploring expedition to the continent of his dreams came in 1768. The astronomers had drawn attention to the coming transit of Venus, which would be visible in the South Pacific, and the Royal Society interested itself in the project. Dalrymple saw himself as the commander of an expedition sponsored by the Royal Society, subsidised by the government and sent to the South Seas for this purpose: then, after successfully doing whatever was required with the planet Venus, the amazing commander would head his ships south, unveil to his shipmates and to the world the Great Continent which was waiting for him, and return home to plaudits which would resound down the ages into eternity.

It was an enthralling vision. Dalrymple pulled all the strings he could, both at the Royal Society and with high personages in the government, to have himself appointed to this post. With the Society, he was successful – after a ballot he received the appointment, and it was taken for granted that he would lead the expedition. He actively entered upon his new duties, including shopping around for a suitable ship for the enterprise, and he is credited with having selected the *Endeavour* (or the ship which later was to be named *Endeavour*) as his first choice. But the Society did not have the funds to purchase the ship, and was forced to appeal to the Admiralty for assistance. The Admiralty agreed, but this changed the nature of the proposed expedition. It was no longer a Royal Society scientific expedition, but a naval expedition, and the Navy was adamant that no Navy ship would sail with a civilian in charge. So Alexander Dalrymple was passed over, and Lieutenant James Cook was appointed to the command instead.

This was a bitter blow to Dalrymple, and he withdrew from the expedition altogether. The traditional view, fostered by R. H. Major and adopted by most subsequent writers, is that in his embittered frustration he became the public enemy of his supplanting rival, and that for the rest of his life his attitude to Cook was marred by jealousy, vindictiveness and spite. Conversely, in the traditional view, Cook reacted to this unfriendliness, and in his turn publicly showed antagonism towards Dalrymple. The subsequent actions and writings of the two men tend to confirm this, and the author must admit that he has always regarded this interpretation as self-evident, although in a recent book Dr Howard Fry has cast doubts on the validity of this traditional view.[11]

Preparations for the voyage got under way. The *Endeavour* was bought, a crew was collected, Green was appointed astronomer to view the transit, Banks and Solander joined as scientists from the Royal Society, Cook and his officers received their briefing from the Admiralty. From all of this activity, Dalrymple kept himself sulkily aloof. He probably had more information about the charts of the area than any man living, but pointedly he made no move to supply Cook with his maps or his advice, and Cook just as pointedly made no move to request it. Dalrymple's book *An Account of Discoveries in the South Pacific to 1764* had already been printed, but strangely, perhaps significantly, had not yet been published. This book contained all known information about the earlier voyages to the Pacific and clearly would have been of much interest to any intended explorer of the Pacific, but Dalrymple did not offer it to Cook, and possibly withheld publication so that he could not see it. The truth is that he had collected and compiled these records to assist himself in the great expedition which he had hoped to lead; when he had been supplanted by Cook, it was not in his nature to make them available to his rival.

But further, Dalrymple's book of maps and early voyages had been compiled and printed, but not published, even before he had been supplanted by Cook, so that even in the days when Dalrymple was strutting the stage as Discoverer-Elect he was withholding publication of his book, and therefore keeping private the information that he had obtained. In this octavo volume there is a good composite map of

Mendaña's Solomon Islands, de Queiros's New Hebrides, Tasman's track south and east of Australia, and Schouten's track along the north coast of New Guinea; and, in addition, the south coast of New Guinea, and Dutch New Holland. In this map the Torres Strait area is clearly shown; and, indicated by a dotted line, is the actual track of Torres from the New Hebrides through Torres Strait to Manila, based on the records of the Arias Memorial.

When Cook was appointed to the command of the *Endeavour* instead of Dalrymple, the latter was bitterly disappointed. His apologist, Dr Howard Fry, at least goes as far as this; while harsher critics of Dalrymple have substituted for the emotion 'disappointment' more uncomplimentary words such as 'spite' and 'malice' and 'jealousy'. In his disappointment or worse, he was not able to approach Cook with a friendly offer of assistance and advice; and he refrained from showing Cook his map, or giving him a copy of it.

But Dalrymple had no quarrel with Banks. As we know from Dalrymple's subsequent letter to Hawkesworth,[12] he gave Banks a copy of his octavo volume, including the map with the dotted line showing the track of Torres through the strait. Cook saw this map on the *Endeavour*, and his reaction to it will be examined in the next chapter.

After the return of the *Endeavour*, Cook's *Journal* was published, edited by Hawkesworth. Certain passages in it appeared to disparage Dalrymple and to snub his pet theories. Dalrymple whipped himself into a rage.[13] Not knowing to what extent Cook was responsible, and to what extent Hawkesworth, he attacked them both. His attack on Cook even descended to taunting him about his seamanship (or lack of it) in running the *Endeavour* onto a reef. His attack on Hawkesworth was so violent that it is believed to have caused his death.

Then, to crown it all, in 1786 (after Cook's death), in his pamphlet on the Chagos Islands,[14] Dalrymple startled the world by disclosing that Captain Cook's triumphant discovery of the east coast was not discovery at all, that he (Dalrymple) had in his possession a map – the Dauphin Map – which showed that Cook had a predecessor who had traversed the coast two hundred years or more before him. To this point

Dalrymple's disclosure was soundly based: the Dauphin Map does show that the east coast had been visited and charted in the earlier century. But, less soundly, Dalrymple went further, implying (or seeming to imply, by innuendo) that Cook fraudulently knew of the Dauphin Map, that Cook dishonestly had it 'under the counter' in his chart-room, that Cook deviously was passing himself off as the Great First Discoverer when he knew all the time that he was only the second. These are fighting words, and the Dalrymple innuendo has been hotly contested. The charge will be examined further when we come to the chapter on Captain Cook.

Dalrymple's cognizance of the Dieppe Maps crops up again in connection with the proposal to colonise Australia. In about 1783 the proposal for the establishment of a convict settlement at Cook's Botany Bay was moving into the realm of practical politics. A few enthusiasts, including Banks, Matra and Young, were pressing the government to implement this scheme. Most people seemed indifferent, not caring whether the scheme proceeded or not. A few people – a very few, it would seem – opposed the scheme. And one of these opponents was Dalrymple.

But the reasons why he was so hysterically opposed to this proposal are, like so much in Dalrymple, hopelessly tangled. Deep down, the old enmity with Cook still rankled, and this proposal to colonise Cook's Botany Bay was too much to the glory of Cook. Perhaps, prophetically, looking far into the future, he could glimpse Cook's ultimate, immortal memorial – the Commonwealth of Australia. Secondly, his loyalty was still to the East India Company, and he feared that this new colony would dent the Company's monopoly: perhaps it would ultimately drive the Company out of business altogether. Above all, this was not going to be the peopling of his own Great Southern Continent, not the foundation of the proud Dominion of Dalrymplea, named after its famous discoverer; it was not going to be the fruition of those dreams that had tormented him on that shore at Madras. It was the peopling of a different continent, honouring a different discoverer. And Alexander Dalrymple instinctively, predictably, understandably, opposed it.

In his pamphlet 'A Serious Admonition to the Public on the Intended Thief Colony at Botany Bay'[15] he called up every argument that he could think of to oppose the proposal, and one of his arguments was that, as Cook was not the First Discoverer of the Botany Bay coast, England had no right to plant a settlement there. He produced the Dauphin Map again, and paraded the evidence which it afforded to show that Cook was not the discoverer:

> 'That the country, be it called New Holland or New South Wales or by whatever name, was discovered before Captain Cook's voyage, is obvious from a very ancient map in which it is described, but I am ignorant what nation can claim the discovery. The map appears to be in date not long subsequent to Magellan's voyage, and I think may be assuredly determined to be above two hundred years old.'

Dalrymple also quoted a Dutchman, Nicolas Struyck, who claimed to have seen a Dutch map which showed the east coast of Australia and therefore (Dalrymple believed) evidenced a Dutch voyage of discovery, also before Captain Cook. There is no evidence that the Dutch ever visited the east coast of the mainland – indeed the reliable Dutch maps and records indicate quite the reverse. The map which Struyk saw must therefore have been one of the Dutch derivatives of the Dieppe Maps, for example that of Cornelis de Jode.[16]

Dalrymple knew that Cook was not the first discoverer of the east coast; but whether, in international law, that affected England's right to annex and colonise is a slender and tenuous line of argument, and Dalrymple himself was only half-hearted in advancing this objection. For the purposes of this chapter, the importance of the 'Serious Admonition' does not spring from this legal quibble, but from the fact that an important geographer in England was making known to the world the existence of the Dieppe Maps and the evidence which they afforded to show that the east coast had been previously explored and charted in the sixteenth century. Whether Cook knew of the Dieppe Maps before the *Endeavour* sailed is a different question altogether.

Chapter 24

COOK AND BANKS

D ID Captain Cook know of these Portuguese maps
prior to his discovery, or rediscovery, of the east coast
of Australia? This is the question that is constantly being
asked. Whenever the author has lectured on this subject, the
one inevitable question asked is the one posed here. And yet,
to the author's mind, the question seems of little importance
to the main purpose of this book. If Mendonça did discover
the east coast, and if the Dauphin Map portrayed it, then it
was so discovered and so portrayed whether Captain Cook
happened to know of this or not.

Captain James Cook was a very great man, and the voyage
of the *Endeavour* was a very great voyage. If in fact he had a
predecessor on the east coast of Australia, that should only
fractionally diminish his glory. Professor Beaglehole, Cook's
greatest admirer, happily speaks of Cook as the 'virtual
discoverer' of his country (New Zealand),[1] not in any way
surrendering because Tasman had made a fleeting visit there
some 130 years before. If tomorrow someone found in the
Torré de Tombo, in Lisbon, some indisputable sixteenth-
century manuscript which afforded cast-iron proof of very
substantial Portuguese exploration – perhaps even temporary
colonisation – of the east coast of Australia, it is not likely that
on the next day we would start demolishing Cook's statues all
over Australia; nor is it possible that he would forfeit the
unique affection and respect which all Australians so justly
feel for him.

It might be that national pride – England's national pride –
would be a little dented if this thesis were widely accepted.
Barbie du Bocage said in a lecture:[2]

'The English pretend that none of these charts [referring to
the Dieppe Maps] were discovered till after the death of
Captain Cook; and thus they had no knowledge of them
when the voyage was made. But their prior existence in
well-known libraries in England may cause this assumption
to be doubted.'

This famous broadside could have one of two meanings – either for reasons of high policies of State, or from considerations of national prestige, England sought to maximise the deeds of her own explorers, and to suppress knowledge of the prior explorations of other nations. If there were such suppression, at national level, at least Cook's personal reputation would not be harmed. But Cook's personal reputation would suffer if it were proved that he, personally, deliberately suppressed knowledge of the Portuguese maps in order to enhance his own reputation. This will have to be examined – but it is an 'if', with many arguments against it.

And conversely, if the Portuguese maps are genuine and authentic, then whether Cook knew of them or did not know of them, whether he used them in his navigation or did not use them, cannot add to or subtract from the authenticity of the Portuguese maps in any way. If, in the extreme case that can be put, Cook did use them in guiding his ship to the haven of Cooktown Harbour after the *Endeavour* had been holed on the Barrier Reef, then that is a dramatic and unsought piece of publicity for the Dieppe Maps. It would go to show how accurate they are in the North Queensland sector of the coast. It would add the august name of Cook to the list of those others, such as Flinders and Burney, who have expressed their faith in them. But Cook's knowledge of or use of the Maps could not make them genuine if they are not genuine, and cannot make them more genuine if they are.

On the other hand, if in some extraordinary way these Portuguese maps are bogus or spurious, as Professors Wood[3] and Scott[4] so strenuously attempt to make us believe, then nothing that Cook thought or said or did could alter that fact. Professors Wood's thesis is that the whole of the Dauphin Map is some miraculously-inspired guess, based on no factual knowledge whatsoever. If this were true, but relying on this bogus piece of cartographical fiction Cook still directed his stricken ship to the fictitious haven so invitingly displayed on it, then Cook was miraculously lucky, and that part of the coast was not only a brilliant guess but a guess which only a benign Providence could have inspired. As Professor J. A. Williamson said so well: 'If the maps were guesswork, they represent the most inspired guesswork ever recorded.'[5]

Nevertheless, the question of Cook's knowledge of the Dieppe Maps must be explored, because it was raised by Alexander Dalrymple one hundred and ninety years ago,[6] and intermittently raised at intervals ever since. In his pamphlet on the Chagos Islands, in 1786, Dalrymple informed the world that he had access to a map (the Dauphin Map) which more than two hundred years before had portrayed the east coast of Australia and which has some 'curious circumstances of correspondence' with Cook's own chart. We already know about the Map and about the coast. We must now consider this charge of 'curious correspondence'.

There have been two classical retorts to this charge. The first is that Dalrymple was so eaten with hate, spite and jealousy that he was just recklessly lashing out against Cook, and so any allegation that he made is necessarily so suspect that the charge is not worth considering. This is in line with the views held by commentators over the centuries, starting with Dr Hawkesworth,[7] when he said that Cook was considered 'except perhaps by Mr Dalrymple to be as good an officer and as able a navigator as the world has ever seen'. The author must admit that he too had always considered this to be the genesis of Dalrymple's charge, and in a previous study wrote:[8]

'Dalrymple, no doubt out of spite, accused Cook of basking in undeserved glory . . ... In the scales the reputation of the honest Cook strongly swings the balance against the shifty and malicious Dalrymple.'

But since then opportunity has intervened to read the careful study by Dr Howard Fry,[9] which seeks to show that this long-held reading is quite wrong. Dalrymple, he claims was not actuated by any hostility to Cook. And if that is the correct reading of Dalrymple, then it is not possible to shrug off the charge which he made in this easy manner, and further consideration has to be given.

The second classical view is that it would have been out of character for Cook to have stooped to deception. His honesty, his personal integrity were such that suppression of information would be an impossibility for him. The desire for

fame which might tempt a lesser man would be scorned by the
upright and modest Cook. But – and here is the rub – in
another direction Cook may have shown more human frailty.
Cook may have kept silent on some points – suppressed
information, if a harsher phrase is required – not for the
sake of exalting himself, but for the purpose of belittling
Dalrymple. The form which he showed on the subject of
Dalrymple's Torres Strait map encourages this view; and an
analogy drawn from his reticence about the Torres Strait map
suggests that there could have been equal reticence about the
Dauphin Map if it also had derived from Dalrymple.

Something was said of the Torres Strait map in the last
chapter. Dalrymple showed the track of Torres by a dotted
line on the map in his octavo volume of maps; and while he
would not give a copy to Cook, he did give a copy to Banks
before the *Endeavour* sailed. Banks showed it to Cook, who
looked at it with disdain. At the best his attitude may have
been 'Very interesting, but of course I cannot navigate my
ship on historical curiosities of this kind.' At the worst – and it
is easy to fear the worst – Cook was showing his distaste for

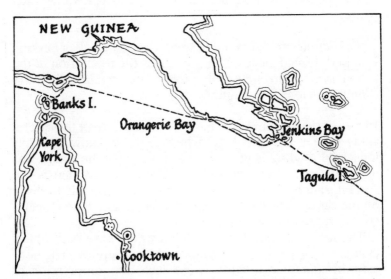

Fig. 24.1 TORRES STRAIT. The approximate track of Torres is
shown by dotted line.

Dalrymple by a studied snubbing of Dalrymple's map. So completely did Cook snub the map that, if it were not for one minor piece of evidence, some scholars would today be claiming that Banks had never shown the map to Cook, and that Cook discovered Torres Strait without any knowledge of Torres at all.

That one piece of evidence can be found earlier in Cook's *Journal*, in the entry of 31 March 1770. In the Eastern Pacific Cook found a minor error in Dalrymple's chart, and was quick to point it out. The French astronomer Pingré had published a book on the Transit of Venus, which Cook necessarily had read, and which he regarded very highly. However, 'Mr Dalrymple [Cook here mentions him by name] and other geographers have laid down Roggeveen's track very different from M. Pingré . . . having laid it down in Lat 27°s.' This, Cook reasoned, is patently absurd: for if Roggeveen had been in Lat 27°s. as distinct from Lat $28\frac{1}{2}$°s. he would have been slavishly following Schouten and Le Maire's track, and no sensible explorer would follow a predecessor's track so precisely, for 'by doing so he must be morally certain of not finding any new land'. It seems a small point. But it is important for us, as it proves that (a) Cook did see Dalrymple's map and (b) he was only too happy to mention Dalrymple by name when he was able to criticize him. So Cook was not likely to throw any bouquets to Dalrymple, or to bring forward any findings which might result in bouquets being thrown to Dalrymple by anyone else.

In that frame of mind Cook contemplated the Australian continent, where Dalrymple so confidently asserted that there was a strait which separated it from New Guinea. Cook approached the Australian coast with Dalrymple's map on board, and with a fierce resolve to 'clear up the doubt' about that strait. The most famous passage in the *Journal* is that of 17 August 1770, where the battered mariner reviews his battered ship and recollects the dangers through which it has passed, but manfully decides to keep plugging on:

> . . . let the consequence be what it will . . . to determine whether or no New Guinea joins to or makes a part of this land. This doubtful point I had from my first coming upon this coast determined if possible to clear up.

This has always been interpreted as a laudable urge to explore, to discover, to extend the world's geographical knowledge, a Ulysses-like itch 'to strive, to seek, to find'. But from what we have just been considering, Cook may have been driven by a less laudable motive. As Dalrymple was the champion of the There-is-a-strait theory, it seems a better possibility that Cook was being eaten by the desire to clear up the doubt the other way – that is, he was hoping that he would find no strait, and thus again discredit Dalrymple. Pingré's book, which has already been mentioned, says that Torres had passed *north* of New Guinea; and we know from Freville that Cook and Banks had arguments on this point, Cook favouring Pingré, Banks favouring Dalrymple. Cook was already coming home to say that Dalrymple's Easter Island was in the wrong place, and that his Great Southern continent did not exist. To this perhaps he could add that his alleged strait was just another Dalrympean misconception.

On 22 August 1770 Cook climbed a hill on an island in Torres Strait, and 'did not doubt but there was a passage'. Dalrymple was right after all. Yet in his *Journal* Cook does not give any credit to Dalrymple, he does not mention him by name, he does not mention that he had a map on board with the clear dotted line showing that another mariner had already passed through the strait. What, then, does Cook say? He could not say 'I discovered this strait', for in his conscience he would know that it was not true. He was not willing to say 'Torres was here before me', for that would be conceding victory to Dalrymple. So he compromises:

> I always understood before I had sight of these maps [he is speaking of Vaugondy's map, not Dalrymple's] that it was unknown whether or no New Guinea was not one continued land . . . however we have now put this wholly out of dispute . . .. I claim no other merit than the clearing up of a doubtful point.

So summarizing Cook's behaviour on the subject of Dalrymple's Torres Strait map:

1 Cook saw no reason why he should mention it.
2 Though he had seen the map, he would not admit that the strait had already been discovered.

3 He argued with Banks about it.
4 When he found that Dalrymple was one hundred percent right, he would not concede victory to him.
5 He side-stepped in his final finding, evading the issue by the phrase 'clearing up a doubtful point'.

And if, for the sake of argument, we consider as a supposition that Dalrymple had also given Banks a copy of the Dauphin Map before the *Endeavour* sailed, how then would Cook have reacted? On analogy with the above five points, we might expect:

1 Cook would not have mentioned it.
2 If he had seen the map, he would not have admitted that the East Coast had already been discovered.
3 He would have argued with Banks about it.
4 When he found that again Dalrymple was a hundred percent right, he still would not have conceded victory to him.
5 But . . .

It is on the fifth point that the rub comes. The first four Cook might have done, in his unwillingness to give any credit to Dalrymple. But here, on the fifth point, Cook did not side-step, he did not prevaricate, he did not seek a way out. Instead, on the fifth point he made this confident and positive claim in his own right: 'From lat. 38° South down to this place I am confident, was never seen or visited by any European before us' (*Journal*, 22 August 1770). If he had had a copy of the Dauphin Map in his hand while he was making this claim, it would have been downright dishonest. And Cook was not a dishonest man.

Yet when he arrived at Batavia, and sent off a letter from there to Philip Stevens, the Secretary of the Admiralty, Cook wrote (23 Oct 1770): 'Although the discoveries made in this voyage are not great . . .' And later, in a private letter to Mr Walker he repeats this phrase. Not great? For a man who had virtually discovered a continent, who was 'confident' that he had just explored two thousand miles of virgin coast never seen or visited by any European before, this seems to be carrying modesty too far. With respect to New Zealand, it would have been proper for Cook to write in this way, implying a distinction between 'discovery' (for Tasman had 'discovered' New Zealand) and 'exploring' – surveying, examining, charting, clearing up doubts, all very great deeds and important achievements in New Zealand waters, for which Cook must be given the greatest credit, even though he did not 'discover' the country. And if Cook did know of the Dieppe Maps, then his letter to Stevens and his letter to Walker could be explained as not coy and perhaps false modesty, but as a factual definition of his Australian achievement, on the same model as that applicable to New Zealand.

The postscript to Dalrymple's pamphlet on the Chagos Islands contains two elements: first, the Disclosure that Cook had had predecessors on the east coast of Australia – a statement which is factual and applicable whether Cook knew of the Dieppe Maps or not; secondly, the Insinuation that Cook did know the maps, indicated by the 'curious circumstances of correspondence' phrase and the circumstances of correspondence which Dalrymple lists. It is only in the second of these elements, in the Insinuation, that Dalrymple implies any culpability in Cook, in the form of deliberate suppression of knowledge.

The passage is undoubtedly a weapon with which to belabour Cook; but whether it was a weapon wielded in spite and hatred (as Professor Beaglehole thinks)[10] or a weapon wielded impersonally and dispassionately in the interests of geographical truth (as Dr Howard Fry thinks) does not affect the Disclosure, though it may affect the Insinuation. The Disclosure is quite definite:

'I have a manuscript in my possession, belonging to Sir Joseph Banks . . .. The very curious Manuscript here mentioned is painted on parchment with the Dauphin's Arms; it contains much lost knowledge; Kerguelen's Land seems plainly denoted; the east coast of New Holland, as we name it, is expressed . . . I have in the hands of the Engraver part of this curious manuscript which belonged to Lord Oxford's collection, as I was informed by my much lamented Friend Dr Solander, who gave it to Sir Joseph Banks'.

To the best of the author's knowledge, this is the first public announcement in the English language of the existence of the Dauphin Map. It is the fountainhead from which the rivers of ink have flowed in the next two hundred years. So far as the above quotation goes, it is impeccable. Dalrymple the geographer had come across this ancient map, and as a fact of life he is announcing its existence to the world. If the effect of this disclosure would be to relegate Captain Cook to the role of rediscoverer, not first discoverer, then let that be, for it would not be Dalrymple's fault. This Disclosure could have equally well been made by someone quite unknown to Cook, it could even have been made by his greatest friend or admirer, for a geographical fact is a geographical fact, and personalities do not come into it. The accident that this Disclosure happend to be made by a man who had a grudge against Cook is unfortunate, but it is irrelevant.

But when we come to the Insinuation, the 'curious circumstances of correspondence', different considerations are necessary. Dr Howard Fry denies that there was any innuendo at all. He claims that Dalrymple was not the kind of man who would make insinuations. But for two hundred years scholars have read an insinuation into the words that Dalrymple used: and, in law, an innuendo is an innuendo not because it was intended that way, but because the ordinary average reader does read it in that way.

The 'curious circumstances of correspondence' to which Dalrymple alludes do not add up to very much. Dalrymple finds, as he must find, that there are bays and capes and islands on the Dauphin Map which correspond with similar bays and capes and islands on Cook's chart. That, of course, proves nothing. If 'the East Coast of New Holland, as we name it, is expressed' – the words are Dalrymple's – on the Dauphin Map, and is again so expressed on Cook's chart, naturally the same features will occur on both, and there will be nothing 'curious' about their circumstances of correspondence. So Dalrymple has to look for any correspondences in the naming of the different features on the two maps, and he finds that the feature named 'R. de beaucoup d'isles' on the Dauphin is named 'Bay of Isles' on Cook's chart, that 'Baye Perdue' on the Dauphin is named 'Bay of Inlets' by Cook.

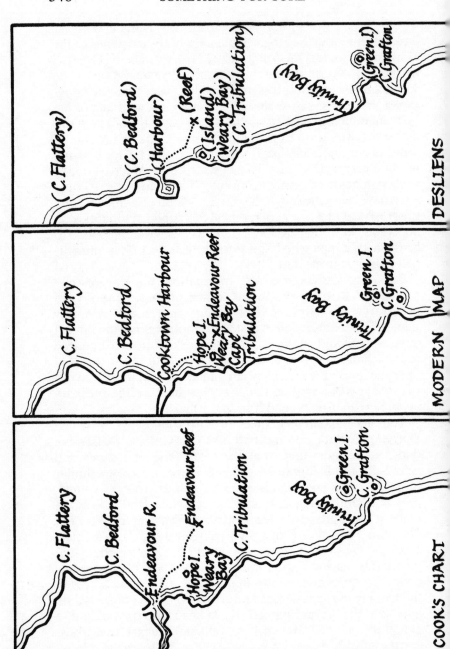

COOK'S CHART

C. Flattery
C. Bedford
Endeavour R.
Endeavour Reef
Hope I.
Weary Bay
C. Tribulation
Trinity Bay
Green I.
C. Grafton

MODERN MAP

C. Flattery
C. Bedford
Cooktown Harbour
Hope I.
Endeavour Reef
Weary Bay
Cape Bay
Tribulation
Trinity Bay
Green I.
C. Grafton

DESLIENS

(C. Flattery)
(C. Bedford)
(Harbour)
x (Reef)
(Island)
(Weary Bay)
(C. Tribulation)
(Trinity Bay)
(Green I.)
C. Grafton

There is nothing very damaging here, and Dalrymple seems to be scratching for bullets to fire: nothing that he is able to list justifies his sarcastic: 'so that we may say with Solomon – There is nothing new under the Sun.'

But soon another pairing, not at first noted by Dalrymple, set tongues wagging. Probably first in verbal discussions on Dalrymple's disclosure in naval and maritime circles someone noticed a further 'curious correspondence' – the parallel meaning of Cook's 'Botany Bay' and the Dauphin's 'Coste des herbaiges'. This is mentioned in Burney (James Burney of all people, Cook's pupil, shipmate and admirer) in the words:[11]

'By extraordinary co-incidence, immediately beyond the latitude of 30° the coast is named Coste des Herbaiges, answering in climate and in name to Botany Bay.'

As Dalrymple had assisted Burney with other material for his book (Rotz's maps, in Burney, came from Dalrymple) it is reasonable to assume that this shaft too – the wording of it, at least, if not its discovery – came from Alexander Dalrymple.

This point was also mentioned by the Frenchman Frederic Metz, who mentioned the point just for the purpose of demolishing it. Metz's argument at least makes sense: if, in common parlance, Cook had the Dauphin Map 'under the counter', then the last thing he would do would be to give away his secret by adopting its nomenclature either directly or in translation. Metz's argument seems to be unanswerable.[12] The only remaining theory that can be advanced – faintly possible, though not at all probable – is that if Cook had been shown the map by Banks or someone else, he might have looked at it briefly without interest, stored 'Coste des Herbaiges' in his subconscious memory, and retrieved it when he was naming his Bay. It is not very likely.

Fig. 24.2 ENDEAVOUR REEF TO COOKTOWN HARBOUR. Place names are shown on Cook's Chart (left) and the modern map (centre). The corresponding place-names are suggested, in brackets, on the Desliens Chart (right). Note how closely the features on the Desliens Chart accord with the modern map, except that Cooktown Harbour is shown as larger than it really is.

What seems a larger point is Cook's behavior after the *Endeavour* struck the reef. Fig. 24.2 gives three charts side by side – one a modern map of that part of the North Queensland coast, one Cook's chart, the other a tracing of the same section of the coast, on the same scale, from Desliens' map. Apart from any other considerations, these maps are interesting for the purpose of comparison, as they demonstrate the accurate correspondence that there is between Desliens and the modern coast. In the figure, modern names have been indicated on the Portuguese map, to help identification. If a present-day yachtsman or launch-owner were to sail the Queensland coast with Desliens in his hand, he could identify his whereabouts point by point and cape by cape. (How he would get on with the under-water hazards is another matter altogether.) The author in fact sailed up this coast on a local passenger vessel, amusing himself with Desliens' chart in his hand, and it was uncanny how each point and each bay showed up in its correct sequence. If Cook had the Desliens, or one of the other Dieppe Maps, in his chart-room, he would undeniably have been able to recognise Cape Grafton, Green Island, Trinity Bay (where he landed) and Cape Tribulation. Even the Endeavour Reef shows on the Desliens as a shoal.

This Endeavour Reef, the reef upon which Cook's ship struck, is much further out to sea than most people realise. When one stands on the Reef, the Hope Islands (so called, because to Cook they seemed his only hope) are just a smudge on the horizon. From the Hope Islands, in turn, the Queensland coast is visible, but only just. It took the *Endeavour* two days of hard battling to make the coast, so the distance involved is not negligible.

And yet, when he wrenched his sinking ship free from the coral and made for the coast, with the pumps just keeping pace with intruding water and the plug in the gaping hole kept in place with sheep's manure, Cook did not make straight for the closest point of the coast by the shortest route – due west. Admittedly, it was just as well that he did not, for his ship would again have foundered on the reefs around Cape Tribulation, but still, a shipwrecked sailor in an unknown sea does not have many options, and his chance of reaching the coast at all was at best a grim race against time. On the other hand, he did not proceed south-westerly, slightly backwards, making for some beach or cove that he had already seen. Instead, he made north-west, into the unknown, towards a coast which he could not see, towards land which might not even exist, towards an area which he had not already inspected, and which might turn out to be worse than anything experienced before – spot-on for the entrance of Cooktown Harbour, the only harbour in a thousand miles of Queensland coast that was suitable for his purposes. He had a boat crew out, and when the beach of Weary Bay was reported Cook still pressed on, despite the weariness of the crew that is signified in the naming of the bay. It was a long, hard and nerve-wracking battle for two days, but at the end of it there showed up this providential harbour, so miraculously nosed out in the wilderness of sea.[13]

If Cook, or any other sailor, were today in difficulties on the Endeavour Reef, with a modern Admiralty chart in his hand, he would undoubtedly run for Cooktown Harbour, as Cook did. And while Cook did not have a modern Admiralty chart, it is historically possible – Collingridge says historically certain – that he had the Portuguese chart. On the Desliens version of this, Cooktown Harbour, identifiably in its correct place, invitingly shows up as a snug, well-sheltered, landlocked harbour (see Fig. 24.2), as close to a little piece of heaven as any shipwrecked mariner could desire. But the Desliens chart does contain one error: on it, Cooktown Harbour is round and spacious, larger than in reality. And it is significant that, as Cook entered the harbour, he 'found [the channel] very narrow, and the harbour much smaller than I had been told.' Of course, he might have been 'told' this by his lookout man, or by the boat crew, or by the man standing beside him on the deck. We do not know: but in the context it was a peculiar remark to make, so peculiar that Hawkesworth altered it to read 'smaller than I had expected'. And above all it seems strange that the one comment that Cook made about his life-saving harbour, the one adjective that he used to describe it, picks up the one point of difference – greater size – which one cannot help but notice on looking at this harbour on Desliens' map.

So far the arguments suggest that Cook did know of the Dieppe Maps. But a very considerable argument on the other side is Dalrymple's timing. Even Dr Howard Fry admits that Hawkesworth's publication of Cook's *Journal* goaded Dalrymple into savage anger.[14] He hit back at Cook (or at both Cook and Hawkesworth, for he did not know which of the two was to blame) with every club within his reach, even jibing at Cook about his maladroit grounding of the *Endeavour*. If at the moment he had had this further club of the Dieppe Maps to beat Cook with, he surely would have used it then, not years later; for it was not until 1786, after Cook's death, that his Disclosure and Insinuation were published. Whether he heard of the Dauphin Map for the first time in 1786 and immediately rushed into print, or whether he had found it as far back as 1772 or 1773, after his white-hot rage had cooled, does not make any difference. Either supposition requires that he did not know of it in 1769 when the *Endeavour* sailed, and that therefore Cook did not know of it either.

But supposing that Cook had seen the Dauphin Map – what would he have made of it? Cook was not a historical geographer, but a practical navigator. A historical geographer attempts to interpret the evidence of features marked on a chart in the light of the circumstances and the age in which the chart was drawn up: a practical navigator judges a chart by its accuracy of bearing and distance, latitude and longitude. For example, Cook, in his *Journal* entry of 31 March 1770, was critical of Dalrymple's map because Queiros's islands of La Encarnacion and S. Juan Baptista are in longitude six degrees too far west, and he condemned it for its inaccuracy. So to Cook's literal and practical mind, the coast laid down on the Dauphin Map – which we know was pushed over one thousand miles in order to join it on to Java and Sumbawa – would not have been in the vicinity of his own track at all. Taking a line from the known longitude of Timor, Desceliers' east coast is approximately in Long. 130°–135° (Greenwich) E. Cook was sailing up a coast in Long. 150°–155° (Greenwich) E – Which would seem to him to be a different part of the earth altogether. If, before he had left England, some Admiralty clerk had shown Cook what maps were available, including (for sake of argument) the Dauphin, and had given Cook the choice of taking some or all of them, Cook probably would have left the Dauphin Map behind.

For again we must remember that we are evaluating the Dauphin Map by hindsight, which hindsight was not available to Cook. The impact of the Dauphin is that anyone who is thoroughly familiar with the modern map of Australia – especially Australians, who see it daily – instinctively and immediately sees its resemblance to the real shape of Australia. But this requires that prior familiarity with the real shape of Australia, and the real shape was only made known by Cook, and was not even visible to Cook until he had reached Cape York, at the end of his traverse of the coast. Dalrymple in 1780, Flinders and Burney in the early 1800s,[15] could look at the Dauphin and say: 'That is New Holland – I can recognise the shape,' because by then they knew the real shape of the continent, having seen it on Cook's chart. Cook could not do this in 1770. It was only as the coast unfolded before Cook's eyes, it was only as his own chart grew under his own fingers, that the resemblance could have become apparent.

When finally Cook reached Possession Island, at the tip of Cape York, the picture of the east coast was complete; and if it had been compared with the Dauphin's east coast at that point its maximum correspondence would have been there to see. It was at that point that Cook could have mentioned the prior chart; or, if he really weré suppressing knowledge, it was at that point that he should have hedged or prevaricated or even remained silent. But he did none of these things. Instead he announced to the world that he was confident that this coast 'was never seen or visited by Europeans before us'.[16] And that seems to have the ring of truth.

In like manner Dalrymple's letter to Hawkesworth[17] seems to brook no contradiction: 'I gave Mr Banks all the information I could, and accordingly he carried with him the Account of Discoveries made in the South Pacific Ocean, with the "Chart".' *All* the information, Dalrymple says – and this information did not include the Portuguese maps.

When Dalrymple published his Disclosure and his Insinuation, Cook was already dead, killed by the Hawaiians at Kealakekua Bay, and so Cook could not defend himself.

Those who seek to belittle Dalrymple say that he deliberately withheld his slur until Cook could not reply to it. Dr Howard Fry hotly contests this, and he is probably right. But Banks was still alive, and the then owner of the Dauphin Map. Banks must have seen Dalrymple's article, for he read learned pamphlets, and mixed with men who read and discussed them. Throughout his life Banks was on friendly terms with Dalrymple,[18] strongly supporting him in the violent schism which rent the Royal Society in 1783.[19] At the time of the article, he was clearly in touch with Dalrymple, having lent him the Dauphin Map for the purpose of having it engraved. In the Disclosure, yes, in the Insinuation too, Banks was abetting Dalrymple. By his collusion, by his silence, by his making the Map available – in all of these things Banks goes far towards affirming the charge that Dalrymple was making.

It may be argued that by this time Banks, too, was unfriendly towards Cook, and would be not unwilling to belittle him. It is true that Banks and Cook quarrelled violently before the departure of Cook's second voyage – so violently that Banks was left behind. But Banks was of a generous nature, and surely he would not have gone out of his way to harm Cook by acquiescing in a damaging innuendo if he knew it to be untrue.

But Banks makes no mention of these maps in his own *Journal*. He was not afraid to mention his disagreements with Cook: there is quite an amusing verbal feud between the 'Continent-Mongers' and the 'No Continent-ers', as Banks dubs them, as the horizon was searched for the Great Southern Continent all the way from Tahiti to New Zealand. It would have been mentioned in Banks's *Journal* if Banks had been keeping a lookout for Portuguese Australia while Cook was poohpoohing the suggestion. But there is nothing in the *Journal* to suggest it.

And lastly, we do not known on what date Banks first heard of the Dauphin Map, still less on what date he acquired it. Dalrymple does give some information:[20]

'This curious manuscript [which] belonged to Lord Oxford's collection, as I was informed by my much lamented friend Dr Solander, who gave it to Sir Joseph Banks.'

James Burney, unearthed the additional facts that when
Edward Harley, Earl of Oxford, died in 1724, the Map was
stolen by one of his servants.[21] Forty-four years later it was
still stolen property ('in concealment', said Burney) but by
now at several removes from the larcenous servant, and
therefore no longer 'hot' property wanted by the police.

How did Dr Solander come to hear of it? If we were asked
to invent a story, we might conjure up the fiction that in 1768,
when the proposed voyage to the South Seas was the subject
of much public gossip, the owner for the time being of the
Dauphin Map suddenly realised that he was holding something that would be of interest to the scientific gentlemen, and
hearing that Dr Solander was to join the expedition he
approached the Doctor and sold him the map. But this nice
story has two difficulties. First, because Desceliers had transposed Australia to its south-of-Java position it would not be
apparent on the face of it that the Dauphin related to the
Pacific at all. Secondly, the extraordinary resemblance which
the shape of the Dauphin Map has to the real shape of
Australia, however great the impact that such resemblance
has for us, could have had no impact at all for people who
were not yet familiar with the real shape of Australia. If
before the *Endeavour* sailed someone had tried to interest Dr
Solander in the stolen map, he probably would not have
responded. It would have been a different story after the
Endeavour returned, when he had become interested in 'New
South Wales', when he had learned and memorized what the
shape of Australia really looks like; when he was in a position
to recognize at a glance that resemblance which Flinders saw,
which Burney saw, and which we see when we look at the
Dauphin Map. Solander acquired it, and gave it to Banks.
Banks treasured it, and in 1790 presented it to the British
Museum, to be housed and maintained in perpetuity for the
benefit of the British people. When the gift was made, the
nation of Australia was already two years old. Banks did not
say so, but no doubt he hoped and intended that it would be
kept in this way for the benefit of the Australian people too.

In 1811 Sir Joseph Banks was asked to write an Introduction to Matthew Flinders' book *A Voyage to Terra Australis*.[22]
He prepared a draft, which returned to the subject of prior
discoveries. In it he discussed the three names 'New Holland,'

'New South Wales', and 'Terra Australis', remarking that the then boundary between New South Wales and New Holland was 'nearly corresponding with the ancient Line of Separation', and he deduced from this fact that the British Government had so fixed the New South Wales boundary for that reason. Translating this into the terms used in Chapter 4 of this book, Banks is in effect saying that the N.S.W. boundary 'nearly corresponds with the Line of Demarcation, fixed by the Treaty of Tordesillas, between Portuguese India Meridional and Spanish Austrialia'. Banks went on to discuss the subsequent Dutch discoveries, and give it as his opinion that they (the Dutch) had every right to colonise New Holland (Western Australia) if they wanted to.

Either Banks thought that it would be prudent to get government approval for this effusion before publication, or else he was ordered to submit it: for on 16 November 1811 he left his manuscript[23] at Downing Street for Sir Robert Peel's perusal. Peel was horrified. He wrote back to Banks on 30 November 1811 (the holograph of the letter is in the Dixson Library in Sydney) saying:

> I have taken the opportunity of showing the enclosed Memorandum to the Earl of Liverpool...[and it is returned herewith amended] to omit any notice of the reasons which are supposed to have informed Her Majesty's Government in placing the western boundary of New South Wales.

He also required deletion of the passage referring to Holland's right to colonise. With this discouragement, Banks did not print his Introduction at all.

The 'present western boundary of New South Wales' referred to in this exchange was Long. 135° (Greenwich) E, a line which runs from the centre of the Arnhem-land coast to the Eyre Peninsula in South Australia. Not only Banks, but later students as well, have wondered why the British Government fixed the boundary at that line, apparently selected so arbitrarily. It was not the western limit of Cook's exploration, or the limit of the land of which he took formal possession at Possession Island: Cook's boundary was Long. 142° (Greenwich) E. So on the one hand England did not

claim the whole of the continent of Australia, and on the
other hand did not limit herself to the land visited and
annexed by Captain Cook, but "cribbed" an extra seven
degrees of longitude (which after all is about 450 miles in
width) between these two meridians, which neither Cook nor
any other Englishman had ever seen, deliberately adding this
slice of territory to the lands within Captain Phillip's Commission. Why was that? Banks had his theory about it, and Peel
was most anxious to prevent it from becoming public.

Banks's theory was that it was intended to be the 'Ancient
Line of Separation'. Peel came down like a ton of bricks.
'Omit any notice of the reasons which are supposed to have
informed Her Majesty's Government in placing the western
boundary of New South Wales!' was the order. The guess
must have been too close to the truth for Peel's comfort. And
indeed it was, as a reading of the political history of the years
1787–1788 shows.[24] The Fourth Dutch War was just over,
but England was most fearful of the overtures which the
French were making towards the Dutch. The effectiveness of
this new French-Dutch partnership was forcibly destroyed
when Prussia invaded and occupied Amsterdam, restoring
the more tractable Stadtholder William V of Orange. Pitt
seized the opportunity, and worked unceasingly to cement an
alliance between Holland, Prussia and England, to thwart any
renewed French flirtations with the Dutch. His overtures
were proceeding favourably in 1787, and were crowned with
success in 1788 when the Triple Alliance of those three
countries was completed.

During the delicate negotiations of 1787 and 1788, leading
up to this desired result, England was clearly not willing to
offend Holland about any distant and unimportant boundary
on the other side of the world. England was willing, more than
willing, to tear up the Treaty of Tordesillas and throw the
scraps in Spain's face, as she did by entering Spain's mare
clausum and occupying a coast well within Spain's territory
under that treaty. But Holland was Portugal's legatee, and the
political situation prevented England from disparaging the
ex-Portuguese rights in the same way. So Captain Phillip's
Commission in effect ordered him to take possession not of
Cook's Australia, but of Spain's Australia, right up to the

Line of Demarcation; but not to cross that line, for that would annoy Holland, the successor of Portugal in India Meridional.

But where did the English officials of the late eighteenth century conceive this Line to be? It is possible that they fixed the 135th meridian as a blind guess; but if it was, it was a guess that had a curious result, for they may have worked it out in this way. The starting point for the Tordesillas calculation is Santo Antão in Lat 17°N, Long 25° (Greenwich) w. The antipodes of this (Lat 17°s, Long 155° (Greenwich) E) is a point on the outer Barrier Reef, somewhat east of the Australian meteorological station at Willis Island. Measuring due west from this point 370 Portuguese leagues, or 1175 nautical miles, finds a point near Anthony Lagoon in the Northern Territory, in Lat 17°s, Long 135° (Greenwich) E.[25] And it was the one hundred and thirty-fifth meridian which was fixed as Captain Phillip's western boundary. See Fig. 24.3.

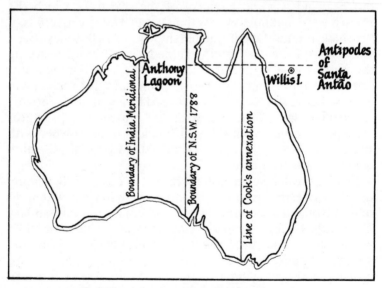

Fig. 24.3 THE N.S.W. BOUNDARY IN 1788

This should have avoided conflict with Holland, and in the short term it did. But there were problems left for the future. To start with, the above calculation fails to take into account the shift in the boundary made at Saragossa: and in 1820 this boundary question again soured relations between the English and the Dutch. By that year Holland was moving east, taking up the rights which she claimed as Portugal's successor. The islands in the Arafura Sea, where Sequeira had voyaged, were annexed by the Dutch. One or two posts were established in New Guinea, and next the whole of West New Guinea was annexed, as far as the present West Irian boundary in Longitude 141° (Greenwich) East.

On 23 January 1824 Sir John Barrow wrote:[26]

> It would be well to bear in mind that the Dutch would have a justifiable plea in planting an establishment on any part of the north-west coast [of Australia] in our example of taking possession of the eastern coast.

And to forestall this, in the following year he took the step of annexing to Britain the whole of Western Australia. There was no longer political need for England to appease Holland, so the policy of 1788 was reversed, and what had been Portugal's India Meridional was now no more.

Chapter 25

MAJOR THE APOSTATE

R ICHARD Henry Major is the enigma-man in these studies. For a quarter of a century he was the Keeper of Maps at the British Museum, where he transformed the records with his systematic thoroughness. It would appear that in the first half of the nineteenth century, and certainly before that, there had been some laxity there, with the result that many maps and manuscripts of real value had been bundled away in store-rooms, without indexing. Possibly the Rotz maps, which had been in the Royal Collection since the time of Henry VIII, were in this category. It was Major's life-work to bring order to this muddle, and to make the cartographical treasures of the British Museum available to scholarship.

Everyone who speaks of him uses the word 'erudite' – '*o erudito conservador da secção cartográfica do Museu Británico*'.[1] There is no doubt that he had a fantastic knowledge of old documents, and through his contacts with his opposite numbers in continental libraries he extended his knowledge to old manuscripts throughout the world. He was a linguist, and his knowledge of languages included Portuguese.

But his writings show him 'erudite' in a pedantic sort of way. Professor Spate calls him 'erratic'. He was a compiler rather than an analyst; his critical ability and his sense of proportion are both somewhat suspect. He was never quite accepted into the higher echelons of scholarship, making his mark rather in addresses to small learned societies and articles in obscure magazines. And so, when opportunity offered, he liked to make the most of it.

It appealed to his vanity to stand before a gathering and say dramatically: 'Gentlemen: I have to inform you that only last week my researches have unveiled a manuscript (or a map) of world-shattering importance. I hold it in my hand. As you can see . . .' Quite often the claim that he was making for his find turned out to be exaggerated; sometimes it exploded in his face. Consequently there is an imbalance in his scholarship, and his reputation suffered both in his lifetime and after his death.

But no one can deny his passion for Portuguese history and the Portuguese people – above all, for the heroes of the Golden Age of Discovery, and for its patron saint, Prince Henry the Navigator. It was really R. H. Major who brought this romantic story to the British public for the first time. His studies fixed the classical pattern for the examination of this theme – from Henry to the Treaty of Tordesillas, Vasco da Gama, the Quest for the Moluccas, and so on. This is the pattern which logic has imposed on this book, as well as all others which have preceded it. Major wrote the first great English-language Life of Henry the Navigator.[2] In it are some moving tributes to the Portuguese people, couched in the rolling rhetoric of his latinised and somewhat old-fashioned style:[3]

'The true heroes of the world are the initiators of great explorations, the pioneers of great discoveries. Such were the Portuguese in the days when the world was as yet but a half-known and puny thing.... England, whose hardy mariners have made a thoroughfare of every sea, knows best how to do justice to the fearlessness of their noble predecessors, who in frail caravels and through an unmeasured wilderness of ocean could cleave a pathway, not only to the glory of their own nation, but to the civilisation and prosperity of the entire world.'

His interest in the Portuguese discoverers naturally led him to the shores of Australia. He was not primarily interested in Australia as such: indeed, in the mid-century nobody was interested in Australian history, not even the Australians themselves. But soon he realised that there was an Australian history that ought to be researched – the great voyages of Tasman, the earlier Dutch contacts of Jantzoon and Pelsaert and Dirk Hartog, the Spanish probes of Mendaña and Queiros, and (when he found the evidence) the even earlier associations of Sequeira and the other Portuguese. These led to his most important work, his collection of early voyages

impinging on Australian history, published under the title of
Early Voyages to Terra Australis.[4]

In a letter to Sir Henry Ellis dated 7 March 1861, Major
formulated, in words which can scarcely be bettered, the
reasons why this research needed to be done. It is, as expressed, the apologia for all subsequent research in this field,
including this present book; and it is worth repeating here:[5]

> 'If any doubt be entertained of the importance of collect-
> ing and embodying in our literature the scattered relics of
> the early history of geographical discovery, the doubt might
> find its answer in the eager curiosity with which the most
> cultivated of Anglo-Saxon inhabitants of America look
> back to every minute particular respecting the early history
> of their adopted country. A vast field of colonisation
> second only to America is rapidly developing itself in
> [Australia]; and we may naturally presume that it will be a
> question of no inconsiderable interest to those who have
> chosen Australia as the birth-place of their children to
> know what were the earliest discoveries of a land so vast.'

This is nobly, if somewhat pompously, expressed. That it is
true, no Australian today would question. But even in this
passage can be seen Major's tendency to magnify the value of
his own labours. There is always the feeling that he thinks that
some achievement is not great because of itself, but because
R. H. Major described it; some manuscript is not important in
itself, but because R. H. Major discovered it. He was probably a little man, puffed up with self-importance, and essentially very vain.

As far back as 1855 he became aware of the existence of the
Dauphin Map, and from that date onwards his main theme
was the pre-Cook, pre-Dutch discovery of Australia by the
Portuguese. Gradually he built up knowledge of the other
Dieppe Maps – the Vallard, in the possession of Sir Thomas
Phillips; the two Rotz maps, in his own department in the
British Museum; the Royal, then held by the French geographer Jomard; the Le Testu, then and still in Paris. He
apparently never made acquaintance with the Desliens. He
expended vast erudition in checking, analysing, verifying and
writing about them. He tracked down the other geographers

who had worked or were working in this field – Dalrymple
and Rennell and Pinkerton in England, Buache, Montbret
and de la Rochette in France. After all of these years of
devoted study, his conclusion is stated loud and clear:[6]

> 'The facts which I have been able to bring together lead me
> to the conclusion that the land described as Jave-la-Grande
> on the French maps to which I have referred can be no
> other than Australia; and that it was discovered before
> 1542 may be almost accepted as demonstrable certainty.'

And again, in another place, he stated his conviction and his
further hopes:[7]

> 'We must therefore come to the conclusion . . . that the
> discovery of the continent of New Holland belongs to the
> Portuguese. It becomes a question of the highest interest to
> ascertain, as nearly as may be, by whom and at what date
> the discovery of this country was made.'

His great hope was that one day he would find a manuscript
which would give both a name and a date to some Portuguese
voyage which would link with the Dauphin Map. In this book
it has been made clear that, in the author's opinion, after
sifting all the evidence and balancing all the probabilities, it
appears that the name is Cristovão de Mendonça, and the
date 1522. With even greater certitude it can be said that in
the whole of the extant documentary and cartographical
evidence, no one except Mendonça measures up to the
requirements. In the 'whodunnit' detective stories of our age
we are instructed to look for three essential ingredients –
means, motive and opportunity. If the reader turns back
through these pages, he will find that Mendonça had all three,
while no one else had them to a convincing degree. R. H.
Major did not become acquainted with Mendonça, so rather
naturally he did not find the name and the date that he was
looking for. He did find Sequeira, and his advocacy is probably one of the facts that has enhanced Sequeira's somewhat
disproportionate reputation.

But if Major could not find the documentary evidence to
link with the Dauphin Map, he was still willing to look for *any*
document or map which would provide cast-iron evidence of

a Portuguese landing on the Australian coast at any time
before the first Dutch sighting in 1606. And in the year 1860
he thought that he had found it. Immediately he rushed into
print. 'Within the last few days I have discovered . . .' so he
starts, with his usual flair for the dramatic:[8]

> 'Within the last few days I have discovered a manuscript
> mappe-monde in the British Museum, with a coast and the
> inscription "Nuca Antara for descoberto no anno 1601 por
> Manoel Godinho de Erédia".'

It was not as early as he would have liked. Indeed the date
1601 was only five years before the first Dutch sighting. But it
was five years before, and the principle was established. 'In
the last few days I have found a document in the British
Museum' (he repeats himself, but how he loved that phrase):

> 'In the last few days I have found a document in the British
> Museum which unequivocally transfers that honour from
> Holland to Portugal. The fact that Australia had in reality
> been discovered more than sixty years earlier [he is refer-
> ring to the evidence of the Dieppe Maps] and in all proba-
> bility by the Portuguese does not, I think, set aside the
> importance of this further fact that the earliest known
> voyage to Australia to which a date and a discoverer's name
> can be attached was made by the Portuguese in 1601.'

This was Erédia's Nuca Antara map, which was mentioned
in Chapter 6. As was said there, Erédia was an eccentric and
confused enthusiast, fired with a vision of the great continent
in the south, call it Nuca Antara or India Meridional or Jave-
la-Grande or what you will, who obtained permission to go
exploring down that way, but because of circumstances
beyond his control never got there. Nevertheless, he drew
maps of his Promised Land, one of which found its way to the
British Museum (where Major found it), and the other was
attached to his book *The Declaration of Malacca*, which
found its way to the Royal Burgundy Museum in Brussels.
The British Museum map, which Major was waving so
triumphantly, is candidly a confused map. In the author's
opinion it is a recollection of Sequeira's Arafura Sea area
(south-west coast of New Guinea, plus Arnhem-land and a

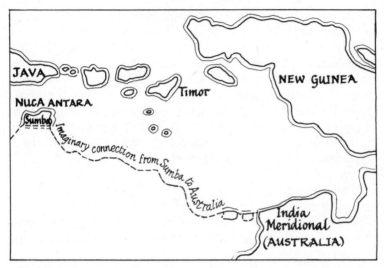

Fig. 25.1 ERÉDIA'S NUCA ANTARA. Interpretative diagram of part of Erédia's map, identifying Nuca Antara with Sumba, incorrectly joined (as shown by dotted line) with Arnhem-land. Note the good representation of the south-west coast of New Guinea (five years before Torres). This outline may have come from Sequeira. Java, Timor and Nova Guiné are named on Erédia's map. Nuca Antara bears a caption that it was discovered by M. G. Erédia in 1601.

hint of Cope York) joined on to the island of Sumba. In Fig. 25.1 a portion of Erédia's map is given, but with the false connection from Arnhem-land to Sumba dotted to give expression to this interpretation. In spite of the confused cartography, Major identified Erédia's land-mass as substantially Australia (as it is); and as it had written on it in black and white that this land had been discovered in 1601 by Manoel Godinho de Erédia, he had some justification in thinking that here was an authentic record of a Portuguese landing on Australian soil, admittedly 60-odd years after the Dauphin Map charting, but still five years before the first Dutch sighting. This is why he was so excited; but the whole of his announcement was based on this curious map, without any knowledge of what was written in Erédia's book, which he looked forward to perusing in due course.

But commenting on the map without first reading Erédia's book was a calamitous mistake. When he obtained a copy of the book from his colleague Charles Ruelens, the librarian at Brussels, the bottom fell out of Major's world. A broken man, he had to stand before his audience again and confess his sins 'Pomposia eating his words,' Professor Spate called it,[9] and perhaps it was; yet we cannot but feel sorry for a man who was experiencing this disappointment and humiliation:[10]

> 'I am sorry to have to report to you that a more unsatisfactory document has never fallen under my notice . . .. It is as when one cracks a fair-looking filbert, and finds one's mouth unexpectedly filled with dust in lieu of the ripe kernel.'

Briefly, recapitulating, Erédia, who was half Portuguese, half Macassarese, had filled his head with dreams of discovering Australia. In a confused way, he knew of the Marco Polo legends, of Portuguese visits to India Meridional, of Malay legends of voyaging in that direction, and (perhaps) of some embroidery that had been born of his own dreams. From these he had built up a composite which did have some relationship to the Kimberley coast.

Then one day a boatload of sailors from a far-distant land arrived at Malacca, almost certainly from the little-known island of Sumba. They seemed to be 'Javanese of another race' – a fair description of the Sumbans, and certainly quite inapplicable for Australian aborigines. And as the 'Nuca' of Erédia's map seems to accord with 'Nusa', the Sumban word for 'island', that island seems to be the place whence they had come. The sketch in Fig. 25.1 is drawn to scale from Erédia's map, and it can be seen that Nuca Antara is in Sumba's position. And as Erédia was a professional, skilled marine surveyor, his evidence on this point cannot be dismissed.

But believing that they had come from the mainland of India Meridional, Erédia made their island and India Meridional one and the same land, joining the two by the false connection which is shown by dotted line in the figure; and he was filled with desire to visit this composite land. He obtained government approval and government equipment, and was about to set out. Like a general striking a 'Victory Medal' before an invasion, Erédia produced a 'Victory Map' – an identifiable outline of the region he was about to visit, with the proud legend 'Discovered by M. G. Erédia 1601' emblazoned on it. Unfortunately, because of Dutch invasion, his expedition never left the harbour; but this map was not destroyed or amended, and lived for 250 years to embarrass, dishonour and professionally ruin poor Richard Henry Major.

Major printed his abject retraction in the magazine *Archaeologia* in 1873.[11] It should have been possible for him to get Erédia out of his hair, to lie low for a while, to recover from his Great Mistake, and to return in due course to his researches. But the shock of the Erédia debacle apparently undermined his confidence in the whole of his life's work – some say that it actually weakened his intellect. He probably realised that after this fiasco nobody would ever have any faith in R. H. Major, or his Portuguese discoverers, or his Dieppe Maps, or anything else that he stood for. And it seems that Major himself did not have the nerve or the character to weather the storm.

We do not know what ridicule and humiliation Major suffered at the hands of others, or what waves of self-pity and self-blame surged through his own mind. This Erédia debacle affected him profoundly, and his next action suggests that it more than affected him – it broke him, possibly deranged him. Anyone can see that this one error in scholarship should not have, could not have, imputed like disgrace into every other line of scholarship in which he had been engaged for the last 30 years, but he acted as though that were the case. In the same issue of *Archaeologia* in which he admitted his Erédia mistake, he also published a second article in which he resigned from the cause which he had espoused so enthusiastically and for so long, withdrew his advocacy of Portuguese discovery altogether, and recanted the heresies with which he had been identified. It was some over-reaction in his hour of disgrace, a form of self-scourging which we can only dimly understand.

This total recantation is in the same format as his recantation of the Erédia mistake – he first claims (pretends, might be a better word) that he had since found a later document which had caused him to change his mind: 'There has recently come into my possession...' – so the familiar opening runs – 'a small map, *Nova et Integra Orbis Descriptio...*' This was Oronce Finé's double-cordiform of 1531.

Finé's map has already been described in Chapter 10. Deriving from Schöner, it shows two huge promontories bulging Equator-wards in the southern hemisphere – one promontory south of India, the other south of Tahiti, separated by a wide V-shaped gulf extending right down to the Antarctic Circle. Diagrammatically it can be envisaged as the shape of the letter M, with the two upper projections separated by the central V-shaped gulf. Across the top of the central gulf Finé shows Java, Amboina and Timor, in approximately their correct positions; and south and south-east of these islands (where Australia ought to be) there is nothing but sea. If a map of Australia on its correct scale is drawn in on Finé's map, either in its true position south-east of Timor and Amboina, or in its Dauphin position south of Java, in either case it occupies an area where Finé shows only sea, with only its far south corners (Cape Leeuwin and Cape Howe) scraping the converging sides of the narrowing gulf. Yet Major took this transparently imaginary map of Finé's – which even if it were genuine would only negative the idea of any land in the Australian area – and forthwith announced that he had found in it overwhelmingly clear proof of a *French* exploration before the Portuguese, so clear that he apologised for his previous mistakes, and withdrew all claims which he had previously made about Portuguese discoveries, and announced that he had now lost all interest in the Dieppe maps. He admitted that patriotic Frenchmen who were experts on Pacific exploration (such as C. C. Montbret, F. Metz and Barbie du Bocage) had not the slightest knowledge of any such prior French exploration, but that did not deter him. As for the Portuguese nomenclature on the Dauphin and other maps, he announced that he could see now that he had been mistaken about that also – those names (he said) were not Portuguese words at all!

This is not an acceptable standard of scholarship, and one is shocked and puzzled at this sudden inexplicable somersault. It can be illustrated by the following analogy, and the reader is invited to look at the map on page 139, produced by Franciscus Monachus of Antwerp, which also shows nothing but sea in the Australian area and therefore is appropriate for use in this illustration. It is submitted that the reader would question the academic integrity and mental stability of the present writer if, after ending the last chapter of this book, he added an Addendum reading:

'Since writing this book I have had another look at the Franciscus Monachus map. In the area which everyone else takes to be an open sea, I can now detect a powerful outline of the shape of Australia. I find that Franciscus's prior knowledge of the existence of Australia is based upon a still earlier Flemish expedition which visited its shores. The Dauphin Map must have followed this Flemish discovery, for I can now see that the supposed Portuguese words are actually Vlaamsch words. I therefore reject everything that I have written in this book, and I no longer believe in the Portuguese Discovery of Australia'.

Yet Major's Retraction is no less confounding than this would be. In five or six pages he dismantled everything which he had so lovingly compiled in twenty-four years of careful study. The reasons he gives are so inadequate, so patently untenable, as to be almost insulting to the reader. A man recanting heresy at a modern-day Inquisition, with the Inquisitor holding a gun at his head, could not be less convincing. 'I hereby retract my Portuguese heresies', he seems to be saying, 'I apologize, I am sorry I ever got mixed up in this business . . . .' Surely if he had really established some prior French voyage (of which modern scholars, again, are quite ignorant) he owed it to his public to elaborate on it. Surely if he had linguistic proof of the 'Catalan' words on the Dieppe Maps (on which, again, all modern linguists contradict him) he would have elucidated it. But he did none of these things. He never wrote again.

Did the Erédia debacle cause some nervous breakdown, or some spiritual extinguishment? Had his mind given way? Was there an element of pique, or of stubborn pride, or of intellectual shame, or of senile stupidity? Or, possibly, was he pushed? After all, he was a public servant, employed by the government; so did someone in authority order him to back-pedal on the subject of the Dieppe Maps, as Banks had been smothered when he attempted to write an Introduction for Flinders's book?

The author has already expressed his personal debt to R. H. Major: his appreciation of the warm humanism of his *Prince Henry*, the usefulness of his researches in the early voyages, the bright Lusophile torch that he lit and carried. But, with regret, it must be said that his Retraction hints at irresponsibility, senility, even insanity. In all charity, it is not the communication of a serious scholar, and before the Erédia debacle Richard Henry Major was a serious scholar indeed.

Major's apostasy did incalculable harm to subsequent scholarship in this field. The collapse of the Erédia 'discovery' should only have demolished the reputation of Erédia; but it transferred its smear to the Dauphin and the Dieppe Maps and to the whole of the Portuguese case. Historians who had previously been looking at this material favourably, or at least with open minds, suddenly fought shy of the whole subject, closing their minds. We have seen this happening in R. H. Major's own brain – whether in his case voluntarily or involuntarily we do not know. It happened to others as well. From that point onwards there were only two camps – those who, like Collingridge, still passionately supported the Portuguese cause; and those, like Wood and Scott, who were just as passionately against it. One camp nailed to its flagpole the earlier writings of Major; the other camp waved his six-page Retraction. So clear is this dichotomy that those in the latter camp, who gleefully adopted Major's Retraction, became known as 'the Detractors'; and it became their obsession to use every opportunity that offered to ridicule, discredit and demolish the Portuguese case. Collingridge probably went too far in trying to uphold his cause. The Detractors certainly went too far in their efforts to deny it. Their bitter controversy, stemming from Major's apostasy, set back the objective study of pre-Cook exploration of the east coast of Australia for just on one hundred years.

Chapter 26

COLLINGRIDGE AND HIS DETRACTORS

THE previous 25 chapters have examined the impact of the sixteenth-century voyages on the old-world countries most concerned – Portugal and Spain, who did the voyaging; Holland and England, their successors; and France, where the Dieppe Maps were published. This chapter will trace the impact of the Dieppe Maps on the country which, in the last analysis, is the one most intimately concerned – Australia, the continent which was sought and discovered. The people of Australia were the last to become aware of these maps; and, in the event, Australia was the country which took least kindly to them.

The British Naval Establishment in colonial Sydney knew of these maps. Matthew Flinders mentions them with approval.[1] Admiral Burney's great book of voyages,[2] which deals with them at length, was undoubtedly in the libraries of Bligh and King and early Sydney's other naval top brass. But these august administrators were in no way representative of the common people of the colony, and these latter – convicts, ex-convicts, remittance men, political refugees, riffraff, flotsam and jetsam of the old world – were neither expert in nor interested in distant European history. The general understanding was that Tasman had discovered Van Diemen's Land (now Tasmania) and that Cook had discovered the continent itself.

But by the mid-century the cultural standard of the infant colonies was beginning to rise. In 1852–3 the first two Universities were founded, complete with schools of British history, and the compilation of Australian history began. Perhaps British–Australian history would be a better term, for it was long before any spirit of Australian nationalism was present to distinguish between the two; and in the golden age of British Imperialism all emphasis was on the glory of British achievement, attaching a taint of heresy to any writer who suggested otherwise. In this atmosphere, as we saw when discussing Major, it was not easy to win or hold public interest in theories about prior Portuguese discoveries.

In November 1881 Mr T. Gill[3] of South Australia saw in an English magazine some reference to the Dieppe Maps, and suggested to the Adelaide Public Library that it should take steps to obtain copies. Inquiry was made, but as the cost of copying was beyond the resources of Adelaide, arrangements were made for Sydney and Melbourne Public Libraries to join in the venture, and about 1883 each of the three libraries received a set of facsimiles of the three maps in the British Museum – the Dauphin, the Rotz Plane, and the Rotz Circular. These facsimiles are still available and in use in the three libraries, and are still the best copies available in Australia.

But in 1883 neither public nor press, political nor academic establishment, was ready to accept the idea that the Portuguese had preceded the British in the discovery of New South Wales. When the facsimiles reached Sydney, they drew an adverse press. With closed minds, the journalists looked at the Portuguese maps and saw 'no resemblance'. There was even criticism of the alleged waste of public funds in procuring the despised facsimiles.

But these maps found one champion in an unexpected quarter. About this time there had arrived in Sydney, as an immigrant, an artist and teacher of painting named George Collingridge. He had been born in England, but had spent his boyhood in France, from whence he and his family had fled during the Franco-Prussian War. He had already made some study of maps relating to early Pacific voyaging; but it must be stressed that he was not a professional historian, not an academic – indeed, not a graduate at all. In political history, he was ill-equipped; but in cartography, and the history of cartography, he was most knowledgeable. Even his adversary, Professor G. Arnold Wood, admitted this.[4] Self-taught though he was in this field, his beautifully illustrated *Discovery of Australia* is still the most comprehensive history of early Australian cartography.[5]

Collingridge's art training, of course, qualified him as a draftsman of maps; and many of his figures (superimposing one map on another for purposes of comparison, and the like) are models of draftmanship. But beyond this, Collingridge, like Desceliers before him, was a pictorial artist. An artist and (by adoption) a Frenchman, he seemed to have rapport with the Dieppe Maps. He was never a wealthy man, and in later life conducted a kind of teashop-museum in the outer Sydney suburb of Hornsby – characteristically named 'Jave-la-Grande' – where he adorned the walls with copies of the Dieppe Maps and expatiated on their significance to goggle-eyed tourists. When he could, he eked out his meagre income by selling painted maps to those who cared to buy, and these Collingridge facsimiles are now collectors' pieces.

He had one further advantage: he was a linguist, skilled in many languages, and unlike his adversaries he could and did read Portuguese. He corresponded with the Royal Portuguese Geographic Society, and was probably the first Australian to go direct to de Barros and the other Portuguese chroniclers. George Collingridge was a better historian, and a better equipped historian, than either his contemporaries or posterity admit, although admittedly he had his limitations.

In 1883, when the facsimiles were under violent attack from the press, Collingridge was asked to examine them and give his opinion.[6] He had not seen the Dieppe Maps before, but immediately recognized the Portuguese content in the nomenclature. This clue, which other Australians had not recognized, guided him to the systematic examination of the necessary historical background – the Treaty of Tordesillas, and all that stems from it – and launched him upon his lifelong study. It led directly to his great *Discovery of Australia*, published in 1895. Despite some limitations, it is a fine work. He tells us:

'Though unable to examine personally some manuscripts of interest and value, I believe I can truly say that I have read every book, and examined every map of real importance to the question which has been produced in English, French, Spanish, Portuguese, Italian and Dutch. I have also corresponded largely during the past four years with many of the most eminent members of the geographical societies of Europe.'

His book, when published, was acclaimed in Europe. The King of Spain conferred upon him the Order of Isabela la

Catolica. The King of Portugal made him a Knight of Santarem.

But in his own country the book was ignored. Sales of the
book were negligible. Press critiques were uniformly hostile.
In academic circles, the fashion was to deride him and his
theme. Financially and publicly, his fine work was an utter
failure. One supporter did come to his side: the NSW Under-
Secretary for Education invited him to prepare a shorter and
cheaper edition, with the promise that it would be prescribed
as a textbook in the government schools. This was done, and
the shorter version was published in 1906;[7] but when it was
about to issue from the press the Under-Secretary died, and
his successor rejected the arrangement. Huge stocks of the
book were left unsold, and again Collingridge suffered great
financial loss. It seems obvious that the new Under-Secretary
sought the advice of the historical establishment, and it will be
seen later with what vehemence Collingridge was opposed in
that quarter.

Collingridge never published again in book form, but
throughout his life he contributed to newspapers and
magazines, for a fee when available, just for the opportunity
of spreading his message when no fee was forthcoming. When
all else failed, he wrote 'Letters to the Editor' on his pet
subject. Admittedly he was tactless, and at times dogmatic,
and that did not help him to make friends. If, for example,
some scientific gentleman wrote an article on the incidence of
dingoes in Australia, using the phrase: 'When Captain Cook
first discovered the east coast of Australia, the dingoes
were . . .' he could expect a thundering reply from Collingridge, deploring the scientist's ignorance: 'I have on my desk,
before me, copies of certain Portuguese maps of the sixteenth
century, demonstrating . . .' and so on. The historical Establishment of Sydney, and particularly Professor G. Arnold
Wood, suffered from this incessantly.

He was uncritical, impetuous, too ready to jump to loose
conclusions. When, very meritoriously, he turned up a letter
from Albuquerque[8] which referred to the expedition of João
de Lisboa,[9] where the ships travelled for three hundred miles
along a 'strait' in Lat. 40°s – which was later proved by the
'Copia' to be the La Plata estuary – Collingridge immediately

jumped to the conclusion that it must have been Bass Strait, that in some unexplained way the Portuguese had got there in 1512, and (here comes the crunch) that this 'proved' that the Mahogany Ship was one of João de Lisboa's. When he saw that Schöner had labelled his Antarctic continent 'Brasillie Regio', he rushed into print with his far-fetched essay 'Is Australia the Baptismal Font of Brasil?'[10]

But on the subject of the Dieppe Maps themselves, he was sane, well-informed and meticulous. Perhaps he strained too much to identify every indentation with some modern bay or inlet, each minor protuberance with some modern cape, each vague 'R.' with some modern river or estuary; and in doing this he lapsed into forced reasoning about unimportant minor features, which had the effect of throwing doubt on the more convincing reasoning which he applied to the maps as a whole. But his interpretations are always stimulating, and the author has often found that some Collingridge theory, which has been dismissed on first reading as quite untenable, turns out later to have unexpected merit.

His greatest error was in trying to explain the westward shift. The reader knows that in the Dauphin the continent is shifted westward a thousand miles, and made to fit under Java and Sumbawa. In Chapter 9[11] it was explained that this arose from Desceliers' 'jigsaw' – an ingenious guess, but still an error – which puts the blame for the error on the Dieppe cartographical editors, not on the navigator who drew the chart. Collingridge did not know of this explanation, and he was obviously worried by this thousand-mile misplacement, realising that the credibility of the Dieppe Maps must suffer if this problem were not cleared up and explained. He did his best to provide an explanation, but on this point his best was not good enough.

Collingridge attempted to explain the thousand-mile westerly displacement by alleging that it was deliberate falsification for political purposes. He knew accurately where the Line of Demarcation crossed the Australian continent – down the present Western Australian boundary. His theory[12] was that Portugal had discovered and partly explored Australia, but was chagrined to find that it was mainly in the Spanish hemisphere, about two thirds of it being east of the

Line. And therefore (so Collingridge alleged) Portugal re-drew and falsified the map to show five sixths, or thereabouts, on the Portuguese side, and only one sixth on the Spanish side.

Now there is no doubt that the Portuguese would, without qualm, falsify, suppress or even destroy a map if some political mileage was to be obtained thereby. But what possible use could this manoeuvre be? At best it could be only temporary, for the continent itself could not be shifted or suppressed: but it is hard to see how it could even be a temporary advantage. If in fact Portugal had wanted to hide her find from Spain, she should have omitted it from the map altogether. If she had been willing to admit the find, but wished to discourage Spain from coming to look at it (or, worse still, from colonising it), she should have shifted the whole continent to the Portuguese side. But by leaving about one sixth of the continent, the slice from Rockhampton to Melbourne, still on the map and on the Spanish side, she was only encouraging Spain to visit and examine this; and as events turned out, it was the very best part of Australia anyway. The Dauphin Map as it stands is a clear invitation to Spain to come and colonise Baie Neufre or Cape Fremose.

But, as we know, the map was being kept so secret that even Portugal's leading mapmakers did not have the chance to see it or publish it. What was the use of a cunningly distorted map if it never saw the light of day? We might descend to very sophisticated cunning and suggest that Portugal first doctored the map and then 'leaked it' for some subtle political purpose; but in that case why was it leaked to France and not to Spain? The Collingridge theory is not viable in any way. Its futility only damaged his reputation and provided ammunition for his enemies.

But Collingridge had another 'falsification theory' even harder to follow. Under this second theory of falsification, he postulated that the Portuguese had transferred Australia from its correct position on the map to the position which it occupies on the Dauphin in order to block up the 'hole' which exists between Java and Antarctica, to fool other nations into believing that no passage existed there, and thus to dissuade them from attempting entrance into the Spice Islands area.

This is a silly and untenable theory under any circumstances, but particularly useless when it is remembered that Spain was the only nation that had to be kept out, and Spain had access to the area along Magellan's track even if that blockage were there. When he realised this, Collingridge then desperately amended his theory to envisage some collusion between Spain and Portugal, both combining to falsify the map to safeguard the area against other powers. Geographically this is impossible, politically it is unthinkable.

This gave Professor George Arnold Wood, Professor of History at the University of Sydney, his chance to attack. Wood was an expert in political history, a good scholar in this department, but he was no cartographer. When it came to reading and comparing maps, he was no match for Collingridge; but once Collingridge stumbled into this political sphere, obviously confusing himself and everyone else, Wood had the advantage. Wood's students all agree that he was a brilliant lecturer – vivid, colloquial, humorous, ironic, sarcastic – and he turned all of these big guns on poor George Collingridge.

Perhaps he was not actuated by personal malice. In his Introduction[13] he pays a courteous, though somewhat condescending,[14] tribute to Collingridge as a collector and drawer of maps. But for Collingridge's theories he was not condescending, but outright contemptuous. For this, his theatre was his lecture-room, his audience his students, his milieu the sarcastic merriment and hilarious 'debunking' for which he was famous. And he turned all of this artillary on his victim. The result was the so-called 'Demolition' of Collingridge's theories which was incorporated, without further research or editing, in Wood's textbook *The Discovery of Australia*. It may have been good vaudeville, but it was not good scholarship.

In logic, in understanding, in information, in scholarship, the Demolition is worthless. A detailed Examen could be made here, itemising point by point the erroneous or threadbare arguments, showing that every point on which he relies is shallow, unfounded and illogical. But there is no need to make that Examen here, for it has already been done with telling effect: in his monograph 'Terra Australis Cognita?'

Professor O. H. K. Spate has unerringly exposed the 'geo-graphical and linguistic limitations' which vitiated the so-called Demolition, sentence by sentence. Professor Spate is an admirer of Professor Wood's abilities in other fields, but he makes it clear that here he has fallen from the standards of good scholarship, and that not only should the Demolition be criticised, but it should and must be rejected.

It will be sufficient for present purposes to concentrate only on the fundamental weakness. Professor Wood's case is almost wholly based on the ipse dixit: 'I, Arnold Wood, can see no resemblance between the Dieppe Map and the real shape of Australia.' And it is no wonder that he could not see the resemblance, for he was looking at the Dieppe Map, if not upside-down, at least so unintelligently that no sensible interpretation was possible. He arbitrarily and wrongly assumed that those portions of the north Australian coast which, throughout this book, we have recognised as Arnhem-land, the Gulf of Carpentaria and Cape York represent only Arnhem-land, the other two ingredients being missing altogether. This is shown diagrammatically in Fig. 26.1, and this figure (drawn by the author, not by Professor Wood) can be verified by comparing it point by point with the lengthy passage on page 78 of Professor Wood's book. For eight pages he continues to harp on his inability to see any resemblance between the Dauphin and the real shape of Australia. And then, after all of these loud assertions, he changes his argument to say that the map is 'too good', that the map-makers knew 'too much', and that he would be prepared to accept the Portuguese map if it were worse.

When he is stuck with the indigestible fact that Matthew Flinders was impressed by the maps, he indulges in face-saving double talk, laced with double negatives and grammat-ical obscurities, which makes his acceptance of Flinders sound like damnation of the Portuguese. When he is cornered, and has to admit of some real knowledge on the part of the mapmaker, then he is quick to assume that the Portuguese must have got that information from the Malays, or from Marco Polo, or from someone else. Never could a nation which had produced Magellan and da Gama sail as far as the Australian coast! Indeed, in one passage he pontificates that,

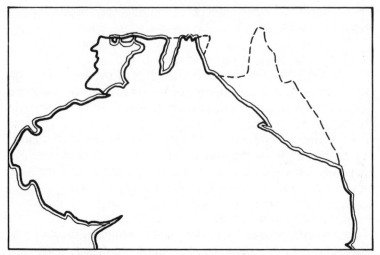

Fig. 26.1 PROFESSOR WOOD'S MISREADING. By viewing the Dauphin's Cape York as part of Arnhem-land, he was then unable to find any feature resembling Cape York on the map. The dotted line shows the missing Cape York, as Professor Wood visualized it.

as Cook had difficulties on the Barrier Reef coast, the Portuguese would not have been able to navigate it at all. And his peroration, praising the Dieppe mapmaker for his brilliant Jules-Verne-like science-fiction, is a monument of hypocrisy and cant.

During his effusion, Professor Wood admits that he had developed a 'hostile prejudice'.[15] No one who has read his unbalanced attack could possibly deny it. If that were all, it would merely be a pity that one blind spot could so damage the reputation of an otherwise commendable historian. But unfortunately, so great was his standing that these ex cathedra utterances poisoned the minds of his students and successors for two generations to come. For half a century his 'Demolition' has been accepted by most historians as a total, authoritative, first-and-final destruction of the whole of the Portuguese case. Most subsequent history books have started with the first Dutch sighting in 1606, adding a footnote to the effect that 'there are rumours of earlier sighting by the

Portuguese, but these have been convincingly disposed of by Professor G. Arnold Wood'.

Professor Sir Ernest Scott, the equally influential Professor of History at Melbourne University, was one who limped after him, adding nothing to the content of the argument, but producing one brilliant theory of his own: that the Dauphin Map was a hoax, a fraud, perhaps a forgery![16] And as even Professor Scott could not pretend that it was a modern forgery, he concocted the theory that it was a sixteenth-century forgery – some hoaxer of the time drew a fictitious map, filled in some Portuguese names to make it look authentic, and palmed it off on old Père Desceliers, who was silly enough to publish it. The resemblance to the real shape which he achieved is then just incredible coincidence.

Every critic who seeks to deny the Portuguese discovery of Australia is faced with the problem of providing an alternative theory to explain away the existence of the Dieppe Maps. If the Dauphin is not the record of real exploration, then what is it? Unless the opposition can produce a viable Alternative Explanation, then, as the logicians say, *Res ipsa loquitur*, the thing speaks for itself. Each detractor has attempted to discharge this onus of proof by dreaming up some Alternative Explanation; but when all of these explanations are extracted and classified and coldly appraised, not one of them stands up to examination. Some of them are quite far-fetched.

The Alternative Explanation classically set up by the detractors of the Wood–Scott school is Chance Resemblance. Some sixteenth-century mapmaker, they say, was drawing a fictitious map, perhaps as an imaginative exercise (Wood), or as a deliberate fraud (Scott), or as a doodle, or for some other reason, not intended to record a real voyage, but deliberately created from the imagination. And then, they say, by a million-to-one chance this 'phoney' map was drawn in almost exactly the same shape as the real continent of Australia. The theory can be fitted into the words of the old adage: if an infinite number of monkeys made an infinite number of squiggles for an infinite number of years, one of them would come up with a map of Australia.

We can only appeal to expert witnesses to tell us whether, in the case before us, this Alternative Explanation is within the realms of possibility; and we are fortunate that we have expert witnesses of the highest credentials to tell us that this hypothesis is *not* acceptable. Matthew Flinders[17] circumnavigated Australia with one of the Dieppe maps in his hand, and his considered opinion is: 'The direction given to some parts of the coast approach too near the truth for the whole to have been made from conjecture alone'.

Surely on a subject such as this the opinion of Matthew Flinders outweighs the theories of a library-full of armchair navigators. Admiral James Burney, who sailed with Cook, said much the same. Professor J. A. Williamson said that if the maps are the result of a guess, it must have been the most inspired guess in the history of the world. And so say many more.

Other suggested Alternative Explanations are more amusing. J. R. McClymont, for example, suggests that someone (perhaps the spy in the Casa da India) was drawing a map of the world, with South America the last part to be inked in. He then folded the map in half, bringing the Java–Sumbawa area into contact with the still-wet ink of South America, impressing a mirrored image of South America on to that area. As McClymont explains it, 'it is necessary to invert them, which can be simply done by placing the chart before a mirror'.[18] When Desceliers saw this inky blot, he mistook it for the outline of a new continent, and incorporated it in the Dauphin Map.

Another set of Alternative Explanations is based upon alleged confusion of scale. Confusion of scale is only a theory, as there are no extant maps in which massive confusion of scale has occurred, but the theory runs like this. Suppose that some cartographical incompetent – say, an imbecile school boy – was instructed to draw a map of England and Scotland. He had no atlas to copy from, but he found a postcard-sized map of England, and a huge wall-poster map of Scotland. Combining cartographical ignorance with native stupidity, he joined these together without adjusting the scale, thus producing a map in which England appeared as a small peninsula on the underside of a continental-sized Scotland. The resulting map might bring a gleam to the eye of a patriotic Scotsman, but it would be impossibly bad cartography.

Yet Professor Heawood[19] invokes this theory as his Alternative Explanation. He suggests that Desceliers took an ordinary map of Java, twisted it violently on to its side, exaggerated its area from 50,000 square miles to 5,000,000 square miles (just a paltry error of 10,000 percent!), drew it in this way on the Dauphin Map, and there rather understandably labelled it Jave-la-Grande – Oversized Java! And what is more, when a map of Java is twisted and blown up in accordance with this recipe, the result shows very little resemblance to the Dauphin Map.

Professor Andrew Sharp[20] has a similar Alternative Explanation based on confusion of scale. He suggests that the Dieppe cartographers took maps of Java and Sumbawa, laid down their top (north) coasts on proper scale, but exaggerated the side coasts (the west coast of Java, the east coast of Sumbawa) this time only 2500 percent – two degrees of latitude expanded to fifty degrees. And again, when this theory is tested by actually re-drawing Java and Sumbawa in accordance with this recipe, the resulting monstrosity demonstrates no noticeable agreement with the Dauphin, certainly less agreement than the Dauphin has with the real coast of Australia. In fairness to Professor Sharp it must be said that this cartographical explanation is not his main argument against the Portuguese Discovery of Australia: his main argument is that Discovery is not complete unless the results are published.

But the real culprit is Professor G. Arnold Wood. Even his sympathetic biographer, Professor R. M. Crawford,[21] indicates in guarded words that his Portuguese chapter is a disaster area in an otherwise fine book; and by way of extenuation he lists the handicaps and difficulties under which Wood worked – lacking knowledge of the Portuguese language, lacking access to Portuguese originals, lacking expertise in cartography. These may explain, but they do not exonerate: a historian with these limitations should not have ventured into this field at all. He may have been driven into it by outside considerations – dislike of the Portuguese, animosity against Collingridge, wounded pride, the plain 'hostile prejudice' which he admits to. Another of his ex-students, in a phrase uncharacteristically uncharitable, puts it thus: 'Professor Wood seemed to be saying "As I, G. A. Wood, do not read Portuguese, it is unlikely that the Almighty would have dared to allow the Portuguese to discover Australia".'

In some other respects, his opposition to the Boer War for example, George Arnold Wood might have been 'a bit of a rebel'. But on this question of the prior discovery of Australia he was as hide-bound as all others of his generation. He was voicing that British nationalism, that Australian Britishism, which pervaded the first decade of the twentieth century. That pre-World War I bias is perhaps hard to understand today: it is now identified with the cliché 'The Wops begin at Calais'. In that era, worship of England meant worship of Cook. Even the Dutch discoveries were under-played, and many Australians, most Australians, indeed, accepted as Gospel truth that 'Captain Cook discovered Australia'. Australian history was and ought to be British history. If the Dutch or the Portuguese had any history, they ought to keep it to themselves. The school textbooks were not deliberately propagandist: they merely mirrored the myopia of the writers of the school textbooks, who in turn mirrored that of Professor G. Arnold Wood.

But Australian history, too, is finding its own feet. As the years go by, time is gradually altering the angle of vision, gradually revealing from a distance what could not previously be seen from too close. No longer is the lecturer who unfolds the case for the Portuguese discovery spurned or discouraged. Never again, it is hoped, will an advocate of the theory suffer the humiliation and denigration that befell poor George Collingridge. The Australian newspapers, the Australian radio and television, the Australian Universities, all now tolerantly, even encouragingly, open their channels to those engaged in the Portuguese Story. It is no longer unpatriotic to suggest that perhaps, after all, it was not the English who discovered the east coast of Australia.

In Portugal, the acceptance is more predictable. There there is, and always has been, a childlike faith in the discoverers of their Golden Age. The Portuguese discovered the whole world, they say, so they must have discovered Australia. What a pity it is, said Camões, that there were not a few more continents – for then the Portuguese would have discovered them too.

In Sagres, in Coimbra, and elsewhere, there are mosaic wall-maps, showing the outline of all of the continents of the world, with proud ribbons radiating from Lisbon along the tracks of the Great Discoverers. The discoverers who reached the shores of Australia are justly entitled to be joined in that distinguished company, and their ribbons qualify to be displayed on those monuments of stone; but more, their deeds deserve to be rescued from oblivion, to be accepted, remembered and honoured in the hearts and minds of living men.

APPENDIX

I: THE HOUSE OF AVIS
Portuguese Kings 1385–1580

João I	1385–1433
Duarte I	1433–1438
Affonso V	1448–1481
João II	1481–1495
Manoel I	1495–1521
João III	1521–1557
Sebastião	1568–1678
Henriques	1578–1580

II: THE CHRONOLOGY OF THE GOLDEN AGE 1394–1606
List of dates mentioned in text

Year	Events	Maps
1394	Henry the Navigator born	
1419	Henry retires to Sagres	
1433	Gil Eannes passes Cape Bojador	
1452	De Tieve discovers Corvo and the Fishing Banks	
1458	Bull of Inter Caetera	
1472	Voyage of João Vaz Cortereal	
1477	Columbus voyages to Iceland	
1487	Bartolomeu Dias reaches the Cape	
1492	Columbus reaches America	
1494	Treaty of Tordesillas	
1497	Vasco da Gama reaches India	
1500	Cabral discovers Brazil	
1505	Ludovico Varthema in the East	
1507	João de Lisboa finds supposed strait	Waldseemüller's Gores
1508	Voyage of Pinson and de Solis	
1511	Albuquerque captures Malacca	
1512	Abreu and Serrão reach Moluccas	
1513	Balboa crosses the Isthmus of Panama	
1515		Schöner's first globe
1516	First settlement of Timor	
1517		Unsigned Reinel chart
1519	Magellan sails from Spain, J. de Albuquerque from Portugal	
1520	Magellan enters the Pacific	
1521	Death of Magellan	
1522	Voyage of Cristovão de Mendonça	
1523		Schöner's lost globe
1524	Junta of Badajoz; Voyages of Verrazano and Loaysia	

Year	Events	Maps
1525	Two voyages of Gomes de Sequeira	
1529	Treaty of Saragossa; Bishop of Viseu exiled	Franciscus Monachus
1531		Finé's double-cordiform
1533		*Carta Anonima Portuguesa*
1535		Penrose Chart
1536		Dauphin Chart
1537	Pedro Nunes discovers the Loxodrome	Viegas (two maps)
1538		Mercator's double-cordiform
1539	Orellano's voyage down Amazon	
1541		Desliens's Dresden chart
1542	*Voyages Aventureux* written	Rotz's 'Boke of Idrographie'
1546		Desceliers's 'Royal'
1547		Vallard
1550	Portuguese settlement in Nova Scotia	Desceliers 1550
1553		Desceliers 1553
1556		Le Testu
1559	*Voyages Aventureux* published	
1561		Bartolomeu Velho
1562	Legaspi in Philippines	
1563		Desliens
1565		Paolo Forlani
1566	Mendaña's first voyage	Desliens
1570		Ortelius publishes atlas
1571	Foundation of Manila	
1578	Battle of Alcazar-Quivir	G. de Jode publishes atlas
1580	Spain annexes Portugal	
1593		C. de Jode publishes atlas
1595	Houtman (first Dutch in Indies); Mendaña's second voyage	Wytfliet's 'Ptolemaic Supplement'
1601	Erédia claims to have discovered Nuca Antara	
1606	First Dutch sighting of Australia; Torres in Torres strait	

CHAPTER NOTES

INTRODUCTION

1 G. A. WOOD, *The Discovery of Australia*, London, 1922, pp. 122–9.
2 E. SCOTT, *Australian Discovery by Sea*, London, 1929, pp. x–xii.
3 R. H. MAJOR, *Early Voyages to Terra Australis*, London, 1859, pp. xvi–xxxvi.
4 O. H. K. SPATE, *Let me Enjoy*, Canberra, 1965, pp. 267–95.
5 J. STEVENS, Translation of Faria y Sousa's *Asia Portuguesa*, London, 1694.
6 J. R. McCLYMONT, 'The influence of Spanish and Portuguese discoveries . . . on the theory of an antipodal southern continent', Reports of the Australasian Assoc. for Adv. Science, Hobart, 1892, vol. IV p. 462.

CHAPTER 1

1 For Cortereal, see p. 35, infra.
2 G. A. WOOD, op. cit., p. 127.
3 J. DE BARROS, *Da Asia*, Nova Edicão, Lisbon, 1777, Dec I liv i cap 4 fol. 9.
4 See IAN CAMERON, *Lodestone and Evening Star*, London, 1965, p. 102.
5 GOMEZ DE AZURARA, *Crónica do descobrimento da Guiné*, Paris, 1841, transl. by C. R. Beazley and E. Prestage, London, 1896, Chapter 9.
6 S. E. MORISON, *The European Discovery of America* (*Northern Voyages*), New York, 1971, p. 229.
7 R. H. MAJOR, *The Discoveries of Prince Henry*, London, 1858, p. 300.

CHAPTER 2

1 For Pedro Nunes, see Chapter 12, p. 161 infra.
2 For magnetic variation, see Chapter 13, p. 183 infra.

3 P. NUNES, *Tratado em defensam da carta de marear*, Obras, Nova Edicão, Lisbon, 1940, fol 119.

4 Cook's *Journal*, 13 March 1771.

5 See A. SHARP, *The Voyages of A. J. Tasman*, Oxford, 1968, p. 68.

6 For more detail, see E. G. R. TAYLOR, *The Haven-finding Art*, London, 1957, p. 117; M. BOAS, *The Scientific Renaissance*, London, 1962, p. 38; J. BENSAUDE, *Histoire de la science nautique portugaise*, Munich, 1914.

7 A full account may be found in E. G. R. TAYLOR and M. W. RICHEY, *The Geometrical Seaman*, London, 1962.

8 e.g., J. H. PARRY, *The Age of Reconnaissance*, London, 1963, p. 106.

9 See A. CORTESÃO, *History of Portuguese Cartography*, Coimbra, 1971, Vol. II, Fig. 141, p. 440.

10 For these tables see J. BENSAUDE, op. cit.

11 NUNES, op. cit., fol 128.

12 J. DE BARROS, op. cit., Dec III liv v. cap 8.

13 E. G. R. TAYLOR, op. cit., p. 190.

14 S. E. MORISON, op. cit., p. 141.

CHAPTER 3

1 S. E. MORISON, op. cit., p. 229.

2 See account in ibid, p. 95.

3 SIR JOHN BARROW, *A Chronological History of Voyages to the Arctic Ocean*, London, 1818, p. 37.

4 A. CORDEIRO, *Historia Insulana*, Lisbon, 1717.

5 G. MADARIAGA, *Christopher Columbus*, New York, 1940, p. 108.

6 Treated more fully in CHARLES GIBSON, *Spain in America*, New York, 1966, p. 32.

7 C. R. BOXER, *The Portuguese Sea-borne Empire*, London, 1969, p. 20.

8 E. PRESTAGE, *Travel & Travellers in the Middle Ages*, London, 1926, p. 209.

9 The text of the letter is given in *Hakluyt's Voyages*, Everyman, London, 1926, Vol. I, p. 216. See Chapter 22, p. 311 infra.

10 For the texts of these treaties see F. DAVENPORT, *European Treaties*, Washington, 1917; P. GOTTSCHALK, *Earliest Diplomatic Documents in America*, Berlin, 1927.

11 G. CLEVELAND, *The Venezuela Boundary Controversy*, Princeton, 1913.

CHAPTER 4

1 For Orellano, see *Cambridge Modern History*, Cambridge, 1933, Vol. II, p. 586.

2 See A. F. Z. CORTESÃO, *Cartografia e Cartografos portugueses dos seculos xv e xvi*, Lisbon, 1935, Vol. I, Estampa xiv, p. 346–8.

3 For an example see L. C. WROTH, *Early Cartography of the Pacific*, New York, 1944, p. 146.

4 J. A. WILLIAMSON, *Short History of British Expansion*, London, 1945, p. 207.

5 See Chapter 12, p. 193, infra.

6 See Chapter 3, p. 44, supra.

7 J. OSORIO, *De Vida e feitos de El Rei D. Manoel*, Porto, 1571; H. HARRISSE, *The Diplomatic History of America*, London, 1897, p. 134.

8 See S. E. HOWE, *In Quest of Spices*, Ann Arbor, 1946, p. 177.

CHAPTER 5

1 JOHN BARROW, Letter to W. H. Horton, Colonial Under-Secretary, 21 January 1824.

2 D. HENIGE, *Colonial Governors*, Madison, 1970, p. 270.

3 H. LEITÃO, *Os Portugueses em Solor e Timor*, Lisbon, 1948.

4 E. DE FARIA Y SOUSA, *Asia Portuguesa*, transl. by J. Stevens, op. cit., Tom I pt ii cap 6, p. 180.

5 A. LAFITAU, *Conquestes des Portugais dans le nouveau monde*, Paris, 1733, p. 430.

6 B. L. ARGENSOLA, *Conquista de las islas maluccas*, in J. Stevens, Collection of Voyages and Travels, London, 1708, Vol I, p. 6.

7   A. GALVÃO, *Discoveries of the World*, Hakluyt Society, London, 1862, p. 165; also in J. KERR, *Voyages and Travels*, Edinburgh, 1811.

8   See R. A. SKELTON, *Explorers' Maps*, London, 1958, p. 35.

9   There is a detailed account of this voyage in A. F. Z. CORTESÃO & A. T. DA MOTA, *Portugaliae Monumenta Cartografica*, Lisbon, 1960, Vol. I, p. 80.

10 J. R. MCCLYMONT, *The First Expedition to Banda*, Hobart, n.d.

11 J. CORTESÃO, *Os descobrimentos portugueses*, Lisbon, 1934, Vol II, pp. 223, 228.

12 A. GALVÃO, op. cit., cap 30. The reference here is to the Kerr version.

13 JOSÉ MARTINHO, *Timor*, Porto, 1943, p. 4.

14 H. FELGAS, *Timor Português*, Lisbon, 1954, p. 220.

15 D. BARBOSA, *The Book of Duarte Barbosa*, Lisbon, 1518, London, 1918.

16 C. E. NOWELL, *Magellan's Voyage*, Evanston, 1963, p. 246.

17 G. GREY, *Journal of Two Expeditions*, London, 1841; Adelaide, 1964, p. 81.

18 P. G. SPILLETT, *Forsaken Settlement*, Sydney, 1972, p. 35.

19 J. L. STOKES, *Discoveries in Australia*, London, 1846; Adelaide, 1969, p. 182.

20 SIR JOSEPH BANKS, *Journal*, 29 September 1770.

21 JAMES COOK, *Journal*, 5 December 1768.

22 WOOD, op. cit., p.127.

23 The Mota Alves map is discussed in Q. DA FONSECA, *A Participão dos portugueses no descobrimento da Austrália*, Coimbra, 1937, p. 412.

24 M. G. ERÉDIA, *Tratado Ophirico*, British Museum.

25 A. SHARP, *Ancient Voyages in the Pacific*, London, 1956, p. 211.

CHAPTER 6

1   Detailed in D. PERES, *Historia dos descobrimentos portugueses*, Oporto, 1945, p. 470.

2   A. DALRYMPLE, *Memoir Concerning the Chagos and Adjacent Islands*, London, 1786, p. 4.
3   SIR H. YULE, *Cathay and the Way Thither*, London, 1916; Marco Polo, Book III, chapters 6–8.
4   G. COLLINGRIDGE, 'Emus and Kangaroos', *Australian Magazine*, Sydney, 1 December 1909, p. 104.
5   M. FLINDERS, *A Voyage to Terra Australis*, London, 1814, pp. 213, 229.
6   G. BARTON, *Historical Records of NSW*, Series III, Vol. 14, p. 662.
7   BARROS, op. cit., Dec III liv iii cap 3 fols 265–73.
8   Ibid, fol 273.
9   J. CORTESÃO, op. cit., pp. 225, 232.
10 Ibid, p. 225.
11 Analysed in SPATE, op. cit., p. 264.
12 M. G. ERÉDIA, *Declaration of Malacca*, Brussels, 1881.
13 R. H. MAJOR, *O Descobrimento da Austrália*, Lisbon, 1863. (Translated by D. J. de Lacerda.)
14 GREY, op. cit., p. 201.
15 A. DA MORGA, *Sucesos de las islas filipinas*, Cambridge, 1971, p. 55.
16 GREY, op. cit., p. 204.
17 EZEKIEL, Chap. xxiii verse 14.
18 GREY, op. cit., p. 205.
19 M. U'REN, *Sailormen's Ghosts*, Melbourne, 1940, p. 23.

CHAPTER 7

1   P. P. KING, *Narrative of a Survey*, London, 1829; Adelaide, 1969, Vol I, p. 113.
2   J. L. STOKES, op. cit., pp. 73, 211.
3   See Chapter 21, p. 306, infra.
4   Tasman's *Journal*, 29 November 1642.
5   A. SHARP, *The Discovery of Australia*, Oxford, 1963, p. 41.
6   Tasman's *Journal*, 14 February 1643.
7   J. C. BEAGLEHOLE, *The Journals of Captain Cook*, (4 vols), London 1955, Vol. I, p. cclxxxiv.

8   Ibid, p. 644.
9   R. DEACON, *John Dee*, London, 1968, p. 52.
10 J. CORTESÃO, op. cit., vol. II, p. 257.
11 A. CORTESÃO, *Cartografia . . . etc*, op. cit., vol. I, p. 21.
12 Ibid, Vol I, p. 23.
13 W. F. GANONG, *Crucial Maps in the Early Cartography of Canada*, Trans. Royal Society of Canada, Third Series, Sec 2, Vols 23–31, 1929–1937.
14 E. C. ABENDANON, 'Missing Links in the development of Portuguese Geography of the Indies', *Geographical Journal*, December 1919, Vol IV No 6, p. 395.
15 Most accounts are based on the eye-witness Pedegache; see *The Historians' History of the World*, London, 1908, Vol XV, p. 525; T. C. KENDRICK, *The Lisbon Earthquake*, London, 1955, Chap. 2.
16 A. F. Z. CORTESÃO, *Nautical Chart of 1424*, Coimbra, 1954, p. xi.
17 Discussed in SPATE, op. cit., p. 284.
18 See CORTESÃO & MOTA, *Portugaliae Monumenta Cartografica*, op. cit., Vol I, p. 34.
19 See H. HARRISSE, *The Discovery of North America*, London, 1892, p. 620.

CHAPTER 8

1   H. HARRISSE, *Découverte et Évolution Cartographique*, London, 1900; *The Dieppe World Maps*, Gottingen, 1899.
2   J. R. McCLYMONT, 'A Preliminary critique of the Terra Australis legend', *Papers and Proc. Royal Soc. of Tasmania*, Hobart, 1886, Vol XII, p. 42.
3   J. A. WILLIAMSON, in *Cambridge History of the British Empire*, Cambridge, 1933, Vol VII, p. 33.
4   H. HARRISSE, *The Discovery of North America*, op. cit.; S. E. MORISON, op. cit.; H. P. BIGGAR, *The Precursors of Jacques Cartier*, Ottawa, 1911; W. F. GANONG, op. cit.; E. C. ABENDANON, loc. cit.; O. H. K. SPATE, op. cit.

5 HARRISSE, *The Discovery of North America*, p. 647.
6 C. H. COOTE, *The Dieppe World Maps*, Bibl. Lindesiana, No 4, Department of Printed Books, British Museum, London, 1898, p. 22. (Includes facsimile.)
7 H. HARRISSE, *The Dieppe World Maps*, Gottingen, 1899.
8 RAYMOND LISTER, *Antique Maps and Their Cartographers*, London, 1970, p. 27.
9 Quoted in DA FONSECA, op. cit., p. 400.
10 C. V. G. COUTINHO, *A Náutica dos descobrimentos*, Lisbon, 1951, p. 119.
11 See R. H. MAJOR, *Early Voyages to Terra Australis*, op. cit., p. xxviii.
12 See p. 74 supra.
13 For the Coste des Herbaiges controversy, see p. 346, infra.
14 G. A. WOOD, op. cit., p. 122.
15 E. SCOTT, op. cit., p. xi.
16 LISTER, op. cit., p. 47.

CHAPTER 9

1 CORTESÃO & MOTA, op. cit., Vol I, p. 34.
2 Ibid, p. 34.
3 JOÃO DE BARROS, op. cit., Dec III liv iii cap 4.
4 DIOGO DO COUTO, *Da Asia*, Nova Edicão, Lisbon, 1778, Dec II liv iii cap 5.
5 For an examination of 'The South Coast of Java', see O. H. K. SPATE, op. cit., p. 270.
6 L. C. WROTH, op. cit.
7 J. C. BEAGLEHOLE, op. cit., Vol I, p. clix.
8 W. F. GANONG, op. cit.
9 G. COLLINGRIDGE, 'Early Discovery of Australia' in *Reports of the Australasian Ass. Adv. Science*, Sydney, 1912, p. 379.

CHAPTER 10

1 Similar discussion in SPATE, op. cit., p. 269.

2   See M. GRAUBARD, *Tidings out of Brazil*, Minnesota, 1957, p. 28.
3   Examined by H. HARRISSE, *The Discovery of North America*, op. cit., p. 582.
4   J. CORTESÃO, op. cit., p. 227.
5   R. V. TOOLEY & R. BRICKER, *A History of Cartography*, London, 1964, p. 245.
6   This was first brought forward by G. COLLINGRIDGE, 'The fantastic islands of the Indian Ocean', *Journal Royal Geog. Soc. of Australasia*, Melbourne, 1894, Vol XI.
7   For Rotz, see p. 207 infra.
8   C. BARRETT, *Pacific*, Melbourne, n.d.; the same point put forward by J. R. McCLYMONT, 'A Preliminary Critique . . . etc', op. cit.
9   Cook's *Journal*, 7 September 1770.
10   See R. V. TOOLEY, *Maps and Map-makers*, London, 1949, p. 122, Fig. 23.

CHAPTER 11

1   Cook's *Journal*, 7 September 1770.
2   S. E. MORISON, op. cit., Introduction, p. viii.
3   W. F. GANONG, op. cit., Vol 23, p. 138.
4   See C. KELLEWAY, *Maps and Map Projections*, London, 1946, p. 78.
5   E. G. R. TAYLOR, op. cit., p. 158.
6   For Finé, see Chapter 10, p. 140 supra, and Chapter 25, p. 366 infra.
7   For these see L. BAGROW, *History of Cartography*, London, 1964, p. 116.
8   CORTESÃO & MOTA, op. cit.

CHAPTER 12

1   'Tratado qu o doutor Pero Nunez fez sobre certas duvidas da navegação'; 'Tratado qu o doutor Pero Nunez fez em defensam da carta de marear', Lisbon,

1537 in P. NUNES, *Obras*, Academia das cienças de Lisboa, Lisbon, 1940.

2   G. A. WOOD, op. cit., p. 122.

3   E. SCOTT, op. cit., p. xii.

4   O. H. K. SPATE, op. cit., p. 269.

5   J. DE BARROS, op. cit., Dec III liv iv Cap 3 fol 92.

6   The fullest description is in J. BENSAUDE, op. cit.

7   See A. CORTESÃO, *Cartografia e cartografos portugueses dos seculos xv e xvi.*

8   Dealt with in M. BOAS, op. cit., p. 205.

9   P. NUNES, *Tratado sobre certas duvidas de navegacão*, Fol 108.

CHAPTER 13

1   For development of compass see A. N. STRAHLER, *The Earth Sciences*, New York, 1965, Chapter 9.

2   CORTESÃO & MOTA, op. cit., Vol I, p. 26.

3   J. C. BEAGLEHOLE, *Life of Cook*, London, 1974, p. 95; R. A. SKELTON, 'Cook as Hydrographer', *Mariners' Mirror*, London, 1954, Vol XL, p. 92.

4   For transatlantic navigation, see R. A. SKELTON, op. cit., p. 62.

5   This very early map by Pedro Reinel is reproduced in H. KUNSTMANN, *Atlas zur Amerikas*, Munich, 1869; and see SKELTON, op. cit., p. 47.

6   E. G. R. TAYLOR, *Tudor Geography*, London, 1930, p. 63.

7   A. SHARP, *The Voyages of A. J. Tasman.*

8   D. W. VAN BEMMELN, *Die Abweichung der Magnetnagel*, Batavia, 1899.

9   See T. YUKUTAKE, *Journal of Geomagnetics*, 1971, Vol. 23 No 1, p. 1.

CHAPTER 14

1   See Fig. 9.3, p. 124, supra.

2   See p. 224 infra.

3   Le Testu also omits this section: see A. BETTEX, *The Discovery of the World*, London, 1960, p. 231.

4   G. COLLINGRIDGE, *The Discovery of Australia*, Sydney,
    1895, p. 173.
5   G. A. WOOD, op. cit., p. 125.
6   E. SCOTT, op. cit., p. viii.
7   FARIA Y SOUSA, op. cit., Tom I Pt iii cap. 3, p. 187.
8   DIOGO DO COUTO, op. cit., Dec III liv iii cap 3, p. 165.
9   For a criticism of the Wood–Scott view, see O. H. K.
    SPATE, op. cit., pp. 270–4.
10 R. A. SKELTON, op. cit., Fig. 46.
11 For Verrazano, see GANONG, op. cit., p. 129.
12 But see H. HARRISSE, *The Dieppe World Maps*, who
    disagrees with this.
13 M. FLINDERS, op. cit., pp. iv–vi.
14 ERNEST FAVENC, *History of Australia*, Sydney, 1888,
    p. 20.
15 S. E. MORISON, op. cit., pp. 225–7.

CHAPTER 15

1   W. F. GANONG, op. cit., Vol XXVIII p.179; but see
    Harrisse's objections, p. 106 supra.
2   J. BURNEY, *A Chronological History of the Discoveries in
    the South Seas or Pacific Ocean*, London, 1803, Vol I pp.
    377–87.
3   J. A. WILLIAMSON, *The Observations of Sir Richard
    Hawkins*, London, 1933, pp. xvii, xx.
4   J. G. KOHL, *History of the Discovery of Maine*, Portland,
    1869, p. 351.
5   See A. ANTHAUME, *Cartes Marines Normandes*, Paris,
    1916, pp. 61–75.
6   See A. BETTEX, *The Discovery of the World*, London,
    1960, p. 231.
7   J. SOTTAS, 'G. Le Testu', *Mariner's Mirror*, London,
    March 1912, Vol II, pp. 65–75.

CHAPTER 16

1   R. A. SKELTON, op. cit., Fig. 42.
2   Ibid, Fig. 197.

3   Ibid, Fig. 125.
4   L. BAGROW, op. cit., plate LXX.
5   J. CORTESÃO, op. cit., Vol II, p. 222; J. MCCLYMONT, 'The influence of Spanish and Portuguese discoveries . . . etc', loc. cit., p. 459.
6   See p. 193, supra.
7   G. DE JODE, *Speculum Orbis Terrarum*, Leiden, 1578, ed. R. A. Skelton, Amsterdam, 1965.
8   F. VAN ORTROY, *L'oeuvre cartographique de G. & C. de Jode*, Amsterdam, 1963.
9   See MCCLYMONT, loc. cit., p. 454; C. KOEMAN, *Collections of Maps and Atlases in the Netherlands*, Leiden, 1961, Vol II, p. 260.
10 C. DE JODE, *Speculum Orbis Terrae*, Antwerp, 1593.
11 H. E. FELGAS, *Timor Português*, Lisbon, 1956, p. 131.
12 G. COLLINGRIDGE, 'Emus and Kangaroos', *Australian Magazine*, Sydney, 1 December 1909, p. 104.
13 C. DE JODE, op. cit., Map 12 (versum).
14 C. WYTFLIET, *Descriptionis Ptolemaicae Augmentum*, Louvain, 1597; Amsterdam, 1964.
15 For Resende, see p. 65 supra.
16 BARROS, op. cit.

CHAPTER 17

1   C. E. NOWELL, op. cit., p. 209.
2   BARROS, op. cit., Dec III liv iv cap 3, fol 413; FARIA Y SOUSA, op. cit., p. 34.
3   FARIA Y SOUSA, op. cit., p. 53.
4   BARROS, op. cit., Dec III liv iv cap 3, p. 413.
5   A. GALVÃO, *Discoveries of the World*, Hakluyt Society, London, 1862, p. 115.
6   BARROS, op. cit., Dec III liv v cap 3, f. 540; Also discussed in DAMIÃO PERES, *Historia dos descobrimentos portugueses*, Oporto, 1945, p. 483.
7   BARROS, op. cit., Dec III liv v cap 3, p. 540.
8   ibid., p. 549.
9   GAGO COUTINHO, *A Nautica dos descobrimentos*, Lisbon, 1951, p. 119.

CHAPTER 18

1 'The Investigator', *Journal of the Geelong Historical Society*, Geelong, June 1975, p. 35.
2 *Geelong Advertiser*, Geelong, 14 September 1847.
3 L. J. BLAKE, *Letters of C. J. La Trobe*, Melbourne, 1975, p. 25.
4 ibid., p. 73.
5 ibid., p. 74.
6 T. RAWLINSON, 'Notes on the Discovery of some keys on the shore formation of Corio Bay', *Trans. Royal Society of Victoria*, Vol XII, Melbourne, 1874–1875, Vol XII p. 33.
7 L. J. BLAKE, op. cit., p. 31.

CHAPTER 19

1 RICHARD OSBURNE, *The History of Warrnambool*, Prahran, 1887, p. 81.
2 J. ARCHIBALD, 'Notes on an ancient wreck near Warrnambool', *Journal. Geog. Soc. Vic.* (1891), Vol IX, pp. 40–8; Archibald Manuscripts, Mitchell Lib. (Sydney), A 1701.
3 OLIVE MILLS, *Why Should Their Honour Fade?*, Hawthorn, 1960.
4 J. MASON, *Argus* newspaper, Melbourne, 1 April 1876.
5 Letter, 3 September 1890, Archibald Manuscripts, Mitchell Library, A 1701.
6 G. G. McCRAE, *The Ancient Buried Vessel at Warrnambool*, Melbourne, 1910.
7 'The Vagabond', 'The Cradle of Victoria', *Argus* newspaper, Melbourne, 15 November 1884.

CHAPTER 20

1 A. SHARP, *The Discovery of Australia*, p. 6.
2 R. H. MAJOR, *Early Voyages to Terra Australis*, pp. xxvi–lxiv.

3 P. B. MALING, *Early Charts of New Zealand*, Wellington, 1969, Plate xxxiv.

4 R. JENKIN, *New Zealand Mysteries*, Wellington, 1970, pp. 15–27.

5 C. G. HUNT, 'Wreck at Ruapuke Beach', Waikato Scient. Assoc., Hamilton, 1955.

6 A. G. BAGNALL & G. C. PETERSON, *William Colenso*, Wellington, 1948, Appendix.

7 D. BARBOSA, *The Book of Duarte Barbosa*, Hakluyt Society, London, Vol II, p. 202.

8 J. CRAWFURD, 'Notes on an Ancient Hindu Sacrificial Bell', *Trans. Ethnological Soc. of London*, London, 1867, Vol V, p. 150.

9 'The Skull-piece of a European Helmet', *The Connoisseur,* Vol XV, London, May–August 1906, p. 187.

10 HENRY KINGSLEY, *The Recollections of Geoffrey Hamlyn*, Cambridge, 1859.

11 P. F. MORAN, *The History of the Catholic Church in Australia*, Sydney, 1895, p. 2.

12 C. M. M. CLARKE, *A History of Australia*, London, 1969, p. 16.

13 SIR CLEMENTS MARKHAM, *The Voyage of Queiros*, London, 1904.

14 J. L. STOKES, op. cit.

15 R. LANGDON, *The Lost Caravel*, Sydney, 1975, p. 211.

16 J. MCKENZIE, *Shipwrecks*, Peterborough, 1974, p. 185.

17 P. HERRMANN, *Conquest by Man*, London, 1954, p. 21.

18 *National Geographic Magazine,* Washington, January 1975, p. 98.

19 S. E. MORISON, op. cit., p. vii.

20 G. N. GRIFFITHS, *Point Piper Past & Present,* Sydney, 1947, pp. 45–52.

21 L. HARGRAVE, Lope de Vega (manuscript), Mitchell Library, Sydney.

22 J. B. JUKES, *Narrative of HMS Fly*, London, 1847, 18 January 1843.

23 E. J. BRADY, *The King's Caravan*, Melbourne, n.d.

24 Collingridge Manuscripts, Dixson Library, Sydney, Q 243 Item 7.

25 S. ROOK, 'They came in hope', *Walkabout Magazine*, Melbourne, April 1973.
26 H. P. WELLINGS, *Benjamin Boyd in Australia*, Sydney, n.d.

CHAPTER 21

1 J. CORTESÃO, op. cit., Vol 2, p. 229.
2 A. GALVÃO, *Discoveries of the World*, in J. KERR, *Voyages & Travels*, Edinburgh, 1811, Vol II, p. 34.
3 Ibid., Vol II, p. 87.
4 Ibid, Vol II, p. 231.
5 F. L. CASTANHEDA, *Historia dell' indie orientale*, Venice, 1577, cap xxvii (translation).
6 JOÃO DE BARROS, op. cit., Dec III liv iii cap 5, p. 491.
7 G. P. MAFFEI, *Historiarum Indicarum*, Antwerp, 1604.
8 R. H. MAJOR, op. cit., p. xxviii.
9 A. CORTESÃO, *Cartografia e cartografos portugueses dos seculos xv e xvi*, Vol II, p. 174.
10 CORTESÃO & MOTA, op. cit., Vol I, Plate 52A, Plate 52C.
11 Ibid., Vol I, Plates 52B, 52D.
12 In C. H. COOTE, *Remarkable Maps*, Amsterdam, 1894–1897, Map I.
13 E. HAMY, 'Commentaries on Old New Guinea Charts', Soc. de Géog., Paris, November 1877, Vol XIV, p. 450.

CHAPTER 22

1 C. JACK-HINTON, 'American Voyage', *Pacific Is Monthly*, Sydney, September 1963, p. 81.
2 Discussed in J. H. PARRY, op. cit., p. 161.
3 J. A. WILLIAMSON, *A Short History of British Expansion*, London, 1945, p. 75.
4 *Hakluyt's Voyages*, Everyman, Vol I, p. 216. See p. 37, supra.
5 See J. CORTESÃO, op. cit., Vol II, p. 229.
6 The text is in F. DAVENPORT, op. cit., p. 146.
7 R. A. SKELTON, op. cit., Fig. 87.
8 F. DAVENPORT, op. cit., p. 156.

9 See p. 298, supra.
10 J. DE BARROS, op. cit., Dec III liv x cap 5 fol 494.
11 CASTANHEDA, op. cit., cap. XXVII.
12 J. CORTESÃO, op. cit., Vol II, p. 230.
13 See Chapter 3, p. 38, supra.
14 J. CORTESÃO, op. cit., Vol II, p. 237.
15 TOOLEY & BRICKER, op. cit., p. 117.
16 *Cambridge Modern History,* Cambridge, 1933, Vol II, p. 569.
17 See BAGROW, op. cit., p. 612.
18 Mentioned in SPATE, op. cit., p. 285.
19 PETER MARTYR, *De Orbe Novo* (McNutt Edition), New York, 1912, Vol II, p. 136.
20 SIR CLEMENTS MARKHAM, *The Voyage of Queiros,* London, 1904, p. 356.
21 Ibid, p. 170.
22 For de Prado, see H. N. STEVENS, 'New Light', J & PRAHS, Vol 17, p. 269.
23 Technical discussion in A. VILLIERS, *Pioneers of the Seven Seas,* London, 1956, p.71.
24 C. M. M. CLARK, *A Short History of Australia,* London, 1964, p. 15.
25 D. M. DOS PASSOS, *Interferencia portuguêsa no descobrimento da Austrália,* Coimbra, 1931, p. 206.

CHAPTER 23

1 A. DALRYMPLE, *An Historical Collection of the Several Voyages and Discoveries in the South Pacific Ocean,* London, octavo volume 1768, two volume edition 1770.
2 For Arias Memorial see p. 330 infra; also see H. FRY, *Alexander Dalrymple,* London, 1970, p. 112.
3 See p. 133, supra.
4 H. FRY, op. cit., p. 52.
5 Discussed in R. ARMSTRONG, *The Discoverers,* London, 1968, p. 97.
6 H. FRY, op. cit., p. 83.
7 J. CALLANDER, *Terra Australis Cognita,* Edinburgh, 1766-8.
8 A. DALRYMPLE, op. cit.

9   J. BURNEY, op. cit.

10 Quoted in R. H. MAJOR, op. cit., p. xvi.

11 H. FRY, op. cit., pp. 270–4.

12 Ibid., p. 274.

13 See G. MACKANESS, 'Dalrymple's Serious Admonition', Sydney, 1943, p. 9.

14 A. DALRYMPLE, 'Memoir concerning the Chagos and adjacent islands', London, 1786, p. 4.

15 A. DALRYMPLE, 'A Serious Admonition to the Public concerning the Intended Thief Colony at Botany Bay', London, 1786.

16 See p. 229, supra.

CHAPTER 24

1   J. C. BEAGLEHOLE, *The Discovery of New Zealand*, Wellington, 1939, p. 1.

2   BARBIE DU BOCAGE, Address to Institute of Paris, in *Moniteur Universel*, Paris, 1807.

3   G. A. WOOD, op. cit., p. 129.

4   E. SCOTT, op. cit., p. xii.

5   J. A. WILLIAMSON, *The Observations of Sir Richard Hawkins*, p. xx.

6   A. DALRYMPLE, 'Memoir concerning the Chagos & adjacent islands', London, p. 4.

7   Cited by H. FRY, op. cit., p. 274.

8   K. G. MCINTYRE, 'Portuguese Discoverers on the Australian Coast', *Victorian Historical Magazine*, Melbourne, Vol XLV No 4, p. 202.

9   H. FRY, op. cit.

10 J. C. BEAGLEHOLE, *The Journals of Captain Cook*, Vol I, p. clxi.

11 J. BURNEY, op. cit., p. 379.

12 F. METZ, *La Revue du Décade*, Paris, 1805, Vol XLVII, p. 261; cited by R. H. MAJOR, *Early Voyages to Terra Australis*, London, 1859, p. xix.

13 Cook's *Journal*, 11 June 1770.

14 H. FRY, op. cit., p. 274.

15 M. FLINDERS, op. cit., p. v; BURNEY, op. cit., Vol I, p. 382.

16 Cook's *Journal,* 22 August 1770.
17 G. MACKANESS, 'Dalrymple's Serious Admonition', p. 9.
18 F. J. BAYLDON, 'A Dalrymple', J & PRAHS, Vol XIII, p. 41.
19 Banks *Letters,* British Museum, London, 1958, p. 62.
20 A. DALRYMPLE, 'Memoir . . .', p. 4.
21 J. BURNEY, op. cit., Vol I, p. 381.
22 H. C. CAMERON, *Sir Joseph Banks,* London, 1952, p. 188.
23 *Brabourne Papers,* NSW Govt. Printer, 1888.
24 W. T. SELLEY, *England in the Eighteenth Century,* London, 1934, p. 152.
25 This same calculation, but for different purposes, was made by Admiral S. E. Morison in his European Discovery of America, Southern Voyages (New York 1974) page 476. To within one half of one degree his answer agrees with the answer given here.
26 J. F. W. WATSON, *Lieutenant James Cook,* Sydney, 1933, p. 6.

CHAPTER 25

(The magazine *Archaeologia* (London) is herein cited as ARCH)
1 Q. DA FONSECA, op. cit., p. 403.
2 R. H. MAJOR, *The Discoveries of Prince Henry,* London, 1868.
3 R. H. MAJOR, 'On the Discovery of Australia by the Portuguese in 1601', ARCH, 1861, Vol. xxxviii, p. 459.
4 MAJOR, *Early Voyages to Terra Australis.*
5 MAJOR, 'On the Discovery of Australia by the Portuguese', loc. cit., p. 439.
6 Ibid., p. 438.
7 MAJOR, *Early Voyages* . . . p. xxxii.
8 MAJOR, 'On the Discovery of Australia by the Portuguese', loc. cit., p. 437.
9 SPATE, op. cit., p. 301.
10 R. H. MAJOR, 'Supplementary Facts on the Discovery of Australia', ARCH 1872–3, Vol. XLIV, p. 242.

11 R. H. MAJOR, 'Further Facts on the Discovery of Australia', ARCH 1872–3, Vol. XLIV, p. 235.

CHAPTER 26

1 M. FLINDERS, op. cit., p. 4.
2 J. BURNEY, op. cit.
3 G. COLLINGRIDGE, 'Early Australian Discovery', *Illustrated Sydney News,* 7 June 1890.
4 G. A. WOOD, op. cit., Intro.
5 G. COLLINGRIDGE, *Discovery of Australia*, Sydney, 1895.
6 B. STEVENS, 'George Collingridge', *Lone Hand Magazine*, Sydney, 1 September 1917, p. 487.
7 G. COLLINGRIDGE, *The First Discovery of Australia*, Sydney, 1906.
8 G. COLLINGRIDGE, 'Early Discovery of Australia', Reports of the Australasian Ass. for Adv. Science, Sydney, 1912, p. 376.
9 For the *Copia*, see p. 137, supra.
10 G. COLLINGRIDGE, *Journal Royal Geog. Soc. A/asia*, Sydney, April 1891, p. 16.
11 See Fig. 9.3, p. 124 supra.
12 G. COLLINGRIDGE, 'Australia – its Discovery', Reports of the Australasian Ass. for Adv. Science, Sydney, 1914, p. 5.
13 G. A. WOOD, op. cit., Intro.
14 O. H. K. SPATE, op. cit., p. 267.
15 G. A. WOOD, op. cit., p. 127.
16 E. SCOTT, op.cit., p. xi.
17 M. FLINDERS, op. cit., p. iv.
18 J. R. McCLYMONT, 'A Preliminary Critique of the Terra Australis Legend', *Papers & Proc.*, Royal Society of Tasmania, Vol XII, p. 51.
19 E. HEAWOOD, *A History of Geographical Discovery*, Cambridge, 1912, p. 4.
20 A. SHARP, *The Discovery of Australia*, p. 10.
21 R. M. CRAWFORD, *A Bit of a Rebel*, Sydney, 1975, pp. 342–4.

BIBLIOGRAPHY

(J&PRAHS = Journal and Proceedings of the Royal Australian Historical Society, Sydney)

ABBOTT, J. H. N., *Out of the Past*, Sydney, 1945.

ABENDANON, E. C., 'Missing Links in the Development of the Portuguese Geography of the Indies', *Geographical Journal*, Vol IV no 6, London, December 1919.

ALBUQUERQUE, Affonso de, *Commentaries*, Hakluyt Society, London, 1877.

ALMEIDA, F. de, *História de Portugal*, Coimbra, 1922.

ANDRADE, F. de, *Crónica de Rey Dom João III*, Lisbon, 1613; Coimbra, 1796.

ANTHAUME, A., *Cartes Marines Normands*, Paris, 1916.

ARCHIBALD, J., Manuscripts Relating to the Mahogany Ship, Mitchell Library, Sydney, A 1701.

——— 'Notes on an Ancient Wreck', Journal of the Royal Geog. Soc. of Victoria, Vol IX, Melbourne, 1891.

ARGENSOLA, B. L., *Conquista de las islas maluccas*, Amsterdam, 1906, in J. Stevens, *Collection of Voyages and Travels* Vol 1, London, 1708.

ARMSTRONG, R., *The Discoverers*, London, 1968.

AZURARA, Gomes de, *Crónica do Descobrimento da Guiné*, Paris, 1841; transl. by C. R. Beazley and E. Prestage, London, 1896.

BAGNALL, A. G. & PETERSON, G. C., *William Colenso*, Wellington, 1948.

BAGROW, Leo, *History of Cartography*, London, 1964.

BAIO, A. (ed.), *Historia do Expansão Português*, Lisbon, 1939.

BANKS, Sir Joseph, *Letters*, British Museum, London, 1958.

BARBOSA, D., *The Book of Duarte Barbosa*, Lisbon, 1518; Hakluyt Society, London, 1918.

BARRETT, Charles, *The Pacific*, Melbourne, n.d.

BARROS, João de, *Da Asia*, Lisbon, 1553–63; Nova Edicão, Lisbon, 1777.

BARROW, Sir John, *A Chronological History of Voyages to the Arctic Ocean*, London, 1818.

———— Letter to W. H. Horton, Colonial Under-Secretary, 22 January 1824.

BARTON, G., *Historical Records of New South Wales*, Sydney, 1910.

BAYLDON, F., 'The Voyage of Torres', J&PRAHS Vol 11.

———— 'The Voyage of Torres' (revised), J&PRAHS Vol 16.

———— 'Alexander Dalrymple', J&PRAHS Vol 13.

———— 'Explorers of the Pacific', J&PRAHS Vol 18.

BAYLISS, A., *Dampier's Voyages*, London, 1945.

BEAGLEHOLE, J. C., *The Journals of Captain Cook*, Hakluyt Society, London, 1955.

———— *The Life of Cook*, London, 1974.

———— *The Discovery of New Zealand*, Wellington, 1939.

BEAZLEY, C. R., *Prince Henry the Navigator*, London, 1895.

BEIRÃO, A., *A Short History of Portugal*, Lisbon, 1960.

BENSAUDE, J., *Histoire de la Science Nautique Portugaise*, Munich, 1914.

BETHUNE, C. (ed.), *Galvão's Discoveries of the World*, Hakluyt Society, London, 1862.

BETTEX, A., *The Discovery of the World*, London, 1961.

BIGGAR, H. P., *The Voyages of Jacques Cartier*, Ottawa, 1924.

———— *The Precursors of Jacques Cartier*, Ottawa, 1911.

BLAKE, L. J., *Letters of C. J. La Trobe*, Melbourne, 1975.

BOAS, M., *The Scientific Rennaissance*, London, 1962.

BOCAGE, Barbie du, Address to Institute of Paris 1807 in *Moniteur Universel*, Paris, 1807.

BOXER, C. R., *The Portuguese Sea-borne Empire*, London, 1969.

Brabourne Papers, Sydney, 1888.

BRADY, E. J., *The King's Caravan*, Melbourne, n.d.

BROWN, Lloyd, *The Story of Maps*, Boston, 1949.

BURNEY, J. A., *Chronological History of the Discoveries in the South Sea or Pacific Ocean*, London, 1803.

CALLANDER, J., *Terra Australis Cognita*, Edinburgh, 1766–1768.

Cambridge History of the British Empire, Cambridge, 1933, Vol VII.

CAMERON, H. C., *Sir Joseph Banks*, Sydney, 1952.

CAMERON, Ian, *Lodestone and Evening Star*, London, 1965.

CASTANHEDA, L., *Historia do descobrimento e conquista de India*, Lisbon, 1551.

CLARKE, C. M. M., *A Short History of Australia*, London, 1969.

CLEVELAND, President G., *The Venezuela Boundary Controversy*, Princeton, 1913.

COLLINGRIDGE, G., *The Discovery of Australia*, Sydney, 1895.

────── *The First Discovery of Australia*, Sydney, 1906.

────── 'Early Discovery of Australia', *Illustrated Sydney News*, 7 June 1890.

────── 'Emus and Kangaroos', *Australian Magazine*, Sydney, 1 December 1909.

────── 'Early Discovery of Australia', Reports of the Australasian Assoc. for Adv. Science, Sydney, 1912.

────── 'Australia, its Discovery', Reports of the Australasian Assoc. for Adv. Science, Sydney, 1914.

────── 'Is Australia the Baptismal Font of Brazil?', *Journal Royal Geog. Soc. of Australasia*, Sydney, April 1891.

────── 'The Fantastic Islands of the Indian Ocean', *Journal Royal Georg. Soc. of Australasia*, Melbourne, June 1894.

────── Collingridge Manuscripts, Dixson Library, Sydney MS Q 243.

COLWELL, J., *A Century in the Pacific*, Sydney, 1914.

Connoisseur, The, 'The Skull-piece of a European Helmet', London, May–August 1906.

COOK, CAPTAIN JAMES, *Journal of the Voyages of the Endeavour*, edited W. J. L. Wharton, London, 1893; edited J. C. Beaglehole, *The Journals of Captain Cook* (4 Vols), London, 1955.

COOTE, C. H., *Remarkable Maps*, Amsterdam, 1894–7.

────── *The Dieppe World Maps*, Bibl. Lindesiana No. 4, Department of Printed Books, British Museum, 1898.

CORDEIRO, A., *Historia Insulana*, Lisbon, 1717.

CORTESÃO, A. F. Z. & DA MOTA, A. T., *Portugaliae Monumenta Cartografica*, (5 vols), Lisbon, 1960.

CORTESÃO, A. F. Z., *Cartografia e Cartografos Portugueses dos Seculos XV e XVI*, Lisbon, 1935.

────── *Historia do Expansão Português*, Lisbon, 1939.

────── *History of Portuguese Cartography*, Coimbra, 1971.

—— *The Nautical Chart of 1424*, Coimbra, 1954.
CORTESÃO, Jaime, *Os Descobrimentos Portugueses*, Lisbon, 1934.
COSTA, F. da, *A Marinhara dos Descobrimentos*, Lisbon, 1939.
COUTINHO, C. V. G., 'Portugueses no Descobrimento da Austrália', *Bol. Soc. Geog. Lisboa*, Vol LVII.
—— *A Náutica dos Descobrimentos*, Lisbon, 1951.
COUTO, Diogo de, *Da Asia*, Nova Edicão, Lisbon, 1778.
CRAWFORD, R. M., *A Bit of a Rebel*, Sydney, 1975.
CRAWFURD, J., 'On an Ancient Hindu Sacrificial Bell', *Trans. Ethnological Society of London*, London, 1867, Vol V.
CRONE, G. R., *Maps and their Makers*, Hakluyt Society, London, 1953.
—— *The Discovery of the East*, London, 1972.
DALRYMPLE, Alexander, *An Historical Collection of the Several Voyages and Discoveries in the South Pacific Ocean Previous to 1764*, London, 1769.
—— 'Memoir concerning the Chagos and Adjacent Islands', London, 1786.
—— 'A Serious Admonition to the Public Concerning the intended Thief Colony at Botany Bay', London, 1786.
DAMPIER, William, *A Voyage to New Holland*, London, 1939.
—— *A New Voyage Round the World*, London, 1927.
DANVERS, F. C., *Portuguese Records Relating to the East Indies*, London, 1892.
DAVENPORT, F., *European Treaties*, Washington, 1917.
DAY, R., *Explorers of the Pacific*, New York, 1966.
DEACON, R., *John Dee*, London, 1968.
DIXSON, W., 'Notes and Comments', J&PRAHS Vol XXII.
Documentacão Ultramarina Portuguesa, Lisbon, 1960.
DOS PASSOS, D. M., *Interferência portuguesa no descobrimento da Austrália*, Coimbra, 1931.
DOS PASSOS, J., *The Portugal Story*, London, 1970.
DUNBABIN, T., 'Early Voyages', J&PRAHS Vol XXII.
EARL, G. W., *Eastern Seas*, London, 1937.
ELDERSHAW, M. Barnard, *Phillip of Australia*, Sydney, 1922.

FAIRBRIDGE, A., 'Terra Australis', J&PRAHS Vol XXXIV.
FARIA Y SOUSA, E. de, *Asia Portuguesa*, Oporto, 1590–1607, transl. by J. Stevens, London, 1694.
FAVENC, E., *Alexander Dalrymple*, Sydney, 1888.
—— *The Exploration of Australia*, Sydney, 1908; Amsterdam, 1967.
FELGAS, H. E., *Timor Português*, Lisbon, 1954.
FLETCHER, C. D., 'Australia and the Indian Ocean', *Australia & New Zealand Historical Studies*, Vol II.
FLINDERS, Matthew, *A Voyage to Terra Australis*, London, 1814.
—— *An Introduction to the Practice of Nautical Survey*, London, 1823.
FONSECA, Q. da, *A Participão dos Portugueses no descobrimento da Austrália*, Coimbra, 1937.
FRY, H., *Alexander Dalrymple*, London, 1970.
—— 'Cathay & The Way Thither', *Australia & New Zealand Historical Studies*, Vol XIV.
GALVÃO, A., *Discoveries of the World*, Edit. Bethune, Hakluyt Society, London, 1862.
GANONG, W. F., 'Crucial Maps in the Early Cartography of Canada', Reprinted from *Transactions of the Royal Society of Canada*, Third Series, Sec. 2, Vols. XX–XXXI, 1929–1937.
Geelong Advertiser (newspaper), Geelong, 14 September 1847.
GIBSON, C., *Spain in America*, New York, 1966.
GOTTSCHALK, P., *Earliest Diplomatic Documents in America*, Berlin, 1927.
GRAUBARD, M., *Tidings from Brazil*, Minnesota, 1957.
GREY, Sir George, *Journal of Two Expeditions of Discovery in North-West Australia*, London, 1841; Adelaide, 1964.
GRIFFITHS, G. N., *Point Piper, Past & Present*, Sydney, 1947.
Hakluyt's Voyages, Everyman, London, 1926.
HALLS, C., 'The Mahogany Ship', *The Mariner's Mirror*, London, 1962, Vol XLVIII No 4.
HAMY, A. T., Herédia, in 'Mémoires Pour Servir', *Bol. de Soc. de Paris*, Paris, 1878.
—— 'Commentaries on Old New Guinea Charts', *Soc. de Géog.*, Paris, 1877, Vol. XIV.

HANTSCH, V. & SCHMIDT, L., *Kartographische Denkmäler*, Leipzig, 1903.

HAPGOOD, C. H., *Maps of the Ancient Sea-Kings*, Philadelphia, 1966.

HARGRAVE, L., *Lope de Vega*, MS. Mitchell Library, Sydney.

HARRISSE, H., *The Discovery of North America*, London, 1892.

—— *Découverte et Evolution Cartographique*, London, 1900.

—— *The Dieppe World Maps*, Gottingen, 1899.

—— *The Diplomatic History of America*, London, 1897.

HEAWOOD, E., *A History of Geographical Discovery*, Cambridge, 1912.

HENIGE, D., *Colonial Governors*, Madison, 1970.

HERRMANN, P., *Conquest by Man*, London, 1954.

HERVÉ, M. R., 'Australia in French Geographical Documents of the Renaissance', J&PRAHS Vol XLI Sydney, 1956.

Historians' History of the World, London 1908, Vol XV.

HOWE, S. E., *In Quest of Spices*, Ann Arbor, 1946.

HUNT, C. G., *Wreck at Ruapuke Beach*, Hamilton, NZ, 1955.

INGAMELLS, Rex, *The Great South Land*, Melbourne, 1961.

INGRAM, C. W. M. & WHEATLEY, P. O., *Shipwrecks: New Zealand Disasters*, Wellington, 1961.

INVESTIGATOR, The, *Journal of the Geelong Historical Society*, Geelong, 1971–5.

JACK-HINTON, C., 'American Voyage', *Pacific Islands Monthly*, Sydney, September 1963.

JENKIN, Robyn, *New Zealand Mysteries*, Wellington, 1970.

JODE, C. de, *Speculum Orbis Terrae*, Leiden, 1593.

JODE, G. de, *Speculum Orbis Terrarum* (ed. R. A. Skelton), Amsterdam, 1965.

JOMARD, E. F., *Les Monuments de la Géographie*, Paris, 1852.

JUKES, J. B., *Narrative of HMS Fly*, London, 1847.

KELLEWAY, C., *Maps and Map Projections*, London, 1945.

KENDRIK, T. C., *The Lisbon Earthquake*, London, 1955.

KERR, J., *Voyages and Travels*, Edinburgh, 1811.

KING, P. P., *Narrative of a Survey*, London, 1829; Adelaide, 1968.

KINGSLEY, Henry, *The Recollections of Geoffrey Hamlyn*, Cambridge, 1859.

KOEMAN, G., *Collections of Maps and Atlases in the Netherlands*, Leiden, 1961.

KOHL, J. G., *History of the Discovery of Maine*, Portland, Maine, 1869.

KUNSTMANN, H., *Atlas zur Amerikas*, Munich, 1869.

KUNZ, E. E., *A Continent Takes Shape*, Sydney, 1971.

LACERDA, D. J. de, *R. H. Major's O descobrimento*, Lisbon, 1863.

LAFITAU, A., *Conquestes des Portugais dans le nouveau monde*, Paris, 1733.

LANGDON, R., *The Lost Caravel*, Sydney, 1975.

LEE, Ida, *Early Explorers in Australia*, London, 1925.

LEGGETT, W., 'Early Visits', *Victorian Historical Magazine*, Melbourne, Vol XXV.

LEITÃO, H., *Os Portugueses em Solor e Timor*, Lisbon, 1948.

LISTER, R., *Antique Maps and their Cartographers*, London, 1970.

LIVERMORE, H., *A New History of Portugal*, London, 1970.

LLOYD, C., *Mr Barrow of the Admiralty*, London, 1970.

McCLYMONT, J. R., 'A Preliminary critique of the Terra Australia legend', *Papers & Proc. Royal Society of Tasmania for 1889*, Vol XII.

———— 'The influence of Spanish and Portuguese discoveries... on the theory of an antipodal southern continent', *Reports of the Australasian Assoc. for Adv. Science*, Hobart, 1892, Vol IV.

———— *The First Expedition to Banda*, Hobart, n.d.

McCRAE, G. G., 'The Ancient Buried Vessel at Warrnambool', *Victorian Geog. Journal*, Melbourne, 1910–11, Vol XXVIII.

McDONALD, A. C., *Early Discoveries*, Melbourne, 1891.

McFADDEN, J., *Bibliography of Pacific Maps*, Sydney, 1941.

McINNES, J. R., *Mahogany Ship*, Melbourne, 1959.

McINTYRE, K. G., 'Portuguese Discoverers on the Australian Coast, *Victorian Historical Magazine*, Vol XLV No. 4, Melbourne, 1974.

MACKANESS, G., 'Some Proposals for Settlement', J&PRAHS Vol XXIX.

——— *Dalrymple's 'Serious Admonition'*, Sydney, 1943.

MCKENZIE, M., *Shipwrecks*, Peterborough, 1974.

MADARIAGA, G., *Christopher Columbus*, New York, 1940.

MAFFEI, G. P., *Historiarum Indicarum*, Antwerp, 1605.

MAJOR, R. H., *The Discoveries of Prince Henry*, London, 1858.

——— *Early Voyages to Terra Australis*, London, 1859.

——— 'On the Discovery of Australia by the Portuguese', *Archaeologia*, London, 1861, Vol XXXVIII.

——— *O Descobrimento da Austrália pelos Portugueses*, Lisbon, 1863.

——— 'Further Facts on the Discovery on Australia', *Archaeologia*, London, 1873, Vol XLIV.

——— 'Supplementary Facts on the Discovery of Australia', *Archaeologia*, London, 1873, Vol XLIV.

MALING, P. B., *Early Charts of New Zealand*, Wellington, 1969.

MALTE-BRUN, J. B., *Précis de Géographie*, Paris, 1810, Livre 22.

——— *Annales des Voyages*, Paris, 1819.

MARKHAM, Sir C., *The Voyage of Queiros*, London, 1904.

MARTINHO, José, *Timor*, Oporto, 1943.

MARTINS, Oliveira, *Portugal Nos Mares*, Lisbon, 1924.

——— *The Golden Age of Prince Henry the Navigator*, London, 1916.

MARTYR, Peter, *De Orbe Novo*, De Nutt Edition, New York, 1912.

MASON, John, *Argus* newspaper, Melbourne, 1 April 1876.

METZ, F., *La Revue du Décade*, Paris, 1805.

MILLS, Olive, *Why Should their Honour Fade?* Hawthorn, 1960.

MORAN, P. F., *History of the Catholic Church in Australia*, Sydney, 1895.

MORGA, Antonia da, *Sucesos de las Islas Filipinas,* transl. by J. Cummins, Cambridge, 1971.

MORGAN, E. Delmer, *Memória lida no Congresso dos Cienças Geograficas*, Berne, 1891.

MORISON, S. G., *The European Discovery of America, Northern Voyages*, New York, 1971; *Southern Voyages*, New York, 1974.

MULLER, F., *Remarkable Maps of the 15th & 16th Centuries*, Amsterdam, 1890.
MUTCH, T. D., 'The First Discovery of Australia', J&PRAHS Vol XXVIII.
NEEDHAM, J., *Science and Civilization in China*, Vol IV, Part 3, Cambridge, 1954.
NORDENSKJOLD, A. E., *Periplus*, Stockholm, 1879.
—— *A Fac-Simile Atlas of the Early History of Cartography*, Stockholm, 1889.
NOWELL, C. E., *Magellan's Voyage*, Evanston, 1963.
NUNES, Pedro, *Obras*, Academia das Cienças de Lisboa, Lisbon, 1940.
NUNN, G. E., *The Columbus and Magellan Conceptions of Geography*, Glenside, 1931.
OSBURNE, R., *The History of Warrnambool*, Prahran, 1881.
OSORIO, D., *Da Vida e Feitos de el Rei D. Manoel*, Oporto, 1571.
PARRY, J. R., *The Age of Reconnaissance*, London, 1963.
PENROSE, R., *Travel and Discovery in the Renascence*, Harvard, 1952.
PERES, D., *A History of the Portuguese Discoveries*, Lisbon, 1960.
PIGAFETTA, A., *The First Voyage Round the World*, London, 1874.
PINKERTON, J., *General Collection of Voyages*, London, 1808–14.
PIRES, Tomé, *The Suma Oriental* (ed. A. Cortesão), Hakluyt Society, London, 1944.
PRESTAGE, E., *The Portuguese Pioneers*, London, 1933, Chapter 17.
—— *Travel and Travellers in the Middle Ages*, London, 1926.
RAINAUD, A., *Le Continent Austral*, Paris, 1873.
RAMUSIO, G., *Il Viaggio*, Venice, 1837.
RAWLINSON, T., 'Notes on the discovery of some keys on the shore formation of Corio Bay', *Trans. Royal Soc. of Victoria*, Vol XII, Melbourne, 1874–5.
ROBERTS, G., *Atlas of Discovery*, London, 1973.
ROOKE, S., 'They came in hope', *Walkabout Magazine*, Melbourne, April 1973.

SANCEAU, E., *Henry the Navigator*, London, n.d.

SANTAREM, Viscount de, *Atlas*, Paris, 1842.

—— *Estudos de Cartografica Antiga*, Lisbon, 1919.

—— *Memoria sobre a Prioridade dos Descobrimentos Portugueses*, Lisbon, 1846.

SANTOS, D. M. dos, *Interferência portuguesa no descobrimento da Austrália*, Coimbra, 1931.

SAYERS, C. E., *By These We Flourish*, Melbourne, 1969.

SCOTT, Sir Ernest, *Australian Discovery by Sea*, London, 1929.

—— *A Short History of Australia*, London, 1922.

SELLEY, W. T., *England in the Eighteenth Century*, London, 1934.

SHARP, Andrew, *The Discovery of Australia*, Oxford, 1963.

—— *The Voyages of A. J. Tasman*, Oxford, 1968.

—— *Ancient Voyagers in the Pacific*, London, 1956.

SKELTON, R. A., *Explorers' Maps*, London, 1958.

SOTTAS, J., 'G. Le Testu', *Mariner's Mirror*, London, 1912, Vol II.

SPATE, O. H. K., *Let Me Enjoy*, Canberra, 1965.

SPILLETT, P. G., *Forsaken Settlement*, Sydney, 1972.

STEERS, J. A., *An Introduction to Map Projection*, London, 1948.

STEVENS, B., 'George Collingridge', *Lone Hand Magazine*, Sydney, 1 September 1917.

STEVENS, H. N., *New Light*, London, 1930.

STEVENS, J. S., *The Portuguese Asia of Faria y Sousa* (translation), London, 1694.

STEVENSON, E. L., *Terrestrial and Celestial Globes*, New Harbor, 1921.

STOKES J. L., *Discoveries in Australia*, London, 1846; Adelaide, 1969.

STRAHLER, A. N., *The Earth Sciences*, New York, 1965.

TARLING, N., *South-East Asia*, Melbourne, 1968.

TAYLOR, E. G. H., & RICHEY, M. W., *The Geometrical Seaman*, London, 1962.

TAYLOR, E. G. H., *The Haven-Finding Art*, London, 1958.

—— *Tudor Geometry*, London, 1930.

TENISON-WOODS, J. E., *Discovery and Exploration in Australia*, London, 1865.

THOMAS, Julian: see 'The Vagabond'.
TOOLEY, R. V., & BRICKER, R., *A History of Cartography*, London, 1964.
TOOLEY, R. V., *Maps & Map-Makers*, London, 1949.
U'REN, M., *Sailormen's Ghosts*, Melbourne, 1940.
'Vagabond, The', 'The Cradle of Victoria', *Argus* newspaper, Melbourne, 15 November 1884.
VAN BEMMELN, B. W., *Die Abweichung der Magnetnagel*, Batavia, 1889.
VAN ORTROY, F., *L'oeuvre Cartographique de G. et C. de Jode*, Amsterdam, 1963.
VILLIERS, Alan, *Pioneers of the Sea*, London, 1956.
WACE, N. M., & LOVETT, B., *Yankee Maritime Activities*, Canberra, 1973.
WALLACE-CRABBE, J., *Fifth Continent Retrospect*, Melbourne, 1958.
WATSON, F., *Lieutenant Cook and his Voyages*, Sydney, 1933.
WEIDER, F. C., *Monumenta Cartografica*, The Hague, 1933.
WELLINGS, H. P., *Ben Boyd in Australia*, Sydney, n.d.
WHARTON, W. J. L., *Captain Cook's Journal*, London, 1893.
WIESEL, F., *Magalhães-strasse*, Innsbruck, 1881.
WILLIAMSON, J. A., *Dampier's Voyage to New Holland*, London, 1933.
—— *The Observations of John Hawkins*, London, 1933.
—— *Short History of British Expansion*, London, 1945.
WOOD, G. Arnold, *The Discovery of Australia*, London, 1922.
WROTH, L. C., *The Early Cartography of the Pacific*, New York, 1944.
WYTFLIET, C., *Descriptionis Ptolemaicae Augmentum*, Louvain, 1597; Amsterdam, 1964.
YUKUTAKE, Takesi, 'Spherical Harmonic Analysis of the Earth's Magnetic Field in the 17th & 18th Centuries', *Journal of Geomagnetism*, 1971, Vol XXII No. 1.
YULE, Sir H., *Cathay and the Way Thither*, London, 1915.

INDEX OF PLACES AND SUBJECTS

MACAO 49, 87
MACASSAR 70, 72, 329
MADAGASCAR 222
MADEIRA 7, 28, 35, 37
MADRID, Treaty of 38
MADURA 120, 307
MAGELLAN, Straits of 301
MAGNA, Ilha de 279
MAGNETIC COMPASS 182, 187
MAGNETIC DEVIATION 183, 186, 187, 189, 190, 201, 202, 248, 252
MAGNETIC ISLAND 189
MAGNETIC POLES 184, 185, 186
MAHOGANY SHIP 263, 265, 266, 267, 269, 270, 271, 272, 273, 274, 275, 276, 278, 281, 288, 373
MALACCA 55, 56, 70, 73, 75, 119, 240, 241, 242, 243, 282, 294
MALUAR 223, 226
MARBIAK ISLAND 246
MARE CLAUSUM 39, 240, 329
MARIANAS 299, 300, 314, 316
MARYBOROUGH GUN, The 246
MARTELOIO, Rule of 20, 21, 22, 23, 26, 47, 147, 175
MAURITIUS 17
MELBOURNE 250, 252, 253, 254, 275, 276, 286
MELVILLE ISLAND 72, 84, 85, 306
MERCATOR'S DOUBLE CON-DIFORM 140, 141
MERCATOR'S PROJECTION xix, 99, 140, 142, 149, 151, 176, 180, 181, 222, 223, 225, 228
MERRI RIVER 265, 272
MICRONESIA 301, 302
MISIMA ISLAND 322
MITCHELL LIBRARY 291
MOLUCCAS 49, 51, 55, 56, 57, 58, 68, 82, 90, 120, 124, 240,

245, 282, 296, 299, 300, 301, 311, 312, 313
MOYNE RIVER 265

NAPIER BROOME BAY 81
NEW CALEDONIA 279
NEWFOUNDLAND 33, 35, 37, 95, 220
NEW GUINEA 86, 87, 122, 124, 139, 146, 223, 225, 226, 227, 230, 231, 232, 233, 235, 244, 245, 246, 297, 301, 303, 305, 306, 307, 315, 316, 320, 321, 322, 329, 330, 331, 334, 341, 342, 357
NEW HEBRIDES 146, 285, 292, 321, 323, 334
NEW HOLLAND 31, 52, 308, 328, 331, 332, 344, 345, 351, 353, 354
NEW JERUSALEM 285, 292, 293
NEW SOUTH WALES 62, 102, 252, 288, 292, 353, 354, 370
NEW ZEALAND 17, 138, 146, 279, 280, 281, 282, 283, 294, 337, 343, 344, 352
NORTHERN TERRITORY 84, 309
NORTH QUEENSLAND 288, 319, 338, 348
NOVA SCOTIA 32, 37, 95
NUCA ANTARA MAP 75, 362, 363, 364
NUNES SPIRAL 167, 177

OBLIQUE LATITUDINAL SCALE 185
OCUSSI 52, 53
ORANGERIE BAY 323

PACEM 72, 241, 243
PACIFIC ISLANDS 283
PAPUAS, OS 231, 246, 306
PATAGONIA 221, 244, 294
PEDIR 243
PENROSE CHART 94, 121, 122, 123

INDEX OF PERSONS